PHILEMON'S PROBLEM

Also by
James Tunstead Burtchaell:

Catholic Theories of Biblical Inspiration Since 1810: A Review and Critique
Cambridge University Press, 1969

Philemon's Problem: The Daily Dilemma of the Christian
ACTA, 1973
(*Living with Grace,* London, Sheed & Ward, 1973)

Marriage among Christians: A Curious Tradition (ed.)
Ave Maria Press, 1977

Bread and Salt: A Cassette Catechism
Credence Cassettes, 1978

Abortion Parley (ed.)
Andrews & McMeel, 1980

Rachel Weeping and Other Essays on Abortion
Andrews & McMeel, 1982
(*Rachel Weeping: The Case against Abortion,* Harper & Row, 1984)
(*Rachel Weeping and Other Essays on Abortion,* Life Cycle Books, 1990)

For Better, For Worse: Sober Thoughts on Passionate Promises
Paulist Press, 1985

A Just War No Longer Exists: The Teaching and Trial of Don Lorenzo Milani
University of Notre Dame Press, 1988

The Giving and Taking of Life: Essays Ethical
University of Notre Dame Press, 1989

From Synagogue to Church:
Public Services and Offices in the Earliest Christian Communities
Cambridge University Press, 1992

The Dying of the Light:
The Alienation of Colleges and Universities from Their Christian Churches
Eerdmans, 1998

PHILEMON'S PROBLEM

A Theology of Grace

James Tunstead Burtchaell, C.S.C.

WILLIAM B. EERDMANS PUBLISHING COMPANY
GRAND RAPIDS, MICHIGAN / CAMBRIDGE, U.K.

© 1998 Wm. B. Eerdmans Publishing Co.
255 Jefferson Ave. S.E., Grand Rapids, Michigan 49503 /
P.O. Box 163, Cambridge CB3 9PU U.K.

Printed in the United States of America

03 02 01 00 99 98   7 6 5 4 3 2 1

Library of Congress Cataloging-in-Publication Data

Burtchaell, James Tunstead.
Philemon's problem: a theology of grace / James Tunstead Burtchaell.
p.   cm.
Includes bibliographical references.
ISBN 0-8028-4549-5 (pbk.: alk. paper)
1. Bible. N.T. Philemon — Criticism, interpretation, etc.
2. Slavery in the Bible.
3. Slavery and the church.
4. Christian life — Catholic authors.
I. Title.
BS2765.2.B87   1998
227'.8606 — dc21   98-35615
CIP

For
Gerry Weber
and
Jake Killgallon
and
Mary Buckley
And for my students
who learned these things with me
and so much else

Contents

A DISTINCTIVE WORSHIP

Preface to the Jubilee Edition

John Elson, whose career was spent as an editor at *Time*, used to tell a story about the magazine's founder, Henry Luce. In his later years Luce had withdrawn from all but the highest policy decisions, yet with an occasional exception. Born of missionaries in China, he had been the first to create a "Religion" page in a major magazine of affairs, and he would sometimes join in vetting candidates for that particular editorial responsibility. Thus he found himself one day with a pomaded young graduate who easily carried the conversation through lunch. Luce was not given to chatter, and stolidly listened. But over coffee he leaned into the Ivy League breeze and interrupted: "Young man, what do you see to be the importance of religion?" Startled by a question that direct, the novice stuttered out some commonplaces about its surely being of heartfelt interest to folks of common insight, and that the recent controversies about Darwin, and all that, now seemed to be getting the attention even of the intelligentsia. Sometimes, he mused, religion was meaningfully entwined with the more significant news sectors such as European or Asian politics, and domestic sectionalism. *Et* much *cetera.* The effort of generating all this twaddle absorbed the young fellow, who failed to notice the clamp of the jaw and the intent ruddiness flooding his prospective patron's face. He jumped as high as his coffee cup when the fist hit the table and Luce, who was often gripped by a strong stammer in moments of urgency, growled deeply, "Y-y-young man, it's God-d-d-damned im-m-m-PORtant!" And so it was, and is.

My first students in the mid-sixties did not arrive with that conviction. They did not welcome lectures in the classroom or sermons in the chapel.

So in theology courses, mostly on the Scriptures, I used much give-and-take as we tried to track the fitful growth of those communal insights remembered by the people of Israel and strewn through the Bible that was more than a millennium in the making. In late-night eucharists where the Scriptures were also explored, we used the dialogue homily: a five minute observation by the celebrant, then twenty-five minutes of reflection and wrangle among the students. I had been provided with a luxurious education, but noticed one day that I had begun learning in earnest only when I began to teach. Those earliest years allowed and obliged me to reflect on the trajectory of belief in the Bible, which is in one sense obsolete since the believing community still continues to develop and restate those inherited insights, while in another sense that old book grabs some of our contemporary predilections by the shirtfront and backs us against the wall with its first-hand assertions of what Jesus died for. Every account of the faith must establish its legitimate development from these classical expressions of the youngest belief.

As I worked to reconstruct for the students the push and swerve of understanding's advance in the Bible, they were constant in their puzzling and questioning and challenging: to find out what the writers were inspired to argue about, and how that inquiry, for all its disorder and sometime lack of perspective, might have been working its way across the long years to conscript them. They made me learn all over again, and better, what I had been trained to teach them. The same study occupied weekend retreats, which we called "advances" because, instead of silent reflection, we spent all day and half the night arguing about what emergent emphases in those old, odd writings were most closely claiming our consciences.

So, in the summers of 1970 and 1971, at two beautiful retreats at Lake Como in the Italian Alps, and Land O'Lakes straddling Michigan and Wisconsin, I tried to elaborate what my students had provoked me to learn from the prophets and the apostles.

An anxious world was not awaiting what I had to say. The religion editors at two major publishing houses had previously solicited manuscripts, so I sent this one out with reasonable confidence. The first editor wrote at some length about what he kindly called "this little masterpiece," but ended with regret that "the writing, and I guess the thought, does not seem to offer more than more sparkle, greater facility, or slightly deeper thrusts in the genre of good pulpit talk." What worse slur was possible? The second was more to the point: "It would not have a wide enough audience to justify our publishing it." A third editor, an old friend, could not see it as a commercial possibility. The fourth, at one of the largest houses, said the religious market was moribund, and the only religion they were printing then was strictly historical, or non-Western. The fifth, another friend from yesteryear, allowed as it was "a very civilized book," turned it down because "we can't sell 'civilized books' at the moment," and asked by-the-bye if I might arrange a lecture booking for him. The sixth sent regrets that the book did not focus on the more concrete interests of immediate concern to readers. At this point I was feeling like Robert the Bruce watching that spider about to cast off on her seventh swing.

Then ACTA, a small nonprofit house run by two streetwise Chicago priests, took the book. The publisher, blessed be he, wrote generously that there were three talks he had heard during his lifetime which had stayed with him, and one had been mine. So in 1973 *Philemon's Problem* appeared. My publishers never liked the title *"Philemon's Problem"*: who knew what it might mean? Who even knew how to pronounce it? I countered that *QB VII* had been on the best seller list then for eight months and nobody knew what that meant. Despite my resistance the book was afflicted with a banal and unwelcome subtitle: *The Daily Dilemma of the Christian.* But worse was yet to come. Sheed & Ward bought the British rights, and retitled it *Living With Grace* without even asking. I angrily demanded a subtitle: *The Memoirs of Prince Rainier.* The American publishers' dislike for my title finally led them, at the fifth reprinting or so, to reverse the typography. I then became the author of

Philemon's Problem

The Daily Dilemma of the Christian

Philemon's added problem was that now the book became known on the street as *Philemon's Dilemma.* So much for assonance.

ACTA advertises by direct mail. Only. The one published advertisement I know of misspelled the title. There were few reviews, mostly brief notices in diocesan newspapers. The longest notice was taken by *The Wanderer,* which concluded: "This is a book about Christian faith, the author tells us. . . . It is easy to see why he thought that he needed to tell us. Otherwise, we might never have suspected it." Nevertheless the book sold heartily.

Reactions have varied. The original manuscript received the then necessary *imprimatur* in one day, but several readers said they wondered how it was acquired at all. Another senior editor at the first publishing house which had turned down the manuscript heard there would be a new edition, and sent out a feeler about acquiring the rights. A group of Samoan high school students sent me term papers they had written on Philemon. A New Jersey priest wrote in earnest rebuke that the Gospel does not charge us to love nonbelievers as brothers, except perhaps when they are in danger of death. As he read all those injunctions to feed, house, clothe, comfort, and otherwise support those in need, the needy were strictly intramural. A lady in Los Alamos explained her re-order: "Naively, I'm amazed the world seems not to have changed completely since its publication. I have!" A woman in Manhattan bought the book on impulse and wrote, "You have crystallized the knotty business of being a Christian in the most outrageous, dramatic, earthy, and beautiful language possible." A Chicagoan missionary in the Philippines said he was retailing the book, page by page, from his pulpit on Sunday mornings in Illongo, the local dialect. Another Chicagoan expressed himself otherwise: "One must have considerable pity for those to whom Father Burtchaell is a source of inspiration. *Philemon's Problem* is an excursion into secular humanism, purely and simply. The theme is that we must care for the temporal needs of our neighbor. . . . It is a perversion of Christ's words to place such emphasis on temporal needs." An Irishman from Braintree said, "I got the distinct feeling that you had written *Philemon* for me. . . . Never before had I uttered aloud while reading, 'of course, of course'." A Jesuit journalist wrote from England: "The moments when one finds ideas painfully arrived at suddenly echoed thousands of miles away are some evidence of the Spirit blowing. But I think it's even rarer to find a book written with such modesty and moderation that still manages to be original on every page. Most are original by adopting some extreme position which common sense rejects. This one has a kind of massive sanity that I personally associate with the Dr. Johnsons and Chestertons. . . . It's just the book I've been longing, with diminishing hope, to see, and which can be given to the non-Christian or the Christian struggling with honest doubts, without a sense of shame or embarrassment."

The book somehow continued to make its way. Sales have abated now, but to have a book remain in print for 25 years is always a comfort for an author. Now it is time for a new edition. Over the years I came to wish for a shift of weight here, a better example there, a thorough rewrite elsewhere. And as students have wrangled me into further insights I have wanted to find room for them here. I once said to my spiritual director, "I know what I want to say; it's just that I can't find the words for it." His reply was that we never know anything until we have the right words for it. There are parts in the first edition I believe I have improved by finally finding better words for them. The newer insights have sometimes come from others, and often from arguing with them. We are, after all, a community of controversy. To give that wise priest's corrective a longer reach, I would say that we don't know anything until we can illustrate it with examples. And over the years I have accumulated some stories that bring out the truth better than before. So I set out to rewrite the entire book. As I did a quarter-century ago, I am persuaded that these are matters about which we must ruminate, and an author's proper ambition is to feed but never satisfy such an appetite.

So this is *Philemon*'s jubilee.

I end with thanks to the Sangre de Cristo Charitable Trust, for a grant which made this writing task possible.

Princeton, New Jersey

Acknowledgments

The greater part of this book appeared in an earlier version: *Philemon's Problem: The Daily Dilemmma of the Christian,* © (1973) ACTA Foundation, and the author is grateful to ACTA Publications, Chicago, for agreeing to the present new edition.

The author and the publisher gratefully acknowledge permission to use extended quotations from the following copyrighted works:

The New Jerusalem Bible, © (1985) Doubleday, a division of Bantam Doubleday Dell Publishing Group, Inc., and Darton, Longman & Todd, Ltd, by permission of Doubleday, a division of Bantam Doubleday Dell Publishing Group, Inc.

Various excerpts copyright © 1973/81/85/87/89/90/91/97 by The New York Times Co.

Commonweal, © Commonweal Foundation

The Early Fathers on War and Military Service, by Louis J. Swift, copyright © (1983) by The Order of St. Benedict, Inc. Published by The Liturgical Press, Collegeville, Minnesota

Wholly Human: Essays on the Theory and Language of Morality, by Bruno Schüller, © (1986) The Georgetown University Press

"Anthems," in *It Will Take a Lifetime,* by Francis J. Sweeney, © (1980) Charles River Books

The Spy Who Came In from the Cold, by John le Carré, © (1963) the author

"Two Hearts," by Brian Doyle, in *Portland,* © 1995 the author

ACKNOWLEDGMENTS

Travels with Charley, by John Steinbeck, copyright © 1961, 1962 by The Curtis Publishing Co., © 1962 by John Steinbeck, renewed © by Elaine Steinbeck, Thom Steinbeck, and John Steinbeck IV. Used by permission of Penguin Putnam, Inc., and by William Heinemann Ltd., London

Cancer and Faith: Reflections on Living with a Terminal Illness, by John Carmody © (1994) the author, published by Twenty-Third Publications ($9.95), Mystic, Conn., 800-321-0411

"End of the March," by Mayo Mohs, copyright © 1970 by Time Inc. Permission granted by Time Life Syndication

"When a Little Child Dies," by Jim Stackpoole, © (1979) *The Michigan Catholic*

Texts from Clement of Rome, Ignatius of Antioch, the *Shepherd of Hermas,* the *Letter to Diognetus,* and *The Martyrdom of Polycarp* are quoted from the translation by Kirsopp Lake in the Loeb Series: *The Apostolic Fathers* (Cambridge: Harvard University Press, 1912-1913).

Introduction

This is a book about Christian faith, Catholic faith. The times are bewildering for faith, for right faith. That may be fortunate. Some of us were reared in days when we were assured there were no sharp bewilderments. For the help of those who also grope about for some sturdy insights in upset days, I offer here a single insight about the Father of Jesus, coherently tracked across doctrine, ethics, and worship. I offer no handbook or summary of Christian belief. Nor do I imply that the point I offer is at the very center of Christianity, or even the most needed for our times. I say only that it is integral to faith in the Father of Jesus, and when it is ignored we stray. When it is not taut and strong in its rightful place, the entire musculature of Christian faith is seized with spasm.

There are few pages here (though 25 years ago there were fewer still), but I hope they are chewy. I leave them so with the expectation that my good readers will graze and ruminate at leisure, and perhaps find, as I find, undeveloped points and hints that invite further development consistent with my theme.

The book is Catholic, as am I. But in these years when Christians from scattered traditions begin to edify one another, to make common cause, and to find they confront common puzzles, I hope that scholars and believers in various churches could find themselves at home here. I am bold to hope even that some who have no Christian faith might find my theme inviting, as King Agrippa listened with sympathy to Paul (Acts 26:27-29). At any rate, I hope they will not be at a loss, like a stand-up comedian in a Trappist monastery.

While I was a boy we brought my great-aunt Mary to town, to lodge in a nearby nursing home. My great-grandfather had come from Ireland as a penniless donkey boy. He died still a devout and faithful Catholic, but meanwhile had become a multimillionaire, and his spoiled children one and all left aside faith in God and his Church. My grandmother was the first to return to her faith. It was shame that did it: the thought that her first grandchild was more than a year old and no one had been Catholic enough to stand for me at baptism.

When her older sister later came, long widowed and anciently aristocratic, to be cared for in our town, she had been many decades apart from God, though not He from her. She was gently restored to Him through the honest services of a young priest. One night we were summoned from the dinner table by a call from the nursing home, and we arrived to find that Aunt Mary, that spunky lady become mellowed, had quietly died. She had at the time been reading Augustine, and I found her *Confessions* marked at this passage in the tenth book:

> Late have I loved Thee, O Beauty so ancient and so new; late have I loved Thee! For behold Thou wert within me, and I outside; and I sought Thee outside and in my unloveliness fell upon those lovely things that Thou hast made. Thou wert with me and I was not with Thee. I was kept from Thee by those things, yet had they not been in Thee, they would not have been at all. Thou didst call and cry to me and break open my deafness: and Thou didst send forth Thy beams and shine upon me and chase away my blindness: Thou didst breathe fragrance upon me, and I drew in my breath and do now pant for Thee: I tasted Thee, and now hunger and thirst for Thee: Thou didst touch me, and I have burned for Thy peace.[1]

This lyric of Augustine meant much to me then, and now much, much more. It puts me in mind of Jesus' own remark at the close of that chapter in Matthew's Gospel which contains the riddles of his parables: "Well then, every scribe who becomes a disciple of the kingdom of Heaven is like a householder who brings out from his storeroom new things as well as old" (Matt. 13:52). I am a scribe. My craft is the tradition, the faith being handed down, which I must study in its antiquity and help to expound for my fellows of this day. I marvel at that faith: primitive yet not stale, and so often loved late. This book draws, I believe, on discoveries so

---

1. St. Augustine, *Confessions* 10:27, trans. F. J. Sheed (New York: Sheed & Ward, 1943), p. 236.

ancient and so new: its striving is to be faithful to a revelation long in the coming, and to be alert to questions never asked till now, yet resigned to the belief that all our best answers are makeshifts in lieu of death and clearer vision in God's peace.

In the 25 years since first writing *Philemon*, in my own unloveliness I have known the sorry pain of journeying into the far country, and then the joy that comes with re-learning the persistence of the Father's welcome to us all. Thus I present this volume renewed, with more steadfast convictions about what Christ demanded from and gave to Philemon and Onesimus.

I begin again with Philemon, an earnest man troubled by a command that could give him no rest, yet offered peace. He was offered a Gospel that he could not quite master. He responded, one trusts, to a summons that drew from him never enough, but more, and then still more, much more even than he had planned to give or thought himself able to give. It put nails through him. It transfigured him. It was worth it.

This book strains after what drew him on.

CHAPTER ONE

Philemon's Problem

From Paul, a prisoner of Christ Jesus and from our brother Timothy; to our dear fellow worker Philemon, our sister Apphia, our fellow soldier Archippus and the church that meets in your house. Grace and the peace of God our Father and the Master Jesus Christ.

I always thank my God, mentioning you in my prayers, because I hear of the love and the faith which you have for Master Jesus and for all God's holy people. I pray that your fellowship in faith may come to expression in full knowledge of all the good we can do for Christ. I have received much joy and encouragement by your love; you have set the hearts of God's holy people at rest.

Therefore, although in Christ I have no hesitations about telling you what your duty is, I am rather appealing to your love, being what I am, Paul, an old man, and now also a prisoner of Christ Jesus. I am appealing to you for a child of mine, whose father I became while wearing these chains; I mean Onesimus. He was of no use to you before, but now he is useful both to you and to me. I am sending him back to you — that is to say, sending you my own heart. I should have liked to keep him with me; he could have been a substitute for you, to help me while I am in the chains that the Gospel has brought me. However, I did not want to do anything without your consent; it would have been forcing your act of kindness, which should be spontaneous. I suppose you have been deprived of Onesimus for a time, merely so that you could have him back forever, no longer as a slave, but something much better than a slave, a dear brother, especially dear to me, but how much more to you, both on the natural plane and in the Master. So if you grant me any fellowship with yourself, welcome him as you would

5

me; if he has wronged you in any way or owes you anything, put it down to my account. I am writing this in my own hand: I, Paul, shall pay it back — I make no mention of a further debt, that you owe your very self to me! Well then, brother, I am counting on you, in the Master; set my heart at rest, in Christ. I am writing with complete confidence in your compliance, sure that you will do even more than I ask.

There is another thing: will you get a place ready for me to stay in? I am hoping through your prayers to be restored to you.

Epaphras, a prisoner with me in Christ Jesus, sends his greetings; so do my fellow-workers Mark, Aristarchus, Demas and Luke.

May the grace of our Master Jesus Christ be with your spirit.

Philemon was a prosperous resident of Colossae in Phrygia (now western Turkey), about 100 miles inland from the Aegean Sea. He was a Christian, and he stood prominently in the band of local believers who used to meet in his house to pray and sup together. Such standing as he enjoys in recorded history derives from the fact that one of his household slaves, called *Onesimos* (which meant "useful," "serviceable," or "handy") fell into ultimate disfavor with him.

There are two plausible reconstructions of what we know. The first is that Onesimus was a runaway who risked savage treatment if captured: flogging, or being branded on the face with a lifetime sign of his servile status, or even crucifixion. Another interpretation is that he had somehow seriously defaulted in his service, and had alienated his master seriously enough to remove the hope of eventual manumission, which was commonly awarded to faithful slaves, especially in urban households. If Onesimus was a fugitive with his very life at stake, then he was looking for a place of safety, a far-off situation where his slave status would be unknown. If he was in disgrace, then he was desperately in need of an influential advocate who might intervene on his behalf with Philemon.[1]

---

1. A third interpretation has been defended by Allen Dwight Callahan: that Onesimus was not a slave, but Philemon's bitterly estranged brother, sent by Paul as his religious representative, with an injunction to Philemon to be reconciled and receive him as his dear brother, now in both flesh and faith. See his "Paul's Epistle to Philemon: Toward an Alternative *Argumentum*," *Harvard Theological Review* 86, 4 (1993): 357-76; Margaret M. Mitchell, "John Chrysostom on Philemon: A Second Look," *HTR* 88, 1 (1995): 135-48; Callahan, "John Chrysostom on Philemon: A Response to Margaret M. Mitchell," *loc. cit.*, 149-56.

In either case it is clear why Onesimus would make for the coastal city of Ephesus. It was a brawling seaport where a fugitive on the run might mingle anonymously and be lost in the transient population that crowded the streets. And it was the place of detention for Paul, who had brought Philemon into the Christian fellowship, and enjoyed honor enough in that household to shelter an offending slave. Certain elements in Ephesus were rallying round Paul, who had been unwelcome there ever since the riots that attended his first visit to the city. Onesimus was somehow drawn to the way of life Paul was expounding despite his confinement, and the slave was baptized into the Christian fellowship, as his master had been earlier.

Apparently his stay in Ephesus was a long one, and this too could be interpreted in two ways. If one presumes that the time required for Onesimus to take Paul's message to heart was likely to be longer than an already impatient master would plausibly permit his slave to be absent from duty, it would seem that Onesimus was a fugitive, not a client soliciting his patron. But if one supposes that it was his "usefulness" to Paul as a respected friend of his master that kept him on in Ephesus, then the journey would seem to have Philemon's permission, if not his blessing. But whatever his plight, this was a slave now desperate for his freedom.

As a fugitive Onesimus may have expected his new Christian comrades to provide him with safer shelter. Paul had a network of connections westward across Achaia and Macedonia to Rome, possibly even to Spain: an underground *via*, so to speak, of fellow believers that could harbor him at a safe distance from the provincial officers who hunted down runaway slaves and returned them in irons to face dire penalties. As a slave who had seen his hope of freedom snatched away, even if he carried Paul's message of commendation, it was a dread thing to come home and submit to the decision of a choleric master. It must have stung when Paul sent him home. To afford Onesimus some security in Colossae, Paul may have sent him along with Tychicus, his courier who was delivering a letter from Paul to the Christians of Colossae. In that letter Paul commends his associate courier "Onesimus, that dear and trustworthy brother who is one of your own" (4:9). Onesimus had been hoping for liberty, whether as a fugitive or as a freedman. In either case he was desperate. But Paul, his only hope, sent him back to the ill-disposed master who held absolute and arbitrary power over his fate.

Onesimus was a slave whose hope for liberation had been snuffed out; the recommendation by Paul still left him entirely at his master's mercy, and Philemon evidently had no other motive to reward him.

7

The Roman world for masters and slaves

The ancient Greek and later Hellenistic slave society was then giving way
to the Roman slave society, where the austerities of bondage were being
routinized by law. Men and women entered slavery by being captured in
war, condemned for crime, forfeit for debts, seized by pirates or kidnap-
pers, abandoned as newborns by parents through either sale or exposure
(left in the wild to be eaten by animals, killed by the weather, or taken as
trover by slavers), or bred by slave parents. They were left with only one
purpose in their lives: work.

It was not likely to be a very moral environment on either side of the
ownership divide. It gave ample evidence for Lord Acton's observation,
"Power tends to corrupt, and absolute power corrupts absolutely." But
one could as well conclude with Edgar Friedenberg that "weakness tends
to corrupt, and impotence corrupts absolutely."[2] The institution corrupted
the parties on both sides of this ruthless bond. Masters were led by their
dominion to become heartless and venal, and slaves were tempted to
become sly and shiftless. Roman law gradually provided that slaves could
earn and own property, and even other slaves. They could mate and bear
children. Slaves also enjoyed various legal protections. Their masters required legal permission to scourge or crucify them. A slave could be freed
from bondage by choice of the master, and if the slave had attained thirty
years of age and one's master were a Roman citizen, he or she when
manumitted also acquired citizenship. Lest one imagine that this was a
far, far gentler destiny than what *Uncle Tom's Cabin* memorialized, it is
sobering to note that slaves could earn only by permission, and whatever
they "owned" was theirs by assignment only, since it all always belonged
to their masters. Sexual opportunity was purposely provided by masters
for slaves to assuage their aggressivity, but slaves could only cohabit and
breed, never marry. Their children were the master's possessions, and sales
records show that partners, parents, and children were commonly sold
separately. Slave matters were within the cognizance of the courts, but
slaves had no standing as parties or witnesses (except under torture), and
once an owner had assured a court of slave malfeasance, the judge could

2. John Emerich Edward Dahlberg-Acton, "Letters to Creighton," *Historical Essays
& Studies*, ed. John Neville Figgis & Reginald Vere Laurence (London: Macmillan, 1907),
p. 504; Edgar Z. Friedenberg, *Coming of Age in America* (New York: Random House,
1965), pp. 47-48. The latter point has been developed by Rollo May, *Power and Innocence:
A Search for the Sources of Violence* (New York: W. W. Norton, 1972).

authorize him or her to impose harsh punishments. The terms of manumission could involve the surrender of lifetime savings to the master, and the obligation to remain thereafter as a dutiful indentured servant in the household.

In a word, the power of the owner was ultimate. This was what made slavery under any circumstance essentially brutal. It was not only those sent to work the mines who "preferred dying to surviving," as Diodorus Siculus put it. Without ancestors or progeny; without birth or death on the public record; without honor in society, property in the economy, or standing in the polity; without the power to name their own children; without the capacity to be either victims or perpetrators of crime (slave torts and crimes created claims or liabilities for their masters) — slaves were already socially dead.

The Greeks had seen a mutual advantage in slavery, since nature had obviously fitted the Barbarians for slave labor, and themselves to be their cultivated masters. The Romans were more inclined to see it as a simple fact of fate and force. On either view of it, a life of effective labor required a life of chastisement and severity. Yet at the same time slaves became the familiars of their masters, serving as wet nurses, nannies, pedagogues, body servants, nurses, physicians, and confidential secretaries. Enslavement thus entailed a bewildering fluctuation between intimacy and estrangement, coercion and blandishments, severity and kindness, atrocity and loyalty.

It is commonly said that chattel slavery in the American South was more savage than Greco-Roman slavery because it was compounded with racism. Here, to educate slaves was a crime, to manumit them was usually illegal, eventual citizenship was not possible, and in some states even public criticism of slavery was criminalized. Nevertheless, what Harriet Beecher Stowe said of our peculiar institution was no more than critics had been saying of its Greco-Roman antecedents. She called it "the sum and essence of all abuse."

> The legal power of the master amounts to an absolute despotism over body and soul; . . . there is no protection for the slave's life or limb, his family relationships, his conscience, nay, more, his eternal interests, but the character of the master. . . .
>
> No southern law requires any test of character from the man to whom the absolute power of master is granted. . . . The physician may not meddle with the body, to prescribe for its ailments, without a certificate that he is properly qualified. The judge may not decide

9

on the laws which relate to property, without a long course of training, and most abundant preparation. It is only this office of master, which contains the power to bind and to loose, and to open and shut the kingdom of heaven, and involves responsibility for the soul as well as the body, that is thrown out to every hand, and committed without inquiry to any man of any character.[3]

In *Uncle Tom's Cabin* she backs away from her narrative to reflect:

Perhaps the mildest form of the system of slavery is to be seen in the State of Kentucky. The general prevalence of agricultural pursuits of a quiet and gradual nature, not requiring those periodic seasons of hurry and pressure that are called for in the business of more southern districts, makes the task of the negro a more healthful and reasonable one; while the master, content with a more gradual style of acquisition, has not those temptations to hardheartedness which always overcome human nature when the prospect of sudden and rapid gain is weighted in the balance, with no heavier counterpoise than the interests of the helpless and unprotected.

Whoever visits some estates there, and witnesses the good-humored indulgence of some masters and mistresses, and the affectionate loyalty of some slaves, might be tempted to dream the oft-fabled poetic legend of a patriarchal institution and all that; but over and above the scene there broods a portentous shadow — the shadow of *law*. So long as the law considers all these human beings, with beating hearts and living affections, only as so many *things* belonging to a master, — so long as the failure, or misfortune, or imprudence, or death of the kindest owner, may cause them any day to exchange a life of kind protection and indulgence for one of hopeless misery and toil, — so long it is impossible to make anything beautiful or desirable in the best regulated administration of slavery.[4]

---

3. Harriet Beecher Stowe, *A Key to Uncle Tom's Cabin; presenting the Facts and Documents upon which the Story is Founded, together with Corroborative Statements verifying the Truth of the Work* (Boston: John P. Jewett; Cleveland: Jewett, Proctor & Worthington, 1853), part I, chapter X, p. 39; II, I, 70.

4. Beecher Stowe, *Uncle Tom's Cabin, or, Life Among the Lowly* (Cambridge: Belknap Press of Harvard University Press, 1962), 1:12-13; 45:453.

From a captivity very much like this, Philemon's slave had tried to break away. Whatever Onesimus' offense was — desertion or default — Paul sat down and wrote on his behalf a brief but very personal and shrewdly ambiguous message to the aggravated master: the Letter (or Postcard) to Philemon. It may be the only extant document which Paul penned in his own hand. And it was all that his convert slave had for his safe-conduct. Onesimus, on his way back to Colossae, was exposing himself to either death or aggravated enslavement — with the difference between the two perhaps not all that great. It all lay in the hands of Philemon.

What could Paul have wanted?

What was Paul asking of this master? The Letter to Philemon is a master-piece of Greek persuasion. After the usual courteous greetings to the householder and his family, Paul notes how well spoken of Philemon was for his hospitality to fellow-Christians. The community there followed the Jewish custom of gathering in the home of its best established members, where itinerant fellow-believers also might find hospitable lodging in the name of the host community. This manifest hospitality encourages Paul to ask Philemon to take Onesimus back peaceably. There is, of course, the question of Philemon's rights and grievances, but Paul never speaks directly to that. He does enter a discreet mention of his own imprisonment, and the chains he bore for his service to Philemon and others. With Paul afoul of the law for preaching publicly the Jesus who was being wor-shipped at private gatherings beneath Philemon's own roof, the gentleman from Colossae was not in a position to be assertive of his own civil prerogatives.

Beyond the law remained the grievance that his chattel slave had been anything but *onesimos*. Paul delicately reminds Philemon that if accounts were ever to be paid off, he himself would be in deepest debt to Paul. Philemon, it seems, had not caught his faith from Epaphras, the itinerant preacher who had brought the Jesus movement to Colossae; he was a personal convert of Paul himself. Thus the apostle enjoyed considerable credit in that household, against which some pretty severe receivables might appropriately be written off.

Following the conventions of Greco-Roman rhetorical persuasion, Paul says he will not impose any duty on his friend. Yet his recommen-dation makes it sharply clear where obligation lies. He asks Philemon to take his slave back, amicably. What he gets is a brother in the bargain; both had been fathered into the faith-family by the same Paul. Ties of faith can bind as tightly as ties of flesh. Even more tightly, to judge by this letter. Then, in the peroration of this tough-but-oh-so-gentle appeal, Paul includes one last request: keep the guest room ready, for he would like to pass by to pay them a visit — though who knew when?

What was Philemon to make of all this? How was he to receive this man "no longer as a slave, but something much better than a slave, a dear brother . . . both on the natural plane and in the Master"? Paul seems to want Philemon to welcome this most culpable member of his household as his covenant brother. He also seems to say, though not with outright clarity, that Philemon should go further, that he should even make Onesimus a freedman, no longer a slave. A less ambiguous order might have made it easier for Philemon. Paul did not mean to be easy.

It was a master's right to discipline Onesimus as an offensive slave, say, by seeking to have him scourged or branded or even crucified if a runaway, or by denying him any further hope of eventual freedom, if a troublemaker. Indeed, some discipline would have seemed imperative, as a lesson to like-minded slaves. One had to maintain discipline to maintain slavery.

But there would always be Paul to face. And even without Paul himself, there was that other letter brought to town by Tychicus:

> You have stripped off your old behaviour with your old self, and you have put on a new self which will progress towards true knowledge the more it is renewed in the image of its Creator; and in that image there is no room for distinction between Greek and Jew, between the circumcised and uncircumcised, or between barbarian and Scythian, slave and free. There is only Christ: he is everything and he is in everything.
>
> As the chosen of God, then, the holy people whom he loves, you are to be clothed in heartfelt compassion, in generosity and humility, gentleness and patience. Bear with one another; forgive one another if one of you has a complaint against another. The Lord has forgiven you; now you must do the same. (Col. 3:9-13)

With that about to be read to comrades in his own house the following Sunday, it could be awkward for Philemon, the master, to sit there while the church welcomed his bloodied bondsman as a newfound brother in the Lord, their common Master.

Alternatively, he might reinstate Onesimus as if no offense were remembered, or perhaps even give him less onerous work. Discipline in the
household would go to pieces, naturally. But even then Philemon might
have qualms, and worry about Paul's threatened inspection tour. Would
this be the adequate welcome Paul requested for his "dear child," his "own
heart," now become Philemon's "dear and trustworthy brother"?

What if Paul was not going to be satisfied with any merely spiritual-
ized brotherhood, or any explanation that conversion itself had already
brought Onesimus the truest freedom of all: moral transformation? What
if, behind the politeness of his letter, he *was* asking Philemon to let his
brother go? The social implications were awesome. If he made this newly
embrothered but miscreant bondsman a freedman, every slave in his
household might be seeking baptism . . . and liberation. Slaves in his
Christian colleagues' homes would follow. Where would it stop? An af-
fluent household could invite family ruin and financial annihilation just
by walking along the new Way.

We have no indication how seriously Philemon felt caught in this
dilemma. Presumably he worked out some amiable solution, for the letter
was shown round the community and eventually enjoyed public circula-
tion. Onesimus, the Colossal hot potato, must have survived, and
honorably.

But most likely neither Philemon nor his contemporaries perceived
the dilemma in its starkest terms: You cannot have a brother who is your
slave; you cannot have a slave who is your sister.

Paul appears not to have pursued his own insights to such radical
conclusions. To the Colossian church he wrote explicitly: "Slaves, be obedient in every way to the people who, according to human reckoning, are
your masters; not only when you are under their eye, as if you had only
to please human beings, but wholeheartedly, out of respect for the Master"
(3:22; likewise Eph. 6:5-6; 1 Tim. 6:1-2; Titus 2:9-10). Indeed, all the household lines of command were to remain stable: wives were to obey their
husbands; children, their parents; slaves, their masters. Despite all his
generic enthusiasm about a "new creation," a "new human being," a "new
covenant in Christ," Paul seemed ready to let old relations, particularly
those asymmetrical relations within the patriarchal household, stay in
place.

Then there were the times Paul sounded as if the new faith had erased
some of the traditional stratifications. The Galatians, like the Colossians,
were told "there can be neither Jew nor Greek, there can be neither slave
nor freeman, there can be neither male nor female — for you are all one

in Christ Jesus" (3:28; likewise Rom. 10:12; 1 Cor. 12:13). Yet of those three contemporary asymmetrical relations Paul used his energies mostly to modify the first. He led a dogged movement to eliminate the hostility and discrimination that excused Jewish Christians from breaking bread with their Gentile brothers and sisters. He sped to Jerusalem (a city he normally avoided) in a fury when a whispering campaign developed there about his supposed softness on the integration issue. He wrote fierce prose to the communities under his authority, and called Peter a hypocrite to his face for being a tokenist. For more than 30 years Paul made good on his word that ethnic animosity and separation had no place among Christians. His other egalitarian exhortations, by contrast, seem less pointed, less concrete.

But we do well to take a close look. Paul made seemingly little overt effort to abolish the ethnic and historic differences between Jews and Gentiles in the Church. What he did instead was remind the two communities that their ability to be in communion in Christ made the most of those established differences. The same Good News had been sent to the two distinct groups, with Peter and Paul as their respective envoys. The elder group had brought to the coalition, not the Law of Moses meant distinctively for Jews, but the Promise to Abraham meant inclusively for all peoples (as it was now newly interpreted). The Old Covenant had been for one people of twelve tribes; the New Covenant was for that same people now opened to take in people from all tribes, tongues, and nations. In Christ the Jews, who were understandably committed to their old sensibilities and customs, now had to live in familial unity with the Gentiles, whose tastes and traditions were strange to Israel but who claimed a welcome in the New Israel. Paul did not argue for homogeneity, nor did he forget who had been the bringers of faith and who, the beneficiaries. Though these two different factions had to sit around the table as one, they still remained distinctive clans within the one people, and that was all right.

Within his apparent conservatism regarding domestic relations, Paul is sponsoring a radical renegotiation of duty. His treatment of traditional subordination, which he appears to leave intact, actually recharacterizes it. Those on the underside of authority are still bound to obey: indeed, to obey as never before. Having stripped off their older behavior, they must now actually obey out of love, not subjection. But those in authority likewise are to exercise their mastery as never before: not to suit themselves, but lovingly to protect and provide for those in their care. To the Colossians Paul puts it in briefest form (3:18–4:1):

Wives, be subject to your husbands, as you should in the Lord. Husbands, love your wives and do not be sharp with them.

Children, be obedient to your parents always, because that is what will please the Lord. Parents, do not irritate your children or they will lose heart.

Slaves, be obedient in every way to the people who, according to human reckoning, are your masters; not only when you are under their eye, as if you had only to please human beings, but wholeheartedly, out of respect for the Master. Whatever your work is, put your heart into it as done for the Master and not for human beings, knowing that the Master will repay you by making you his heirs. It is Christ the Master that you are serving. Anyone who does wrong will be repaid in kind. For there is no favouritism. Masters, make sure that your slaves are given what is upright and fair, knowing that you too have a Master in heaven.

Everything has been turned on its head. The Christian slave, as Paul tells the Corinthians, has become "a freedman of the Master," and the owner is now a "slave of Christ." Though the social and legal conventions seem to be left in place, Paul claims that for Christians they can no longer function as before. Since all "have been bought at a price" by Christ with his blood, and since their submission to the Father confers dignity instead of degradation, how could they either demand or offer the old slavishness or servility between echeloned human beings (1 Cor. 7:22)?

Paul's slyly ambiguous injunctions were subversive of the old ways, as the obligations of the party in authority — husband, parent, master or mistress — became further redefined. Ephesians, a later text, says it differently: wives and husbands should "be subject to one another. . . . Husbands should love their wives, just as Christ loved the Church and sacrificed himself for her . . . and let every wife respect her husband. . . . Parents, never drive your children to resentment but bring them up with correction and advice inspired by the Lord" (5:21–6:9). To masters: "Never forget that everyone, whether a slave or a free man, will be rewarded by the Master for whatever work he has done well. . . . Treat your slaves in the same spirit; do without threats, and never forget that they and you have the same Master in heaven." Likewise 1 Peter: "Husbands must treat their wives with consideration in their life together, respecting a woman who, though she may be the weaker partner, is equally an heir to the generous gift of life" (3:7).

Wives and children and slaves, Paul was telling them, were to be all the more biddable toward their masters — as to the Master himself. Having thus enjoined those in inferior positions to identify their masters and mistresses with Christ, Paul might then have suggested a more radical reciprocity, by also identifying those in subjection with Christ. After all, he had written to Philippi that Jesus had assumed the condition of a slave (2:7). Yet he does not do that. Instead, he urges husbands and parents and masters and mistresses to be fair and compassionate because they have a common Master to face in judgment. The traditional authority could remain, but now to be exercised in ways the tradition had never known. Paul's Gospel asserts *force majeure,* even over Roman law, and subordinates husbands, parents, and owners to its higher authority. But he seems to leave wives, children, and slaves in their place.

Yet Paul had undermined the old understanding of domination and submission. The prophetic tradition in Israel had undermined the monarchy by idealizing the king as a shepherd in the line of David, just as the scribes later idealized him as a sage in the line of Solomon: both identities required royal power — whether of force or of wisdom — to be reversed, and used thenceforth to protect or to reconcile the people. Similarly, when Paul imposes on the master the duty to call his slave "brother," and to show him heartfelt compassion, generosity and humility, gentleness and patience, fairness and forbearance and forgiveness, the worm is in the wood. Ownership is no longer the guarantor of authority and privilege. It has been changed into the responsibility to serve, with self-restraint.

Looking downhill from their very modern standpoint, some scholars are chagrined that the old tradition of household authority was so ingrained that Paul, with decades of scars from his single-minded struggle for inter-ethnic fellowship between Jews and Gentiles, could not bring himself to see and say as plainly that faith in the Father of Jesus could have no peace with slavery. But before writing Paul off as a shill for the established order we might ask which would really have been the more radical: flatly to deny that any human could own another, or to demand that no traditional relation, *even* that of master and slave, owner and owned, could cancel or compromise their radical equality and solidarity in Master Christ?

Slavery as a master metaphor for Christian discipleship

One salient reason why abolition was not a perpetual plank in the platform of the early Christians was that slavery was an element in their own new self-identification. To understand this point one must take notice that translators have sanitized our New Testament by rendering *doulos* and *oiketēs* — both of which mean "slave" — as "servant." Accordingly, *kyrios* is rendered as "lord" in many places where its association with slaves would be brought out best by "master," which is sometimes unambiguously represented by *despotēs*.

Translated thus, the stories Jesus tells sound different. No slave can take orders from two masters. After his slaves and his son sent to collect the rents are abused and killed by his sharecroppers, it is the master, not just the "landowner," who deals with them. It is slaves who find the weeds in the wheatfield and ask their master what is to be done. It is the conscientious bailiff-slave of the household who will be doggedly awake and on duty whenever his gratified master makes it home, and it is the shiftless slave who is not at his post, and will inevitably be sold off. The unforgiving debtor is a slave, and his feckless sub-debtor is a fellow slave; were he a servant he might have been put into bondage to work off the debt, but since he is already a slave he is sent to be tortured instead. The king sends his slaves to scout out revelers for his son's ill-attended wedding feast. It is a master who distributes cash to his various slaves for them to invest and sustain the household income in his absence, and who then harshly disciplines the one good-for-nothing slave, for the harsh truth is that the slaves work the fields but the harvest is the master's. The prodigal father has his slaves set out a great banquet when his shiftless younger son returns home; then he hears out his embittered firstborn who has slaved for him and been taken for granted.

In the Gospel narratives recounted *about* Jesus, the centurion comes to plead for the life of his slave, not a servant, and he assures Jesus that his slaves are as prompt as his soldiers to jump at his command. It is the high priest's slave who loses an ear at Gethsemane. Later that evening slaves huddle with soldiers outside in the courtyard during Jesus' arraignment.

Thus the stories told by Jesus are strewn with slaves, and the stories about Jesus report Roman and Jewish slaves. These slaves are expected to do what they are told and take what comes. Some are indolent and some are trustworthy. Taken together they provide the overtones to one of the New Testament's primary analogies for the Christian believer. Thus we read that Jesus' disciples, even with all duties accomplished, will still call themselves "useless slaves who have done no more than our duty." Whoever would be great among them must be a *servant (diakonos)*, but whoever wishes to be first of all must be the *slave* of all.

A most powerful Gospel use of the image is in Luke's infancy narratives, where Mary listens to the heavenly courier's bewildering message and replies simply that she is the Master's slave-girl, on duty and waiting for orders. She blesses the Master for having passed over so many celebrities to single out an insignificant slave for such intimate service, and she foresees how God will up-end the social order when he comes with faithful love to rescue his slave Israel. Old Simeon later sings out his request to be excused after his long seasons of attentive waiting, "Now, Master, please let your slave go off duty, in peace."

Paul, Timothy, Epaphras, James, Peter, Jude, the seer of Patmos — and Moses, the prophets and martyrs and saints and worshippers — are all presented in the Scriptures as slaves of God, and of Jesus Christ the Lamb. Paul says further that he and his co-workers have been seconded by the Lord to be the slaves of the Christians they care for, from church to church. But since he acts on his Master's orders he is determined to serve his fellow Christians' needs, not their whims. Paul says that slavery had always been their status: but previously they sold themselves into slavery to sin which led to their death; and now they are bound over to uprightness as they were instructed, and it has rewarded them with holiness.

Like Jesus, Paul gives the slave analogy further resonance by crossing it with other analogies. When the Spirit enters their hearts and prompts them to address their Master audaciously as "Abba" — "Daddy" — then they are obviously no longer slaves but his children and heirs. This is God's emancipatory gift, not their escapade. They must have the same attitude as Jesus, who though he was the Master's Son, accepted enslavement, and enslavement's ultimate jeopardy: chastisement, abuse, humiliation, crucifixion. For that God had every creature hail and honor him, not as a manumitted Freedman, but as the exalted younger Master now settled into his own inheritance. So Paul could equally well say they are children and heirs, *and slaves*.

Supporting the entire Christian belief, like the main pole under a great tent, is the one Hebrew image that allowed the Christians to understand Jesus' own failure and death as glorious achievement: the cycle of songs in Isaiah which had interpreted a humiliated Judah as God's Suffering Slave (a.k.a. the Suffering Servant) who, meek as a lamb led to slaughter,

18

loyally accepts unjust abuse and gives up his life to provide the redemption-price for many. It was those prophetic lyrics which taught the early Christians in retrospect that Jesus, as a Suffering Slave, had to be slain in order to be able to rule as a glorious King.

No slave can be greater than his or her Master. How had Jesus won the hearts and loyalty of his disciples? He had been a nobody: a carpenter's son from Nazareth — could anyone of worth come from there? From Galilee, where everyone spoke with a backward accent. Never the pupil of any sage, he brassily began to speak out in the synagogues, and got a reputation for being audacious. When his speech began to take on a prophetic edge, and to nick the egos of people of station and piety, his own family was embarrassed and tried to take him back home under wraps. But then he lost all sense of his rightful place, and began to stir the poor of the countryside. His unsheathed voice, like John's, began to reach higher and higher. He was a peasant, an uppity peasant, and they were whispering about him as one sent to rule; that meant *overthrow*. By the time it all came crashing down in sudden violence, and he was given a slave's death, all those who had followed him as their Joshua, their David, their Maccabee, their Spartacus, had run for cover and pretended they had never heard of him or taken him seriously.

Then, in no time at all, there he was once more: returned to settle accounts. And what was that Suffering Slave's retribution? Reconciliation. What was his revenge? Forgiveness. What was his reward? He, the Slave who stood silent before his perjured accusers, who had been bound, tortured, and crucified for no other reason than for being a faithful Slave, was now their faithful Master. And they, who found it in themselves to be his faithful followers only late (though not too late), realized that their discipleship was a blessed bondage. For now it was their calling to follow his will, to obey his orders, to have their service taken for granted, to accept a unilateral life of speaking the truth at whatever cost — offering their labor thanklessly, and counting themselves happy to be able to be slaves for the Almighty.

In the lengthened perspective of John's Gospel the analogy of slave/discipleship is reworked somewhat. In one passage Jesus says his disciples are friends, not slaves, for slaves never know their master's purposes, only his orders. When Jesus' invitation to follow him causes some to bristle that they are sons of Abraham and have never slaved for anyone, he alertly replies that those who stand to their duty for him really *are* family, not slaves, for the household is their abiding home, unlike slaves who are always at risk of being sold off. For if, in the general New

Testament perspective, these are slaves, they are also sons. That set every-one's imagination on its ear.

The early Christian policies on slavery

With blessed bondage as a master metaphor for their own calling, the early Christians were not instinctively driven to rise up and abolish chattel slavery. They had all accepted a life of exposure to outrage. Taking their lesson from what had happened to Jesus, the Baptist before him, and Stephen and all those others after him, they knew that if they were faithful they would enjoy no more standing than slaves did. They knew they were the man-slaves and woman-slaves Joel had foretold would have the Spirit poured out upon them. In affliction they prayed as slaves: "And now, Master, take note of their threats and help your slaves to proclaim your message with all fearlessness." They had no hope to win the world in any normal sense, for their intent was to emancipate people from — yet through — suffering. And in any case, they had more moral concern for masters and mistresses, who were likely to be more in thrall than were their slaves.

In the Greco-Roman world there was already a contemporary social critique of slavery, and Paul would have been familiar with it. The Greek Sophists had derided the established belief that Greeks were as naturally given to mastery as Barbarians were to slavery. Most enslavement, they replied, was a matter of either violence or luck, certainly not of relative excellence. More recently the Roman Stoics had been insisting that slavery was ultimately irrelevant: the truly free person is the virtuous person, while any corrupt person is truly servile. Seneca contrasted great acts of nobility by distinguished slaves with craven behavior by some masters, and he taunted the latter for being enslaved by their appetites for sex or food. If anyone was owned, he said, it was really the masters: by their prostitutes. Despite all this critique, however, no one in Paul's time had yet imagined a society without slavery.

Slaves, we know, are humans, and should not, cannot, also be prop-erty. Throughout the sadly prolonged history of slavery, that would eventually become the gravamen of the abolitionists. But that was not the Christian grievance with slavery. Paul never presents Onesimus to Philemon as his fellow human. He sends him home instead as his dear brother in Christ, and that would become the more radical doctrine. Paul's moral imperative exceeded even the claim that one cannot have

20

a brother who is one's slave; and that one cannot have a slave who is one's sister. Instead of forbidding slavery he imposed fellowship. Instead of saying that no Christian person can belong to another, that no person can own human property, he insisted that every Christian person must belong to all others, and that we Christians must all take and treasure one another for our own. And he insisted that this relation master all others.

In the Christian view of it, abolition, both in theory and in actual history, would be as incomplete as manumission: it does no more than set slaves free to fend for themselves. That much liberty can be desolate. Our age hears a great deal of talk about emancipation of every kind, but our age tends to think of liberty as what we award to people with whom we wish to have no further burdening associations. One social service executive put it well many years ago in commenting on her work for the poor, when she pointed out that abortion is the one social service that emancipates us from further social service.

The early Church was naturally restless with the low-level fever that came from Paul's injunction to write off grievance, debt, and wrong as freely as the Lord had done for the sinful woman who had bathed his feet with her tears (Luke 7), for the Roman centurion, for the Good Thief, and for Peter. The restlessness refused to go away, because it was not just Paul who said fellowship with Christ depended on our fellowship with one another, and not just Paul who promised to visit and see for himself how Philemon had set his heart at rest. It was Jesus. And when he shall have come, the obscure injunction to take one another as brother and sister would prove more captivating and enthralling and breakaway, than any command to set one another free.

There was thus no mass movement for emancipation in the early Church. But slavery was an essential issue. One of our earliest hints is another passage from Paul, to the Corinthians:

> Everyone should stay in whatever state he was in when he was called. So, if when you were called, you were a slave, do not think it matters — even if you have a chance of freedom, you should prefer to make full use of your condition as a slave. You see, anyone who was called in the Lord while a slave, is a freeman of the Lord; and in the same way, the man who, when called, was a free man, is a slave of Christ. You have been bought at a price; do not be slaves now to any human being. Each one of you, brothers, is to stay in the state in which you were called. (1 Cor. 7:20-24)

The passage has thrown interpreters into turmoil because of Paul's elliptical ending to the second sentence. It might mean that if Christian slaves were offered their freedom, they should decline. But it might carry the contrary meaning instead: that they should not struggle for manumission; but if freedom were offered, it would not be wrong to accept. In either case, Paul seems radically indifferent to whether believers are enslaved or free. One's circumstances are utterly insignificant by comparison with how one treats his or her fellows.

We know that some Christians did take unusual measures to set slaves free, and that their efforts proved controversial. Clement, bishop of Rome, wrote in the late 90s that many in the Church had sold themselves into bondage and used the proceeds to buy the release of others, or to feed the poor. Ignatius, bishop of Antioch, on his way to martyrdom in Rome about 15 years later, instructs Polycarp, bishop of Smyrna (who would himself later be a martyr) that no Christian should treat slaves high-handedly, nor should slaves put on airs: "Let them rather endure slavery to the glory of God, that they may obtain a better freedom from God." Thus far the message is traditional, but he goes on: "Let them not desire to be manumitted out of the common purse, lest they prove themselves slaves of lust." Apparently Ignatius, whose abiding concern was peaceable unity within the churches under their presiding bishops, had word that local congregations were breaking into hostile factions when their common funds were being used to purchase the freedom of church members. One can easily imagine the political atmosphere if potential converts had their eye on this as an incentive, or when some members' favorites were emancipated and others' not, or when the slaveowners were also Christians and drove hard bargains with the Church for full market value. Such wrangles over the common fund had not brought out their philanthropic best. Compared with that, Ignatius regards even continued bondage as preferable. Writing as a prisoner in chains on the way to capital punishment he can compare himself to Peter and Paul, whose authority he invokes: "They were apostles, I am a convict; they were free, I am still a slave. But if I suffer I shall be Jesus Christ's freedman, and in him I shall rise a free man."[5]

Pity for slaves continued. Throughout the second, third, fourth, and fifth centuries we hear of Christian communities using their common funds to assist widows, orphans, the destitute, and "afflicted souls," "to redeem from distress the slaves of God," "those in chains," for "the redemption of the saints, the deliverance of slaves," "to purchase a slave,

5. 1 Clement 55, 2; Ignatius to Polycarp 4, 3; Ignatius to the Philippians 6, 2.

22

and save a soul." Constantine decreed that slave families were henceforth to be kept together instead of being sold off separately, and he proscribed branding on the face as punishment for runaways, a punishment so particularly resented by Christians.[6]

Despite all that, Christians continued to own slaves and, since those slaves were often themselves Christians, the Church's way of handling this became very ambiguous, as this passage in Augustine reveals:

> All slavery is filled with bitterness: all who are tied to slave chains complain at having to serve. But you must not be afraid of the service of this [divine] Master: there will be no groaning, no grumbling, no dissatisfaction here. No one wishes to be sold away from this household [the Church], since it is so wonderful that we should all have been redeemed. It is a great joy, my brothers, to be a slave in this great household, even a slave with chains on his feet. You must not be afraid to trust your Master, chained slaves: blame your own deserts for your chains; have faith in your chains, if you want them to become like adornments. It was not without meaning, nor without listening to people, that the Psalmist said, "May the groaning of those who are in chains reach unto your presence" (79 [Vulgate 78]:110).
>
> "Serve the Master in joy." The Master's slavery is free; slavery is free when charity, and not necessity, is what enforces it. "You, brothers, have been called to be freed," said the Apostle; "only you must not let your freedom give an opportunity to the flesh; you must be slaves to one another, because of the charity given by the Holy Spirit" (Gal. 5:13). Charity makes you a slave, after the truth has made you a free man. "If you remain faithful to my Word," said the Evangelist, "You will really be my pupils, you will recognize the truth, and the truth will set you free" (John 8:31-32). You are both a slave and a free man; you are a slave, because that is what you were made; but from that status you have become free, because you love Him who made you. Do not complain at having to serve; your complaints will not bring it about that you cease serving, only that you serve as a bad slave. You are the Master's slave, and the Master's freedman;

---

6. The Shepherd of Hermas, *Similitude* 1, 8; *Mandate* 8, 10; Justin, *Apology* 67, 6; Tertullian, *Apologeticus* 39, 6; *Martyrium Pionii* 9, 3-4; *Didascalia Apostolorum* 19; *Apostolic Constitutions* 2, 62, 4; 4, 9, 2; 5, 1-2; Henry Chadwick, "New Letters of St. Augustine," *Journal of Theological Studies* 34 (1983): 432-33; Lucian of Samosata, *Peregrinus* 12-13.

you shouldn't want to be set free with the result that you leave the household of Him who set you free.[7]

There is some Stoic doctrine here, but much transformed in Christian usage. By Augustine's time the Christian treatment of slavery had become fairly stabilized. As long as the agricultural economy, the customs of warfare, and criminal justice continued to make slavery a common practice, Christians evangelized and welcomed slaves as believers, urged them to serve honestly and cheerfully, tried to alleviate the rigor of their lives by charity, and occasionally purchased or granted their freedom. Paul's injunction to slaves to be wholeheartedly obedient in every way to their masters lives on in pastoral admonitions. Already in the second century Christian slaves were being chided for presuming wrongly on their fellowship and becoming uppity. On any reading of history, this was a radical message: that slaves in the hellhole of helplessness should put a brave face on it and treat their masters and mistresses fondly and fairly. It certainly stretched the sense of "fairness," however, as viewed from the privileged moral perspective of the slaves.

Christian compromise and abolition

We look in vain for the truly radical message that Christians should no longer hold slaves, and that they should set them all free forthwith. We read of collections being taken up to pay some owners for their slaves, but we do not read of owners being shamed into freeing any. As the lash beat time over those long years, there was pastoral evidence in plenty to show that the Pauline exhortation to mutual fidelity between owners and owned was not really symmetrical. It was an act of exquisite, daily martyrdom to obey an owner who was by definition a despot; it was gracious, but hardly heroic, to command shiftless slaves patiently.

As a result, the pastors of the church fell easily into the hands of the owners, and their message showed the result of that. Consider one late example. The Anglican Bishop of London expounded Paul thus to the Masters and Mistresses of the Southern Colonies in America in 1727:

> Christianity, and the embracing of the Gospel, does not make the least alteration in Civil Property, or in any of the Duties which belong

7. St. Augustine, *Commentary on Psalm 99 [98]: 7*; in Migne, *PL* 37: 1275.

to Civil Relations; but in all these Respects, it continues Persons just in the same State as it found them. The Freedom which Christianity gives, is Freedom from the Bondage of Sin and Satan, and from the Dominion of Men's Lusts and Passions and inordinate Desires; but as to their *outward* Condition, whatever that was before, whether bond or free, their being baptized, and becoming Christians, makes no manner of Change in it. . . .

And so far is Christianity from discharging Men from the Duties of the Station and Condition in which it found them that it lays them under stronger Obligations to perform those Duties with the greatest Diligence and Fidelity, not only from the Fear of Men, but from a sense of Duty to GOD. . . .[8]

This might seem to make the Gospel unevenly appetizing to the slave-owners. On a longer view of it, however, since the system was already more likely to corrupt master than slave, and since the masters' Lusts and Passions and inordinate Desires were likely to be more enflamed by slavery than those of their chattels, we could even fault the bishop with prejudice for attending so little to the salvation of the gentry.

This all bears out the modern observation of Abbé Pierre:

We have come to this point: One no longer dares to preach the fullness of the Gospel in churches because the faithful manage to pamper the clergy so much that priests can no longer preach the true Gospel without being embarrassed. This is a very sound collective ruse which places the clergy in a bourgeois state which neither the Lord nor His apostles knew. Thus, it is pretty sure that certain pages of the Gospel will be preached no longer.[9]

8. Edmund Gibson, Bishop of London, "Letter to the Masters and Mistresses of Families in the English Plantations Abroad: Exhorting them to encourage and promote the Instruction of their Negroes in the Christian Faith," 1727, in *An Historical Account of the Incorporated Society for the Propagation of the Gospel in Foreign Parts,* ed. David Humphreys (London: Joseph Downing, 1730), pp. 265-66.

9. Abbé Pierre, "A Prophet in America," *Jubilee* 3, 2 (June 1955): 11. Abbé Pierre, a charismatic French priest and Resistance activist during World War II (Henri de Grouès was his original name), organized the ragpickers of Paris to work together in "Emmaus" communities and build homes for one another with the proceeds of what they could scavenge from the city dump.

Much better was the exhortation by George Keith to his fellow Friends, or Quakers, in 1693. He began where Paul did:

> Seeing Our Lord Jesus Christ hath tasted Death for every Man, and given himself a Ransom for all, to be testified in due time, and that his Gospel of Peace, Liberty and Redemption from Sin, Bondage and all Oppression, is freely to be preached unto all, without Exception, . . .

but then he wheeled in a quite different direction from that of the Bishop of London:

> Therefore we judge it necessary that all faithful Friends should discover themselves to be true *Christians*, by having the Fruits of the Spirit of Christ, which are *Love, Mercy, Goodness, and Compassion* towards all in Misery, and that suffer Oppression and severe Usage, so far as in them is possible to ease and relieve them, and set them free of their hard Bondage, whereby it may be hoped, that many of them will be gained by their beholding these good Works of sincere *Christians*, and prepared thereby, through the Preaching the Gospel of Christ, to imbrace the true Faith of Christ.

And then he concludes what even Paul did not:

> And to buy Souls and Bodies of men for Money, to enslave them and their Posterity to the end of the World, we judge is a great hinderance to the spreading of the Gospel and is occasion of much War, Violence, Cruelty and Oppression, and Theft & Robbery of the highest nature. . . . Therefore, in true *Christian Love*, we earnestly recommend it to all our Friends and Brethren, Not to buy any Negroes, unless it were on purpose to set them free, and that such who have bought any, and have them at present, after some reasonable time of moderate Service . . . they may set them at Liberty, and during the time they have them, to teach them to read, and give them a Christian Education.[10]

10. George Keith, "An Exhortation & Caution to Friends Concerning Buying or Keeping of Negroes," 1693, said to be the first printed protest against slavery in North America, in *Source Book and Bibliographical Guide for American Church History*, ed. Peter G. Mode (Menasha, Wis.: The Collegiate Press, George Banta, 1921), pp. 554-55. In the next century Friends were urged to "manifest their disunion" with any of their fellowship who continued to hold slaves; ibid., pp. 555-57.

Harriet Beecher Stowe

Another most powerful counterexample to that lamed Christian tradition was provided by *Uncle Tom's Cabin,* the nineteenth century's runaway best seller in the English language. Harriet Beecher Stowe explained that there was only one audience capable of understanding her story: "The great object of the author in writing has been to bring this subject of slavery, as a moral and religious question, before the minds of all those who profess to be followers of Christ. . . . May they unite their prayers that Christendom may be delivered from so great an evil as slavery!"[11]

The burden of her tale is that while there were admirable examples of integrity among both the slaving and the owning classes, there was a heroic quality to the sanctity of George and Eliza and especially Tom that was impossible for Eva or Mr. Shelby, though both groups would have done well by Paul's twofold injunction. But the novel quite powerfully depicts what Paul never discussed: that slavery itself had the tendency to corrupt everyone involved precisely because slavery gave dominion so easily to lusts and passions and inordinate desires — on both sides of ownership. Christian duty required not simply that people cope as best they could within the institution, but that they abolish the system itself. For slavery could corrupt even insightful but inert bystanders like Augustine St. Clare. One conversation between him and his cousin from the North concerns the intractability of young Topsy:

> "I don't see," said Miss Ophelia to St. Clare, "how I'm going to manage that child, without whipping her."
> "Well, whip her, then, to your heart's content; I'll give you full power to do what you like."
> "Children always have to be whipped," said Miss Ophelia; "I never heard of bringing them up without."

11. Beecher Stowe, *A Key,* iii-iv. Beecher Stowe manifests her integrated Christian perspective by the way she amalgamates her vocabulary. Thus, she ushers her reader into a slave warehouse (*Uncle Tom's Cabin,* 30:334):

> Then you shall be courteously entreated to call and examine, and shall find an abundance of husbands, wives, brothers, sisters, fathers, mothers, and young children, to be "sold separately, or in lots to suit the convenience of the purchaser;" and that soul immortal, once bought with blood and anguish by the Son of God, when the earth shook, and the rocks rent, and the graves were opened, can be sold, leased, mortgaged, exchanged for groceries or dry goods, to suit the phases of trade, or the fancy of the purchaser.

"O, well, certainly," said St. Clare, "do as you think best. Only I'll make one suggestion: I've seen this child whipped with a poker, knocked down with the shovel or tongs, whichever came handiest, &c.; and, seeing that she is used to that style of operation, I think your whippings will have to be pretty energetic, to make much impression."

"What is to be done with her, then?" said Miss Ophelia.

"You have started a serious question," said St. Clare; "I wish you'd answer it. What is to be done with a human being that can be governed only by the lash, — *that* fails, — it's a very common state of things down here! . . . In many cases, it is a gradual hardening process on both sides, — the owner growing more and more cruel, as the servant more and more callous. Whipping and abuse are like laudanum; you have to double the dose as the sensibilities decline. I saw this very early when I became an owner; and I resolved never to begin, because I did not know when I should stop, — and I resolved, at least, to protect my own moral nature."[12]

Now let us return to the still bewildered Philemon, whose problem antedated all the later glosses and double-talk and efforts at discipleship. He was one of the few slave-owners in history to whom Christ's spokesman would authoritatively intimate that his slave was now a truly dear brother — a line of thought whose inner dynamic moved honestly to the insight that the brothers had better be master and slave no longer. Neither Paul nor Philemon could foresee or even imagine a society without slavery. But the simple designation of "brother," which Paul had launched at Philemon's conscience, was like hydrofluoric acid: so corrosive it would dissolve almost any kind of container.

For Christ's sake he was asked to receive back into his house, to cherish as a brother (indeed, to cherish as he would Paul himself), a man who in their surrounding society was beyond brotherhood. Paul had bidden him take a slave as a brother. Yet even Paul did not clearly — and probably could not — assert the full, explicit reach of his own request. To serve Jesus' Father, to heed Paul, to embrother Onesimus, Philemon would have had to fly in the face of the society, the polity, and the economy; disenthrall his slaves one and all; and stir up a social upheaval ruinous enough that all might become brothers and sisters. And he would have to act out of brotherly love, from start to finish.

12. Beecher Stowe, *Uncle Tom's Cabin*, 20:252. I am grateful to a former student, Colm Connelly, Esq., for having pointed out this passage.

Philemon's problem is our problem, the problem of any believer. All societies are poised on inequities — some concealed, others noticed — that make brotherhood and sisterhood unfeasible. Every age and locale has its particular and familiar — too familiar — bondages. Regardless of our status, we believers, exploiters and/or exploited, are similarly nearsighted about the oppressions we may unwittingly have learned to live with. No one cries out: neither the strong nor the weak, because for opposed reasons they dare not. Perhaps this is unfair: it might seem that slaves would sense injustice that masters ignore. But even slaves have their eyes and feelings dulled; one cannot long entertain hope for what seems unattainable. So, rather than live in perpetual frustration, even the enslaved will not allow their consciences to become too sensitive.

Yet we are bidden to take all men as brothers, all women as sisters. And the sight of Christ crucified, all mangled yet magnificent, should warn us what the cost will be, must be. Christians are tempted to receive Paul's commands as domesticated slogans, ever trying to live at peace in societies where people cannot effectually be brothers and sisters as they are told to be. Whereas political, social, and economic revolution are continually indicated by integral Christian faith, we usually prefer to come to terms with what we have grown to regard as familiar and congenial. Christ's baptism of fire is quenched so disappointingly by our own rites of water. Christians do not usually refuse fellowship; but they often fail to see what it requires, because they cannot bear to see it.

Philemon's problem goes even deeper. It is not only that he fails to receive clear, concrete imperatives from his Church; nor that his vision of what Christ requires is perforce obscured by his own vested interests and the blurred perspective of his own time and home; nor that massive sacrificial generosity would be required for him to turn his life inside out on behalf of his brother, his sister, his neighbor, and his enemy; nor even that he may lack the clout needed to foment a social reform in the world order that lies beyond his own household. It is the very social order that inhibits Philemon from loving Onesimus, and Onesimus from loving Philemon, as Christ has loved them both. Yet there is no social order, no revision of the economy, no reform in politics, no imaginable world situation, and indeed no imaginative anticipation of any future human environment, that adequately conforms to the Gospel or makes room for its full realization. There is no revolution that does not in large part eventually redistribute injustice. And it must always be in a world that is flawed with compromise and blindness and greed and inequity and well-intentioned violence that Philemon lives. The Kingdom of God is near at hand, yet never quite comes; his will must be done, yet it never quite is.

To understand better the ways we flinch at the Gospel, as Philemon must have done, consider the different stances taken, only a few decades apart, by Edmund Gibson and George Keith. Keith the Quaker took the society of faithful response to be his community of faith, while Gibson the Anglican took the nation to be the addressee of the Gospel. Gibson believed that the "established" church, the protégée of the civil state, should take Paul to heart, while Keith expected civil society to be largely threatened by Christian imperatives and hostile to Christ's concerns. One man expected society at large to heed the Gospel without being corporately transformed; the other never expected British society at large to be able to hear or heed what the Society of Friends must. Gibson was an ancestor of those today who set out to transform "the world" or "society" without seeking first the Kingdom of God in the Church. That is folly — and not the folly of the Cross.

We have not yet considered what may have been the knottiest feature of Philemon's story, and of ours. We have not attended to *Onesimus'* problem. He was asked to return to a disgruntled master, with Paul's writ in his hand but no knowledge or assurance of what his master was going to make of it, and no say-so in Philemon's decision. Onesimus, on his faith, was bidden to put himself back in the hands of another man's faith. He was asked to take his master as a brother, in the uncertain hope that his master could give up his corrupting advantage, in the uncertain prospect that whatever fraternity Philemon could summon up would be wholehearted. Thereby Philemon was faced with a man who for Christ was voluntarily surrendering into his master's hand all his hopes for a voluntary life.[13]

Beecher Stowe gives us a feel for Onesimus' problem in the conversation between Mr. Wilson, the sympathetic white man, and George the slave:

> "Well, George, I s'pose you're running away — leaving your lawful master, George — (I don't wonder at it) — at the same time I'm sorry, George, — yes, decidedly — I think I must say that, George — it's my duty to tell you so."
>
> "Why are you sorry, sir?" said George calmly.
>
> "Why, to see you, as it were, setting yourself in opposition to the laws of your country."

13. I owe this insight to a former student, James T. Lehner, M.D.

"*My* country!" said George, with a strong and bitter emphasis; "what country have I, but the grave — and I wish to God that I was laid there!"

"Why, George, no — no — it won't do; this way of talking is wicked — unscriptural. George, you've got a hard master — in fact, wicked — well he conducts himself reprehensibly — I can't pretend to defend him. But you know how the angel commanded Hagar to return to her mistress, and submit herself under the hand; and the apostle sent Onesimus back to his master."

"Don't quote Bible at me that way, Mr. Wilson," said George, with a flashing eye, "don't! for my wife is a Christian, and I mean to be, if ever I get to where I can, but to quote the Bible to a fellow in my circumstances, is enough to make him give up altogether. I appeal to God Almighty; — I'm willing to go with the case to Him, and ask Him if I do wrong to seek my freedom."

"These feelings are quite natural, George," said the good-natured man, blowing his nose. "Yes, they're natural, but it is my duty not to encourage 'em in you. Yes, my boy, I'm sorry for you, now; it's a bad case — very bad; but the apostle says, 'Let every one abide in the condition in which he is called.' We must all submit to the indications of Providence, George, — don't you see?"

George stood with his head drawn back, his arms folded tightly over his broad breast, and a bitter smile curling his lips.

"I wonder, Mr Wilson, if the Indians should come and take you a prisoner away from your wife and children, and want to keep you all your life hoeing corn for them, if you'd think it your duty to abide in the condition in which you were called. I rather think that you'd think the first stray horse you could find an indication of Providence — shouldn't you?"[14]

Mr. Wilson was described as "much tumbled up and down in his mind," and George was pressing him to clear his mind. St. Clare, whose mind was always clear, finally came to his own conclusion: "My view of Christianity is such that I think no man can consistently profess it without throwing the whole weight of his being against this monstrous system of injustice that lies at the foundation of our society; and, if need be, sacrificing himself in the battle." But St. Clare did not become a Christian "because I have had only that kind of benevolence which consists in lying

14. Beecher Stowe, *Uncle Tom's Cabin*, 11:114-15.

on a sofa, and cursing the church and clergy for not being martyrs and confessors."[15]

We who tend to be like Mr. Wilson but need to be like George must make our own ways forward, wary of self-gratifying illusions. Hoping to catch fresh provocation from the origins of our belief, this book will begin with the New Testament and draw from it implications that seem simple yet are hard to look at. It is a touchy task. The New Testament was written by believers timebound and myopic like ourselves, folks who could not quite stretch their minds to the full measure of the Mystery. Their inspired message was ambiguous, and sometimes at odds with itself. Their lifestyle was something less than best, though perhaps missing the mark less than ours.

Abolition would not be the definitive compliance, long overdue, with Paul's Letter to Philemon. Taken apart from Paul's great taunt to Philemon, abolition would be not very lifegiving at all. The British Parliament, for instance, was able to abolish slavery in 1834, and in that same year it enacted the New Poor Law designed to incarcerate British paupers in workhouses where husbands would be separated from wives, and both sexes would be subjected to slavelike labor, regimentation, surveillance, and discipline.[16] Abolition by itself was one of those potentially great moral events that have both succeeded and suffered from near-sighted sponsorship. Theoretically and historically, the mere outlawing of slavery belonged to a much shorter agenda than Paul's injunction to brotherhood.

In one sense there could be no response to Paul's request short of liberation and fraternization. In another sense, whether or not the two men remained master and slave was not central to their moral transformation in Christ. Sympathize with Philemon! And sympathize with Onesimus (though perhaps not quite so much, for his moral risk was probably the lesser)! Sympathize with any believer in Jesus Christ, for whom the impossible becomes mandatory, eternal life ruinous, brotherhood and sisterhood fatal. Like Philemon, we do not have the challenge put squarely to us in so many words. It grows out of a Gospel that taunts us to make slaves and masters into brothers and sisters, yet feels like only a provocation, not an empowerment. There is no social order a Christian should not overthrow. But there is no living without a social order, and no social order that is ever going to embody successfully the imperatives of Christ, or

15. Beecher Stowe, *Uncle Tom's Cabin*, 28:320-21.

16. David Brion Davis, *Slavery and Human Progress* (New York: Oxford University Press, 1984), p. 122.

even invite us to imagine their full grasp. We find ourselves wringing our hands in frustration at being — not "unprofitable servants," but shiftless slaves.[17]

Paul's demand required of believers endlessly more than abolition: both before any laws could be changed, and after. Those who take the Gospel to heart often make poor subscribers to moral manifestoes and petitions and coalitions, because their imaginations usually run more wildly and deeply beyond the specific grievance at hand. Once the Christian mystery has hold of their moral imaginations, they can appear, or be, immobilized, like Augustine St. Clare, and Tolstoy, because the unbounded searching of their consciences prompts them to so many possibilities, so many imperatives. The imagination is the first of the human faculties to become a catechumen, and it can nag both mind and will with the limitless generosities implicit in any of Jesus' or Paul's throwaway lines. If Philemon had no imagination, or a dull and defensive one, then his problem was puny. But if his imagination was lively and fearless, as I suspect it was at Paul's prompting, then his problem was as great as the Gospel. Please God ours will be like that.

The theologian's dangerous venture is to catch the glow of Christ's fiery face reflected in the eyes of Matthew, Mark, and those others. This book is one attempt to accept the New Testament's urging to go beyond itself. Undeveloped as that Testament may be, it is the classic collection of prophetic messages to which the Church is answerable, and before which all of us must squirm. Open-eyed study and experience will see that in our midst there abide superstition, weasel-wording cowardice, ennui, and persistent exploitation. So it ever was. This book proposes not to ignore

17. "Edmund Biot articulated precisely the ideology that dominated antislavery thought until it was finally repudiated by radical abolitionists. Explaining why Christianity had accepted ancient slavery as a 'given condition,' directing its efforts less to remedial legislation than to 'the morality of men,' Biot concluded:

It is evident that laws too favorable to the slaves would have strongly tended to upset the whole world edifice, already crumbling under the repeated blows of foreign invasions. It was preferable, in order to maintain public tranquility, that improvements in the lot of the slave be brought about progressively through the improvements of the master.

"This faith in the indirect benefits of Christianization — like the faith in the indirect benefits of political and economic freedom — gave way only slowly and incompletely to the belief in a new or second dispensation, distinguished by conscious decision, collective effort, and mobilization of public opinion." Davis, *Slavery and Human Progress*, pp. 114-15.

that unhappy sight, but more emphatically to share the vision of better joys put before us. I cannot decide whether it is a comfort or a disappointment to launch an undertaking with the knowledge beforehand that it is too wonderful to allow of present satisfaction.[18]

18. This discussion of slavery and its consideration by Christians is indebted to the following: S. Scott Bartchy: *MAΛΛON XPHΣAI: First Century Slavery and the Interpretation of 1 Corinthians 7:21* (Missoula: Society of Biblical Literature, 1973); idem, "Philemon, Epistle to," & "Slavery: New Testament," *Anchor Bible Dictionary* 5:305-9; 6:65-73; K. R. Bradley, *Slaves and Masters in the Roman Empire: A Study in Social Control* (Brussels: Collection Latomus [*Revue d'Études Latines*], 1984); Moses I. Finley, *Ancient Slavery and Modern Ideology* (New York: Viking, 1980); J. Albert Harrill, *The Manumission of Slaves in Early Christianity* (Tübingen: J. C. B. Mohr [Paul Siebeck], 1995); Orlando Patterson, *Slavery and Social Death* (Cambridge, Mass.: Harvard University Press, 1982); Joseph Vogt, *Ancient Slavery and the Ideal of Man,* trans. Thomas Wiedemann (Cambridge, Mass.: Harvard University Press, 1975); Wiedemann, *Greek and Roman Slavery* (Baltimore: Johns Hopkins University Press, 1981).

A Distinctive Doctrine

CHAPTER TWO

The Father of Jesus, and Strange Gods Before Him

Voltaire once wrote in his notebook, "God made man in his image and likeness, and man has returned the favor."[1] Like Caiaphas before him, the cynical French deist occasionally enjoyed the gift of making religious observations that were truer than he knew. For a character study of deities in the mythologies and theologies of various religions discloses enough pettiness and outrage to confirm Voltaire's suspicion that most gods are patterned after their worshipers, rather than vice versa.

Indeed, gods are often likened to the worst of their worshipers. "Homer and Hesiod have attributed to the gods everything that is a shame and reproach among men, stealing and committing adultery and deceiving each other."[2] The gods of the Greeks, later adopted by the Romans, were a promiscuous lot. The mythologies of both peoples display the kind of family quarreling, incest, and fratricide which explain how the gods managed to slip unnoticed into the battles of the men and the beds of the women of Athens and Rome and other similarly devout cities. As Clifford Howell once said of Olympus, "Concerning their goings-on up there the less said the better!"[3] The massacres of war prisoners necessary to satiate

---

1. *Voltaire's Notebooks*, ed. Theodore Besterman, vol. 1 (Toronto: University of Toronto Press, 1952), p. 231. See also his *Oeuvres complètes* (Paris: Garnier Fràres, 1880), 26:330, 29:545-46, 30:4-5; *Correspondance*, ed. Besterman, vol. 67 (Geneva: Institut et Musée Voltaire, 1961), pp. 106-7, no. 13588. I am grateful to Professor Thomas Schlereth for drawing my attention to these passages.

2. Xenophanes, *Fragments*, 169.

3. Clifford Howell, S.J., *Of Sacraments and Sacrifice* (Collegeville, Minn.: Liturgical Press, 1952), p. 96.

37

Huitzilopochtli and his annual roster of 365 associate divinities suggest that the Aztec gods were as bloodthirsty as the Aztec people. Christianity records similar degradations. Saints may not be gods, but they are believed to be like God. What would God be like for devotees of the traditional protector against fires: "Holy St. Florian, Save our house; Let someone else's burn down!"? In a similar vein, the blessing of a flag in the old *Roman Ritual* virtually called on God to curse the home country's enemies.

Power may be the occupational hazard of being a god. There seems, in fact, to be a repeated alignment of gods with the ugly purposes of homicide. Benvenuto Cellini, for example, tells us in his memoirs of the time when he was besieged with Pope Clement VII within Castel Sant' Angelo by Charles V's troops during the sack of Rome. Boastful of his marksmanship, Cellini let fly with a small artillery piece and blew in half a Spanish officer standing far off in the trenches.

> The Pope, who was expecting nothing of this kind, derived great pleasure and amazement from the sight, both because it seemed to him impossible that one should aim and hit the mark at such a distance, and also because the man was cut in two, and he could not comprehend how this should happen. He sent for me, and asked about it. I explained all the devices I had used in firing; but told him that why the man was cut in halves, neither he nor I could know. Upon my bended knees I then besought him to give me the pardon of his blessing for that homicide; and for all others I had committed in the castle in the service of the Church. Thereat the Pope, raising his hand, and making a large open sign of the cross on my face, told me that he blessed me, and that he gave me pardon for all murders I had ever perpetrated, or ever should perpetrate, in the service of the Apostolic Church.[4]

An interesting contrast with Cellini is General George Patton, whose memoirs betray somewhat more uneasiness about the divine good pleasure:

> The first Sunday I spent in Normandy was quite impressive. I went to a Catholic Field Mass where all of us were armed. As we knelt in the mud in the slight drizzle, we could distinctly hear the

4. *The Life of Benvenuto Cellini*, trans. & ed. John Addington Symonds (New York: Heritage [n.d.]), p. 47.

roar of the guns, and the whole sky was filled with airplanes on their missions of destruction . . . quite at variance with the teachings of the religion we were practicing. . . .

An arresting sight were the crucifixes at road intersections; these were used by Signal personnel as supplementary telephone posts. While the crosses were in no way injured, I could not help thinking of the incongruity of the lethal messages passing over the wires. . . .

Christmas dawned clear and cold; lovely weather for killing Germans, although the thought seemed somewhat at variance with the spirit of the day.[5]

Nevertheless, when the winter rains of 1944 immobilized his armored equipment, Patton impatiently directed his chaplains to lead prayers for dry weather. Shortly before Christmas he summoned Father O'Neill, Third Army chaplain:

General Patton: "Chaplain, I want you to publish a prayer for good weather. I'm tired of these soldiers having to fight mud and floods as well as Germans. See if we can't get God to work on our side."

Chaplain O'Neill: "Sir, it's going to take a pretty thick rug for that kind of praying."

General Patton: "I don't care if it takes the flying carpet. I want the praying done."

Chaplain O'Neill: "Yes, sir. May I say, General, that it isn't a customary thing among men of my profession to pray for clear weather to kill fellow men."

General Patton: "Chaplain, are you teaching me theology or are you the Chaplain of the Third Army? I want a prayer."

Chaplain O'Neill: "Yes, sir."

The prayer, printed by Army Engineers and distributed on cards with Patton's holiday greetings on the reverse side, besought the Deity thus:

Almighty and most merciful Father, we humbly beseech Thee, of Thy great goodness, to restrain these immoderate rains with which we have had to contend. Grant us fair weather for Battle. Graciously hearken to us as soldiers who call upon Thee that, armed with Thy

5. George S. Patton, Jr., *War as I Knew It* (Boston: Houghton Mifflin, 1949), pp. 95-96, 202.

power, we may advance from victory to victory, and crush the oppression and wickedness of our enemies, and establish Thy justice among men and nations. Amen.[6]

Of his great goodness God, we may infer, responded promptly with the Battle of the Bulge.

In the same spirit George Bush's Presidential Proclamation calling for a National Day of Prayer on 3 February 1991 on behalf of Operation Desert Storm, wove together the themes of God and Nation in a way that would have served the needs of any King of Samaria:

> As one Nation under God, we Americans are deeply mindful of both our dependence upon the Almighty and our obligations as a people He has richly blessed. From our very beginnings as a Nation, we have relied upon God's strength and guidance in war and peace. . . .
>
> Today the United States is engaged in a great struggle to uphold the principles of national sovereignty and international order and to defend the lives and liberty of innocent people. . . . Our cause is moral and just. However confident of our purpose, however determined to prevail, we Americans continue to yearn for peace and for the safety of our service men and women in the Persian Gulf. With these great hopes in mind, I ask all Americans to unite in humble and contrite prayer to Almighty God. May it please our Heavenly Father to look upon this Nation, judging not our worthiness but our need, and to grant us His continued strength and guidance. . . .
>
> "All this being done, in sincerity and truth," as President Lincoln once wrote, "Let us then rest humbly in the hope authorized by the Divine teachings, that the united cry of the Nation will be heard on high, and answered . . ." by Almighty God, our refuge and our strength, our rock and our salvation.[7]

6. Patton, *War as I Knew It,* pp. 184-85.

7. George Bush, "For a National Day of Prayer, February 3, 1991, By the President of the United States of America: A Proclamation," The White House, Office of the Press Secretary (Fort Stewart, Georgia), 1 February 1991. The same theme came out in the President's radio address promoting the prayer day:

At this moment, America, the finest, most loving nation on Earth, is at war. At war against the oldest enemy of the human spirit — evil that threatens world peace.

At this moment, men and women of courage and endurance stand on the

Gods are imagined to be so like ourselves as often to be unsavory. Thomas Hardy implies as much in his *Return of the Native* when he comments on the heroine:

> Eustacia Vye was the raw material of a divinity. On Olympus she would have done well with a little preparation. She had the passions and instincts which make a model goddess, that is, those which make not quite a model woman. Had it been possible for the earth and mankind to be entirely in her grasp for awhile, had she brandished the distaff, the spindle, and the shears at her own free will, few in the world would have noticed the change of government. There would have been the same inequality of lot, the same generosity before justice, the same perpetual dilemmas, the same captious alternation of caresses and blows that we endure now.[8]

The hope, in fact, is sometimes expressed that could God manage to be no more decent than we humans are, that would be gratifying enough. "If I were God," said Sidney Webb, "and he were I, I'd forgive him." Something of the same lay beneath the well-known English gravestone:

> Have mercy on my soul, Lord God
> As I would do, were I Lord God
> and you were Martin Elginbrodde

With equal imagination Paul Bryan Crowe, a high school dropout and foundry worker in Louisville who late in life discovered Melville, Elizabeth Barrett Browning, and Shakespeare, has done some instinctual reflecting on God from his own experiences:

---

harsh desert and sail the seas of the Gulf. By their presence they're bearing witness to the fact that the triumph of the moral order is the vision that compels us. . . .

So many of us, compelled by a deep need for God's wisdom in all we do, turn to prayer. We pray for God's protection in all we undertake, for God's love to fill our hearts, and for God's peace to be the moral North Star that guides us.

"Radio address by the President,"
White House press release, 2 February 1991

8. Thomas Hardy, *Return of the Native* (New York: Harper, 1905), p. 77.

My father was a drunk, like a lot of people. He was rough as a cob, born and raised in Portland and damn proud of it. He was a sheet metal worker for the L&N for 32 years. But he lived until he was 83, and there's 51 years I can't account for. He was 56 when I was born, and didn't have a hell of a lot of time for a new kid. I remember a fight we had on Christmas Eve when I was 17. I grabbed the old man, who was 73, and threw him down on the ground and told him I thought I'd break his neck.

You know what he did? He spit right in my eye. I was so stunned I didn't know what to do. So I walked away and didn't speak to him for six years. Finally I decided I wanted to talk to him again, and he said, "Whatever you want." Under different circumstances I might have loved him, but his drinking got in the way. But I can't wait until I get over to Glory and have the opportunity to sit down with him and get to know him better.

This leads Crowe to thoughts on God and the Hereafter. His God is a good guy who

eats chicken, drinks beer, loves moonlight on the river and would even smoke a joint if you offered it to him. I can't believe what churches and so-called religious people say. I had eight or ten people tell me that the tornado of '74 was God's warning. My God isn't in charge of tornadoes. He wouldn't throw one at you just for kicks. My God's waiting over there with a table laid for me. When I get there, he's going to say, "I'm God, and I love you. Forget all the bull you heard on earth."[9]

John Steinbeck offers a wonderfully wry send-up of the Christian affinity for a vengeful God in *Travels with Charley*, his memoir of a drive around the country in Rocinante, his pickup truck, with Charley, his faithful hound:

Sunday morning, in a Vermont town, my last day in New England, I shaved, dressed in a suit, polished my shoes, whited my sepulcher, and looked for a church to attend. Several I eliminated for reasons I do not now remember, but on seeing a John Knox church I

9. Paul Bryan Crowe as quoted in John Flynn, "Blue collar, silver tongue: Books made carouser a philosopher," (Louisville) *Courier-Journal*, 21 January 1977, B1.

drove into a side street and parked Rocinante out of sight, gave Charley his instructions about watching the truck, and took my way with dignity to a church of blindingly white ship lap. I took my seat in the rear of the spotless, polished place of worship. The prayers were to the point, directing the attention of the Almighty to certain weaknesses and undivine tendencies I know to be mine and could only suppose were shared by others gathered there.

The service did my heart and I hope my soul some good. It had been long since I had heard such an approach. It is our practice now, at least in the large cities, to find from our psychiatric priesthood that our sins aren't really sins at all but accidents that are set in motion by forces beyond our control. There was no such nonsense in this church. The minister, a man of iron with tool-steel eyes and a delivery like a pneumatic drill, opened up with prayer and reassured us that we were a pretty sorry lot. And he was right. We didn't amount to much to start with, and due to our own tawdry efforts we had been slipping ever since. Then, having softened us up, he went into a glorious sermon, a fire-and-brimstone sermon. Having proved that we, or perhaps only I, were no damn good, he painted with cool certainty what was likely to happen to us if we didn't make some basic reorganizations for which he didn't hold out much hope. He spoke of hell as an expert, not the mush-mush hell of these soft days, but a well-stoked, white-hot hell served by technicians of the first order. This reverend brought it to a point where we could understand it, a good hard coal fire, plenty of draft, and a squad of open-hearth devils who put their hearts into their work, and their work was me. I began to feel good all over. For some years now God has been a pal to us, practicing togetherness, and that causes the same emptiness a father does playing softball with his son. But this Vermont God cared enough about me to go to a lot of trouble kicking the hell out of me. He put my sins in a new perspective. Whereas they had been small and mean and nasty and best forgotten, this minister gave them some size and bloom and dignity. I hadn't been thinking very well of myself for some years, but if my sins had this dimension there was some pride left. I wasn't a naughty child but a first rate sinner, and I was going to catch it.

I felt so revived in spirit that I put five dollars in the plate, and afterward, in front of the church, shook hands warmly with the minister and as many of the congregation as I could. It gave me a lovely sense of evil-doing that lasted clear through till Tuesday. I even con-

43

sidered beating Charley to give him some satisfaction too, because Charley is only a little less sinful than I. All across the country I went to church on Sundays, a different denomination every week, but nowhere did I find the quality of that Vermont preacher. He forged a religion to last, not predigested obsolescence.[10]

The only common reason people would resort to gods is that the latter were believed to exercise considerable power in this world's affairs. No wonder, then, if they were imagined to be as pouty and peevish as most powerful human rulers. No wonder either that the gods have been appreciated and imagined as back-up authorities for those who govern others on earth. Christians seem as inclined this way as others, past and present. We have long believed that our God does not share in the primitive crudities of the pagan deities, but there is evidence to the contrary. Indeed, much of the primitive distortion in our notion of God is introduced in the primitive period of our lives: our childhood. The youthful unfolding of the individual in some ways recapitulates the development of humankind. From the parents a child learns of a god who strongly disapproves of disobedience, and hitting one's sisters and brothers, and telling lies. The youngster goes to school, and finds that God also shares many law-and-order concerns of the teachers. At church, the god of the pastor displays a more focused set of priorities: emphasis is laid upon mass and confession and communion and on collecting food for the poor and clothes for the homeless. The youngster may notice out of the corner of her eye that God is also moved by concern for the fiscal participation of her parents. When she reaches the age for high school the child finds that God's own preoccupations have kept pace with hers: they share strong but conflicted interests in sex, drink, and drugs. Much later, after emerging from the years of youth, she may notice — not without some resentment — that the God had been used as a sanction by all those who were responsible for her discipline. A mother goaded beyond her patience might threaten her child with a yet more dread reckoning at the end of the day — vengeance is mine, saith the father. But when both parents together are at their wits' end, there is always the no-nonsense option of delivering children into the hands of the living God. God is thus associated, unwittingly but with a deep and powerful durability, with fear.

There has always been a traditional alliance between religion and rule.

10. John Steinbeck, *Travels with Charley* (New York: Viking, 1962), pp. 77-79. Mary Lee Freeman, a former student, first drew this text to my attention.

Karl Marx insisted that religion, "the sigh of the oppressed creature," had been used by the ruling class as a sedative for the exploited working class. Others have observed that the basically conservative interests of state and church (and thereby the church's God) have made them congenial allies throughout history.

> It is thus possible to say that Churches, understood as monopolistic combinations of full-time experts in a religious definition of reality, are inherently conservative once they have succeeded in reestablishing their monopoly in a given society. Conversely, ruling groups with a stake in the maintenance of the political status quo are inherently churchly in their religious orientation and, by the same token, suspicious of all innovations in the religious tradition.[11]

The gods have repeatedly been associated with power figures of home, tribe, and nation, and they have not much benefited from keeping such company.

The Father of Jesus: a much stranger God

Divinity seems to face three occupational hazards. First: gods are strange. Not simply in Isaiah's sense that God's thoughts are not our thoughts, nor his ways our ways — but more by way of caprice. Part of the fear we have of gods is that there is no one to whom they have to account for their moods — hence they tend to indulge themselves and to act arbitrarily. Since the ancient and (perhaps) less savage days when the divine hand was seen in flood and earthquake, stillbirth and plague, humans have been bewildered by the divine mood-swings between wrath and complaisance. One can never be secure in anticipating what a god will do, still less how a goddess will react. Such a god was in the mind of the third-grader who was retelling the parable of the Sheep and the Goats: "Then the king will say to the ones on the left side, 'Get out of my sight. You make me nervous.'"

This evokes the second hazardous trait of divinity: gods are powerful. This makes the caprice of deities all the more worrisome: in their hands they hold the keys of life and death, prosperity and destitution, war and

11. Peter L. Berger & Thomas Luckmann, *The Social Construction of Reality: A Treatise in the Sociology of Knowledge* (New York: Doubleday, 1966), p. 113.

peace. Oddly enough, gods are usually not acknowledged to hold such sway within the human heart. Instead, they bear down upon us from without, with all that fortune or misfortune can effect.

Thirdly, gods concern themselves with what we humans do. It is not because they care for us that much, nor that the demands they make are moral, but they do scrutinize human behavior and treat us according as we please or displease them.

It is this combination of divine qualities — unknown, mighty, and judgmental — that makes most gods distinctly unpleasant. Most gods are not quite as appealing as your better friends. Far from hankering after an eternity of their companionship, most people would probably not be anxious to spend a weekend with their particular god or anyone else's. By a strange reversal of spookery, heaven has become haunted with the ghosts of humankind: humans who are as persistently impersonal and fearsome as those who dominate among us. If power tends to corrupt, and absolute power corrupts absolutely, to whom would it apply better than to gods? In assimilating deity to our familiar and exploitative rulers, we have created a heaven that is peopled by the least appealing ghosts possible. We have corrupted god, and no wonder that we are not attracted by a god of our making who can be as peremptory, punitive, and petty as we are in our worst (that is, omnipotent) moments.

Yet there has been, in Israel and the Church, a strange and inexorable resistance to this human corruption of God. Our theological tradition has been continually obscured, infected by the malignancies which, as we have argued, commonly prey upon every religion, to the point where Jews and Christians have sometimes worshipped a god scarcely different from those of their pagan neighbors. Nor can we claim any method different from the common one: extrapolating from our human knowledge — illuminated, as we believe, by inspired insight — in the hope of reaching and clarifying a concept of who lies beyond. No one has seen God; we have only humans as suggestive paradigms.

But what Christians rejoice in is a better knowledge of a better God, since we have a new image and likeness to behold: Jesus of Nazareth. Those who believe that Jesus is the Onlybegotten Son of God are not so much making a statement about Jesus as they are confessing that *he* is the one who embodies God in our midst. Like Father, like Son. Jesus, who dies for those who connive at his murder, is the best — indeed, the ultimate — model we have of what God is truly like. Jesus' life, death, and appearances after his resurrection are only a hint, and even an unsatisfying hint, of God. God, after all, cannot be adequately revealed in human affairs, nor utterly incarnated. All that we can see, even in Jesus, true God and true man, is a suggestion, an allusion to what eye has not seen clearly nor ear heard precisely because the Lord is too awesome to be displayed fully on earth to the human heart or the human cosmos.

Nevertheless, the Father that Jesus reveals is the put-down and antithesis of our other gods. For one thing, he is not strange. He is indeed a mystery: not in the sense that he is unintelligible, or an enigma who throws us into confusion, or is wrapped in darkness, but, on the contrary, there is so much to understand that we can never get to the bottom of it; such a depth of light is exposed to us, we can never take in all that it reveals. In that sense he is a mystery: he is unfathomable yet invites us to know him ever more. And what is strikingly knowable and welcome to know is that he has no moods or caprice, no arbitrary seasons of change. He has a single relentless stance toward us: he loves us. Nor is the Father of Jesus revealed to us as possessed of force. Jesus, who shuns all political influence, and refuses to call even his own followers to his aid, let alone legions of angels on full alert, is helpless before the power of any human who does him violence. Yet it is by his very bruises that we are healed. He emerges, unlike even our strange gods, as capable of touching the human heart. He is not the god of storms or of wars, but the Son of him who can leave us our freedom yet display his power in us. It is the greatest power, transforming from within. Lastly, the Father of Jesus does not scrutinize our lives. He does not judge us, because he loves even those who are evil.

In a word, the Father of Jesus loves sinners. He is the only God humankind ever heard of who loves sinners. Gods despise sinners, but the Father of Jesus loves all, no matter what they do. And, of course, this is almost too incredible for us to accept.

The Father's love embodied in Jesus is characteristically different from our natural human way of loving. But before getting some clarity on that, we must beware that the very word "love" has become equivocal in most languages. In one sense it means a benevolent, self-sacrificing loyalty, an act of the will. In another, almost contrary, sense it means "liking," an instinctual desire for something or someone, an act of the senses and emotions. For instance, I am drawn to "love" various things and persons. I "love" the Oregon coast at sunset, the Brandenburg concerti, asparagus, and my eighth grade teacher. No matter how one cares to name these reactions — savoring, "loving," liking, desiring, appreciating — there is a common dynamic in them all. I am attracted by certain qualities in these other persons and things, qualities that willy-nilly I find congenial and appealing. I did not decide to like asparagus. Indeed, there were early years when asparagus went unappreciated (likewise, perhaps, the eighth grade teacher). But somehow since childhood my apprehensions and evaluations have changed — not by choice — and here I am liking asparagus, and Sister Kathleen Clare. When I "love" as a man, I am drawn inexorably by the good perceived in the other. I "love" someone for what I sense in him or her. The contrary is also true. There are some people who repel us, and we cannot decide to have it otherwise. We can be civil, we can be kind or loyal, can marry them, but we cannot like or "love" them.

Yet we can love them. Love, in the proper sense of that word, is a matter of choice, of behavior that can be decided. Human love is quite unlike human "loving," or liking, for our likes are autonomous reactions and often run athwart our choices. It is possible for humans to move beyond their native, self-centered concern into a care for others that transcends likes and preferences. I am the object of my likes, but the subject of my loves. Unfortunately, by calling both movements "love" we obscure how radically different an act of true love is from that other kind of response, best called liking. True love requires a self-expenditure that disentangles us so strenuously and single-heartedly from the snarl of our likes that it is possible, Christians believe, only by God's liberating enablement. It can best be seen as embodied in Jesus, who in turn displays the kind of Father he has, that Father to whom John simply gives the name "Love."

Unlike ourselves, the Father loves us, not for what he finds in us, but for what lies within himself. It is not because we are good that God loves us, nor only the good among us whom he loves. It is because he is so unutterably good that God loves us all, good and evil alike. Put most clearly: the Father of Jesus loves sinners. He loves the loveless, the unloving, the (for unaided us) unlovable. He does not detect what is congenial, appealing, sound, or attractive, and respond to it with his favor. Indeed, he does not respond at all. He initiates. His is motiveless love, radiating forth eternally. And because the Father of Jesus is creative, his love originates good rather than rewarding it. Augustine had this divine priority in mind in his aphorism, *Quia amasti me, fecisti me amabilem*. "By loving me, you made me lovable."

Jesus, who lives for those whose likes are all awry and whose love is dead, and who dies that his killers might live, reveals a Father who has no wrath. The Father cannot be offended — nor can he be pleased — by what we humans do. This appears to be indifference, but it is the very opposite of indifference. The Lord who searches the heart and reins of humans, who hears our most casual word, who has an eye cocked always

48

on the sparrow, does not cherish us as we deserve — were it so we would be desolate — but he loves us as he must, he is unwilling to do otherwise. He *is* Love. Hard as it is for us to believe, for we neither give nor receive love among ourselves in this way, we yet believe, provoked by the life, death, and glorious reconciling appearances of the Carpenter-Messiah, that his Father is more loving, more forgiving, more cherishing than Abraham, Isaac, or Jacob could have dreamt.

What this says simply is that the Father of Jesus is gracious. His love is gratuitous. In one sense a person loves gratuitously in that she is favorable to another person without his deserving it. It is a deeper and more poignant grace to be favorable to one who denies her his favor, and is hostile and injurious. The supreme grace is to be implacably favorable without any regard to another person's behavior. Jesus conveys that there is no motivation in God, no *quid pro quo*, nothing he stands to gain. His love is utterly gratuitous in a way, as I have said, that defies our imagination. As a response to grace there is a corresponding spectrum of gratitude, which becomes supremely necessary when evoked by this supreme grace: necessary, not for God's sake, but for ours. For most gods it is a slight if they fail to receive their due worship from the humans they have favored, but for the Father of Jesus there can be no such misfortune. Our gratitude fills no need of his, though it does fulfill a need in ourselves. God, then, is gracious in a way that can only be hinted at in human events, and it is this unspeakable, incredible grace of his that most particularly sets him apart from all strange gods that humans have entertained before him.

Most gods and goddesses, patterned as they have been after human lords and ladies, have been more wanton than benevolent. While gods have at critical moments proven useful and have been invoked with regularity, they are not persons you would care to have around in your more casual moments. Gods, like powerful patrons, are to be consulted in time of human need, but not supped with overly often. Most religions present humankind with the prospect of joining the gods after death. That prospect is far from appealing, if truth were told. If the Father of Jesus has sometimes evoked a similar and characteristic dread and diffidence, it is precisely because he has been unwittingly likened by our traditions to those pagan gods whom alone he is not prepared to tolerate. For, beside them, he really is by far the Strangest of All.

Scripture: Memoir of the Church

The Christian vision of God might best be illuminated at this point by reference to the earliest and classic documents of Israel and the Church. But before turning to Scripture I should clarify one or two principles of understanding which I shall be using.

First of all, the Bible is a collection of books that reflect more than ten centuries of religious tradition within one developing people. It was an argumentative millennium, and the controversies, revisions, reversals, and breakthroughs of thought that marked the ideological development of God's people during this period that all later generations must regard as classical, are represented in and recoverable from these books chosen from among all those that were produced. A book written in the third century, B.C., for example, when compared with a document dating back to the tenth century, will be found to repudiate or correct some of the views in the more ancient document, while refining others. And even single books that have been revised by numerous hands over as much as 700 years will display a diversity of theology that has not been obliterated by successive updating. The Bible is not systematically homogeneous, and it presents its interpreter with a scatter of different beliefs and prospects that are or seem to be somewhat askew of each other. It is not the task of the biblical reader simply to tease out the best and most enlightened theology available in the Bible, since the process of development which has left a millennial residue in Scripture has continued on unabated ever since. In a sense everything in the Bible is obsolete for every subsequent believer. Yet as the tradition unfolds from within itself, as earlier belief is continuously telescoping forward into later elaborations of the same belief, the interpreter must try to plot the trajectory of faith in its growth and unfolding.

This is itself a creative act. There is no system of baseline norms by which one can examine and evaluate Scripture, since the ancient traditions can be studied only from the mobile vantage point of the believing community. This is why I insist it is a creative as well as a critical task. The modern critic must be continually making choices about what is primitive and what advanced, what regressive and what revolutionary, within the various books. Her own viewpoint is fixed in a certain time and culture and era of the Church. Thus her angle of retrospect is like that of no other time, and her interpretation must perforce be affected by it. It is nothing she can avoid, nor should she. But when she evaluates the texts that lie before her, she cannot simply claim to be repeating what Jeremiah or Paul or Luke meant. She is offering a synthesis for which she herself, standing where she does, must claim responsibility as they did. Of course it is nothing she does alone. It is the Church who understands her own Bible.[12]

This responsibility for understanding and interpreting is open to abuse. Thus, for example, in 1925 Bruce Barton published *The Man Nobody Knows*, which made out that Jesus was the original advertising executive, the harbinger of our consumer-oriented society. In 1952 the *Olive Pell Bible* appeared, wherein Mrs. Pell had systematically excised all mention of sex, violence, and meat-eating, much as Martin Luther was once of a mind to omit the Letter of James from the New Testament since it conflicted with his theology of faith and works. Pier Paolo Pasolini's film, *The Gospel According to Saint Matthew*, produced in the cutting room a Jesus who is an exact replica of an Italian communist cell leader. These are but a few of the violent hands that have been laid on the Bible by interpreters who were anxious for it to speak with but one voice, and that voice to be in harmony with their own. Yet despite these and so many other examples, there is no utterly disengaged standpoint possible. The Bible is not uniform within itself, for it contains the choice and collected residue from the earliest age of belief, which was then selectively gathered and successively published and republished as the classical collection to which all future belief, in order to develop authentically, would have to be tethered, and would have to serve as its legitimate continuation.

The Bible is the Church's family album. And since the Samaritans broke with the Jews, then the Jews with the Christians, then the Protestants with the Catholics, then the Mormons with the Protestants (and in all cases, vice versa), all these continuing communities of belief have finalized their distinctive canonical lists and editions of the books that track and justify the ongoing trajectory up to each one's particular point and angle

---

12. What Anglican biblical scholar Charles F. D. Moule said about moral matters may be applied to doctrinal ones as well:

> What is written is an indispensable aid to meeting God; but it is not in the inanimate writings, but in the living encounter — jointly shared with others and checked in mutual debate — that the divine guidance is to be sought. While there is obviously a truth in the saying, "The Church to teach; the Scriptures to prove," for ethics the formula might rather be "The Scriptures to lead to God in Jesus Christ; the Holy Spirit in the Church through Jesus Christ to teach." . . . The organ of perception through which the Holy Spirit may be expected to speak with distinctively Christian moral guidance is the *Christian worshipping congregation listening critically.*

"Important Moral Issues," The Expository Times
74, 12 (September 1963): 373, 372

of differentiation, and secure their respective traditions of subsequent belief that have continued to develop and differentiate after their canons were closed, just as they had been developing throughout their classical, scriptural eras. These distinct communities all have their own self-understandings, but the Church believes that the same Spirit which inspired the prophets and apostles and their fellow-seers to write and re-write as they did, was needed by the Church to have the intuition and judgment to recognize the books in which its faith was rooted, and is still needed by the Church to read them and construe them instinctively, and faithfully to elaborate and expound the successor-faith of those ancestors.

Thus one same charism empowers one continuous community to write, accredit, read, and cultivate the faith once — and still being — delivered to the saints. To read the Bible, then, is an undertaking both passive and active, preservative and creative, antiquarian and innovative, for the Church confesses that these Scriptures are her inspired capstan of fidelity, and also believes that she, too, has the Spirit. The Bible is her genealogy, her memoir, her credential; it is also her provocation and her inspiration.

If anyone would have a hermeneutic advantage in approaching the Bible, it would be the believer who stands most correctly — through faith, communion, prayer, and openness to the corrective of communal debate — within the ongoing trajectory of belief as it passes through our time. Thus I shall in no way maintain that the particular theology of grace which this book expounds is to be found unchallenged within the biblical documents. There are various views of grace mingled there. In arguing that this understanding grows from the view that thrusts forward out of a common heritage with Israel, and that it is the emergent and distinctive contribution of Christianity, I must still take responsibility for the hindsight I claim, and realize that it depends not simply on a scholarly handling of the literature, but on the pastoral and theological and prophetic worth of my own stance today. It is a view that claims to be inspired by the Bible. But other views, some quite adverse, have claimed to rely upon similar inspiration. My remarks on the proper use and meaning of Scripture are not extensive here, and will be more by way of illustration than of proof, since the view of grace offered here has not so much been explicitly denied by Christians as it has been inadvertently neglected, or felt to be too incredible to accept. This is something to be displayed, not proved.

The gracious God in Scripture

The literature of Israel broods repeatedly over the problem of its relation to Yahweh. On the one hand, his choice of Abraham, Isaac, Jacob and the tribes of Israel is understood as gratuitous, and since he is in sovereign control of Israel's affairs, he is mighty enough and more than enough to ensure the faithful fealty of his people. On the other hand, there is the constant worry that, no matter how gracious their Lord, the Hebrews could always anger him beyond recall. The tension between these two views is embodied in two distinct covenant arrangements. The covenant made by the Lord with David and his house is strong on grace: God unilaterally chooses David, the inauspicious shepherd boy, to be king, and promises outright that his descendants will rule over Israel forever. God would adopt David's son as his very own. Should he stray into infidelity, never fear: the Lord would whup him briskly enough to bring him round. The theology of this covenant of guaranteed grace is most clearly expressed in 2 Samuel 7. The covenant with Abraham (Gen. 12ff.) is patterned after that of David: God intervenes on his own initiative, and makes promises to his chosen people that he means to make them his client nation with a dynasty to boast of. He makes promises that have no conditions attached, and he guarantees that his purpose shall not be thwarted.

The covenant with Moses at Sinai, by contrast, is bilateral. The Lord is still the initiator: the rescue from Egypt was by his design and repeated intervention. But his choice of the children of Israel requires that they bind themselves to follow his law, and understand well that should they fail in the undertaking then he will most assuredly abandon them. Beside the long passages in Exodus which describe this covenant, it may perhaps be best seen in Deuteronomy 28 and Joshua 24, where Moses and Joshua clearly put to the people their two choices: obedience and life, or neglect of the law and death.

Neither of these two models ever quite quenched the other. The davidic covenant was naturally favored by the monarchy, and the mosaic covenant inspired the prophetic critics of the kings. Most often they are not seen as clearly antithetical, as in this syncretic passage:

"Yahweh set his heart on you and chose you not because you were the most numerous of all peoples — for indeed you were the smallest of all — but because he loved you and meant to keep the oath which he swore to your ancestors: that was why Yahweh brought you out with his mighty hand and redeemed you from the place of slave-labour, from the power of Pharaoh king of Egypt. From this you can see that Yahweh your God is the true God, the faithful God who, though he is true to his covenant and his faithful love for a thousand generations, as regards those who love him and keep his commandments, punishes in their own persons those that hate him. He destroys anyone who hates him, without delay; and it is in their own persons that he punishes them. Hence, you must keep and observe the commandments, laws and customs which I am laying down for you today." (Deut. 7:7-11)

There seem to be two Gods here. On the one hand, a Lord who chooses Israel irrespective of her merits. On the other, a Lord who will continue to cherish Israel only on the ground of her merits. The Old Testament oscillates between the two ideologies, trying to sidestep the hazards of each. If you have a God who is totally gratuitous, then what urgency could there be in your being righteous? But if being at peace with God depends upon your being righteous, how can you call his blessing a gift?

One theme which strove to weave the two theologies together was that of continual forgiveness and reconversion. In the Book of Judges a repeated cycle is set up: apostasy, punishment, reconciliation, and deliverance. Over the course of a dozen generations, each time the people forget Yahweh and dally with supplemental gods he unleashes some of the hostile neighboring peoples upon one or more of the Hebrew tribes. The Hebrews, lethally overwhelmed, repent, and meet an initially aloof hostility, but they eventually prevail:

"When Egyptians and Amorites, Ammonites and Philistines, when the Sidonians, Amalek and Midian oppressed you and you cried to me, did I not rescue you from their power? But it is you who have forsaken me and served other gods; and so I shall rescue you no more. Go and cry to the gods whom you have chosen. Let them rescue you in your time of trouble."

The Israelites replied to Yahweh, "We have sinned. Treat us as you see fit, but please rescue us today." They got rid of their foreign gods and served Yahweh, who could bear Israel's suffering no longer. (Judges 10:11-16)

Yahweh emerges as a Jewish mother

When Judah was finally crushed by Babylon and her best and brightest were taken into exile, Jeremiah thought briefly that there was finally a rightful end to this ignoble cycle of apostasy and forgiveness. The Children of Israel were now to be repudiated once and for all, as they had so chronically deserved. But his fellow prophets off in Babylon quickly insisted that there was really no end to the softheartedness of their God. In his long and poignant oracle comparing the history of his people to a long marriage wherein a forgiving husband endlessly reclaims his promiscuous wife, Ezekiel concludes with the Lord's final words: " 'I shall renew my covenant with you; and you will know that I am Yahweh, and so remember and feel ashamed and in your confusion be reduced to silence, when I forgive you for everything you have done — declares the Lord Yahweh'" (Ezek. 16:62-63). We find a similar view in Isaiah:

> Shout for joy, you heavens; earth, exult!
> Mountains, break into joyful cries!
> For Yahweh has consoled his people,
> is taking pity on his afflicted ones.
> Zion was saying, "Yahweh has abandoned me,
> the Lord has forgotten me."
> Can a woman forget her baby at the breast,
> feel no pity for the child she has borne?
> Even if these were to forget,
> I shall not forget you! (Isaiah 49:13-15)

> I did forsake you for a brief moment,
> but in great compassion I shall take you back.
> In a flood of anger, for a moment
> I hid my face from you.
> But in everlasting love I have taken pity on you. (Isaiah 54:7-8)

This theme of dependable compassion brings with it the suspicion that Yahweh was a patsy who could not really get on without Israel, and that his *raison d'être* as God was irrevocably tied up with this people he was codependently sponsoring. How could you take the anger of such a God seriously? How could you take this God seriously? Indeed, how gracious was he, really, if he apparently had no choice but to cherish Israel? And how could his love be seen as anything but a corrupting love? There is this constant paradox: God could at any time reject Israel, yet they knew he wouldn't. He was not the sort who rejected his own.

The paradox flows over into the New Testament. There one is commonly reminded that only those who do the will of Jesus' Father will enter the kingdom (Matt. 7:21). Those who engage in fornication, idolatry, sorcery, drunkenness, etcetera will certainly not inherit the kingdom (Gal. 5:19-21). Jesus' closest neighbors who fail to take him seriously and repent will be cast down to hell (Matt. 11:2-24; Luke 10:13-15). Yet it is never the will of the Father in heaven that any of his weak ones be lost (Matt. 18:12-14; Luke 15:3-7). He will leave the ninety-nine in order to search for the single stray.

The entire purpose of Jesus' mission is to reconcile humans to his Father, and it is this notion of purpose that suggests a *unity* within the paradox.

The Gospel, growing in scope and size and insight and perspective through its editorial history, is first concerned with the events of that final weekend; later its interest moves backward in reminiscence over his public career; finally it speculates on his identity and divine mission. Thus the Gospel first fastens its interest upon a moment, then reaches backward through time, and finally lets its concern break out of time entirely.

The inner core of the Gospel is the story of Jesus' death and resurrection. The Gospel assigns responsibility for this tragedy-turned-triumph to various persons: to Judas, to Peter and the other disciples, to the Romans, to the Sanhedrin and the various sects and offices it held together (Pharisees and Sadducees, scribes and priests), to the Jews in Jerusalem and those scattered around the horizon of their world, to Jesus, and to his Father. More simply put, Jesus' death is ascribed by Peter to the whole world — the people of Israel, and "those outside the law" — the Jews and Gentiles acting in sinister concert (Acts 2:14, 23). The only on-stage characters exempted from blame are the women who followed and stood by silently, and John who was so young that, like the women, he was not at risk. The disciples are not present at Jesus' death and are bewildered by his resurrection; most likely they are out of town, fleeing to their northern homes and jobs when the end, which is also the new beginning, comes. Yet they had contributed in their way to the tragedy: stirring up hopes of a nationalist revolt, then deserting when their bravado backfired. Judas seems to be slightly more purposeful, but only slightly. He acts in a definite way; nevertheless he acts in confusion and, to judge by the outcome, aimlessly. The Romans perform the actual execution, yet this too is purposeless, since Pilate knows there is no merit in the charge of sedition. The Jews claim responsibility for the death, yet the very mob that is so sure he should be liquidated is the same that hurrahed him into their city brief days before. Theirs is even greater confusion. Satan is anxious for Jesus' death, yet his venture is his undoing.

Only Jesus is truly purposeful about his death: he has seen it coming, he accepts it as inevitable, and he yields up a life he refuses to lead in any other way. But the Gospel's deepest insight is that Jesus' Father had intended his death from the first, and proposed all along to raise him then to new life, and others after him, so that the whole world, both those within and those beyond the law, might be reconciled to himself. It is this insistence on the priority of God's purpose which is a constant theme in the Gospel, and one of its most effective ways of expressing the divine grace. This forehanded initiative, which theologians sometimes call prevenience, invests the entire New Testament.

A literary tradition somewhat later than the passion and resurrection narrative is the Gospel of Jesus' ministry. Here too there is a strong emphasis on Jesus' purposefulness. He is basically an itinerant prophet. He heals the sick, blurts out the raw truth about moral compromise in every direction, and talks of repentance. In all his roles Jesus is said to be led by the Spirit of his Father. Preaching and healing form a single mission: to bring life to men and women who are limp and listless. His healing is the introduction and illustration of his word, which is all about unsolicited service to one's neighbor in need. It is clear, as the story moves on, that Jesus is in opposition to the religion of the land as is. It is also clear that everyone has plans for him, but that he evades them all to continue what he had from the first decided upon: to seek people out and rally them to his life-giving mission. Once again, he is a man of purpose, of prevenience, of grace.

The latest portion of the Gospel to be elaborated is that which purports to describe his youth, while in reality dealing with his origins behind time. The "infancy Gospels" never really dwell upon his family origins, which were either obscure or uninteresting to the people who wrote them, but on Jesus' role as one sent into history to fulfill eternal plans. Here it is that grace is most strongly asserted: the Father destined his Son before ever Abraham was, to join and gather the children of God. As the Bible ages, its retrospective gaze plunges backward: from David to Moses to Abraham to Adam to the Beginning (before every other beginning) when the Word was with God. All that had happened in Israel, everything since Adam and Eve, and indeed everything before Adam and Eve and before the light was let be, was coiled within a prior purpose. The inference of Jesus' prior existence is not a dry doctrinal statement of his divinity, but an affirmation of grace, in that the Father's characteristic generosity is anterior to all human hopes or performance. If Jesus is divine, then he is utterly prior to all human affairs. If there is talk of an eternal mystery, a surprise the Father holds in store for humanity in the final era, then this underlines precisely how we are like sparrows in his hand, and how that hand is home.

There is nothing very astonishing about a God who loves us relentlessly, except that we generally do not believe in one. The hope of this book is to examine what differences such a belief would make to our doctrine, our ethic, and our ritual, which have too often been directed to a god of whom we have really, at heart, been warily and cautiously afraid.

And what difference would such belief, such a God, make for Philemon? So many persons press in upon him as he deliberates about his slave. He would somehow do a kindness to Onesimus, placate Paul, keep his other slaves submissive, maintain his family estate, offer the most magnanimous example to his comrades in the faith, retain the trust of his fellow slaveowners in the neighborhood, and serve the Father's purpose — all this, and all at once. But he cannot do justice to all those claims. If he yields to the most insistent, he chooses what is expedient. If he seeks to do justice as best he can, he chooses to be ethical. If, however, he consider himself not so much plagued by impossibly competing duties, but haunted by a God whose love comes at him with relentless and incredible energy, then he will burst out of the muddle. Decision, not forced on him by the issue itself, is summoned from him by another call. Philemon's life is energized, not simply by the moral situations he faces, but by his own inward character, which is driven beyond what is just to what will release the intensest response of love to the Father.

CHAPTER THREE

His Father's Son,
Firstborn of Many Children

A principal disclosure of Christianity is the unyielding love of the Father of Jesus. As we pointed out, Christians flinch at this as do others, yet this is the God we are charged to preach. Much more before our eyes, however, is Jesus of Nazareth, his Only Son, a man among us, flesh of our flesh and bone of our bone. It is in seeing Jesus that we catch our best glimpse of the God we cannot see. It is one of Jesus' Jewish titles, Messiah (from the Hebrew, meaning the "Anointed One," as does "Christ," from the Greek), that has given us our own religious name. Yet Jesus the Messiah, the Christ, and the God he embodies, cannot be rightly understood unless we clear up one very grievous and ancient misunderstanding. Jesus does not save us from the Father.

Much conventional Christian preaching nevertheless implies that the Father and Jesus are disposed differently toward our sin. This might best be understood in the context of what I call the "Savior Myth," which is commonly put abroad by Christian spokespersons.[1] This is a belief that is rarely expressed in so many words, but can easily be reconstructed from catechisms the world over, with a slightly different turn or flavor in this or that context. It runs basically thus:

> In the beginning God created humans good. They were at peace
> with one another, and with the Creator. Through some primeval sin

---

1. By "myth" I do not mean a tale of the affairs of gods, but an account of God's dealings with humans in simple story form, to evoke some facet of the vast mystery.

man[2] snubbed a divine command and was punished by being left to his rebel self in a deservedly antagonistic environment. The spirit of disobedience was passed on from parents to children rather like a hereditary curse or a genetic defect. Human affairs went from bad to worse as people perpetrated ever new outrages upon one another. Yet, even as God turned in anger from his contumacious creatures, in his heart of hearts he hankered to have them back, and slowly prepared the way for a reconciliation. His only Son became man himself, and since he brought into human flesh and fellowship that perfect obedience of Son to Father, he lived without sin, even into the anguish of a violent, victim's death. At last there was one human being who, from start to finish, had justly deserved the Father's good pleasure. In rewarding him God not only exalted him as a man into the glory of his native intimacy with himself, but for the Son's sake God turned his face once again toward all fellow humans who would associate themselves with Jesus, would gratuitously receive the salvation earned by Jesus' passion, and would live in the same ultimate heroic acquiescence that had marked his life and death. The gates of heaven were once more opened in welcome, and salvation offered to all who would believe in Jesus as Onlybegotten Son of God.

This little salvation history, however it be formulated, stumbles in several directions. To begin with, the character of God as recounted is curiously inconsistent. If God does turn from mankind in wrath, how serious can it be if he is all the time planning to undo the catastrophe? If he is benevolent enough to hand his only Son over to infamy, torment, and death in order to reclaim his human creatures, what need does he really have to be appeased? Is redemption carried out simply for the sake of protocol? You must either take God to be radically alienated by sinful humans, in which case the Savior could hardly be acting under his Father's auspices, or believe in a God who is not really all that wroth, only sullen enough to pout for a few millennia, in which case the atonement would seem to be a way of truckling to his injured feelings. Neither God has much dignity or appeal.

2. This book avoids throughout the use of "man" as a collective name for human beings — not without some sense of loss for that euphonious Anglo-Saxon monosyllable. But in this particular passage, with its unmistakable overtones of the two creation myths in Genesis 1–3, it is right to use that most original of all uses of "man" for "Adam," the primal man from whom woman and all their offspring came.

Secondly, if Jesus' death and resurrection were the necessary prerequisites to salvation, what of the vast throngs of human beings born and dead before the event? Are so many thousands of generations of Adam's children excluded from grace by being born out of due time? Theologians have speculated that grace was in fact made available to them by a sort of Keynesian deficit spending on God's part: he advanced his grace in anticipation of Jesus' accomplishment. But aside from this unfortunate economic metaphor, no hopeful or satisfying explanation is offered why the Savior, coming quite late into history, leaves behind so many brothers and sisters. And, indeed, if salvation is given by faith in Jesus Christ, there is the further distribution problem that the Christian message has never been adequately conveyed to more than a minority of those who have lived after the event, nor can one reasonably presume that it is ever going to be otherwise. How bent upon saving humankind can God really be if the event touches but very few?

The real objection to this makeshift Christian myth, however, is that it is basically blasphemous. It glorifies Jesus by discrediting his Father. It denies precisely what Jesus has disclosed about the Father: that he never turns away from us no matter how far we may turn from him, that he has no moods or temper, and cannot be provoked or offended. The flaw in the myth is that it is one more device adopted by those who cannot quite bring themselves to believe there is a God who loves us, without exception, in an unyielding love. They must somehow imagine him turning away and needing to be reconciled by some appropriately meritorious event upon earth. The fact that the Savior is himself the divine Son become man does not purge the myth of this inconsistent but antiChristian suggestion that there had to be at least one utterly deserving human to justify a restoration of God's love for humankind.

The growing understanding through the Old Testament

The earliest Christians, of course, inherited their understanding of Yahweh's mind and purposes from Israel. In the early Old Testament the Lord is generally hostile toward the foreign nations primarily because they are the rivals or enemies of his own people, whom he cherishes *because* they are his own. Thus his wrath toward Egypt, Moab, Amalek, Ammon, Edom, Canaan, the Philistines, Syria, and Assyria fairly paralleled and justified the antipathies of the Hebrews, whose proud and possessive patron he is. God hears his people groaning under the lash of the Egyptian taskmasters (Exod. 2:22-25), vows to "blot out all memory of Amalek under heaven" (Exod. 17:14), provides that "the stars fought from heaven, from their orbits they fought against Sisera" (Judges 5:20), curses Israel's false friend Tyre "because they have handed hosts of [Israelite] captives over to Edom [and its slave-trade], heedless of a covenant of brotherhood" (Amos 1:9), and snorts with contempt at the already doomed Assyrian emperor's arrogant boast:

> "Like someone collecting deserted eggs,
> I have collected the whole world
> while no one has fluttered a wing
> or opened a beak to squawk." (Isaiah 10:14)

Toward his own people also — the children of Abraham, Isaac, and Jacob — Yahweh's oracles beat a steady tattoo of anger for their infidelities. Elijah, the scourge of Israel, exultantly orders his countrymen to slaughter the 400 priests of Baal (1 Kings 18). Jeremiah provocatively smashes a large pottery jug to smithereens in the infamous Valley of Ben-Hinnom outside Jerusalem to evoke Judah's irreparably broken covenant, and he utters Yahweh's doom:

> "They have filled this place with the blood of the innocent; for they have built high places to Baal to burn their sons as burnt offerings to Baal, a thing I never ordered, never mentioned, that had never entered my thoughts. . . . I shall make them fall by the sword before their enemies, by the hand of those determined to kill them; I shall give their corpses as food to the birds of the sky and the animals of the earth. And I shall make this city an object of horror and derision. . . . I shall make them eat the flesh of their own sons and daughters: they will eat one another during the siege . . ." (Jer. 19:4-9)

Ezra tears his beard and his clothes in horror at the filth and pollution of his people, and forces every Jew — beginning with the priests — who had acquired foreign wives during the Exile, to expel the wives and their children from the country "until our God's fierce anger over this is turned away from us" (Ezra 10:14).

These domestic imprecations against Israel and Judah were different from those uttered against alien nations. They were constantly neutralized by appeals to return to their old loyalty, and oracles promising that he, their Lord, meant to win them back — by wooing or whupping, whatever it took. "I will not destroy Ephraim again, for I am God, not man, the Holy One in your midst, and I shall not come to you in anger" (Hosea 11:9). "The nations will know that the House of Israel were exiled for their guilt; because they were unfaithful to me, I hid my face from them and put them into the clutches of their enemies, so that they all fell by the sword. I treated them as their loathsome acts of infidelity deserved and hid my face from them. . . . Now I shall bring Jacob's captives back and take pity on the whole House of Israel and show myself jealous for my holy name . . . and they will know that I am Yahweh their God. . . . I shall never hide my face from them again, since I shall pour out my spirit on the House of Israel" (Ezek. 39:23-29). Despite his continual assertions of anger, it is always the indulgent initiative of the Lord that draws Yahweh's fickle people back to his embrace.

After the Exile and Return of Judah, the new discovery that there really are no other gods alters this picture significantly. Once monotheism takes hold, it is not foreign gods but foolish idols that contend for the loyalty claimed by Yahweh, and idols seemed weaker rivals than gods are. But there is also a dark side to the advancing belief: if there be only one God, and he turns out to be Israel's God, it is not all good news for Jews. Naturally they are bucked up to know that theirs is the only show in town. Except . . . if Yahweh is the only God, it meant that he had created the heavens and the earth. That part wasn't hard to take. But it also meant that he had created Adam and *all* Adam's children, a massively larger act of patronage than directing the geopolitical fortunes of the children of Jacob. This would mean — so sadly for the Jews — that the abominable Egyptians, Moabites, Amalekites, Ammonites, Edomites, Canaanites, Philistines, Syrians, Assyrians, and Babylonians were all their brothers and sisters. The books of Jonah and Ruth were written to drive that point home (as a counterforce to Ezra and Nahum and Esther and Judith with their nationalist bias). A new and bittersweet biblical message was that, as far as Yahweh was concerned, the *goyim* might be more to be pitied than censured.

The dominant teaching throughout this development was: (1) that their Lord had summoned Israel, had made a blood covenant with them, and was jealous for their loyalty; and (2) that he had continuous cause to divorce them as unfaithful, yet was continually inclined to want to forgive them and win them back.

There was, however, another intervening motif in the Old Testament. Certain figures were described as capable of intervening with Yahweh in his seasons of anger, and of prevailing upon him to relent. A mob of 250 beefy Levites under Korah had revolted against the resented restriction of priesthood to the clan of Aaron, and in the midst of their showdown with Moses and Aaron, rather like the confrontation between Elijah and the 400 priests of Baal at Carmel, at a word from Yahweh the earth opened and swallowed them, their families, and all their belongings — so the story goes. When a sympathy campaign for the Korahites then flared up among the rest of the community, Yahweh replied with a virulent plague. It was only Aaron's initiative in performing a rite of expiation in the midst of the camp that brought Yahweh to relent — not before nearly 15,000 dissenters had been annihilated (Num. 17:6-15). This was a striking instance of the general obligation of the Aaronic priesthood to mollify the divine anger with prayers and sacrifices.

Israel's God allowed himself to be talked down from his rages by certain leading figures. Abraham was remembered for having bargained with him to save the people of Sodom from their doom (Gen. 18). When the Midianite women at Peor seduced the Israelite men into worshipping their local god, Yahweh punished his people with a plague which abated only after Pinchas, grandson of Aaron, appeased Yahweh's anger by virtuously impaling with a single thrust of his spear an Israelite and a Midianite temple prostitute in sacrilegious embrace. Pinchas "has deflected my wrath," Yahweh said, and earned "a covenant of peace and the authority to perform rites of expiation for the people" (Num. 25; Ps. 106:30-31; Sirach 45:23-24). It was often said that Yahweh remained faithful to the royal house only because of his fondness for David (Pss. 89, 132), and that prayer and sacrifice in Solomon's Temple would have a special power to placate him in his anger (1 Kings 8:30). Elijah, who had wasted Israel and the surrounding territories with a three-year drought, was billed to return before the final reckoning "to allay God's wrath before the fury breaks . . . and to restore the tribes of Jacob" (Sirach 48:10).

But the grandest Old Testament figure whose intervention was invariably able to placate Yahweh's anger was Moses. After the fracas of the Golden Calf it was Moses who stayed his hand:

> "Yahweh, why should your anger blaze at your people, whom you brought out of Egypt by your great power and mighty hand? Why should the Egyptians say, 'He brought them out with evil intention, to slaughter them in the mountains and wipe them off the face of the earth?' Give up your burning wrath; relent over this disaster intended for your people. Remember your servants Abraham, Isaac and Jacob. . . ."

64

Yahweh relented, and Moses immediately went back to clinch the deal: "Oh, this people has committed a great sin by making themselves a god of gold. And yet, if it pleased you to forgive their sin . . . ! If not, please blot me out of the book you have written" (Exod. 32:11-14, 30-35; Deut. 9:7-21; Ps. 106:23).

Yahweh assures Moses, "I know you by name and you enjoy my favor," and Moses comes right back at him: "If indeed I do enjoy your favour, please, my Lord, come with us, although they are an obstinate people; and forgive our faults and sins, and adopt us as your heritage" (Exod. 33:12; 34:9). When Yahweh is angered by all the grumbling in the desert and his fire begins to scorch the camp, "the people appealed to Moses who interceded with Yahweh and the fire died down" (Num. 11:1-2). During the rebellion at Kadesh, when the impatient crowd is ready to stone Moses and Aaron, Yahweh loses all patience. "How much longer will these people treat me with contempt? . . . I shall strike them with pestilence and disown them. And of you [Moses and Aaron] I shall make a new nation, greater and mightier than they are." But Moses replies,

> "If you kill this people now as though it were one man, then the nations who have heard about you will say, 'Yahweh was not able to bring this people into the country which he had sworn to give them, and so he has slaughtered them in the desert.' No, my Lord! Now is the time to assert your power as you promised when you said, 'Yahweh, slow to anger and rich in faithful love, forgiving faults and transgression. . . .' In your faithful love, please forgive this people's guilt, as you have done from Egypt until now."

Yahweh does give in: "I forgive them as you ask" (Num. 14:10-21). One begins to feel as if the relationship between Moses and his Lord was that of a codependent wife with an alcoholic and abusive husband. Of the two, Moses clearly seems the more irrepressibly benevolent.

But this is to misunderstand. All of those privileged intercessors serve as literary foils for a Yahweh whose serious demands on renegade Israel require that he be deadly serious, but whose ultimate will is to convert his people, not to destroy them.

The settled understanding of Yahweh is that of Nehemiah in his lengthy profession of faith: "They grew disobedient, rebelled against you, and thrust your law behind their backs . . . so you put them at the mercy of their enemies . . . and when they called to you, you heard them from heaven and, because of your great compassion, rescued them many times. . . . You were patient with them for many years and warned them by your spirit through your prophets, but they would not listen . . . you did not destroy them completely nor abandon them, for you are a gracious, compassionate God, the Mighty and Awe-inspiring One, maintaining the covenant and your faithful love . . . you acted faithfully while we did wrong . . ." (Neh. 9:26-37).

Thus, in the Old Testament, there is really no serious motif of benign human mediators soothing a hell-bent divinity. Moses, like Pharaoh and Nebuchadnezzar, was in the service of the "Savior of all" (Wisdom 16:7), because it was Yahweh who ultimately arranged to be mollified.

As Jewish expression shifts into Greek from the native Hebrew, the nemesis of his people is not the Lord. The older analogies are still in use, but insofar as they represent hostility or malevolence to humankind, they have their origins no longer in an angry God, but in various spiritual "forces" or personified abstractions. The Wisdom of Solomon speaks of an avenging Justice who will let no wrong go undetected or unpunished (1:8-11), and of Death with whom the godless foolishly flirt (1:16), and of malevolent Hades (1:14), and Retribution, and Hostility, and the Destroyer (18:20, 22, 25). The Master of creation, because he is sovereign and these created forces are not, is always inclined to forbearance:

> You show your strength when people will not believe in your absolute power,
> and you confound any insolence in those who do know it.
> But you, controlling your strength, are mild in judgment, and govern us with great lenience,
> for you have only to will, and your power is there.
>
> (Wisdom 12:17-18)

Radical developments in the New: no wrath in God

In the New Testament the texture of this understanding changes further. One of the strong and continual motifs in the Old Testament had been the anger and fury of the Lord, mentioned hundreds of times.

> In fear be submissive to Yahweh;
> with trembling kiss his feet,
> lest he be angry and your way come to nothing,
> for his fury flares up in a moment. (Ps. 2:11-12)

"I shall enslave you to your enemies
    in a country you do not know,
for my anger has kindled a fire
    that will burn you up." (Jer. 15:14)

"Look, I shall gather them in from all the countries where I have driven them in my anger, for fury and my great wrath. I shall bring them back to this place and make them live in safety." (Jer. 32:37)

In the New Testament Scriptures, however, this traditional wrath-motif fades to a handful of verses. The angry retribution of God is provoked by the unjust and deceitful and greedy (Rom. 1:18; 2:8; Eph. 5:6; Col. 3:6). Revelation speaks of the "wine of anger," "fierce anger" poured out for those in Babylon (Rome) who worship false gods (Rev. 14:8, 10, 19; 16:19; 19:15), and of plagues of anger poured over the earth (15:1, 7). The Baptist warns the Pharisees and Sadducees to flee the "coming retribution," the "wrath that is to come" (Matt. 3:7; Luke 3:7), and Paul claims that Jesus does save his followers from that final retribution (1 Thes. 1:10). Acts shows that Ananias and Sapphira are struck dead for lying to the Holy Spirit in the Church; a terrified Simon Magus asks Peter's prayers to head off the doom he has earned by racketeering from the pulpit; and when Herod Agrippa was eaten by worms and died, it was seen as God's right reckoning because the fool of a king had fancied himself divine (Acts 5:1-11; 8:9-24; 12:20-23).

Yet retributive anger in the New Testament is increasingly disjoined from God himself. Matthew and Mark recount Jesus' warnings, but usually the consequences of sin are their innate evil, not a vindictive retaliation by the Lord. It is the wide and spacious road that leads to destruction; the blood of the slaughtered prophets and honest victims is on the heads of the scribes and Pharisees (Matt. 7:13; 23:34-36).[3]

---

3. This too has its beginnings in the later books of the Old Testament. Moses, for instance, is said to have averted the destruction of his people, not by God, but by personalized abstractions of evil:

    . . . for a blameless man hurried to their defense.
    Wielding the weapons of his sacred office,
    prayer and expiating incense,
    he confronted Retribution and put an end to the plague,
    thus showing that he was your servant.
    He overcame Hostility not by physical strength,
    nor by force of arms;
    but by word he prevailed over the Punisher. (Wisdom 18:21-2)

Retribution, the old stock-in-trade of the tradition, is still about, and the traditional imageries of final judgment are still there. God will cut, thresh, and winnow his harvest and then burn the chaff (Matt. 3:12; Luke 3:17-18). Jesus has been appointed Son of Man (Dan. 7) to conduct the final judgment of all nations (Matt. 26:64; Mark 8:38; Acts 10:42-43; 2 Tim. 4:1). All will arise, wicked and righteous alike, but those who are banished from God's fellowship will see what they have forfeited, and will forever weep and gnash their teeth in frustration (Matt. 8:12; 13:42, 50; 22:13; 24:51; 25:30; Luke 13:28). Those who die in their sins will be cast down into burning Gehenna (Matt. 5:22, 29, 30; 10:28; 18:9; 23:15, 33; Mark 9:43-47; Luke 12:5). Gehenna, often translated "hell," is a New Testament metaphoric allusion to that smoldering, desecrated area in the Valley of Ben-Hinnom, the gully outside Jerusalem mentioned in Jeremiah.

Lacking in this redirected tradition of the New Testament is much purposeful connection between the doom that awaits evildoers, and the personal wrath of God. Still less does it teach or assume that Jesus is the sinners' friend and advocate who will shield them from his Father's retribution. It is a commonplace, especially in Matthew and Luke-Acts, that Jesus is the New Moses, but always as a leader, never as a defensive pleader. The only mention of Moses standing before God in the context of judgment portrays him as the accuser of Jesus' adversaries (John 5:45-46).

A central preoccupation of the non-Gospel parts of the New Testament, some younger than the Gospels and others older, is the mystery of Jesus' death. Despite their varied analogies and vocabularies, these books converge in their resolution to that puzzle.

Jesus obediently accepted death — a wicked, tormented, and abandoned death — as our Passover lamb (1 Cor. 5:7). He has been made perfect through suffering (Heb. 2:10); "he offered up prayer and entreaty, with loud cries and tears, to the one who had the power to save him from death, and, winning a hearing by his reverence, he learnt obedience, Son though he was, through his sufferings; when he had been perfected, he became for all who obey him the source of eternal salvation" (Heb. 5:7-9). "For the sake of the joy which lay ahead of him, he endured the cross, disregarding the shame of it, and has taken his seat at the right of God's throne. Think of the way he persevered against such opposition from sinners . . ." (Heb. 12:2-3). "He offered himself, blameless as he was, to God through the eternal Spirit" (Heb. 9:14), and his heroic endurance both makes and shows him to be the faithful Witness (Rev. 1:5), the Firstfruits of all who have fallen asleep (1 Cor. 15:20), the Firstborn from the dead

(Rev. 1:56), the Living One who holds the keys of death and Hades (Rev. 1:17-18), the Beloved (Eph. 1:6), the Upright One (Acts 3:14; 7:52), the Yes to all God's promises (2 Cor. 1:20), Leader of life, faith and salvation (Acts 3:15; Heb. 12:2; 2:10), Prince and Savior (Acts 5:31), Lord of peace (2 Thes. 3:16), Chief Shepherd and Guardian of their souls (1 Peter 5:4; 2:25), Lord and Judge of both the living and the dead (Rom. 14:9; Acts 10:42), Great Shepherd of the Sheep (Heb. 13:20), Lion of the Tribe of Judah, the Root of David who has triumphed (Rev. 5:5), the rejected stone now set in place as the Keystone (Acts 4:11), the Lord and Messiah whom God has made (Acts 2:36), the Son of Man coming on the clouds of heaven to judge all nations. "Everyone will see him, even those who pierced him, and all the races of the earth will mourn over him" (Rev. 1:5-7; 5:5). "Death has no power over him any more" (Rom. 6:9).

The effortlessly sovereign Father responded by raising him — Jesus the champion, his own Son — to glory. "The whole House of Israel can be certain that the Lord and Christ whom God has made is this Jesus" whom we crucified (Acts 2:36). He was lifted "above the angels" (Eph. 1:21); he "has entered heaven and is at God's right hand, with angels, ruling forces and powers subject to him" (1 Peter 3:22; Heb. 4:14). And, as "forerunner on our behalf," he clears the same path for us (Heb. 6:20).

The Father also empowered Jesus to breathe the divine Spirit into his elect. Jesus "lavishly sends the Spirit to you, and causes the miracles among you" (Gal. 3:5).

Jesus died for the benefit of humankind. He "was handed over to death for our sins and raised to life for our justification" (Rom. 4:25). "He offered himself for us in order to ransom us from all our faults and to purify a people to be his very own and eager to do good" (Titus 2:14).

Humans then entered mystically into his death and resurrection, through faith and baptism. If Jesus could speak of his own death as a baptism (Mark 10:38-39; Luke 10:50), his disciples can speak of their baptism as a death. And those who have died thus have risen transformed. Paul can say, "I have been crucified with Christ . . . it is no longer I, but Christ living in me" (Gal. 2:19-20). "All who belong to Christ Jesus have crucified self with all its passions and its desires" (Gal. 5:24; 6:14, 17). Christians have been buried in Christ's death through baptism and raised with him through faith (Rom. 6:3-6; Col. 2:12).

Jesus' death was a sacrifice. This analogy is used in several ways: "an offering and a sweet-smelling sacrifice to God" (Eph. 5:1); "a sacrifice for sin" (Rom. 8:3), "to purify our conscience" (Heb. 9:14); a sacrifice in which he offered himself, "once and for all," for the sins of the people (Heb. 7:27).

Jesus, the Great Shepherd of the Sheep, has sealed an eternal covenant with his own blood (Heb. 13:20), and by one single sacrifice "has achieved the perfection of all who are sanctified" (Heb. 10:14).

It is a covenant of reconciliation and peace (Rom. 3:25), creating a community that would dissolve old antagonisms. Through Christ God wanted "to reconcile all things to himself, everything in heaven and everything on earth, by making peace through his death on the cross" (Col. 1:20). God "reconciled us to himself through Christ and he gave us the ministry of reconciliation. I mean, God was in Christ reconciling the world to himself, not holding anyone's faults against them, but entrusting to us the message of reconciliation" (2 Cor. 5:18-19). Gentiles and Jews "have been brought close, by the blood of Christ. For he is the peace between us. . . . His purpose was . . . to reconcile them both to God in one Body; in his own person he killed the hostility" (Eph. 2:13-16).

What Jesus did was to liberate us. Jews were liberated from the law (Col. 2:14-15; Gal. 3:12) once they were led by the Spirit instead (Gal. 5:18). The elect were liberated from the sinister worldly power of the material and spiritual forces that had controlled creation (Gal. 4:3). "Through his blood, we gain our freedom, the forgiveness of our sins" (Eph. 1:7).

No difference between Father and Son

Jesus, then, is resolutely gracious to us. We are "justified by his grace" (Titus 3:7). But he is never so portrayed at the implied expense of his Father. Threaded through this understanding there are apparent, periodic allusions to Jesus shielding us from his Father. But it is never implied that Jesus' benevolence is nudging a less gracious Father. They are always in concert. One analogy is that of substitutional suffering: "Christ died for us while we were still sinners . . . and we shall be saved through him from the retribution of God" (Rom. 5:8-9; 1 Thes. 1:10). Yet this was on the Father's initiative: "God loved us and sent his Son to expiate our sins" (1 John 4:10). It is the same with the redemption analogy: "You have been bought at a great price" (1 Cor. 6:20; 7:23), "not in anything perishable like silver or gold, but in precious blood as of a blameless and spotless lamb, Christ" (1 Peter 1:18-19). The Lamb "bought people for God of every race, language, people and nation" (Rev. 5:9; 2 Peter 2:1). Yet the ransom was not paid to the Father, who "marked him out before the world was made," "revealed him at the final point of time," "raised him up from the dead and gave him glory" (1 Peter 1:20-21). In 1 John we find the analogy of intercession: "If anyone does sin, we have an intercessor *(paraklētos)* with the Father, Jesus Christ, the upright. He is the sacrifice to expiate our sins" (1 John 2:1-2). Yet it is the Father who traditionally provides reassuring consolation *(paraklēsis)*.

All that Jesus wrought was done in dutiful obedience to the Father's will. Thus it is the Father who initiated the entire rescue. "God destined us not for his retribution, but to win salvation through Our Lord Jesus Christ" (1 Thes. 5:10). Jesus "gave himself for our sins to liberate us from this present wicked world, in accordance with the will of our God and Father" (Gal. 1:4). "God, being rich in faithful love, through the great love with which he loved us, even when we were dead in our sins, brought us to life with Christ — it is through grace that you have been saved — and raised us up with him and gave us a place with him in heaven, in Christ Jesus" (Eph. 2:5-6). Paul also describes the Father's initiative as carried out by the Spirit: "if the Spirit who raised Jesus from the dead has made his home in you, then he who raised Christ Jesus from the dead will give life to your own mortal bodies through his Spirit living in you" (Rom. 8:11). If Jesus' disciples are to set no bounds on their love, it is because they know first-hand that their heavenly Father sets none on his (Matt. 5:48). So it is "the living God" who is "the Saviour of the whole human race" (1 Tim. 4:10). The "acts of saving justice" wrought by Jesus and by the saints are ascribed to his Father too (2 Peter 1:1; Rom. 5:18; 10:3; Rev. 15:4; 19:8). By putting forward Jesus as a paragon of righteousness, God showed his own "saving justice . . . first for the past, when sins went unpunished by his hand; and now again for the present age, to show how he is just and justifies everyone who has faith in Christ Jesus" (Rom. 3:25-26).

This total comity of Father and Son in Jesus' redemptive work is put forward powerfully in the hymn in Philippians:

Make your own the mind of Christ Jesus:
Who, being in the form of God,
    did not count equality with God
    something to be grasped.
But he emptied himself,
    taking the form of a slave,
    becoming as humans are;
and being in every way like a human being,
    he was humbler yet,
    even to accepting death, death on a cross.

And for this God raised him on high,
   and gave him the name
   which is above all other names;
so that all beings
   in the heavens, on earth and in the underworld,
   should bend the knee at the name of Jesus
and that every tongue should acknowledge
   Jesus Christ as Lord,
   to the glory of the Father. (2:6-11)

The Christian writers of the following century did not swerve from this account of Jesus and his Father. Their notion of moral evil as dooming is traditional, but they likewise affirm God's relentless forgiveness. Clement, bishop of Rome writing at the end of the first century, says that those engaged in covetousness, strife, malice, fraud, hatred of God, gossip, and vainglory are "hateful" to the Master of the Universe and "enemies" of his Son Jesus, but goes on to say that the Master does only good, "especially to us who have fled for refuge to his mercies through Our Lord Jesus Christ" (*1 Clement* 35:6; 20:11). Ignatius, bishop of Antioch on his way to a martyr's death in Rome, says we must "either love the grace which is present or fear the wrath to come" (*Eph.* 11:1). The Shepherd of Hermas, in an apocalyptic moral treatise of the mid-second century, believes that intercession by the churches and by the poor and by those who are fasting is welcomed by God (*Mandate* 9:9; *Similitude* 2:6; 5:3:8); indeed, "the Lord [Jesus] is very merciful and gives unceasingly to all who ask from him" (*Sim.* 5:4:4). The Father is approachable by sinners: "Be not at all double-minded about asking anything from God, saying in yourself, 'How can I ask anything from the Lord and receive it after having sinned so greatly against him?' Do not have these thoughts but 'turn to the Lord with all your heart,' and ask him without doubting, and you shall know his great mercifulness, that he will not desert you, but will fulfill the petition of your soul. For God is not as humans who bear malice, but is himself without malice, and has mercy on that which he has made" (*Mand.* 9:1-3; *Sim.* 9:23; 4:5).

The *Letter to Diognetus,* of the later second century, describes the Master of the Universe as uninterruptedly "kind to man," "long-suffering," and "free of wrath" (8:7-8), who sent his royal Son as "human to humans" — to save, to persuade but not to compel, to call but not to stalk, and to judge (7:4-6). The gospel of the sub-apostolic period is well put by this author:

But when our iniquity was fulfilled and it had become fully manifest, that its reward of punishment and death waited for it, and the time came which God had appointed to manifest henceforth his kindliness and power (O the excellence of the kindness and the love of God!) he did not hate us nor reject us nor remember us for evil, but was long-suffering, endured us, himself in pity took our sin, himself gave his own Son as ransom for us, the Holy for the wicked, the innocent for the guilty, the just for the unjust, the incorruptible for the corruptible, the immortal for the mortal. For what else could cover our sins but his righteousness? In whom was it possible for us, in our wickedness and impiety, to be made just, except in the Son of God alone? O the sweet exchange, O the inscrutable creation, O the unexpected benefits, that the wickedness of many should be concealed in the one righteousness, and the righteousness of the one should make righteous many wicked! . . . [He is] nurse, father, teacher, counsellor, physician, mind, light, honour, glory, strength, life, and provider of clothing and food. (9:2-6)

This was a God whom human evil provokes to a re-creation more revealing and more extravagant than creation. And there is nothing revealed or wrought by Jesus that does not proceed from his Father, the Master of the Universe. So the two are utterly at one: there is no request from the Son that does not originate in the Father.

The traditional nomenclature of retributive anger, propitiation, redemption, and final doom remains in the Christian vocabulary, and Jesus is the one who bears the fearsome brunt of the insult to the Father's dignity. Jesus is both priest and victim of the expiatory sacrifice, and he purchases our freedom at the price of his own blood. But the analogies are now truncated into metaphors, for it is not the Father who crouches in wait for sinful prey, or nurses his wrath against the final reckoning, or demands reparation for human transgressions. The Christian mind had instinctively discerned that redemption through Jesus was not a divine Plan B, but the wondrously intended divine Whoopee: now, after the most *felix culpa* ever planned, God could be known among his creatures — with the angels as gape-mouthed and astonished as everyone else — by his furthermost creative disclosure: as the persistent and transforming lover of sinners.

Theological confusion

As it happened, however, this signature insight in the Christian revelation eventually began to be compromised, mostly by believers who had lost all sense that their faith was a pilgrim always on the move, and who began to construe the older biblical memoirs as if they were on par with the growing tip of revealed understanding, in the New Testament and in the Church that continued to telescope forward from there.

It was Anselm of Canterbury (†1109) who claimed there was a critical deficiency in the conventional explanations for the incarnation. His treatise, *Cur Deus Homo (Why a God-Man?)*, tried a new approach in an effort to make sense of the incarnation on grounds of reason alone. Every rational creature, he argues, naturally owes it to the Creator to be submissive. A human being who denies God rightful obedience is guilty of sin, but since it involves contempt for God's dignity, it cannot be forgiven simply by the sinner's return to obedience, because the dishonor is a contemptuous act of *lèse-majesté* that requires further amends. Satisfaction for sin requires that both God's sovereign claims and God's honor be indemnified. It is unthinkable that God could simply waive this double injury by a gratuitous act of mercy, fictitiously treating the sinner as though he or she were no longer sinful. God is bound by his own justice not to reward a sinner for sin; he has no choice but to exact full satisfaction.

Humanity allowed itself to be seduced by the Devil, and thereby crippled itself by both weakness and mortality. Therefore, Anselm figured, humanity is impotent either to free itself from the Devil or to reconcile itself with God. Anyway, it is absurd to imagine that God would or even could respond positively to a request for mercy, because it would contradict God's justice. For humanity to be reconciled to God now requires full satisfaction for both the offense and the indignity. Since the duty to atone is incumbent on humanity, no one but a human could make amends. Since the amends exceed the wherewithal of all creation, only God could make adequate amends. Therefore, concludes Anselm in the algebraic riddle he has made of the mystery, only a God-man could make reparations so fully that God could honorably re-admit humanity to favor. *Voilà.* Since God has a stake in rescuing his original creative purpose, which was bliss for all human beings, a divine incarnation in humanity is the obvious way for God to rehabilitate his own undertaking.[4]

4. St. Anselm of Canterbury, *Cur Deus Homo*, 1:1-19; 2:4-7, in *S. Anselmi Cantuariensis*

Anselm was veering seriously from the trajectory of orthodox specu-
lation. Athanasius, for instance, had seen the Father as humanity's redeemer, not its financier. "The Word of the All-good Father was not un-
mindful of the human race that he had called into being; but rather, by
the offering of his own body he abolished the death which they had
incurred, and corrected their neglect by his own teaching. Thus by his
power he restored the whole nature of man." The divine reckoning, on
the Father's behalf, is with the Devil, death, and corruption, not with the
Father.[5] The point within all that older theology was central: Jesus cannot
be the loving Son of an unloving Father. This was the widespread understanding in the patristic period.

Anselm's view that the Father could not love humanity as long as it
was sinful, without compromising his own natural demand for satisfaction, found a strong echo in the magisterial Reformers of the sixteenth
century. Indeed, since their animosity toward Church authority induced
them to identify Scripture as independently sovereign and sufficient, they
felt obliged to make every portion of the biblical text equally authoritative,
and were inclined to treat the oldest Hebrew texts as peers of the New
Testament rather than as steps toward it.

Luther (†1546) put it thus:

> Because an eternal, unchangeable sentence of condemnation has
> passed upon sin — for God cannot and will not regard sin with favor,
> but his wrath abides upon it eternally and irrevocably — redemption
> was not possible without a ransom of such precious worth as to atone
> for sin, to assume the guilt, pay the price of wrath and thus abolish sin.
>
> This no creature was able to do. There was no remedy except for
> God's only Son to step into our distress and himself become man, to
> take upon himself the load of awful and eternal wrath and make his
> own body and blood a sacrifice for the sin. And so he did, out of his
> immeasurably great mercy and love towards us, giving himself up
> and bearing the sentence of unending wrath and death.
>
> So infinitely precious to God is this sacrifice and atonement of
> his only beloved Son who is one with him in divinity and majesty,

---

Archiepiscopi Opera Omnia, ed. Franciscus Salesius Schmitt, O.S.B., vol. 2 (Edinburgh:
Nelson, 1946), pp. 47-101.

5. St. Athanasius of Alexandria, *De Incarnatione Verbi Dei*, 9-10, trans. A Religious
of C.S.M.V., *The Incarnation of the Word of God* (New York: Macmillan, 1946), pp. 34-36.
Translation amended.

that God is reconciled thereby and receives into grace and forgiveness of sins all who believe in this Son.[6]

Calvin (†1564) tends to see a premonition of this theology in the psychological experience of sinful dread:

> No one can descend into himself and seriously consider what he is without feeling God's wrath and hostility toward him. Accordingly, he must anxiously seek ways and means to appease God — and this demands a satisfaction. No common assurance is required, for God's wrath and curse always lie upon sinners until they are absolved of guilt. Since he is a righteous Judge, he does not allow his law to be broken without punishment, but is equipped to avenge it. . . .
>
> Suppose someone is told: "If God hated you while you were still a sinner, and cast you off, as you deserved, a terrible destruction would have awaited you. But because he kept you in grace voluntarily, and of his own free favor, and did not allow you to be estranged from him, he thus delivered you from that peril." This man then will surely experience and feel something of what he owes to God's mercy. On the other hand, suppose he learns, as Scripture teaches, that he was estranged from God through sin, is an heir to wrath, subject to the curse of eternal death, excluded from all hope of salvation, beyond every blessing of God, the slave of Satan, captive under the yoke of sin, destined finally for a dreadful destruction and already involved in it; and that at this point Christ interceded as his advocate, took upon himself and suffered the punishment that, from God's righteous judgment, threatened all sinners; that he purged with his blood those evils which had rendered sinners hateful to God; that by this expiation he made satisfaction and sacrifice duly to God the Father; that as intercessor he has appeased God's wrath; that on this foundation rests the peace of God with men; that by this bond his benevolence is maintained toward them. Will the man not then be even more moved by all these things which so vividly portray the greatness of the calamity from which he has been rescued?

6. Martin Luther, "Sermon for the Twenty-Fourth Sunday after Trinity," on Col. 1:3-14, Erlangen ed. [2], vol. 9 (1868), p. 369; *Sermons of Martin Luther*, ed. John Nicholas Lenker, trans. Lenker et al., vol. 8 (Grand Rapids: Baker, 1988), pp. 376-77. See also Luther's "Lectures on Galatians — 1535," Weimar ed., pp. 40-40[2]; *Luther's Works*, ed. Jaroslav Pelikan, vols. 26-27 (Saint Louis: Concordia, 1963).

Calvin is not entirely unaware of the conflict within this explanation: how could such a baleful Father beget such a benevolent Son? He therefore qualifies himself: "God is in some way hostile *(quodammodo infestum)* to us." How account for sympathy on the part of the Father toward Christ's unbounded affection for these cursed creatures? "Because the Lord wills not to lose what is his in us, out of his own kindness he still finds something to love . . . he is moved by a pure and freely given love of us to receive us into grace. . . . But until Christ succors us by his death, the unrighteousness that deserves God's indignation remains in us, and is accursed and condemned before him."[7] But this is a possessive love, not a convincingly disinterested love like that of Jesus. Calvin reaches out to Augustine for a little support, but Augustine's formula is only a little less problematic than Calvin's own theory:

> God's love for us is incomprehensible: it cannot change. It was not after we were reconciled to him through the blood of his Son that God began to love us. He loved us before the world was created, so that before we were, we would be his children along with his only-begotten Son. Christ his Son reconciled us to God through his death, but not that he could shift from hating to loving us, as if enemies had become friends and shifted from hating to loving each other. We have been reconciled to one who already loved us while, by our sin, we were hostile toward him. The Apostle vouches for this: "So it is proof of God's own love for us, that Christ died for us while we were still sinners" (Rom. 5:8). He directed charity toward us, while we were hostile toward him and evil in what we did, though it was ever so truly said that "You hate evildoers, Lord" (Ps. 5:7 Vulg.). In his marvelous, divine way he both loved and hated us. He hated us insofar as we were no longer what he had created, but because our evildoing had not utterly wrecked his handiwork in each one of us he managed to hate what we had made, and to love what he had made.[8]

Lest anyone imagine this was a theory to which the Reformers claimed copyright, here is the Catholic *Catechism of the Council of Trent* explaining

7. John Calvin, "How Christ has fulfilled the function of Redeemer to acquire salvation for us," *Institutes of the Christian Religion* 2:16, 1-3, ed. John T. McNeill, trans. Ford Lewis Battles, vol. 2 (Philadelphia: Westminster, 1960), pp. 503-9.

8. St. Augustine, *Commentary on John's Gospel* 110:6, Migne, *PL* 35:1923-24.

that satisfaction which appeased God and rendered him propitious to us; and for it we are indebted to Christ the Lord alone, who, having paid the price of our sins, most fully satisfied God on the cross; for no created being could be of such worth as to exonerate us from so heavy a debt; and, as St. John testifies: "He is the propitiation for our sins, and not for ours only, but also for those of the whole world" (1 John 2:2).[9]

This is pure Anselm. But the Council itself, unlike the theologians who later wrote the catechism, clove to the older tradition. The Reformers' doctrine of salvation by faith understood all humans to be so corrupted and incapacitated by sin that they could not be healed or restored; instead, if humankind but accepted it, they were rehabilitated by God's crediting to them, while they really remained sinful, the redemptive righteousness of Christ. Trent, on the contrary, asserted that the sinner was inwardly reborn to righteousness — always by God's grace and best (but not always) by faith — and drawn into a process of sanctification that involved the disciplined purification of his or her human powers. This rightly construed forgiveness, not as a change in God, but as a change in humans. Thus the Council spoke of "satisfaction," not as accomplished by Christ to appease an intransigent and injured Father, but as a therapeutic and rehabilitative rigor undergone by recovering sinners through Christ under the oversight of a magnificently generous Father.[10]

Luther, Calvin, and most others who see Jesus making propitiation to an estranged Father for sinful humanity have unwittingly reversed the ancient belief that Jesus reconciled sinful humanity to the loving God, not a wrathful God to sinful humanity.

Thus the doctrine of Jesus' salvific and atoning death is preserved from drastic misunderstanding only if we understand that God's Son took our flesh, accepted death at our hands, and was raised glorious, not in order to wreak any change in his Father, but to intensify the change in us. The silent, pervasive, perpetually saving work of God's Spirit would now find voice and witness and thankful praise in the community of his disciples who would vouch for what they had seen and heard and touched and undergone. Jesus does indeed save: by revealing the character of the

9. *Catechismus ad Parochos* (Rome, 1567), 2, 5, 60, authorized by the Council of Trent, Sess. 24, can. 7, and published by Pius V. English ed.: *Catechism of the Council of Trent*, trans. J. Donovan (Dublin: James Duffy, 1867), p. 257.
10. Council of Trent, Sess. 14, can. 9.

Father who has all along been drawing his children into salvation. What he reveals is a Father who all along loves us before and after he has enabled us to love. One of the tragic Christian confusions has been to suppose that Jesus died to change the Father, not us. Another has supposed that neither Father nor Son nor Holy Spirit could change us.

Abelard the reformer

One who sensed this was Peter Abelard (†1142), who was from the first put off by Anselm. Abelard addressed sin less as an atrocious action than as an inward corruption. Salvation was correspondingly on the spiritual level: not a cosmic transaction but an inner transformation. Sin as corruption can injure people even if they have not themselves engaged in contumelious actions, and to be remedied it requires not simply meritorious acts but inner change. Christ saves us, not by the solo act of his dying, but by his living and his dying, all of it offered lovingly to his Father. Abelard engages some of the traditional language to explain this, but in the traditional sense that does not portray Christ appeasing a wrathful Father. Jesus, he says, redeems us from sin by showing us his love, and attracting us into it. Christ's submissive example inspires us, while the Spirit's inner force empowers us, to join in Christ's submission to the Father. Justification is no momentary *tour de force*; it is a long, disciplined, and persevering fidelity: "No one is acknowledged as righteous for acting honestly from time to time; it requires a habitual disposition." Justification is not an event within God; it occurs when humans move from sin into love — by God's perpetual grace.

> We believe that we are justified by the blood of Christ, and reconciled to God by the singular grace shown unto us whereby his Son took upon him our nature, and in it taught us by word and by example and so endured unto death, and thus drew us closer to himself by love: so that fired by so great a benefit of divine grace true love should not be afraid to endure anything for his sake. This benefit indeed we do not doubt kindled the early [pre-Christian] Fathers also (who looked forward to it by faith) into the highest love for God, no less than the men in these years of grace. . . . Therefore our redemption is that supreme love which exists in us through the passion of Christ, which not only frees us from the servitude of sin, but wins for us the true liberty of the children of God, so that we fulfill all things by love of him rather than by fear of him, who showed such

grace that cannot be excelled, as he himself bore witness, saying, "Greater love hath no man than this, that a man should lay down his life for his friends."[11]

Abelard never elaborated this into a coherent doctrine, for he was a controversialist, not a theory-maker. He was a dialectician who saw what was amiss in the legalistic theories of expiation that were becoming the mode in his day. One scholar writes appreciatively:

> In Anselm's presentation Christ is, as it were, conducting an argument in Heaven, and we have the very atmosphere and language of the law-court. Abelard on the other hand has much more in mind Christ going about in the marketplace and touching men at every turn. Anselm is concerned mainly with Christ's attempts to please God: Abelard with his attempts to win *us*. . . . [Abelard] would admit that redemption is a mystery, but not in the sense that it cannot be found out, but rather that when it is found out we are struck dumb with wonder that it should be at all! The mystery to him, as to St. Paul, is that while we were yet in our sins Christ should die for the ungodly. It is in other words a mystery of divine grace, a moral mystery, not a metaphysical puzzle. . . .
>
> The "prevenient" grace of God arises not because He thereby does something which He need not do, but because He loves us, and He loves us all the time. By "grace" Abelard means not the, as it were, social condescension of a superior to an inferior, but simply "disinterested love." . . . The whole scheme calls out our wonder and awe far more than that view of atonement which, while it postulates a mystery, proceeds to discuss it as a proposition in logic.[12]

---

11. Peter Abelard, *Commentary on the Epistle to the Romans,* in *Opera Abelardi,* ed. Cousin, vol. 2 (Paris, 1859), p. 207; previous quotation, p. 231.

12. A. Victor Murray, *Abelard and St. Bernard: A study in twelfth century 'modernism'* (New York: Barnes & Noble, 1967), pp. 133-35.

Hastings Rashdall believes that Anselm, originally trained in the law, was somehow snarled in his own theories:

> Anselm appeals to justice, and that in all good faith: but his notions of justice are the barbaric ideas of an ancient Lombard king or the technicalities of a Lombard lawyer rather than the ideas which would have satisfied such a man as Anselm in ordinary human life. . . . A God who really thought that His honour was increased by millions of men suffering eternal torments, or that

This is not unlike that theological observation of Paul Bryan Crowe: "My God's waiting over there with a table laid for me. When I get there, he's going to say, 'I'm God, and I love you. Forget all the bull you heard on earth.'"

For contrast, one need only remember Jonathan Edwards's famous Connecticut sermon, "Sinners in the Hands of an Angry God," to which John Steinbeck might profitably have listened had he worshipped in Enfield, Connecticut, instead of Vermont, back in 1741:

> They deserve to be cast into hell; so that divine justice never stands in the way, it makes no objection against God's using his powers at any moment to destroy them. Yea, on the contrary, justice calls aloud for an infinite punishment of their sins. . . . They are already under a sentence of condemnation to hell. They do not only justly deserve to be cast down thither, but the sentence of the law of God, that eternal and immutable rule of righteousness that God has fixed between him and mankind, is gone out against them, and stands against them; so that they are bound over already to hell. . . .
>
> Yea, God is a great deal more angry with great numbers that are now on earth; yea, doubtless, with many that are now in this congregation, that, it may be, are at ease and quiet, than he is with many of those that are now in the flames of hell. . . . The wrath of God burns against them; their damnation does not slumber; the pit is prepared; the fire is made ready; the flames do rage and glow. The glittering sword is whet, and held over them, and the pit hath opened her mouth under them. . . .
>
> [N]atural men are held in the hand of God over the pit of hell; they have deserved the fiery pit, and are already sentenced to it; and God is dreadfully provoked; his anger is as great towards them as to those that are actually suffering the executions of the fierceness of his wrath in hell, and they have done nothing in the least, to appease or abate that anger, neither is God in the least bound by any promise to hold them up one moment; the devil is waiting for them, hell is gaping for them, the flames gather and flash about them, and would fain lay

---

it was a satisfactory compensation to Himself that in lieu thereof an innocent God-man should suffer upon the cross, would not be the God whom Anselm in his heart of hearts really worshipped.

The Idea of Atonement in Christian Theology, Bampton Lectures for 1915
(London: Macmillan, 1919), pp. 355-56

hold on them and swallow them up; the fire pent up in their own hearts is struggling to break out . . . all that preserves them every moment is the mere arbitrary will, and uncovenanted, unobliged forbearance of an incensed God. . . .[13]

The theory of an expiatory Jesus appeasing the Father's just and wrathful retribution continues on with vigorous conviction mostly in serious Calvinist circles.[14] But it prowls about more widely here and there as a rogue doctrine. This nineteenth-century hymn provides a typical example:

Man of sorrows, wrapt in grief,
Bow Thine ear to our relief;
Thou for us the path hast trod
Of the righteous wrath of God;
Thou the cup of fire hast drained
Till its light alone remained.
Lamb of God, we look to Thee!
Hear our mournful litany. . . .
Man of sorrows, let Thy grief
Purchase for us our relief. . . .[15]

Many who read or pray or sing these texts will encase them within the understanding that what Jesus suffers is meant to pay our debt to a demanding God. Thence the occasional reassurances that the Father is not as bad as we feel obliged to suspect:

Judge not the Lord by feeble sense,
But trust him for his grace;
Behind a frowning providence
He hides a smiling face.[16]

13. Jonathan Edwards, "Sinners in the Hands of an Angry God, Sermon preached at Enfield, July 8th 1741, At a Time of great Awakening; and attended with remarkable Impressions on Many of the Hearers," in *The Works of President Edwards*, vol. 7 (Worcester, Mass.: Isaiah Thomas, 1809), pp. 486-502.

14. It is still strongly served by the classical exposition of Archibald Alexander Hodge, *The Atonement*, published first in 1867 by the Presbyterian Board of Publication.

15. Matthew Bridges (1800-1894), adapted.

16. "God moves in a mysterious way," William Cowper, 1774.

He will not always chide;
He will with patience wait;
His wrath is ever slow to rise,
And ready to abate.[17]

All this tangled confusion about salvation arises from the one central misunderstanding: that human sin necessarily prompted a hostile reaction in God, which could be relieved only by God's Son who submitted on our behalf to becoming a man like us in all things but sin itself, and underwent a hideous death to justify a reconciling shift by the Father — from being wrathful, punitive, and hostile, to his restored and native character: gracious, reconciled, welcoming.

In this heterodox scenario of atonement the one thing missing is real forgiveness. When Jesus has finished, the Father need not forgive because by now his benevolence has been fully deserved. He may emerge reconciled and welcoming, but not gracious, for the reconciliation has been infinitely purchased. Reconciliation through Jesus on this view of it comes by right, not mercy. It is a settlement, not an act of clemency.

Obviously this theological contortion is possible only if we agree to imagine a schizoid Godhead: a stringent Father and a compassionate Son. We must also mistakenly imagine that the drama of divine salvation, as understood by Christians, demands with equal insistence that God must change and that we need not because we cannot.[18]

Philemon and his contemporaries were being coaxed out of a conventional understanding of their relationship to the Lord who had made Israel a people. There were, so to speak, two languages in use to understand their liaison: one tended to weigh obligations, to calculate debt, to reckon who deserved what. The other swept all that off the table with a great swing of the forearm, and spoke of all the ledgers being lost and all the mortgages burned. If Philemon favored the dutiful consideration of debts owed and contracts made, Paul's letter would have set him to thinking about how to deal somehow differently with his bondsman. But if he had

17. "O bless the Lord, my soul!" James Montgomery, 1819.

18. Vincent Taylor, in his otherwise appreciable study, *The Atonement in New Testament Teaching,* admits that the entire doctrine rests upon the axiom that since the divine righteousness does not permit God to "look upon the evil and the utterly contrite with the same eyes," reconciliation requires a transformation in God's atttitude toward sinners. This he admits is adverse to the New Testament view that God reconciles humans to himself, rather than being reconciled to them. Second ed. (London: Epworth, 1945), p. 193.

been lured into this radically New Way of consideration and speech, he could not think of his slave as a slave without thinking of himself as a slave. That would have made all the difference.

CHAPTER FOUR

What Need for Jesus,
If the Father Already Loves and Saves?

If what Jesus conveys about his Father is true, then God's benevolence knows no seasons. His favor toward us is perpetual. The full complex of his gift-giving can never be intermittent. There can be no periodic suspension of grace, understood either as the Father's favorful attitude at work through the Spirit, or as its saving effects for and within humans. In brief, there can be no story line of salvation, if by that one meant that God's grace was interdicted in time, and then made available once more because of Jesus' accomplishments.

What I wish to argue here is that it is *not* the peculiar and exclusive mission of the incarnate Jesus to *save* humankind. The particular purpose for which the Son was sent was precisely to *reveal* to us that there is a God who is always saving, to disclose that his Father and ours has no wrath, and that he unleashes his saving gratuity upon all people no matter what their condition or understanding.

Jesus the revealer

At all times and in all places the Father is at work, touching human hearts invisibly by his Spirit to draw them out of selfishness into love. Before Abraham was, and further than the Gospel has reached, there is the Father always at work. Or, to put it in other terms, the visible mission of Jesus, understood as comprising its preliminaries in Israel and its follow-through in the Church, is a limited and particular human movement spread by the Gospel and a Gospel-responsive faith. The visible mission is not nearly as universal as that other, invisible divine mission of the Spirit, whereby the Father reaches out to all people in history, to most of whom the Gospel may never have effectively reached. Just as no one can come to Jesus unless drawn by the Father who sent him (John 6:44), and just as the Spirit who raised Christ Jesus from the dead has made a home in Jesus' disciples (Rom. 8:11), this same Spirit prowls and wafts at will, exerting that quiet, tidal pull toward the Father even in the hearts of those who know not Jesus.

Jesus' revelation is not only an insight into his Father. It is a double disclosure. He also reveals how, though God cannot turn from us, we can and sadly do turn from God. By his death for those who slay him, Jesus displays their own evil to those who have eyes to see — a chastened capacity which is itself the infused gift of the Spirit. The alienation is on our part: it is not God who must be transformed, but ourselves.

Jesus does not come to perform before God. He comes to call us — by revealing to us the character of his Father, and that of ourselves. The actual work of saving human beings, of purifying them from sin and drawing them into love, has gone on unremittingly as long as there have been human beings. But our understanding of this was given a jolt of trans- forming insight in the coming of Jesus Christ. In this sense Jesus is dis- tinctively understood as a Revealer of the gracious Father who also saves through his unseen, unheard Spirit.

If Heaven has gates — and walls and locks and the other foreboding symbols of aloofness — then the Father of Jesus does not live there. It is really *our* world that is hemmed in and secluded, while meanwhile God's home is thrown open in welcome . . . a much snubbed welcome.

It is strange how Christians may confess God to be radically gracious, yet falter when it comes to believing that he should be entirely so. There is, for example, the folk tale, or myth, of Mary.

A man died and went to Heaven to seek admittance. St. Peter checked his credentials at the gateway, but the record was very bad and he was told to go to Hell. He appealed. When Christ came to the entry to render judgment his aspect was more severe and forbidding than Peter's. The man was very definitively sent on his way. In despair and bewilderment he wandered round the walls for one last wistful look, when a back door opened and a very motherly woman emerged. She asked him why he looked so woebegone. When he told his story, her heart was moved with motherly pity. Taking him by the hand she drew him inside, and went off to speak a word in his favor

86

to her Son. The Son, who could never be severe with his own mother, agreed to relent for her poor protégé. And thus one more sinner made it into the Kingdom.

The point of the story, of course, is that in popular Christian senti- ment Jesus is not as approachable or as compassionate as some human beings. Over the centuries Jesus of Nazareth has been progressively divinized, and has strangely emerged as less than humane. The farther he was focused back into the remote inaccessibility of the Lord, the more Christianity has resorted to stand-in mediation by Mary and the saints. Over recent centuries, it is noteworthy that most Catholic visionaries have been visited, not by Jesus, but by his mother: a seemingly more approachable person, more welcoming, easier to converse with. The cult of the saints, moreover, both in biography and in worship, sometimes suggests that believers turn to them (or to romanticized images of them) as congenial (even homely) and well-connected advocates who are willing to act as go-betweens with the Lord, who does not himself suffer sinners so gladly.

There seems to be a similar persuasion behind the theological move- ment in our time which would insist that Jesus was far more human than is generally thought; that he knew all the misgivings and bewilderment and perhaps the doubt of any prophet faced with violent death; that he suffered the same weaknesses and temptations and failures to which we are commonly subject; and that he had a human father as we all do. Thus, it is felt, he will be more *simpatico*, more encouraging, because more human and thus more truly gracious. On this view of it, the acceptance of humans in their weakness is not seen as a typical divine quality.

I would find Jesus more reassuring if he did not have the foibles, faults, and failures that make me untrustworthy. But the issue is this: to the extent that this folk-view influences the Christian mind, to the extent that to be divine is seen effectively as inferior to being human in respect of benevolence, the incarnation has failed. What the very adventure of the Son in our human flesh strives to convey is that there is a welcoming love, an unconditioned acceptance, a relentless and eternal affection in the Father which so far exceeds our own experience that even the selfless career and death of Jesus can only hint at it. The very substance of our faith is the belief and hope that behind this hint lies love beyond measure, too intense for us now to bear the full sight of it.

As for mediation, it is not we who must resort to go-betweens in order to approach a remote and intractable God, but God who must use all manner of intermediaries to break through the distraction of a stiff-necked, blind, and timorous people. If there is alienation it is we who back away, not he. If anyone is inaccessible, it is not God but us, lost in ego. Our hearts are no mystery to God; it is God's heart that we find either uninteresting or incredible. The whole initiative and thrust of mediation comes from God to us, as God's self-disclosure breaks though our all-too-human non-chalance. We need no mediator to gain his attention. It is his attention which holds us in being.

If, then, the Father of Jesus cannot but love his humans, he is at work unremittingly in the world, reconciling us to himself whether or not we are explicitly aware of him. The *distinctive and peculiar* mission of Israel, of Jesus, of the Church, had been, has been, and is *to reveal* that God is always actively at work saving us, in ways both seen and unseen. The work of salvation is universal; the work of revelation is historically limited. Furthermore, revelation is not necessary. With or without the incarnation, the Father's love would inexorably continue through silent ingratiating by the Holy Spirit, deep down within. Jesus' coming is not a necessity: it is a grace, a luxury, an absurd abundance of bounty. What is absolutely necessary to humanity is that we be saved: that through God's gracious enablement we emerge from our selfishness to become loving persons. If, in addition, we also discover now that this is of eternal significance, so much the better for us. As I shall later contend, revelation is itself most powerfully salvific . . . indeed, *it has no other purpose* than to overwhelm us by the sight of God's single-minded determination to save us. Nevertheless, salvation and revelation are distinct and often separate realities.

Salvation beyond Church

That so many fail to see this is probably due to Paul and Augustine. They were the two grand influential writers on grace. Each underwent a con-vulsive change in the course of his life through a fulminant conversion experience. Both later looked back on their preconversion days with con-siderable self-reproach. One feels there may have been some exaggeration in the way they both disparaged their respective days of youth. But be-cause for each of them the moment of conversion involved a shattering revelation that burst him free of his former depravity into belief in Christ and baptism into the Church, each took his own experience as the para-digm of what every person must undergo. For both Paul and Augustine the salvation event coincided with revelation: thereafter they naturally tended to overlook the distinction.

Thus under their aegis the Christian tradition has been inclined (though never persuaded) to consider non-Christians as depraved sinners (never overlooking, though, that Christians also sin), and that faith and baptism are the only avenue of salvation. Extrapolating still further, they have writ this large over human history, and argued that in the long era before the release of salvific grace in Christ, all humans had wallowed in sin, as a *massa damnata*. Paul, in refuting the Judaizers, and Augustine in his arguments with the Pelagians, both tried to establish the prevenience of God's grace by seeing it as a sort of chronological priority. Both species and individual, they said, pass through an early stage of depravity, and what saves them from it is Christ: in his death and resurrection for the human species, and in faith and baptism for the human individual. Both Paul and Augustine are so earnestly anxious to share their own life-giving experience with others, like returnees from a charismatic weekend or survivors of a crash diet, that they give little thought to the possibility — indeed, the assurance — that God has other, more covert but similarly powerful ways of converting others who have never heard of Christ, or who have rightly disliked what they heard from some Christians.

It was Cyprian of Carthage (†258), Augustine's North African predecessor by almost two centuries, who is credited with having put it most blatantly: *Extra ecclesiam nulla salus,* "There is no salvation outside the Church." Both the formula and the idea behind it have hectored the Christian mind ever since.

The activity that most brings this to the fore is missionary work. Francis Xavier, the saintly Jesuit who introduced the Christian faith to vast areas of India, Sri Lanka, China, and Japan was not untypical in his attitudes. At Malindi (near Mombasa in present-day Kenya) he had had some contact with Islam which he regarded as loathsome.

> The Moors were edified by seeing how we Christians lay our dead to rest. One of them, a man highly respected in the city, asked me whether our churches were much frequented, and if our people prayed with fervour. He said that devotion had declined markedly among his own community, and wondered if the same thing has happened to the Christians. . . . He could not understand why there had been such a serious falling-off of devotion, and gave as his opinion that it must have resulted from some great sin. We argued the point a long while, but he was not satisfied with my solution, that

God, the all-faithful, abided not with infidels and took no pleasure in their prayers.[1]

Contempt for the infidel surely had much to do with the brutality used by the early Christian *Conquistadores*, who easily adopted the view of João de Barros that "though the Moors and Gentiles are certainly rational creatures and so potential converts to Christianity, yet since they show no disposition to be converted, we Christians have no duties towards them."[2]

Xavier grew very attached to one ship's captain, a Chinese, who conducted him through some very dangerous waters and proved a more trustworthy comrade than most of the profiteering, Christian Portuguese sailors.

> They were brothers under the skin, both of them kindly and daring souls, though in different fashions, and but for that execrable idol [kept by the captain] they might have been the best of friends. Before the year was out, Francis wrote from Japan to Dom Pedro da Silva to say that poor Ladrão was dead. "All through the voyage," he continued, "he was good to us, and we were unable to be good to him, for he died in his infidelity. Even after death we could not help him by our prayers to God, for his soul was in Hell."[3]

Such an arrogant theology would, when confided to a great and holy man like Xavier, simply blind him to some of the good and godliness he confronted every day — and to the Lord who had enabled it. In the hands of the European adventurers and other Christian explorers, traders, theologians, and soldiers, such blind theology would underwrite all manner of savagery and contempt, and cause the spread of European influence to disparage and smother flourishing cultures and gentle people in all corners of the earth.

Attitudes in later years have softened. Whether from a feeling of indifference, or camaraderie, or just simple good sense, Christians are no longer anxious to consign all heathens to Hell. Integrating this attitude into their theology has not been all that easy, however. If unbelievers must grudgingly be believed salvageable, theologians have been unwilling to

1. James Brodrick, S.J., *St. Francis Xavier* (New York: Wicklow, 1952), pp. 107-8.
2. Brodrick, *St. Francis Xavier*, p. 117.
3. Brodrick, *St. Francis Xavier*, p. 357.

imagine it possible without giving at least indirect credit to the Church. Thus, one speaks of "baptism of desire": those who are virtuously disposed, yet through no fault of their own do not know of their summons to become Christians, are deemed to be as if they had been baptized. They are sometimes called "crypto-Christians," or "anonymous Christians." Theologians talk about a sort of associate membership in the Church, an affiliation unwittingly enjoyed by all people of graced good will. This would naturally have irritated someone like Gandhi, who was not at all ignorant about either Christ or Christians, and had no desire to join them. He once wrote to a woman who had pressed her faith upon him:

4 September 1932

Dear Sister,

I have your letter. Why do you think that the truth lies only in believing in Jesus as you do? Again why do you think that an orthodox Hindu cannot follow out the precepts of the Sermon on the Mount? Are you sure of your knowledge of an orthodox Hindu? And then are you sure again that you know Jesus and his teachings? I admire your zeal, but I cannot congratulate you upon your wisdom. My forty-five years of prayer and meditation have not only left me without an assurance of the type you credit yourself with, but have left me humbler than ever. The answer to my prayer is clear and emphatic that God is not encased in a safe to be approached only through a little hole bored in it, but that He is open to be approached through billions of openings by those who are humble and pure of heart. I invite you to step down from your pinnacle where you have left room for none but yourself.

With love and prayer,
Yours, M.K.G.[4]

Shortly after World War II Leonard Feeney, a Boston Jesuit, became obsessive and articulate in support of Cyprian's old dictum *Extra ecclesiam nulla salus*. This he construed quite literally: only members of the Catholic Church can be saved. That is probably just what St. Cyprian had in mind, and many others, like Boniface VIII and Vatican I, who had endorsed his

4. Mohandas K. Gandhi, Letter to Satyavati Chidamber, *The Collected Works of Mahatma Gandhi*, vol. 50 (Ahmedabad: Ministry of Information and Broadcasting, Government of India, 1972), p. 21.

doctrine down the centuries, thoughtlessly or thoughtfully. But the *ecclesia* had been clearing its mind about *salus* in the meantime, and Father Feeney eventually found his own self, for all that loyalty, *extra ecclesiam:* by bell, book, and candle.[5]

It is surely time for the Church more bluntly and more instructively to disavow Cyprian's maxim, and to admit that *extra ecclesiam* there is plenty of *salus.* This need be no grudging admission. It is the very commission the Church has received: to publicize that God's effective grace knows no bounds. The Christian Church can and should claim no exclusive distributorship for God's grace. We are perhaps one of the rare religious enterprises that confesses it is *not* necessary. It calls attention, not to itself, but to a Father who is already reconciling people to himself. As the roadside signs used to say, "Jesus saves." But so do many others, yet we believe they can do so only by enablement of the Spirit of the same Father. The Church is commanded to go public with the secret — to its members and to all people — that there is a God who loves us beyond our imagining. Membership in the Church embodies a response to that giveaway: belief in the good news, and a commitment to love in return, beyond measure. The Church is not the exclusive assembly of the saved; it is the assembly of those who know and give thanks through his Son that there is a saving God carrying on wherever he pleases . . . and that means everywhere.

Obviously I speak of what should be, rather than what actually is. The Church's continual shortcomings in carrying out the terms of her original warrant have led her into two misfortunes. First of all, what Christians preach is sometimes bad news, not good. Approaching our fellows with the presumption that they are all reprobate, we may arrogantly offer them (on terms) a way out of their sinfulness. But the Christian can make no legitimate presumption about anyone. We have good news to offer anyone: to the selfish, to sinners, that they be encouraged to repent; to the redeemed, the selfless, that they learn how they became so, and how much more so they might be.

5. The Vatican explanation of the Feeney decision held on to Cyprian's formula, but then explained that membership is not required for salvation: it might suffice to be united with the Church by some kind of inexplicit desire. Vatican II ignored Cyprian and put it more straightforwardly: "There are those who without any fault do not know anything about Christ or his church, yet who search for God with a sincere heart and, under the influence of grace, try to put into effect the will of God as known to them through the dictate of conscience: these too can obtain eternal salvation." Vatican II, Dogmatic Constitution on the Church, *Lumen Gentium,* 16.

The Church cannot meet the world armed only with presumptive condemnation. For many people our message must bring the contrary — enthusiastic congratulation: "You are doing what we are describing!" When strangers seem to be living for their neighbors, to be spending themselves on others in their need, the Gospel is meant to encounter them not with reproach but with commendation: they are apparently living by God-given grace. The Christian comes not just to tear down and uproot, but also to build up and to plant. Too much woe has come from our coming at people with eyes shut and mouth open, bent on gifting grace to a graceless world.

There is a further misfortune. By fancying herself as God's unique channel of salvation, the Church inevitably degenerates into institutional egotism. Clerics tend to fret about Church membership, and attendance at services, and "vocation" trends, losing sight of other substantial signs of human compassion, wisdom or welfare — all telltale indices of God-grace on the move. The Church's ultimate task is not to spread the Church; it is to spread the faith in order to spread costly love and prophetic service. Those who hear and heed this faith from the Church will coagulate and group into the Church, but this is not the furthest purpose; it is the Way to it. The Church is not convoked throughout the world with an uncommon work to do. We are sent with an uncommon, revealed insight to join in a most blessedly common work: salvation.

Here one is reminded that Jesus was remarkably unpreoccupied about the future of those who believed through him. His attention went rather to those who were deprived: to the running sores of the leper; to the milky, sightless eye; to the dragging, withered leg; to the slack-mouthed village idiot; to the shrunken belly; to the faceless leper banished to the wilderness. With all these he shared out life as they had need. To those others otherwise deprived, who had no such needs, he gave harsh warning that if they did not share their substance with their brothers and sisters in need, then they were — *were,* not *would be* — even more dreadfully blighted.

For his disciples themselves, he seemed strangely to have little care and few words. They were to follow him, joining in the work. His day was spent facing those who did not believe: working for them, speaking to them. The believers were more taken for granted. He did not face them. He expected them to be at his side, sharing the same work and word. In the evening, perhaps when supper had given way to a weary reverie around the fire, he might turn to them with a few words.

Left to themselves, they set about organizing. He reacted impatiently, and likened them to heathen politicos contending for power. Let them imitate slaves and servants, he said, and more work would get done. Some have concluded that Jesus had no intention of founding a Church. A wiser observation would be that he had no illusions about how to found one. His consuming desire was spent in walking about, doing the work and spreading the word. Those who believed would fall in step with him, and thus a Church was being formed as long as they faced and moved as he did, and did not turn inward upon themselves. His followers might well organize as groups do, and this they eventually did when they were no longer welcome in their home synagogues and had to regroup, with officers and laws, fiscal resources and approved rituals and other provisions Jews commonly made to preserve the purpose and integrity of their fellowship to be passed into the waiting hands of future generations. Israel already had all this, and Jesus' people grouped together in those traditional ways.

Jesus' kingdom is assured and assembled, however, not by Church organization, but by individual conversion. For this one cannot organize. Though people are sometimes converted in groups, no group was ever converted. The human heart is touched and broken and healed most personally by the finger of God. Only individuals are converted. Only individuals are holy. Only individuals love or believe. Thus, if Jesus' work of revelation is continued, there will be a Church. But the mere fact that the Church continues gives no guarantee that Jesus' mission will thrive.

Before going further, let me recapitulate. Jesus reveals to us a Father who loves us even when we fail to love. Thus though we are easily turned away from him, he remains steadfastly turned toward us. We do not transact directly with God, but in reacting to our neighbor and worshipping with our neighbor we are, under it all, reacting (in Christ, if we are Christians) through the Spirit to the Father. Salvation occurs whenever anyone emerges by God's gracious enablement from her native selfishness into generous love, and opens her heart to her neighbor. This change of heart is verified and embodied in the service of one's fellow humans. Now this goes on here and there, yet never simply on our own strength, for we are not to the manner born. We begin very much wrapped up in ourselves, and for us to turn to our neighbor requires that God enable us to wish it and to do it. This we call a favor, his grace. And grace, like bacteria, is everywhere. God loves all human persons, favoring them at all times and drawing them toward his love, wittingly or unwittingly. Grace is no monopoly of Christians. The Church has been given no exclusive franchise on God's favor. The unbeliever and the believer are both saved in exactly the same way: by accepting God's transforming enablement and by loving

94

and serving their neighbor in need. The difference is that the believer has been alerted to the fact that in this transaction eternity is at stake and the Eternal Father is drawing them into his force-field.

The purpose of Jesus is the Father's purpose — to save human persons — and his peculiar and particular way of doing this is not simply to touch them with his and our generosity, but to reveal to them that this is an intimation of what the Father is like. The Church is to continue this: to join the universal, human work of bringing people from death to life, and to undertake the distinctive, ecclesial work of revealing that everything which passes between us is a function of our relationship to God. Unlike most religions, Christianity has no special set of actions that provide a short cut around or a remedy for the day-to-day transactions people have between themselves. Christianity, instead, fastens deeper attention on these crucial, non-religious activities.

It is not only the case that religion runs the perpetual risk of hypocrisy, but that religion is not the substance of salvation. When Jesus himself talks about how we will fare before the face of the Judge, it is noteworthy that religion does not come into the discussion. Jesus talks of taking in the orphans from the streets, providing a home for the widow who has neither family nor food, speaking up for the abused, burying the bodies left to rot, pacifying those who are violent, abiding those who injure us, caring for the people with contagious diseases. The very things Jesus preached are in no way intrinsically religious. The purpose of religion is to lead people knowingly to salvation in these ways, not to replace these salvific acts with others of its own choosing or making.

Why, then, the Church?

The only place we can find the Father is in his sons and daughters, and in the transaction of goods and services which will help those brothers and sisters to become nourished and to grow. If this is so, the Church dare not offer its activities as a short-cut around the practical love of one's neighbor. No one has ever seen God. And the only words we can speak to him with sincerity are those verified by our dealings with our brothers and sisters. No one can love the Father he does not see, without loving the brother and sister he does see.

Thus the crucial activities of Christians are not peculiar to Christians. Christianity must be dedicated to what is not particular to Christianity (though it is peculiar to Christianity to realize that). Ours must be a most outward-facing fellowship. It must be an agency of individual and group service, with the knowledge that in washing the feet of the world one is kissing the Father's cheek. What marks this agency of service and forbearance is the conviction of those who serve and suffer that they are responding to the boundless love of the Father, and are drawing others to respond as well, whether or not those others see and believe and enter our fellowship of belief. Faith, that precious gift which reveals all gifts, is something we could do without. Indeed, at the end of time, Paul notes, it will vaporize along with hope in the flame of final love. Love is something no one can ever do without.

A bill was once introduced into the Oregon legislature, intended to remove the tax exemption granted to athletic associations, churches, and fraternal lodges, meanwhile affirming the exemptions granted to orphanages, hospitals, and similar institutions. The bill was defeated, but what is more significant is that a good number of legislators felt they should draw the line between organizations that serve themselves and those that serve the unserved. They thought they knew on which side the churches fell. Their observation should strike the Church as a radical accusation and a call to refresh our original purpose. The Church must be an organization that serves the afflicted, acting in the privileged belief that its service must be prophetic and revelatory as the service of Jesus was. Its purpose goes beyond the secular succoring of neighbor; it is the conveyance of more than bread alone, in the belief that whoever gives bread in love, gives more than bread alone.

If Jesus is our Lord, it is our business to seek his kingdom as he did. We do this first of all by giving life and its provisioning to those who have them in short measure; that life is love. Further, we try to share our life-giving secret: that in serving our sister and brother we are reconciled to our Father, who loves us and calls us to himself. Revelation, though unnecessary, is a most precious extravagance which has no purpose but to save us.

Still, some will feel, the Church does not then seem all that important. I often believe that this complaint arises most from those believers who, leaving little trace of any real contribution to the world, must prop up their self-esteem by thinking they are important to have around. Yet taking this query at face value, we might put it into its bluntest terms: what real gain does faith afford a person who is already living by grace in love? Why need the Church bother someone who is already redeemed?

What does revelation add to salvation?

What can revelation add to salvation that is not necessary, yet beyond all value, all trade? Paul Horgan's novel, *Whitewater,* tells a story about that.[6] Fictional Belvedere, pop. 5,453, is a small, isolated town in West Central Texas, punctuated by a single water tower standing high above the flat, dry prairie. Three chums are nearing the end of their high school years there: William Breedlove, Marilee Underwood, and Phillipson Durham. Billy is the nervy blond Adonis of the senior class and indeed of the town: first in sports and first in trend-setting, striking fear in the hearts of the attractive girls' mothers. His mild evangelical parents — silent and sourly patient — already stand off at a bewildered distance from his energy. Bright and perky Marilee is only one of so many who have been drawn into Billy's attractive spell, but she is the one he most means to possess. Her widowed mother, who willingly takes on the color of any background, seems to have passed on that chameleon gene. Phil is new to the town (five years is not time enough really to belong), the only son of a grey and wretched father increasingly debilitated by syphilis contracted when Phil was a baby, and a mother who went to bed for life the day she learned of it. Phil knew why their lives had been blighted, and he was just coming to realize how they were blighting him as well.

Billy wanted to do all and Phil wanted to know all. Billy wanted what was possible and usually got it. Phil would settle only for the impossible. As the story begins Billy was having the easier time of it because all he thought of doing was to be found in Belvedere. Phil needed the world, but was trapped in Belvedere by the poverty and the needs and the wants of his parents.

Phil found a unique confidante in Victoria Cochran, a local girl who had not succeeded in her ballet career in New York and Paris. She had been hungry for something far beyond the plains, and she came home still hungry. She had married an older federal judge who retired back to his mansion in Belvedere. After being widowed (when he was 80 and she only 41), she had made her quiet and frugal life in the old house furnished with his library and his art collection. The only invitation to town involvement she accepted was a seat on the school board, and her interest in bright and promising students (who might need to be freed from Bel-

---

6. Paul Horgan, *Whitewater* (New York: Farrar, Straus and Giroux, 1969). So much of the précis that follows is extracted *verbatim* from the text that most quotation marks are omitted. Explicit quotations are from pp. 132, 239-41, 160, 222, 334.

vedere) made her the willing hostess to the three chums, but she quickly saw it was Phil who appreciated her free and critical spirit and the culture of her household. Victoria knew how important it was for young people like Phil simply to have someone to listen. She welcomed him to her house, but never coaxed him to come more often than he wished. She made him aware of how ugly and narrow and foolish the town was, but prodded him to look for the beauty beyond the banality. She bred him for a wider later life after Belvedere.

He encountered an odd combination of eccentric lyricism and raw good will — the first in those aspects of seasonal sweetness and wide grandeur in the landscape which took any newcomer a long time to get used to and to love; the other in the puzzled gracelessness of many people he knew in their use of each other and their stated opinions. He later found that various distant cultures, as he put it with irony, were also concerned with the inescapable failures and shortcomings of humanity, but some had other, more confident conventions of responding to these, publicly and privately.

The youngsters were not a crowd entirely to themselves, and in their small town they saw and sensed blighted lives, violent marriages, and daily madness. But Phil had moments of discovery. One day the drunken, stroke-stricken town banker took him for a wild ride and under an anaesthetic of Old Forester told him why the only happiness he had found was refuge from his wife in daily trysts with the divorcée who sold perfume in the dry goods shop:

"You want to know somethin, young feller? I'll tell you the most lonesome thing in the world is not to have anybody to know what you are really *like*. . . . It wouldn't have mattered a-tall what I did if someone just knew what I was *like*. . . . Now, boy, you take and you marry a girl who knows what you're really like, and you be sure of her, so she won't try to make you over into what she *thinks* you're like, which only means what she thinks you ought to turn into to suit *her!*"

This was not entirely at odds with Vicky Cochran's observation:

"Oh, I think anybody could be happy forever, if they had ever been sure that they were necessary, réally necessary, to the life of somebody else."

Eventually Billy possessed Marilee. Shortly afterwards, he was killed by a fall from the water tank he insisted Phil help him paint with a victory graffito the night before his big game. When Marilee found out a few weeks later that she was pregnant, she and the child joined Billy in death by taking a pickup and driving it into a lake. Phil's father, on being informed of the night's full tragedy, said only, " 'Oh, shit' . . . As he said it, it was not an indifferent obscenity, but a weary comment on life as he knew it."

Phil's life is shut down with the sorrow of it all, and after graduation he seems permanently interred in Belvedere when he takes a job in his father's print shop. One day the mayor comes by to tell Phil that a citizen's committee had voted to award him a scholarship that would pay his way to any university, all the way to the doctorate. Vicky tips him off that the anonymous donor was probably the banker's wife, who had always been a little sweet on him. When he dithers over leaving his increasingly feckless parents, she insists the only hope they now have is in *his* fulfillment, and gives him the nerve to take the grant. Phil goes far away to a good college, finds a good wife, earns his doctorate, and settles into adulthood as a very thoughtful historian of culture. His mother dies and is buried before he can come for the funeral. He does come home, though, to bury his father, and only then learns that Vicky too lies in the graveyard.

At the time of his marriage she had written him that she believed he must not need her any further. He should give himself, and even his memories, to his wife. He protested this, and he and his wife would write her from time to time, but always without a reply. He then began to realize that the love Victoria had borne him was far more than he had suspected. He visited the old mansion a last time, empty of the beloved old artworks now — the Canova, the Van Ruisdael, the Corot, the choice Manet — but especially empty of its mistress. On his way back home, a stopover in Chicago offered the time to visit the Art Institute.

> Feeling anonymous and at peace, he went up the wide stone stairway and idled his way into the galleries. Almost at once he was unexpectedly thrown back into the midst of what he thought he had bidden goodbye to forever.
>
> There, on the wall, he saw it — the jade green sea off Boulogne-sur-Mer, with the black fishing boats moving toward the darker horizon of the painted sweep of grey sky. [It was his and her favorite, the Manet.] With hot thought, he came close to read the frame, and saw that the painting was a purchase of the Romson Fund in 1949, and

for the first time he knew where the means had come from to give him his life. His bitterness at the impossibility of acknowledgment made him fear for making a public spectacle of himself. He was stricken with a gratitude made equally of wonder and shame.

Putting on his dark outdoor glasses to hide behind, he returned to the lobby and at the book counter . . . found a postcard reproduction in color. He now keeps the postcard on his study desk, under a silver lamp with a green glass shade. Every time he thinkingly regards it, it tells him of the time when life turned outward for him, and of Victoria, through whose lightly given experience his imagination at last left town forever.

What difference would it have made for Phillipson Durham to live out his life never knowing that unwittingly he had been loved by Victoria Cochran, who sold her favorite paintings to give him his education, who forwent the only life-giving company she was likely to enjoy in Belvedere, and — since she knew him to be stymied by indebted relations — never let him become dependent upon her? What was now the force of that postcard, that sacramental evocation of his having been loved, been saved, by a woman who was as purposefully and generously attentive to him as he had been inattentive to the sacrificial fullness of her care? Because of her gifts she had already given him the enablement to become a thoughtful, knowing, and loving man. His salvation was in place.

Yet what a further gift the revelatory discovery was for him: that his adult life had been a personal gift! He was overwhelmed to find that this woman had loved him well beyond his capacity then to appreciate it. And he would not for all the world have missed later learning that truth. The revelation is a disclosure to him that he has been rescued in an incomparable way, and he turns now to his wife and children and students in that gratitude with an even more acute and effectual dedication, for he is now more deeply and efficaciously convinced that it is only the deft and self-denying sharing of one's wherewithal that makes one well-to-do. The joy of the revelation, though it overflows into his work as a father and as an educator, has a value that escapes measure. Now he is more than generously wise; he is enabled to propagate his wisdom generously.

So it is for anyone, no matter how sensitive, self-giving, and courageous: the discovery that Jesus of Nazareth died to show him or her the Father's unrelenting love speaks to the heart and wreaks a deep transformation. For some, it might be inaccurate to speak of a conversion, but the discovery of being loved, without our knowing and beyond our imagining, has the power to touch our heart at its deepest, and change our lives so mightily that the best people will speak of it as if they had been struck down in mid-journey and had their eyes opened — as if they had been blind before. Salvation and revelation are distinct, but eventually they crave to be joined together.

In Jesus' light we see light, and can appreciate all manner of other insights found from other revelations. John Carmody has put it thus:

> Only once did the Word spoken eternally in the bosom of the Father take flesh of a sister and so fix eternity to a specific personal history, make one lifetime the story of God.
>
> I think it is important to get all the clarity one can on this matter. People are not saved by the words they create, the ideas they have, the orthodoxy they do or do not seem to manifest. People are saved by the love in their hearts, the yes they say in their depths to the joys and sufferings God gives them. . . .
>
> Though I find goodness and wisdom in many places, those other places, those personal revelations, are less adequate expressions, incarnations, translations of the goodness of God, the graciousness of the absolute future, than what I find in Jesus. So I make Jesus the explicator of the salvation available in those other places, and I make Jesus the explicand at their heart or foundation. Jesus is both what I must explain, if I am to clarify the history or enfleshment of what Muslim or Buddhist holiness entails, and how I am to explain it.[7]

If Philemon was disposed to think of the conversion to Jesus as having converted everything in his life from benefit to gift, how could he have prevented himself from imagining the possibility for him to do a like thing for his Onesimus?

---

7. John Carmody, *Cancer and Faith: Reflections on Living with a Terminal Illness* (Mystic, Conn.: Twenty-Third Publications, 1994), pp. 141-42.

A Distinctive Morality

CHAPTER FIVE

Does Moral Behavior Matter,
If It Makes No Difference to the Lord?

Why please this God, who persistently loves us regardless of our moral worth?

In the foregoing pages we inquired into one of the insights in the New Testament which we took to be a load-bearing element in the transformed faith, and we pursued the clues it offered for understanding the character of God and the purposes of Jesus his Son and the mission of their Spirit. The middle chapters to follow will turn, now, from doctrinal to moral inquiry. Immediately we encounter a problem. If, taking Jesus as the *alter ego* of his Father, we believe that God is love, that in the teeth of our infidelities he relentlessly cherishes and pursues us; if he can be neither pleased nor offended since our behavior is no cause for his love; then what need have we of moral behavior? If he has a welcome for us whether we keep his moral imperatives or not, why bother with them?

Commandments have made many modern theologians restless, since they seem to diminish our free-standing maturity. Other, postmodern thinkers seem more agreeable to accepting the ancient ethic, but only if it is theirs to interpret without regard to its native meanings. It is not only the laws of Moses, however, that would be neutralized. They take exception to any precept that presumes to say in advance to anyone else, sometimes regardless of circumstances and alternatives, what is right or what is wrong. General guidelines, folk wisdom, experienced advice — yes, that might offer some help. But there can be no commandments, it is said, no generic and abstract prescriptions to tell people in advance how to behave, especially in ambivalent situations. And these modern revisionists see all situations as morally ambivalent.

Yet there is much to be said in favor of commandments as a high form of moral discourse. They are one of the clearer literary genres for making the benefits of human experience and moral reflection available to future generations. In most societies the only effective way moral wisdom can be made publicly available and durably effective is through commandments. Justice, people commonly believe, will more surely be done when ordered by authority than when expounded by learning. Most people would give no notice at all to the exotic moral inquiries of thinkers like Amen-em-ope, Plato, Lucretius, or Boëthius, yet might heed the same ethical insights if they came on the say-so of authorities: the Sun-God Amon, Alexander of Macedon, Emperor Theodosius, or even the local pastor. Within the Christian tradition the clergy have often chosen to give commands (whether in God's name or their own) as preferable to ambiguity. However — so this revisionist line of argument proceeds — though the ruler may use a language different from that of the sage, moral wisdom is what they are both trying to foster.

A commandment is one of several possible syntaxes of moral discourse. Some argue that it is preferable and more mature to say, "This is good," than to say, "Thou shalt do this." But every imperative statement ultimately resolves itself into a declarative one. When a father forbids his son to sleep round the town, he is really warning him that if he does, he will offend social custom, or incur a paternity suit, or get the clap, or be disinherited, or hurt some woman, or go to Hell, or become a meaningless and loveless man. Even in the case where the father backs up his command with his own deterrents, he is still warning his son of more substantive evil to be visited upon him, just as surely as if he had used the straightforward syntax of advice instead of command.

But this may be a hasty criticism, particularly in the Jewish and Christian traditions. As observed earlier, most gods tend to come across as unknown, mighty, and judgmental. The primal human reaction to such gods is fear, even terror. God's expectations are so impossible; God's pleasure is so hard to anticipate; God's anger can be so disastrous. In this context, the disclosure of commandments might be more a rescue than a burden. It would surely seem so in Israel. Knowing what the Lord demanded was a gift, a protection, a clear advantage over the Gentiles.

---

1. Arbitration between tribes came to be reserved to some established national hero who had roused the lethargic tribes from isolationism to join in a war of mutual defense: this kind of charismatic guerilla leader who had displayed a greater loyalty to the entire nation than to his or her own tribe earned the trust and title of "Judge."

Of course, to know commandments is not to keep them. Still, guilt from sin seemed less fearsome than the dread of not knowing Yahweh's paths. Thus the Torah came to be seen as a gift, a delight. In its very complexity, the web of further legalisms that were spun around it by the Jewish rabbis and then the Christian divines with their cocoons of casuistry, was in the believer's favor: even in extraordinary eventualities one could know what God wanted done.

Commandments, then, are one syntax for sharing the moral yield of experience (by which I mean, not events, but the fruitful insights those events can provoke in us) with those who follow. But the New Testament is ill at ease with commandments as a form of moral discourse, and I would propose that we stand to learn from that disinclination.

Law in Israel

Hebrew law has roots reaching down deep into the Exodus and the Conquest. After invading Canaan and Gilead the tribes settled in scattered pockets throughout the territory. The task of settling disputes between tribesfolk, easily accomplished by the central leader during the earlier nomadic days on a smaller scale, now fell to the local chiefs.[1] By a combination of the reading of omens, or the throwing of magical lots, or folk wisdom, they had to see justice done well enough that grievances would not fester into feuds. In time, landmark decisions came to be publicized and remembered. There was the time, for instance, when an engaged girl was caught *in flagrante delicto,* and claimed that she had been raped. Not so, said the shrewd elder: she was in the village, and could have called for help. Had she been in the countryside with no one to hear, the presumption would be in her favor, and the judgment would lean toward acquittal. The sentence: both parties to be stoned to death (Deut. 22:23-27).

There was another famous case of the ox that gored to death an ox in a neighboring field. The usual settlement was that the surviving ox must be sold, the two owners to divide the proceeds and also to divide the carcass of the dead animal between them. But in this case the goring ox had been known to be of vicious temperament (there had been other incidents), yet was never fenced or tied properly. The verdict: since the incident involved criminal negligence the live ox was forfeit to the aggrieved owner and the careless owner was left with the dead animal (Exod. 21:35-36).

As the memory of particularly wise decisions served as precedents for future judgments, and gradually accumulated into a common law, they were transformed from narrative — "A man was caught doing such-and-such, and Moses said, 'This man must be put to death'" (Solomon's judgment between the two harlots claiming the one baby is remembered in this form) — into imperative: "If anyone does such-and-such, you will put him to death." By being cast in the syntax of legislation rather than that of judicial precedent, they would enjoy enhanced authority by ascription to God through Moses, rather than through any of the lesser venerated judges. In even more ancient days justice had been decided more by divination and lot (safer for the arbiters if the verdict went against a powerful family). The result was thus attributed to God and could be accepted without rebellion. As human judgment first augmented and then replaced magic or ordeal, it needed to be grounded on comparable authority. This was first done by tracing the legitimacy of elder-judges to Moses, and thence to Yahweh (Exod. 19:13-25; Deut. 1:9-18; 16:18-20). Later, as the common law was being converted to writing, their decisions were translated into commandments. They were no longer remembered as the decisions of inspired, shrewd men. They were, by literary convention, put in the mouth of Moses; thus they could be more readily recognized as God's judgment, or Word.

One way the moral tradition preserved its needed suppleness was by supplementing the Torah with a continuous oral interpretation and application. Young scribes were quizzed at the feet of elder sages, asking them questions and being interrogated in return. The anecdote about Jesus staying behind in the temple as a youth evokes just this sort of teacher-disciple exchange that can still be seen in the Orthodox Jewish and Muslim traditions. It combines a retention of the ancient texts by memory, with a trained personal initiation into making further casuistic or midrashic applications.

The New Testament builds on that base. When John came baptizing, for example, his message was a call to repentance. Luke mentions that various classes of people approached him with questions that called for the usual sort of rabbinical answers. John's syntax shifts abruptly from the prophetic to the casuistic:

> He said, therefore, to the crowds who came to be baptised by him, "Brood of vipers, who warned you to flee from the coming retribution? Produce fruit in keeping with repentance, and do not start telling yourselves, 'We have Abraham as our father,' because, I

tell you, God can raise children for Abraham from these stones. Yes, even now the axe is being laid to the root of the trees, so that any tree failing to produce good fruit will be cut down and thrown on the fire."

When all the people asked him, "What must we do, then?" he answered, "Anyone who has two tunics must share with the one who has none, and anyone with something to eat must do the same." There were tax collectors, too, who came for baptism, and these said to him, "Master, what must we do?" He said to them, "Exact no more than the appointed rate." Some soldiers asked him in their turn, "What about us? What must we do?" He said to them, "No intimidation! No extortion! Be content with your pay!" (Luke 3:7-14)

The questions put to John were the standard queries likely to be addressed to any sage, particularly one of a reformist persuasion: how should one lead a life righteously in the sight of the Lord? His answers are in the highest tradition of Israel . . . or, more precisely, in two of the highest traditions: that of the prophet and that of the sage. What he enjoins is the highest equity, and the forgoing of self-aggrandizement in the face of a neighbor's deprivation.

The inadequacy of commandments

But as soon as we examine the ethical injunctions of Jesus, we see a different approach, a moral tradition at once more traditional and more radical. Jesus finds the syntax of law too stifling a translation for the syntax of prophecy. Compare the anecdote about John recounted above with the reply of Jesus to virtually the same sort of questions:

And now a rich man came to him and asked, "Master, what good deed must I do to possess eternal life?" Jesus said to him, "Why do you ask me about what is good? There is one alone who is good. But if you wish to enter into life, keep the commandments." He said, "Which ones?" Jesus replied, "These: *You shall not kill. You shall not commit adultery. You shall not steal. You shall not give false witness. Honour your father and your mother. You shall love your neighbour as yourself."* The young man said to him, "I have kept all these. What more do I need to do?" Jesus said, "If you wish to be perfect, go and sell your possessions and give the money to the poor, and you will have treasure in heaven; then come, follow me." But when the young man heard these words he went away sad, for he was a man of great wealth.

Then Jesus said to his disciples, "In truth I tell you, it is hard for someone rich to enter the kingdom of Heaven. Yes, I tell you again, it is easier for a camel to pass through the eye of a needle than for someone rich to enter the kingdom of Heaven." When the disciples heard this they were astonished. "Who can be saved then?" they said. Jesus gazed at them. "By human resources," he told them, "this is impossible; for God everything is possible."

Then Peter answered and said, "Look, we have left everything and followed you. What are we to have, then?" Jesus said to them, "In truth I tell you, when everything is made new again and the Son of Man is seated on his throne of glory, you yourselves will sit on twelve thrones to judge the twelve tribes of Israel. And everyone who has left houses, brothers, sisters, father, mother, children or land for the sake of my name will receive a hundred times as much, and also inherit eternal life." (Matt. 19:16-29)

Jesus reverses the order followed by John. He meets the conventional questions with what starts out to be a conventional casuistic response. The man is pleased with this response: he has done well by the law. But then Jesus goes on. Abiding by the law is not sufficient. There is more to do. If he really wishes to lay hold of eternal life, the man may have to liquidate all his assets, abandon the proceeds to the poor, and follow Jesus on his mendicant wanderings.

Some interpreters have suggested that the passage offers a double standard: a set of minimum requirements for everyday observants who must keep the commandments, and a higher way for those elites in the Church (monks, nuns, mendicants, and the like) who are zestful enough to follow a more exacting regime of self-denial. But the Gospel cannot support such a meaning. Jesus is presenting a single way of life, the only one he urges as successful. The plight of his interlocutor is sad: his assets are many and his courage is slight. He disappears in the opposite direction. The point of the story is one of the master points of Matthew's Gospel: the young man might not attain eternal life, even though he has abided by the commandments. The Mosaic law is to be honored, but it is a developing start: it does not nearly reach what Jesus prophetically demands, nor does it know all that is required to be reconciled with the Father.

The inspired tradition of Israel and of the Church was always developing. But it did not grow continuously, like the wheat that puts forth blades, leaves, stalks, ears, and whiskers. It grew continually, like the crab that periodically wriggles out of its shell, quickly expands to a new stage of growth, and then swiftly hardens its skin into a new shell. The molting phase of the inspired tradition occurred when it would be restated, especially in writing. The new might go beyond the old, by way of omission, or expansion, or revision, but because the contemporary interpreters thought of themselves as restating and preserving a revealed insight once handed down to the saints, even at their most innovative they were at pains to disavow any break with the past upon which they had been nourished.

Jesus had it both ways, so to speak. In the same breath he would insist that no part of the Torah — not the smallest letter, or even the flourish of the pen at the end of the smallest *yod* — was to be vacated, and then he would insist that no matter what they had heard, *he* had something more to lay on them. This baffling double claim of continuity and of break was his way of coaxing them further into the mystery. Jesus is contrasting the previously understood claims of Israel with his own. When a young man came of age he encountered the law. He was served notice of what the Lord demanded of him. He knew what he was getting into: he ratified the covenant with his eyes open. If he undertook to follow Jesus, however, he did more, though it seemed quite the contrary. Jesus, whose moral imperatives could be counted on to overflow any code, invited men and women further: to undertake commitments whose concrete follow-through was unknown, to make promises whose full measure could never be taken, to ratify a covenant whose terms could not be previously foreseen even with the most open of eyes. He was asking more, however, not less. Much more.

Much of the comfort in the law came from its precision: through it one was supposed to know whatever God required. But Jesus insists that the divine demand knows no known limits. In founding a covenant of faith, more than of obedience, he invites disciples to make their response, not within the limits of prior conditions mutually accepted, but in terms of the true needs of the person to whom fidelity is pledged. And since Jesus represents all neighbors in need, there is no end to the service required.

Jesus does not reject commandments. He reaffirmed the old prohibitions against murder, adultery, robbery, perjury, fraud, and abandonment of elderly parents. But from those who hankered after eternal life he asked more, with an excruciating, open-ended vagueness: "Come, follow me. . . . Repent, and believe in the Gospel" (Mark 10:17-22; 1:15). He had no trust in the compliance of those whose moral agenda was limited to and by the concrete requirements of the Torah, for they were the sort who looked without seeing and listened without understanding (to avoid changing their ways); they gave lip-service without heart-service, and always found a way to degrade the divine Law into human commandments (Mark 4:12; 7:6-7).

They defiled preaching and tithing and washing by using them as camouflage for their dislike of "the weightier matters": justice, mercy, and good faith (Matt. 23:13-32).

Jesus rejects a moral life whose master metaphor is a canonical set of commandments, because an ethic whose template is law can alway delude one into thinking that God's demands are contained by the law, or all law. The claims of Jesus' Father found an early understanding in the law, but our inspired understanding of his claims continues to develop. They exceeded the law — not by leaping over it but by running ahead of it. They burst the law. The law is not demeaned or abrogated or reversed, but Jesus proposes what one might call a Gospel ethic: a claim as large as the needs of the world!

Jesus says he wants not simply that the Torah be obeyed, but that its "purpose" be achieved. To abstain from killing is no good if anger survives; or from adultery if lust lives; or from perjury if deception remains at work; or from feuding if retribution is the price of peace; or from violence against kinsmen if violence against foreigners is the price of that peace (Matt. 5:18-48). The aim of the Torah was to create a people loyal to one another with a minimum of violence. The greater aim of Jesus was to create a people loyal to one another and to all others, with no violence. It would mean going the extra mile, supping with sinners, taking suffering from brothers but not giving any, bringing judgment to bear without a word of condemnation, being *kosher*-pure in both intake and output, forgiving the unforgiving, and entering the City of Treachery, not on the warhorse but on the donkey of peace. His idiom is that of the prophets and the sages, and his parables are like hot peppers that burn in the conscience long after they are spoken.

In setting aside law as an analogy too weak to convey his preaching, Jesus replaces it with a much more rigorous alternative. His moral imperatives are limitless, open-ended. His claim is such as to devour a person's life, to allow a person no rest. Of course, Matthew's story of the rich young man is not to be spoiled by thinking that Jesus is speaking only of wealth.

In the end he makes it clear that all the supports one might cling to must be released: kin, house, and land — in a word: home. A person must not remain focused on those who belong to him, who must serve him back. A person must be on the move, like the Master prowling for the unfortunate sisters and brothers who have need of him. Like the law, home represents a claim that would be limited and controllable.

Jesus as neither lawgiver nor judge

Note that throughout the Gospels Jesus encounters many specific queries. "Why is it that John's disciples and the Pharisees fast, but your disciples do not?" "Look, why are they doing something on the Sabbath day that is forbidden?" "Why then do the scribes say that Elijah must come first?" "Why did Moses command that a writ of dismissal should be given in cases of divorce?" "Is it permissible to pay taxes to Caesar or not?" "Good master, what shall I do to inherit eternal life?" "Who is my neighbour?" Jesus, unlike the Baptist and Paul, is not in the habit of offering specific answers. Nor does he respond with more abstract principles of general morality. Often he responds with riddles or stories suggestive of a larger vision that renders the original question petty or needless. He always has more to say than their queries call for: their questions are too puny for his answers. He declines to be a lawmaker. He is not calling Jews back to Moses. He is calling Jews and Gentiles forward to a measure of devotion Moses never dared demand, but toward which he was already on the move.

The extraordinary character of Jesus' ethic can also be found in his long series of injunctions in the Sermon on the Mount (Matt. 5:20-48). His disciples must have a virtue deeper than that of the scribes and the Pharisees, who claim to abide by the law. They have learnt how it was said to their ancestors . . . but he says to them. . . . The old ordinances fail by default. They seem to put curbs on obligation while imposing it. There must be a new integrity, a reckless generosity. The quality and measure of service that Jesus calls for can only partially be summed up in the Golden Rule, which so many writers use to suggest a parity between the ethic of Jesus and that of other religions. "Treat others as you would like people to treat you" (Luke 6:31; Matt. 7:12). It is better captured in that other maxim: "This is the first commandment: 'Listen, Israel, the Lord our God is the one, only Lord, and you must love the Lord your God with all your heart, with all your soul, with all your mind and all your strength.' The second is this: 'You must love your neighbour as yourself'" (Mark 12:29-31). Best of all it is suggested in John's quotation: "You must love one another just as I have loved you" (13:34). The New Commandment begins with no more limits than Jesus' own example, an incitement to how wantonly one might love.

Jesus, the new Moses, strikes a new sort of covenant between the Lord and his people. He has but one master command: that people love one another as he has loved. He does not oppose the Torah or reject it: he takes it for granted. He sweeps past all systems of law, which presume to define and thus to limit the Father's claims and human possibilities. Jesus charges each person with full responsibility for the needs of each needy brother and sister, and renders the analogy of law inadequate for the Christian conscience. Thus he is no lawgiver, no legislator.

Nor do the Gospels care to call him judge. John's Gospel illustrates this. Jesus heals a man who had for 38 years been a helpless paralytic. It is the Sabbath, and certain onlookers challenge Jesus for instructing the man to break the prescribed rest by trying out his walking legs and carrying his mat around. Jesus meets the criticism by claiming exemption from the Saturday rest. "'My Father still goes on working, and I am at work, too.' But that only made the Jews even more intent on killing him, because not only was he breaking the Sabbath, but he spoke of God as his own Father and so made himself God's equal" (John 5:17-18).

His reply, at first mystifying, bears explanation. Despite the first chapter of Genesis, it was a contemporary belief that the Lord did not, in fact, cease all his activity to rest on the Sabbath. There were two divine responsibilities he did not delegate to his heavenly subordinates who otherwise served as his factotums in running the universe: life-giving and judging. The rabbis noted that children were born indiscriminately on Saturday as plentifully as on any day of the week. People died, too, without respect to the calendar. Each occasion — birth or death — required that the Lord exercise in person one of those two sovereign powers: life-giving or judging. Thus the opinion that the Lord was ceaselessly on call. Jesus' claim to share the Father's seven-day work week implies that he shared those two exclusively divine powers. The implication was not lost on his critics, and he was accused of claiming equality with God.

As Jesus' discourse further unfolds, John implies that life-giving and judging in the deeper sense do not occur at what they knew as the two ends of a lifetime — at first breath and last — but at life's climax: the moment of encounter with the Lord. A person who for virtually a lifetime (40 years was the round number for a generation) had been as good as dead, encounters Jesus. He is given life — not simply the ability to walk, but what that was meant to stand for: the strength to walk in God's paths, to stay clear of sin. There was an immediate reaction among the bystanders, this way and that. Some said it was God's kind of good work; others fell to grumbling about the Sabbath infraction. According to John, Jesus simply confronts the crowd with an act of raw, vitalizing benevolence, and their reactions to him reveal their own hearts. Some cherish the itinerant healer for doing good, while others revile him for doing it on the wrong day. There is no quarrel over whether or not he is divine, but simply over whether he is a good or a lawless man. Unwittingly, by taking opposing sides when the divine benevolence is exposed to them, they judge themselves. Some show their life; others display their death. The unleashing of God's graciousness in human affairs makes it unnecessary to wait until death for humans to be divided: the cleaving judgment is in the ever contemporaneous Now.

John inverts the traditional sense of judgment. The radical sense of the New Testament word for judging, *krínein,* is "to cleave, to divide." Jesus can claim, "I judge no one" (8:15), for it is not he who scrutinizes a person's life and declares where he or she stands. He enters a village and gives heart and life to someone in need of both. By the time he leaves, everyone has taken sides: they have been divided, judged. What this reveals is not simply what kind of person *he* is, but what kinds *they* are: how they stand in regard to benevolence, to grace, to the Father. The encounter with prophetic benevolence provokes people to judge themselves by taking sides, *pro* and *con.*

> Thus, as the Father raises the dead and gives them life,
> so the Son gives life to anyone he chooses;
> for the Father judges no one:
> he has entrusted all judgment to the Son,
> so that all may honour the Son
> as they honour the Father.
> Whoever refuses honour to the Son
> refuses honour to the Father who sent him.
> In all truth I tell you,
> whoever listens to my words,
> and believes in him who sent me,
> has eternal life;
> without being brought to judgment
> such a person has passed from death to life.

In all truth I tell you,
the hour is coming — indeed it is already here —
when the dead will hear the voice of the Son of God,
and all who hear it will live.
For as the Father has life in himself,
so he has granted the Son also to have life in himself;
and, because he is the Son of Man,
has granted him power to give judgment. (5:21-27)

The Gospels do identify Jesus as lawgiver and judge, but go to great pains to show that these analogies are transfigured far above their conventional meanings. I am inclined to doubt that Christian moral theology has continued to notice the startling innovation that Jesus was evidently at such pains to offer. For the old themes of legislation and judgment are often worked into our preaching in ways that would make Moses happier than they would Jesus.

Paul might have been put forward before Jesus on this matter of the law, as he so often is. Before our Gospels were published he had made a rumpus round the Mediterranean, insisting that Jesus was not the new Moses, but the fulfillment of the Promise made to Abraham, who had fathered the chosen people long before there was any talk of Torah. Torah came later, Paul said, to humiliate Israel by her inability to live up to it. And with the release of the Spirit in full force by Jesus' death and rising, and the begetting of a New People with new strength, now drawn from every nation under God, the booster-stage Torah was left behind and disciples were no longer to be committed to it by circumcision (Rom. 4–5).

Two salvation metaphors

The rudimentary structure beneath almost all Christian moralizing is what I suggest calling the "Forensic Metaphor." Like the "Savior Myth," it is nowhere set down in simple and brief fashion, but let me try to sketch it out:

Human beings live under the legitimate authority of God, whose sovereign rights as creator are limitless. God has established a law, a code of commandments for humanity, which he makes known in various ways. First, there is the subtle, stirring voice of right-and-wrong in everyone's conscience (sometimes called the natural law). Then there are the laws of Moses revealed to Israel, and the latterday

116

insights provided through Jesus to the Church. Although God's statutes bind all humans, they are not evenly known from person to person. All, however, are expected to have a grasp of at least the basic obligations. Thus warned, each person has a lifetime of freedom to act at will, but in the end every person will be judged on how well he or she has kept the law. God will then call them all to account for everything they have done, though taking into consideration all the extenuating circumstances that might modify guilt: ignorance of the obligation, a strong impulse or passion that may have swept someone into more evil than he or she really chose, lack of foresight about the harm that resulted, and so forth. After all this is summed up in a net outcome, a final verdict is issued, and the person is consigned appropriately to either eternal reward or eternal punishment.

The Forensic Metaphor, even in briefest form, suggests how the commonly held folk-ethic of Christians is at odds with the Jesus-ethic in the Gospel. In imitation of the civil law, God is seen as both legislator and judge. He gives the laws to begin with, and at the end holds humans responsible for having observed them. His legal demands, even if numerous, are limited. There is little hint of the Gospel call to give one's whole heart, to unleash one's full strength, to follow Jesus whithersoever in search of all human sufferings and want. Nor is there any room for the changeless benevolence of Jesus' Father, who loves without restraint.

When ethics are cast into the traditional mold of law (rather than incorporating law as the explicand of some other master metaphor), sin risks being portrayed, not as an intrinsic disorder and disaster within the person, but as a disobedient rejection of authority, disastrous *because* it is recorded and punished. Virtue is no matter of growth within the person, but of conformity whose reward is given by an observant God. In a word, the Forensic Metaphor undergirds an ethic that is extrinsic. The law is an advertisement, not of what corrupts a creature or makes a person grow, but of what God forbids or imposes, and enforces.

Admittedly every metaphor must be allowed a little limp, but I am arguing that this one — so popular in Christian teaching — obscures some of the very points the Gospel aims to emphasize. In its place I would offer what might be called the "Confrontation Metaphor."

All persons have their lives to live. During that brief, critical time they must grow. Beginning as totally self-centered infants, they must be transformed into persons who are totally given to others in gener-

117

ous love. They interact with their fellows, immensely affected by them yet picking their own way along the path that offers many turning points. They may know what kind of God cares for them, and what kind of persons they themselves are becoming. But also, they may know neither God nor themselves. If they do, so much the better. What is essential, however, is that they grow to fullest human stature, that they become men and women who love heartily and serve respectfully. At death, as far as we can know, time will end and growth will cease. What each person has by then become, that will each person remain forever. At death each one confronts God. If a person has grown from selfishness into love, she will draw near and cleave to him — as she has gone out of herself to her fellow humans before death. If a person has only become more wrapped up in himself, then he will come face-to-face with the Lord, but not notice him any more than he has noticed his fellow humans. Death is the occasion for fullest revelation — yet only those with eyes to see will see.

According to this analogy, God does not alter his attitudes in response to human behavior: his is an unyielding welcome. Since good and evil, growth and corruption, are values in themselves, morality comprises, not simply what humans intend and accomplish or avoid, but what and who they become as a result. And revelation is a gift, since it discloses to us what it is to our advantage to see. In the Forensic Metaphor, virtue and sin are oddly symmetrical: both are possessed only insofar as a person is consciously and purposefully eager and active. If anything, the conscience of the sinner is portrayed as the more active, because the more agitated. In the Confrontation Metaphor sin is seen, not as the conscious choice of evil, so much as the subtle and obstinate avoidance of neighbor-need, and the self-inflicted anaesthesia of conscience. Sin involves the smothering of responsibility; it is less defiance than autistic avoidance. In the end a person is not judged for what he or she has responsibly done right or wrong. The person is simply presented to God as is, and relates to him accordingly, like those villagers in the Fourth Gospel.

Perhaps the point can be illustrated by several anecdotes. The first is provided by Jesus himself in the parable of the Rich Man and Lazarus (Luke 16:19-31). There was a man who dressed well, ate well, and went to Hell. No crime is held against him; there is no accusation of debauchery. But during all those years of satiety there had been a man nearby who should have been his neighbor but never was. This man who haunted the nearby alleys did not eat well, since he could not even win access to the rich man's garbage. Nor did he have much more than his own sores for wearing apparel (one thinks of the dreaded pellagra or kwashiorkor that come from famine). During all those years the rich man had come and gone upon his own business, never noticing Lazarus. It is therefore fitting that the rich man has no name, no *persona*. The great gulf that separated him from Lazarus was of his making, and it widened each time the rich man passed Lazarus without noticing him. When the two men died, the gulf between them had long been fixed, and it remained. Lazarus went to be comforted in the company of Father Abraham, and the rich man stood off at the same distance, but now at the other end of circumstance. Abraham cut off his agonized appeals. The rich man made a last, desperate request that Abraham warn his five brothers of what they too would face. Abraham replied that if his five brothers were as blind as he to needy others, then not even a messenger from the land of the dead would be able to break through to them. They, like he, would see and hear what they wished to see and hear. This reinforces Jesus' claim elsewhere that those who cannot hear what he is saying or see what he is doing have closed themselves off to their brothers and sisters, and thereby to him and to the Father. The "great gulf" between them and the "torment" and "flames" had not been "fixed" by heavenly anger; indeed, Father Abraham speaks in sorry candor, not in anger. The love of God is not punitive, but neither is it sentimental: it pours forth lavishly, but unless human beings allow themselves to be helped to open to it (in the rich man's case, by Moses and the prophets), they will surely be destroyed: by their own hand. In the end it will be in vain that God has loved us, if we do not meanwhile become people who see, and love.

Another suggestive text is found in *The Towers of Trebizond*, an otherwise bizarre travel story by Rose Macaulay. The scene in question finds her poking through the ruins of a Byzantine church in Trebizond, near the east end of Turkey's Black Sea coast.

> It took me some time to make out the Greek inscription, which was about saving me from my sins, and I hesitated to say this prayer, as I did not really want to be saved from my sins, not for the time being, it would make things too difficult and too sad [she was at the time having an affair with someone else's husband]. I was getting into a stage when I was not quite sure what sin was, I was in a kind

2. Rose Macaulay, *The Towers of Trebizond* (New York: Farrar, Straus & Cudahy, 1956), p. 150.

of fog, it makes a confused sort of twilight in which everything is blurred, and the next thing you know you might be stealing or anything, because right and wrong have become things you do not look at, you are afraid to, and it seems better to live in a blur. Then come the times when you wake suddenly up, and the fog breaks, and right and wrong loom through it, sharp and clear like peaks of rock, and you are on the wrong peak and know that, unless you can manage to leave it now, you may be marooned there for life and ever after. Then, as you don't leave it, the mist swirls round again, and hides the other peak, and you turn your back on it and try to forget it and succeed.

Another thing you learn about sin, it is not one deed more than another, though the Church may call some of them mortal and others not, but even the worst ones are only . . . a chain, not things by themselves, and adultery, say, is chained with stealing sweets when you are a child, or taking another child's toys, or the largest piece of cake, or letting someone else be thought to have broken something you have broken yourself, or breaking promises and telling secrets, it is all one thing and you are tied up with that chain till you break it, and the Church calls it not being in a state of grace.[2]

The third anecdote bearing on judgment as a life-offering confrontation is an adaptation of Pinocchio. The hero of the story is a very self-centered young puppet who heedlessly takes for granted the generous attentions of his maker and master Geppetto. To cure him of his egotism, he was given an increasingly long nose, but it seems that even this disfigurement failed to evoke the desired repentance. More draconian measures were needed. Pinocchio was therefore taken on a guided tour of Hell, in the hope that the sights there might shock him into virtue. The first person he encountered in the underworld was a ballerina. She was dancing with great concentration when he approached to interview her. He found that she danced right past him, and no amount of agile effort on his part succeeded in catching her attention. Moving along, he came upon a carpenter hard at work: sawing, fitting, and gluing his woodwork. He too proved impossible to interrupt, no matter how insistently the little puppet-man tried to catch his eye or ear. It was at this point that Pinocchio saw, in a flash, that in Hell everyone is left to themselves, free to do only what they wanted to do, and to take notice of no one else. Then he remembered that some people were like this already on Earth. He returned to the upper world a wise and repentant puppet.

In proposing that Christian moral understanding ought not be shaped on the armature of law, I am not denying that the Church instinctively proclaims many of the old commandments and formulates new ones besides. She does. But the mystery of how she knows which to retain and which to forget is a sense as deep as her faith, and as authoritative as the voice that first delivered the tablets of stone. She uses those older mandates to allude to obligations now more expansively understood. I am trying to highlight the more stringent and more internalized ethic implied in the Gospel, the explicator of the legal explicand.

Classical theology has maintained that one could sin only when aware of it. This flies in the face of common observation. We do not notice — we do not allow ourselves truly to notice — human needs that we are unwilling to go out of our way to relieve. Sin brings the hardened heart, the deafened ear, the unseeing eye, the astigmatic conscience: the very opposite of awareness and responsibility. Sin is like leprosy, which destroys the nervous system as it progresses. Active love, like that of Jesus, is searching and sensitive, and discovers without being told: who is suffering, who lies neglected.

It is precisely the person who lies helpless in self-incurred blindness that needs revelation. For ignorance of oneself is not bliss. We have need of our neighbor to pierce through our distraction and disclose to us that we are wretched and pitiably poor, and blind and naked too. If the rebuke comes as part of the authentic Christian revelation, it brings two singular advantages. First, we discover that our selfishness and estrangement are of eternal significance. Second, in the forgiveness of the Father, embodied in the humble and humane bluntness of the sister or brother who holds the mirror before our imagination and memory, we find the support it takes to see ourselves as we really are. Revelation in time is a grace, for it opens our eyes to dare see the blinding welcome that waits beyond time.

Strange doctrine, strange morality

Jesus, who became unbearable to his generation for the truth he spoke and the good he did, went to his violent and lonesome death stripped of every friend for whom loyalty meant risk. Yet he bounded forth gloriously from that death to seek out those defaulted disciples. He broke their hearts with his greeting of peace, and breathed into them enough of his Spirit for them to believe that, while they had not loved him, he had loved them. Then they could see the Father in him, a Father whose relentless love had touched them through his Son, in their own flesh. After that there was no stopping them. And what possessed them, what they could not stop saying every which way, was the revelation that the Father of Jesus, the Master of the Universe, loves sinners. Indeed, now they could think of no reason for him ever to have created the cosmos if not to share with a creature-people the thrill of seeing Jesus — "my Son, the Messiah!" — on display, for what Paul called "the praise of his glory" (Eph. 1). The blinding center of that cosmos was no Sun or galaxy of suns, but his Son given up on Calvary, dying for those who killed him, and determined to reinvigorate them by his Spirit so that they could then bear the sight of his love, and bear to believe that they were undeservingly called into it, into Him.

It was a belief almost too hot to handle.

Arius, the great heretic of the East, would not believe that God could so stoop to conquer — actually to become one of us, to manifest in his own person and our own nature the love which he is. Arians thus refused to accept Jesus as the Divine Son incarnate, and honored him instead as an exalted spokesman. Thus we sinners could have God's love only on a creature's say-so.

Pelagius, the great heretic of the West, would not believe that our human nature had been disabled by sin to the point of helplessness. Gift and grace through Jesus came to us from the Father; he could never be accepted unless humans still had their natures intact enough to welcome him. Grace came, he insisted, and was readily accepted by willing humans, heads held high. Pelagius refused to acknowledge that sin kills both our relish for the good and our desire to love. On his view of it, Jesus gave us a helping hand up, but not life out of death.

Both beliefs were beguiling, for Christians found themselves too ashamed to believe that God himself in Jesus had reached out from the Cross to take sinners into his embrace, and too arrogant to admit that he could find no responsive welcome from them. The Arians could not believe it was God himself on the Cross; the Pelagians could not believe that they were standing there in the lineup alongside Peter, Judas, Pilate, the Sanhedrin, and Satan. It is so doubly demanding to confess that he, so loving, had to pursue us, so unloving.

Those deviant companions in heresy were given a thrashing in the fourth and fifth centuries but, like the Sun, what Jesus revealed was always hard to gaze at. It was all so new, yet also very familiar. The first Christians were all Jews, and Jews were beginning to look for understanding beyond the Scriptures. Likewise the Christians, in coming to know Jesus crucified and risen, realized that though their faith had got a running start in Israel and found expression in Scripture, there was hardly a clause in it that was not sprung open by what they had been shown. For instance, the New Testament says easily and often that Jesus died and rose according to the Scriptures; that it had been written that the Messiah had to die and thus enter into his glory. One didn't have to be a Yeshiva pupil like Saul of Tarsus to realize that there is no single phrase or clause in those Scriptures that foresaw the Lord's Anointed as a victim. Quite the contrary, they were waiting for the Messiah to come and annihilate his enemies, and thus to provide them with a final peace. The catch-phrase, "according to the Scriptures," did not refer here to any proof texts. It was their entire horizon that had been stood on its head, and now they could see that every one of the Lord's initiatives had been squandered on his people; every prophet could expect deaf ears; every king would be more venal and craven than Samuel's worst premonitions. In hindsight the Jesus people saw that for Israel and Judah hope was never planted in anything but disaster. Indeed, if the Exodus was their heroic inaugural, the Catastrophe when Jerusalem fell was a rebirth to a more heroic and chastened honesty. Now that they thought about it, the disciples realized that as Jews they already knew about resurrection. Yet they knew they had known nothing much about it. Now they were living on the strength of a resurrection that offered a life much more beyond the political prosperity and peace of a single people and country: indeed, their hope now was for an exodus of a new people drawn from all peoples, moving on through this world and its life to another homeland and another fullness of life.

Arius and Pelagius were two of many who had flinched at this faith. The demon that Anselm, whom we studied earlier, would set loose was as old as Arius and Pelagius, but perhaps warier and road-wise, and thus of a stronger virulence. Anselm's new deviance was reminiscent of Arianism, because the Father could not be believed as unremittingly loving: from Adam's sin until Jesus' death, he could not bring himself to forgive. The new deviance's resemblance to Pelagianism was by inversion: because Pelagius believed sin had never stricken humans to the heart, because their will remained intact, salvation was a big help but did not make a radical difference. Anselm's new deviance had a fierce enough account of sin, but by identifying salvation as a change within God rather than a change within humans, and by saying that salvation was "imputed" to people and not "accomplished" within them by grace, he also meant that it made no radical difference in them.

Only those who held tight to the mystery and confessed that God was in Christ reconciling the world to himself managed to hold its astonishing elements together. They could easily express themselves in the old language of redemption — for instance, that "our Lord Jesus was handed over to death for our sins and raised to life for our justification," with the understanding that it was done to transform us, not to transform the Father. All the old vocabulary of sacrifice persisted in the Christian repertoire of understanding, but within the new faith its analogical sense had been up-ended. Jesus fell willing victim to *our* hostility, not the Father's. Rather than commending feckless us to a recalcitrant Lord, Jesus was commending an ecstatic Father to recalcitrant us. So much old language is put to topsy-turvy use in the New Testament. For instance, John's Gospel and John's first Epistle say Jesus' Spirit is to replace Jesus as the disciples' *Paraklētos* = Paraclete: their advocate, intercessor, loyal go-between. Yet the larger story encasing these statements is that Jesus and the Spirit are both working on Heaven's behalf to appeal to us. The advocacy, the *paraklēsis,* was all God's doing, because the Father is so steadfast and we are so renegade.

Thus the first Christians experienced some beneficent doctrinal whiplash when they took in that unthinkable thought: that there was nothing they could do to alienate the love of God. Their understanding of the moral life underwent more upheaval than their traditional vocabulary might suggest. They still spoke of judgment, but now it was a gift instead of a threat. It came upon us, not as a *dies irae* at the end of our days but, like Dante's journey of discovery (begun on Good Friday, yet a comedy), "midway along the path of this life." And because it was meant as salvific, it can disclose both sin and salvation to us, and make good news of both. Our desperate need to act well rests not upon God's command and our jeopardy. Quite the opposite, our moral imperative is God's will — not as an arbitrary act of sovereignty, but as a benevolent appeal that we walk into life, not death. Right action and right forbearance are enjoined because they are good; they are not good because they are enjoined. And if we draw away and destroy ourselves by our immoral omission and commission, we are lost to his affection, not his indignation. The old language of judgment and retribution is still on duty in the classical Christian documents, but it makes sense only if we understand it in the new order of things. Jesus has come to judge: he has let us have our way with him, in order to give us a lifesaving glimpse of who we are because of how we have acted, and thereby to enable us at last to come to him and be saved. That privileged revelation, the long light he continues to beam steadily at us from that stroboscopic lightning stroke at Calvary, is at once a flash of life-giving and of judgment. We are offered the nerve to look at both, because the light flows from the Father whose love for us is the cause, not the effect, of such good service and forbearance as we allow him to wreak in our lives.

That is the nerve which might have empowered Philemon to look at his new and unexpected brother Onesimus, and to suspect that to free his slave and set him up in a life of his own within the community might not be as drastic a change in his moral relationships as some others that were dawning on his imagination.

Thus the outcome of our moral behavior, of the disciplined pattern of initiative and forbearance in our lives, will not be to assure that the Lord loves us, but to assure that we love the Lord. The moral worth of what we achieve and what we accept will be the changes it effects within ourselves, not any change we could imagine by way of pleasure or displeasure in the Lord. Commandments are one of several syntaxes whereby we urge on one another what we have learned about the outcomes of various patterns of behavior: whether they are life-giving or death-dealing, and how. The texture of our moral discourse will be composed of the wisdom the Church has been able to draw off its long experience: the reflection, the misunderstandings, the wrangles, the reconsiderations. And rather than finding the prospect of judgment an uneasy one, judgment is something we must pray for: for the enlightened insights that refresh and sometimes overturn our settled understanding of what is life-giving, and what is corrupting. Each individual's life is at stake, but only the Church's communal conscience and memory and moral nerve are lucid enough to light all of us individually on our way to him whom the *Dream of the Rood* calls "the young Hero . . . the mighty Prince . . . the victorious Lord . . . the Lord of Life."

CHAPTER SIX

Old Morality or New?
The Moral Force of Action and Forbearance

If, in the light of an authentic Christian faith, the foremost outcome of a purposefully moral life is that by enablement of the Spirit we become assimilated to Jesus the Son, and increasingly capable of cleaving to the Father — that is, that our humanity be enlivened and enhanced in love — then we need a tried and shared wisdom about the personal effects that certain patterned behavior naturally impresses upon whoever acts that way, or in that way forbears to act. To achieve this we do well to become critically familiar with recent revisionist schools of thought that contend otherwise.

Situation Ethics

One such ethical approach that drew a strong following in recent memory is Situation Ethics. To review what is perhaps more a movement than a theory, because it has been propounded with somewhat different emphases by various ethicists, we can examine *Situation Ethics,* the immensely influential book by the late Joseph Fletcher, who was the most lively proponent of this approach. Fletcher revealed posthumously that in his adult life he had not been a Christian believer, though most of his career was spent teaching in a seminary and his views continue to influence preachers today. He had been active in ethical debate since the days when the Old Morality was the Newest Thing around, and his espousal of Situationism is clear and attractive, but defective.[1]

---

1. Joseph Fletcher, "Memoir of an Ex-Radical," in Kenneth Vaux, ed., *Joseph Fletcher:*

Dr. Fletcher repudiated the Old Morality because he saw it as legalistic. It takes the form of a code, a list of commandments that assign an invariable moral value to various acts. The circumstances attending these acts may modify their morality, but the ultimate and invariable index of good and evil is the very nature of the acts. Against such a view Fletcher urges that no action is good or evil in itself. It cannot be judged in isolation from its meaningful and meaning-giving context of circumstances. The morality of any action is correlative to the love it expresses. Admittedly there are many deeds that are *usually* sinful (e.g., abortion, lying, arson, extramarital intercourse). Yet this is not because they are intrinsically evil acts, but because they most often embody selfishness, exploitation of one's neighbor, or irresponsibility. In certain extraordinary circumstances these actions might so bespeak commitment, caring, and sincerity that, viewed in their contextual totality, they would be adjudged good and virtuous. Thus, since morality is not intrinsic to acts, we can never resort to inflexible ethical laws or norms. At best we can employ maxims, for which we must always be prepared, in some situations, to deviate.

We are limited, says New Moralist Fletcher, to three ethical approaches. There is legalism, which lays down a code of predetermined norms: commandments that establish which acts are invariably good and which are evil. Catholics have tended to derive their laws from natural reason, while Protestants customarily extract theirs from the Bible. But there is little difference: both pharisaically reduce Christian ethics to a manual of absolute rules for mechanical consultation. Secondly, there is antinomianism, which reckons every human event to be so singular and incomparable that no principles could possibly have universal validity. One must wait until the moment of decision, and trust the guidance of the Spirit to inspire a spontaneous moral judgment "on the spot."

Situationism is deftly presented as the moderate option between these two extremes. "The situationist enters into every decision-making situation fully armed with the ethical maxims of his community and its heritage, and he treats them with respect as illuminators of his problems. Just the same he is prepared in any situation to compromise them or set them aside *in the situation* if love seems better served by doing so." Fletcher will neither be bound by norms nor discard them entirely. He accepts them, but only as cautious generalizations, working rules that are expected to break down in extraordinary circumstances. He "keeps

Memoir of an Ex-Radical, Reminiscence and Reappraisal (Louisville: John Knox, 1993), pp. 55-92.

principles firmly in their place, in the role of advisers without veto power!"[2]

Natural-law ethics has customarily claimed to deduce its first principles from a study of humanity and society. Dr. Fletcher states that the first principle of Situation Ethics cannot be deduced, validated, or even discussed. There is no metaphysic that can lead the mind up to faith, by proving that God exists. Likewise there is no reasonable argument which can prove that humans ought to love. It is the irrational, arbitrary leap of faith that posits love as the *summum bonum,* the supreme good. Christian morality sets out from a decision, not from a deduction. "Any moral or value judgment in ethics, like a theologian's faith proposition, is a *decision* — not a conclusion. It is a choice, not a result reached by force of logic, Q.E.D. The hedonist cannot 'prove' that pleasure is the highest good, any more than the Christian can 'prove' that love is!"[3]

Situation Ethics, our author tells us, is no system, no computerized conscience with answers to moral dilemmas. He nevertheless consents to formulate the insights of his method in six propositions:

1. Only one "thing" is intrinsically good; namely, love, nothing else at all.

Fletcher sides firmly with the nominalists, who say that goodness is only a predicate, never a property: nothing possesses moral value by itself; it can only be assigned value by reference to persons. "Hence it follows that in Christian Situation Ethics nothing is worth anything in and of itself. It gains or acquires its value only because it happens to help persons (thus being good) or to hurt persons (thus being bad)."[4] Goodness, then, is nothing intrinsic or objective; it flows solely from the loving purpose with which one acts for the benefit of other persons.

2. The ruling norm of Christian decision is love, nothing else.

Immature Christians would always rather escape the burdens of responsibility. Law ethics has been a comfort to such folk, because it replaces freedom with security. In that system there are no dilemmas to be faced, only statutes to be consulted. The Situationist, rejecting the plea of Dostoevsky's Grand Inquisitor, claims that there is only one absolute obligation: love. All other laws will sooner or later conflict with love, and are therefore only relative, unauthoritative, voidable.

2. Fletcher, *Situation Ethics* (Philadelphia: Westminster, 1966), p. 55.
3. Fletcher, *Situation Ethics,* p. 47.
4. Fletcher, *Situation Ethics,* p. 59.

3. Love and justice are the same, for justice is love distributed, nothing else.

Fletcher employs the traditional theological distinction between justice and love (justice gives a person her due, and is obligatory; love gives a person beyond his due, and is optional). Real love, he says, seeks the greatest good for the greatest number of persons. It is calculating, prudent, shrewd, and efficient; it uses its head, it figures all the angles. What might at first sight seem to be loving behavior to one's immediate neighbor could, on a broader social calculus, show up as hurtful to the common weal. Conversely, treatment of individuals that is usually considered immoral might sometimes be justified by the benefits it brings to the community.

4. Love wills the neighbor's good whether we like him or not.

With Bultmann he states, "In reality, the love which is based on emotions of sympathy, or affection, is self-love; for it is a love of preference, of choice, and the standard of the preference and choice is the self."[5] Authentic love is not liking, nor a feeling of benevolence. Feeling, in fact, is not capable of being commanded as love is. Love is impartial in that it focuses its concern, not on those neighbors who are liked, but on those neighbors who are more numerous or more in need.

5. Only the end justifies the means, nothing else.

Means are neutral tools, with no moral content but what the ends give them. Fletcher insists he is not advocating the choice of evil means to a good end; any means to a good end becomes, by that fact, good. He gives the example of two episodes in the American pioneer West, when parties of settlers were being pursued by Indians. "(1) A Scottish woman saw that her suckling baby, ill and crying, was betraying her and her three other children, and the whole company, to the Indians. But she clung to her child, and they were caught and killed. (2) A Negro woman, seeing how her crying child endangered another trail party, killed it with her own hands, to keep silence and reach the fort."[6] Fletcher infers that the second woman made the right Situationist decision. Taking one innocent life was good because by it many innocent lives were saved. The only self-validating end for a Christian is love; all means and subordinate ends must be justified by reference to that.

5. Fletcher, *Situation Ethics*, p. 104.
6. Fletcher, *Situation Ethics*, pp. 124-25.

6. Love's decisions are made situationally, not prescriptively.

Since it is impossible to know in advance, in ignorance of the situation and consequences of an act, whether it is loving or not, one must await the moment itself and make the ethical judgment then, not by consulting a prefab set of rules.

It is disappointing that Professor Fletcher's proposal, intended mainly as a critique of the Old Morality, did not locate very accurately his real grievance with the traditional system. Ethics, especially Catholic ethics, has been much more situational than he seems to notice. It is very difficult, perhaps impossible, to find a single act which of its definition, stripped of all motives, foreseen effects, and circumstances, was presented as absolutely immoral. The Old Moralists used to say that blasphemy, strictly defined as cursing God, might be the only intrinsically immoral act they could think of — but, like suicide, it is difficult to imagine it as a sane act. In fact, the traditional prohibitions of the Old Morality have all been situational. Lying, murdering, stealing, etc., include situational elements. Lying is evil, they said, but unlike simple "falsehood" it was complexly understood: telling a direct and deceptive falsehood to someone who has a right to the truth, except in jocularity, etc. Murdering is evil, and unlike simple "killing" it was described as homicide, except when resorted to as a last means of self-defense against murderous assault, or as the only available means to protect a community from serious criminal harm, etc. Stealing is evil, and unlike simply "appropriating" it involves taking the property of another unjustly, which would not include seizure to redress injustice, official expropriation for the public good, or claiming the necessities of survival from others whose need is not comparable. . . .

The Old Morality never said that the situation was ethically negligible. On the contrary, it simply asserted that once certain combinations of disqualifying factors are present, no additional situational elements can redeem that default. Once it is established that the person with whom one performs the sexual celebration which is destined to mean unconditioned commitment is not in fact the person to whom one is so committed, i.e., one's spouse, then the act is seen to be evil, no matter what other situational variables you care to add. And once it is established that the human being one intentionally slays is entirely innocent, e.g., an unwanted child, no situational variable can purge the act of its evil. Both Old and New Moralities are situational; but the one denies and the other affirms that a fundamental evil in the action can be outweighed by further situational factors.

What Fletcher and others want is a set of maxims of general but not invariable validity, a system of guidelines with allowances for extraordinary situations that could justify otherwise sinful acts. On the level of popular morality this would, of course, conflict with the notion of commandments. But the real disagreement is much deeper. The Old Morality has held it as axiomatic that any human action involves four distinguishable moral factors: (1) the motive of the agent; (2) the intrinsic nature of the act; (3) its foreseen effects; (4) the modifying circumstances. For an action to be morally good, all four factors must be good; for it to be evil, it suffices that a single factor be evil. Thus the theorem: *Bonum ex integra causa; malum de quocumque defectu.* A single evil factor corrupts the whole act.

The fixation of Catholic Old Moralists on sin was due, not simply to the fact that they wrote manuals for confessors, but also to the divergent attitudes of this theorem to good and to evil. Determine that an action is good, and you say only that it *may* be done; numerous other good options may be appropriate. Establish that it is evil, and you say it *must not* be done. In dietetics they say that green and yellow vegetables, legumes, meats, wines, cereals, cheeses, and fruits are all possible features of a wholesome diet, but no single item is a must. On the other hand, it can be said definitely that prussic acid is a must-not. So with the soul: pathology is more definite than physiology; imperatives are attached much more easily to evil than to good actions.

The Old Morality has held that goodness is indivisible: for an act to be good each separate factor must be good. The Situationist New Morality seems to contend that goodness is divisible: the evil of one factor might be redeemed by the prevailing good of others.

Morals, the making of a person

Despite its name, Situation Ethics does not revolve on situation at all. Fletcher moves about — messily at times — from motive to consequences to situation. But the crucial factor in the method is motive. The system really should be called intention ethics. What is novel about it is the claim that any action, in any situation, with any consequences, is good if it is an action of love, and evil if it is an action of nonlove. All ethical judgment must therefore revolve about what today would be called "attitude." It is essentially indifferent to the forms a person's behavior takes, provided this behavior be the outward expression of inward caring. No one can ever be blamed if his or her intentions were good. In other words, the moral value of one's deeds is wholly contained in the purpose one brings to them. It is precisely this axiom which is both the pivot and the weakness of the entire system. The New Moralists are saying that the moral value of an act is what you put into it. They neglect that it also involves what you get out of the act.

On a phenomenological view, human behavior consists of countless day-to-day actions scattered across the surface of our lives. Generally we put very little of ourselves into any particular act. We do not often manifest our full and true person in any one moment. If we should be voluntarily crucified or something like that, we would most likely be drawing ourselves up to full strength, so to speak — but we are not often voluntarily crucified. Single actions are not usually expressive of our total character nor utterly decisive in our life. But over a period of time certain characteristic trends and traits appear, personality patterns emerge, an overall direction of our affairs is felt and observed. In a certain sense it is right to speak of a duality here: not a severance between intention and deed, but a dialectic between this fundamental bearing (let us say, our fundamental selfishness or selflessness) and the complex of individual actions. What I do and what I am are constantly interacting upon one another. My character discloses itself in what I do. My life works from the inside out and also from the outside in. In Christian terms the state of grace and the state of sin refer to this deep level of fundamental orientation which is forming and stabilizing itself over the course of a lifetime. It would be difficult to localize conversion or serious sin within any singular act or abstinence, and unobservant to assert that there could be much short-term oscillation between one fundamental orientation and its opposite. Yet these states are slowly entered and reinforced or debilitated by the swarm of minor daily deeds.

Fletcher, it appears, acknowledges only a one-way traffic: he points out — quite well — how purpose shapes deeds, but neglects that conversely deeds shape purpose. This is illustrated by a case he presents elsewhere:

> How are we to "judge" the Puerto Rican woman in Bruce Kendrick's story about the East Harlem Protestant Parish, *Come out the Wilderness?* She was proud of her son and told the minister how she had "made friends" with a married man, praying God she'd have a son, and eventually she bore one. The minister, dear silly man that he is, told her it was okay if she was repentant and she replied,

"Repent? I ain't repentin'. I asked the Lord for my boy. He's a gift from God." She is *right* (which, by the way, does *not* mean a situationist approves in the abstract of the absence of any husband in so many disadvantaged Negro and Puerto Rican families).[7]

In response to this argument, Dominican Herbert McCabe retorts:

> No, not in the abstract, just in the concrete. "She is right" is a betrayal of the revolution that is required in East Harlem. Of course such a woman, caught up and lost in the jungle of the acquisitive society, may be blameless, may be a saint, and of course the first thing that matters is to understand and sympathize with her immediate position; but she is *wrong*. To say she is right is to accept, as she does, the social situation in which she lives. A genuine moral judgment cuts deeper than that; it questions such a "situation" in terms of something greater. When we say "You can't apply the same high moral standards to slaves as you do to us" we accept slavery as an institution. Of course to punish or condemn the slave for lying or stealing is to hit the wrong target; it is the masters who bear the blame, but the blame is for the slave's wrong action.[8]

Here we have a paradigm of the various moralities. The minister, representing the Old Morality, says the woman has acted wrongly, and is guilty. Fletcher says that her motives were good; in light of the local situation she has acted rightly, and is not guilty. McCabe says that in light of the total situation she has acted wrongly, but is not guilty (the guilt accrues to Harlem's makers). But all three positions are caught up in a superficial praise-and-blame morality. Fletcher does not adequately suggest that often the Christian's duty is not to conform to the situation but to repudiate it, even to refashion it. And even McCabe cannot be urgently committed to a revolution in East Harlem, if it is likely that "such a woman, caught up in the jungle of the acquisitive society, may be blameless, may be a saint." The most terrible thing about Harlem is that it tends to smother the integrity of its people, it tends to make them evil people. Harlem's makers are those who kill the soul as well as the body, and this

7. Joseph Fletcher, "Love is the Only Measure," *Commonweal* 83, 14 (January 1966): 428.

8. Herbert McCabe[, O.P.], "The Validity of Absolutes; Rejoinder — The Total Context," *Commonweal* 83, 14 (January 1966): 440.

is why Harlem is Hell. It is never radical enough to admit that an evil situation has made the poor woman act wrongly, while leaving her blameless; it has wreaked a far more tragic evil upon her by drawing her to absorb its evil values. The same, of course, might be said of Grosse Pointe or San Sebastián or Rome.

The myopia in a praise-and-blame ethic is that it ignores the dynamic interaction between singular acts and overall orientation, between deed and intention. A morality that is concerned with guilt or innocence thinks of acts only as responsible *expressions* of the moral self, and neglects that — moral or not — they are also *shapers* of the moral self. The fact that repetitive evil actions incur guilt is extrinsic; the intrinsic, and more important, fact is that they make the doer less loving. A young boy who grows up in Harlem may, through little conscious fault of his own, take his recreation by slashing tires, robbing drunks, petty thieving, and pushing heroin. A police officer on patrol in Harlem may, through little conscious fault of his own, augment his pay by protecting a chop shop, shaking down drug dealers, taking bribes, and roughing up youngsters like the one just described. It is absurd to suggest that, since there is little malevolence involved and they are creatures of their situation, they are doing right. It is irrelevant to say they are doing wrong, but that the guilt falls upon others. The tragedy is that morally they themselves have been destroyed by a course of actions they may have entered with no noticeably evil intent.

A young woman who knows no better may take to bed a new boyfriend every week, simply because in her milieu this is the accepted way of showing affection and holding a partner. It is not meaningful to call her guilty or guiltless. What can be said is that through unwitting misuse she has corrupted her own capacity to love. A coal mine owner in the last century might have taken it for granted that young women and children were effective workers if put to crawling through tunnels, dragging loads of coal. He probably did not choose overtly to exploit them, yet gradually and imperceptibly (to him, at least) the situation was set to make him exploitative, and to kill his sensitivity and respect for personal dignity. A child brought up in an unstable home has harm done to her loving power that is not of her own choosing. Sin has too often been imagined as a responsible decision to do evil. Instead, it is a suffocation of responsibility through repetitive actions that generally avoid any open decision. We have made "good" and "evil" into a legal metaphor corresponding to "responsibility" and "guilt"; in a world where there is all too little responsibility but much evil, it seems not to be the most helpful metaphor for theology,

Old or New. Remember that in Matthew's judgment parable ("I was hungry and you never gave me food") they are sent away for offenses that were unwitting; by doing unloving things they had become unloving — and much to their surprise.

Consequently our distress for the East Harlem woman is that with even the best intentions, in the worst situation, she had done something that injured her: whether or not it hurt, it ruined her. And my distress with the New Morality is that it is shallow and legalistic. It ignores that there are false, exploitative, and evil actions which, regardless of our felt motives for performing them, can corrupt our ability to love, and that for this reason moral value is somehow objective as well as subjective. Situational variables may anaesthetize us to moral pain or mitigate the damage, but the damage is there. We cannot long go through the motions of lovelessness without one day waking up to discover we have killed our love. Like Pontius Pilate.

One of the chief weaknesses in the Old Morality was its refusal to allow for extraordinary exceptions to its absolute laws. Indeed, *the* weakness is using the notion of law at all. The New Morality's criticism of this weakness is disappointing because it is so half-hearted and conservative. It shares the Old idea that morality has to do with guilt or innocence: with responsibility. It thus ignores that much of the evil we do and absorb is not due to our evil intentions and purposes, but to the evil values our cultural milieu invites us to snort to the point of addiction. Situation Ethics should recognize more clearly that our situation is to a large degree wanton, and that our worry should be to defend ourselves against the toxic values accepted in our society. Ethics cannot afford to be individualistic, when so much of the lovelessness in individuals is contracted from a brazen culture. Our Christian duty is so often to fight free of our situation, though we may apparently be destroyed in the effort. Like Christ.

Innocence has often been considered like virginity: as a quality with which we all begin, but usually lose. On the contrary, innocence is a mature, adult character trait that we must grow into, painfully. Like virginity, it is the ability to possess oneself firmly enough to aim one's actions at a virtuous purpose. Those who ricochet through life are not innocent in any profound sense. They are often not legally responsible, insofar as they have lost their self-determination. But that is not innocence, or immunity from moral evil. A drunk is morally responsible (no matter what may be said of legal responsibility) for the damage he or she does while under the influence, for the drunk is responsible not to have forfeited responsibility, and the victim of society is responsible to have fought his or her way free to responsibility. The same applies to anyone for whom evil has become habitual and inadvertent.

This was the same problem we saw imposed on Philemon by this same Christ: the memory of crucifixion and the vision of resurrection summoned him beyond his plans, desires, and struggles to be a man transformed. There was no longer any question of what he could settle for. His plans were dissolved; his desires, rendered puny; his struggles, not so fatiguing. Likewise for any Christian: instead of reaching for those good actions he must or may accomplish, he is drawn after possibilities of love that stretch endlessly on. Situation ethics (as also that tepid ethical hand-me-down it wished to supplant) shrinks back from this very surrender of self that Christian faith is all about. It seeks to foreclose alternatives: not what might be more excusable, but what might be more creative or generous or honorable. The best hope for any Philemon is that he be somehow enabled to see beyond his situation to an ethic of a better day.

Proportionalist Ethics

While Fletcher & Co. were re-grading the Christian road more smoothly up the arduous slope of moral probity, a companion venture was underway elsewhere. Though Situationism had been gathering a fair following among Catholics, there was a fellowship of revisionist moral theologians, all Catholics, who were trying to do something similar.[9] Bruno Schüller, S.J., in Germany would become the leading strategist of what has come to be called Proportionalism, and Richard A. McCormick, S.J., has advocated and interpreted the theory most effectively in the United States.

Situationism and Proportionalism began in the same period, but the latter was much slower to catch the public imagination. Their starkly different literary genres probably had something to do with that. The following excerpts, though they do not treat of the same issue, display that difference.

9. Peter Knauer, S.J., Alfons Auer, Joseph Fuchs, S.J., Franz Böckle, Louis Janssens, Bruno Schüller, S.J., Franz Scholz, Richard A. McCormick, S.J., Charles E. Curran, and Garth L. Hallett, S.J., are among the more articulate.

Fletcher:

Pettifogging morality is the issue in N. Richard Nash's play *The Rainmaker*, when the father of the family defends the love affair of his spinster daughter with a rascal passing through town, because it promises to renew her confidence in her womanly qualities. To his self-righteous and violent older son who wants to stop it at once, he points out that he is so fiercely concerned with what is "right" that he cannot see what is good!

Yet another feature of moralism's triviality, in addition to its petty ethics, is its *easy* ethics. Moralistic people tend to be perfectionists who assume that we can be righteous and fulfill the requirements of "the moral law" if we sincerely want to. This is, of course, a tragic failure to see how complex righteousness can be or become in concrete situations. Any business manager compelled to shape decisions involving conflicts of interest between investors, customers, workers, and competitors is bound to see the moral myopia of any ethical viewpoint which supposes that selfishness ("sin") is easily transcended. Moralism's distortion of morality reduces it to petty ethics — easy ethics — mostly irrelevant to the actual decision-making pressures of business management.[10]

Schüller:

The expression "bad means" would be a *contradictio in adiecto* if in this context we understood "means" as the *bonum utile*. Because as a *bonum propter aliud*, the *bonum utile* only participates in the value of the end for whose attainment it is suitable. As a result it is analytically evident that what is nothing else than the means to a good end cannot be other than good.

Accordingly, what is meant by "bad means"? It is a state of affairs (a), which is brought about only because it leads to a state of affairs (b), which must be valued as something good, while the state of affairs (a) must itself be judged bad for some reason. A good end justifying a bad means would thus mean that causing something bad to happen becomes morally justified by the fact that this occurs for the sake of realizing something good. Yet what should be understood by "bad" or "something bad"? Two sharply divergent meanings of the word suggest themselves. By "something bad" we mean: (1) moral evil (*malum morale, peccatum*); (2) non-moral evil (*malum naturae sive physicum*), an evil, therefore, such as sickness, pain, poverty, and error.[11]

10. Joseph Fletcher, *Moral Responsibility: Situation Ethics at Work* (Philadelphia: Westminster, 1977), pp. 163-64.

11. Bruno Schüller[, S.J.], *Wholly Human: Essays on the Theory and Language of*

You see what I mean. Proportionalism may be no more morally rigorous than Situationism in practice, but it requires a more rugged stamina to get through a page of its theory. Yet in their very different forms of discourse these two moral endeavors are pleading the same cause and case: that the moral value of a human act derives from its intention, not from the dynamic of the act itself.

The sexual revolution of the sixties had provided Situation Ethics with both its energy and its agenda. Proportionalism was also provoked by a specific sex-related issue, which at first seemed to give the movement a narrower concern and scope. Contraception, for which reliable and inexpensive techniques had become available in the fifties and sixties, had gradually won such broadly based moral approval that rejectionist Catholic teaching, abruptly reiterated in 1968 by Paul VI in *Humanae Vitae*, seemed to isolate the Church in the company of only a few conservative religious bodies. Since on virtually all other issues Catholics were then taking liberal positions, this one anomalous hold-out doctrine became an embarrassment, and it was the felt need to come to terms with birth control that motivated the imaginations of the Proportionalists.

These men had all been well trained in casuistry, an experience-based method whereby the Church brought its pastoral savvy to bear in testing possible moral developments. Traditional Catholic ethicists — since the Baroque period, that is — had used this dialectical method for both their arguing and their teaching. Insofar as there had been any movement or renewal in that period, it had tended to emerge from casuistic conflict.

The "cases of conscience," usually set forth in the brief write-up of a perplexing conflict faced by a hypothetical character, provided a method whereby the pastoral experience and instincts of the clergy could be brought to bear on moral issues. They sometimes explored behaviors that challenged long-settled moral judgments, and these were published and

---

Morality (Washington: Georgetown University Press, 1986), p. 163. See also his "Direct Killing/Indirect Killing," in *Moral Norms and Catholic Tradition: Readings in Moral Theology*, ed. Charles E. Curran & Richard A. McCormick, S.J., vol. 1 (New York: Paulist, 1979), pp. 138-57 (essay first published in 1972); idem, "Various Types of Grounding for Ethical Norms," *Moral Norms*, pp. 184-98 (first published in 1976); McCormick, "Does Religious Faith Add to Ethical Perception?" in *The Distinctiveness of Christian Ethics: Readings in Moral Theology*, ed. Curran & McCormick, vol. 2 (New York: Paulist, 1980), pp. 156-73; idem, Appendix: "The Principle of the Double Effect," *How Brave a New World? Dilemmas in Bioethics* (Washington: Georgetown University Press, 1981), pp. 431-47; idem, in *Doing Evil to Achieve Good: Moral Choice in Conflict Situations*, ed. McCormick & Paul Ramsey (Chicago: Loyola University Press, 1978).

widely argued to the point where some intelligible new distinction emerged, and gradually found support. Occasionally this could lead to a major revision in the tradition. The corrective distinction bore a double burden: to make sense to the pastoral experience of the times, and to be coherent with the tradition.

When changes were accepted the system itself was rendered more stable by being able to account for this new kind of behavior. In the eighteenth century, for example, the old biblical prohibition against usury was still being upheld: those with means were theoretically obligated to lend to those in serious need without demanding repayment of more than was lent. But it gradually became recognized that many loans were really not acts of charity; they were investments, and under this new interpretation a sort of mutually promising transaction could honestly be made with a mutual expectation of interest. By being differently described, the act deserved a different moral appraisal.

But casuistry could also reaffirm a traditional ethical judgment. At the end of the nineteenth century, for instance, the consensus still defended a penalty of excommunication imposed on duellers, their seconds, and even physicians or clergy willing to stand by in case of need. Defending one's safety, according to the tradition, and even one's honor, had been morally acceptable, even when there was risk of injury or, in the most serious eventuality, death. But after considerable debate it was agreed that the duel could not be justified by this general principle: it was not a morally sound form of self-defense, because it was based on a pathological sense of honor that was a mixture of vanity and pride. On any wholesome sense of it, the man of authentic fortitude and virtue should ignore society's foolish contempt, rather than ever risking bloodshed. Thus the excommunication was upheld.[12]

At the very time the Proportionalists were beginning their innovative project, Catholics were in a large casuistic dispute over a variety of newly inflamed moral questions: contraception, masturbation, sterilization, eugenics, artificial conception, abortion, homosexual relations, euthanasia, nuclear warfare, the socioeconomic prerogatives of the state, racial relations. For liberal scholars of the time, contraception seemed the most problematic, but there was the hope that a revised consensus about birth

---

12. Benedict XIV, *Vix pervenit*, Encyclical to the Bishops of Italy, 1 November 1745; Leo XIII, *Pastoralis Officii*, Letter to the Bishops of Germany and Austria, 12 September 1891, sustaining a Response of the Holy Office to the Bishop of Poitiers, 31 May 1884.

control might lead to a major enlargement of perspective that would help the other issues to find some better resolution.

What most of these moral quandaries had in common involved another element of Catholic tradition, the "principle of double effect." Actions undertakeable for well-intentioned and arguably good purposes might have concomitant negative outcomes. Could those evil effects ever be permitted for the sake of the good effects?

The rigorous moral imperatives of the earliest years had hardly left room for such a question to be entertained. There was no allowance whatever for apostasy, for example. The duty, when challenged, to profess the Christian faith in the teeth of death was absolute. So too was the obligation of monogamous marital fidelity. And the repudiation of bloodshed was so strenuous that early Christians began to be uneasy about military service. So rigorous was their moral understanding in some of these matters that for centuries the Church did not firmly believe itself competent to forgive and reconcile members guilty of these three sins: apostasy, adultery, and murder.

When the emperor himself became a Christian, things began to change. Now Christians could give him their first allegiance, and not notice that he might be every bit as much Christ's rival as Diocletian had been. Now they might kill in his service and feel it was nothing that needed forgiving. Christians willing to bear arms for the pagan emperors had had misgivings that the new, ostensibly Christian rule eventually relieved. Articulate pastors like Ambrose and Augustine who had deplored the use of force for self-defense (though it might be justified to defend innocent and helpless third parties), did not see the same problem when the emperor defended the empire. But as the great empire and its *Pax Romana* fractured into so many wary, rival, ethnic principalities, and as continual bloodshed became the more obvious price of local survival, the Church's capacity to condemn homicidal violence was increasingly compromised.

Nearly a milleniunm later Aquinas turned his attention to this, and argued that one might strike a blow for peace, provided that one acted in self-defense, and provided also that it was a person's own survival, not the adversary's death, that was in the forefront of his intent. Here, on the best authority, was a rudimentary antecedent of what would come to be the "principle of double effect." Here too began a legitimate worry: if the Church was going to accommodate society's disorderly purposes, it needed to worry about Paul's old warning never "to do evil that good may come of it" (Rom. 3:8).

By the latter years of this century that deft moral wisdom about how to handle evil and remain good had become more finely elaborated. In one of the classic dilemmas, it was held by some that if a pregnancy in its early stages were to prove unavoidably lethal, and thus likely to destroy both mother and child, it would be licit to deliver the child (who was too premature to survive, and whose delivery would thus be an abortion) and thereby save the mother. In another case — of a person dying very painfully yet very slowly, say, of cancer — it was found ethical to increase the dosages of morphine as required to suppress the pain, even though it might also gradually suppress respiration and bring on a swifter death.

The long years of casuistic discussion were grounded on Aquinas's early insight that an action with mixed but inseparable outcomes, good and bad, could be redeemed if the good were urgent and truly intended, and the bad sincerely regretted. Moralists eventually agreed upon four requirements for this formula to be honestly applied: (1) the causative action must not be evil in its own right; (2) its bad effect must not be sought, but only endured; (3) the bad effect must be the concomitant but not the cause of the good; and (4) the good intended must be proportionately worthwhile to justify the bad.

The most classical and pervasive invocation of the "principle of double effect" for self-justification by Christians had been to rationalize "defensive" warfare (all warfare seems to be "defensive"), even at the risk of civilian casualties. After the formula had been jingoistically invoked on behalf of the bombing of civilian populations as a belligerent strategy to break the willingness of opponent nations, as at Rotterdam and London, Dresden and Berlin, Tokyo and Hiroshima, even theologians began to see how disreputably the principle could be misused.

No "exceptionless norms"

But only a few years later some of these same theologians were roused to redeploy that principle when Catholic traditionalists and Roman authorities flatly denied its applicability to matters of sex. The principle of double effect could never justify contraception, sterilization, or artificial insemination — so the Vatican argument ran — because the natural purposefulness of the sexual powers was so imperatively directed to propagation that they could never rightly be actuated while blocking their essential fertility.

Most resistance to the Vatican ban argued from the changed context. In previous ages the loss of children through miscarriage, stillbirth, and infant mortality had by itself tended to hold down family size in many households. Ironically, the improvements in public health were now imposing impossibly large families on the poor. But the Vatican teaching undercut all consideration of outcomes, by asserting that "artificial" contraception was intrinsically disordered. If the causative action was evil in its own right, there was little point in arguing about desirable and undesirable outcomes.

At this point a number of innovative proposals were floated by different scholars in what was becoming the Proportionalist group. Some now felt that the notion of an "indirect" intention to permit the bad "side-effect" of an action was strained. What freed the responsible person from blame for the obliquely caused bad outcome was the presence of a "commensurate" or "proportionate" reason. If the good outcome was valuable enough to make the bad outcome tolerable, then why not simplify things and stipulate that the good outcome alone provided the sole motive for the action, and thus determined its overall moral character? Since the bad outcome would not then enter into the definition or character or meaning of the action, it was displaced from the moral meaning of the event, so that it no longer mattered all that much whether it was indirectly or even directly intended.

After that it was natural to propose that if many actions were indivisible in their nature but had composite effects, it didn't matter so much even if the bad effect actually produced the good one, because it was primarily the altruistic attitude of the person acting that clothed the whole event, including any proportionately reasonable use of otherwise bad means to good effect. This was thought to bond the various elements of a composite action into a tighter unity, and to justify the good effect, whose moral yield so outweighed the bad sequelae that the total outcome was one of unalloyed and uncompromised goodness.[13]

Another very potent and imaginative suggestion followed. No bare action, abstractly considered in advance as a concept, is yet actually good or evil. Passing on an infection, taking someone else's car, killing a child, altering a ledger — each concept is still morally neutral when considered in the abstract without specifying the agent or circumstances or motives or foreseen outcomes, by someone who is merely speculating about the act and its various imaginable outcomes as a possibility. Only when actuated do these potential acts acquire their moral dimension. A volunteer

13. Peter Knauer[, S.J.], "The Hermeneutical Function of the Principle of Double Effect," trans. John T. Noonan, Jr., *Natural Law Forum* 14 (1969): 132-62.

in an AIDS clinic unwittingly becomes infected and passes it on; a bystander at a traffic accident commandeers an unattended taxi to rush a victim to the emergency room five blocks down the street; a three-year-old is kidnapped for sacrifice in a demonic ritual; an FBI agent cooperating with management doctors the books of a corporation and sets up a sting operation to uncover a drug ring. Those are morally identifiable scenarios for passing on an infection, taking someone else's car, killing a child, and altering a ledger. Once the generic possibilities have been fleshed out with specified purposes and circumstances and outcomes, one can prepare a prospective moral appraisal, and then when the decision is taken and put into action, the act is finally vested with its net moral valence of goodness or badness.

Since a *potential* action identified by its barest behavioral definition is not yet a moral event, not even an intended one, whatever good or evil it might potentially entail is not "moral" good or evil. The Proportionalists began to call it "physical," or "premoral," or "nonmoral," or "ontic" good or evil. If, in pursuit of an appropriately good or evil purpose, that action could be enfolded in a larger scenario of purpose and outcome, and enacted — say, the FBI drug sting — then the undesired but tolerable side-effect of the falsified ledger that, abstractly considered, was a "premoral evil" (or a "disvalue," as some daintily like to put it), is justified by the intended nature of the overall operation, which is declared to be morally good. No more ambiguity, no compromise, no net difference of bad subtracted from good. *Amor vincit omnia.*

The more they thought about these matters together, the more the Proportionalists came to the natural conclusion that what they had discovered was not just an intellectual device for negotiating certain conflict situations, but a new formula for morally interpreting just about any human undertaking. After all, if one takes the long view of it, most human initiatives beget mixed results. A happy family vacation on Padre Island may lead to one of the teenagers getting smitten by a local boy, and pregnant. A teamster wins the Illinois Lottery, and ten years later every member of his family has been corrupted by greed, anger, and resentment. An alienated young man who joins the Army to get away from his family comes home after four bleak years with most of the snarls combed out of his soul.

In this new, as-it-were unified field theory of morality, many actions, whatever their evil aspects and outcomes, might receive their moral definition and justification from their allegedly proportionate and selectively highlighted good aspects. Critics have complained that this was precisely "doing evil that good might come of it." But the Proportionalist defense has been that where evil did abound, there did good yet more abound. The overall undertaking — act, intention, circumstances, and foreseen effects — was globally good because the outcome good-naturedly designated as the defining one, was good enough to justify the negatives. Thus now one was actually doing *good* that the good might come of it.

At this point Proportionalism had come to pretty much the same conclusion as Situationism: it is intention that clothes an action in its moral meaning. They, too, spoke of all factors combining to produce moral meaning, but the outcome pivoted on good or evil disposition.

What originally provoked the Proportionalists to construct their revisionist theory was their determined sense that contraception somehow had to be justified: for couples, for individuals, and for the human species. Their tactic in this struggle was to find some general way to disallow moral absolutes, or "exceptionless norms." There can have been no premonition that this doctrine would have a headlong quality to it, and would impel them later to contemplate the moral acceptability of behaviors they might never have imagined themselves justifying: adultery, torture, slavery, and nuclear weapons.

It might have been noted, however, that this innovative moral doctrine had sidestepped rather than confronted the older notion that to be morally good an act must be good both in itself and in its direct and directly intended outcomes. This was indeed noted by authorities in the Church, and to address and neutralize that resistance the Proportionalists moved to redefine the very nature of their moral discourse.

No distinctive moral discourse in the Church

It was an old Catholic doctrine that Christian ethics constructed its moral norms through a reasoned examination of nature. The Proportionalists took this notion more seriously than their predecessors and concluded that theirs was a philosophical task, not a theological one, and that Christian ethics was an autonomous discipline not subject to Church scrutiny. They also expected their findings to make good sense to outsiders: nonbelievers as well as other religious or Christian scholars. They had accepted from their own teachers that there was not a single moral obligation imposed by Jesus that they could not justify independently by a reasoned study of human nature. Thus the Catholic agenda, the Christian agenda, they said, was really no more or less than the human agenda.

Moral theology could not be ecclesially distinctive because the philosophical level at which the moralists do their work is more fundamental and hence more reliable than the level at which the Church operates. Moralists work philosophically to discern the "natural law." Of course Israel and the Church have laid down their own "positive laws" — but these are only house rules: derivative enactments of good sense but certainly not of fundamental principle. These community norms were grounded on the discretionary judgment and choice of the lawmakers, whereas the more fundamental natural law they usually aimed to apply was grounded on the authority of God, as implied by the rational patterns created in human beings and human society. So, for instance, revisionist Catholic scholars are confident that the fundamental obligation not to "bear false witness" is of divine origin and universal authority, and could plainly be expounded and defended without any reference to Exodus or Deuteronomy or the New Testament. Any country's civil or criminal laws on perjury, and even any religious precept about oath-taking, are all derivative from that natural obligation and simply represent some community's serious attempt to articulate that natural imperative. Therefore Christians should not imagine that they would have any privileged insights or moral norms on the subject, or any peculiar norms that would set them apart from their fellow citizens. They apply the norms well, but there is nothing Christian about them.

Thus the Catholic revisionists insisted, on the one hand, that they were dealing rationally and professionally with moral norms of divine authority, and on the other, that the Church lacked the standing and the competence to criticize their conclusions.

An obvious objection to this claim would refer to the plentiful moral content in the Bible. The Proportionalists have never overlooked that objection, and in attempting to answer it they have made it possible to understand better the enormity of their dissent.

One Proportionalist reason why a correct moral doctrine could not depend upon a particular faith was their very distinctive view of the Bible. Bruno Schüller claimed that the Bible preaches but does not teach. Since in moral matters it speaks only in exhortation (*parenesis*, from the Greek), and exhortation conveys no moral mandates, the Bible aims at effect more than at truth. It does not legislate; it motivates. Schüller thus agrees with Bultmann that there is no specific Christian ethic. Whatever the force of its moral injunctions, Christian exhortation has no substantive ethical demands to make on the believer. For the content of our moral obligations we must turn to philosophy. Rational inquiry will tell us the "what" and the "whether" of moral behavior; intramural preaching will tell us Christians only the "why" and the "for whose sake." Christians must discipline themselves therefore not to expect the Bible to authorize any specific moral standards. Schüller expressed impatience with biblical scholars who failed to join in this doctrine, which of course was another assertion of autonomy for the ethicists.[14]

In the 1960s Father Schüller expressed annoyance at Catholic colleagues who were driven to identify something distinctive about Christian morality, and had become fixated on the Sermon on the Mount. Christians, they insisted, live under the uncommon command to love their enemies. Schüller did not deny this, but observed that people without any religious faith also can and do understand that they may not hate their enemies.

In any case, a close study of the moral materials in Scripture will only lead one back to the natural law. Schüller finds the Golden Rule ready and waiting right in the middle of Deuteronomy. The whole point of the Decalogue is, as he reads it: "Yahweh acted justly toward the Hebrews; therefore they must act justly towards one another." The Gospel, he says, would later intensify that command from justice to love. What that means is that the Christian believer must now "act in a morally good way," and "show goodness (as far as he can) to everyone."[15]

The ineptness with which the Proportionalists deal with Scripture is not reassuring. Schüller notes that Hebrews were able to purchase and own Hebrew slaves, but were obliged to liberate them at seven-year intervals (Exod. 21:2-4; Deut. 15:12-15). He sees here the Golden Rule of natural law at work. The reason for manumission is given: "Remember that you were once a slave in Egypt and that Yahweh your God redeemed you; that is why I am giving you this order today" (Deut. 15:15). Schüller paraphrases: "Yahweh acted justly towards you; therefore you must act justly towards others."[16] But the Israelites would have been stupefied to be told that Yahweh was acting *justly* when he brought them forth from bondage in Egypt, with an outstretched arm and a mighty hand. If all Yahweh had done for Israel was to "act justly," then what were the prophets raving about? His affection for them was not generically just; they knew it to be particular, extravagant, inexplicably and prodigally forgiving. Their duty to free their indigent fellow-Hebrews, unlike enslaved foreigners, rested on the fact that

14. Schüller, *Wholly Human*, p. 30.
15. Schüller, *Wholly Human*, pp. 19; 16-17.
16. Schüller, *Wholly Human*, p. 18.

they were *their* covenant-fellows, and had to be treated with a staunch benevolence like they had all received from *their* Lord.

The Proportionalists seem unaware that the Decalogue was not understood by Israel as a code of generic human moral obligation. It was part of the communal agenda for a chosen people, and its obligations were a matrix of social duty that bound them simultaneously to their Lord and to their kinspeople, their Hebrew "neighbors." This was no Golden Rule. It was a pact of solidarity between centrifugally inclined tribes that nevertheless agreed to stand by one another to the death, if need be, against a hostile world. It was familial. Sectarian, actually.

Schüller's understanding of the New Testament is even more stinting: "The Christian acknowledges that God has shown him nothing but (moral) goodness and love. In virtue of this acknowledgment he is challenged to imitate God as his model and, like God, to show goodness (as far as he can) to everyone." Apart from its terminal triteness, this misreads the New Testament's moral genre. God and Christ, he insists, are put forward only as didactic paragons of goodness, not as actual standards for that goodness. After all, he writes, "Only God can forgive sin. . . . God effects the salvation of the human race. Human beings, on the other hand, can at best actively work for the well-being of others." On the contrary: Christ sent his disciples — without exception — to forgive sins, and first of all those of their fellow Christians; there is hardly an obligation more fundamental. And they are to understand that this is how his salvation is effected.

In their concern to disallow any normative moral teaching in Scripture, they have rejected any biblical authority for the Catholic tradition of indissoluble marriage. Since it is only a biblical exhortation, not a rule, says Schüller, we first have to reckon rationally what sort of marriage best befits human nature, and then decide what sort of fidelity best suits it . . . that is, suits us. That might conceivably lead us to oppose, not adultery as such, but only adultery that is "unchaste" or "irresponsible."

Neither Paul nor the evangelists imagined they were transmitting "requirements of morality" that would bind all, for the morality of Jesus was given to his disciples and was the new code of behavior for the New Israel, his Church. To the extent that the Church could live by these norms credibly enough, then others might come to join them in bearing this yoke that was so light. And they would become, to use Schüller's phrase, "wholly human" . . . but only by becoming supernaturally more-than-human.

Even the Decalogue, which was adopted by the Church as if it were under their copyright, is presented in the New Testament in transfigured meaning. Christians had already begun their usefully anachronistic habit of reading Christian duty into those primitive laws of Israel. The "Lord" was now known differently and so were his names; the "neighbor" was different too; the "Sabbath" would later be observed on a different day in a different way; and the injunctions against murder and adultery and stealing and covetousness and perjury were blooming into great positive imperatives in the consciences of Christians whose transformation agendas for their anger, lust, greed, and cunning drove them beyond the old restraints, to seek and succor their (newfound) neighbors in their (newly known) needs. These were not matters that could be taught to strangers . . . unless they became brothers and sisters.

The early believers did not make cheap copies of their upgraded Decalogue available in campus bookstores as outside reading in philosophy courses for the required lecture on "moral requirements." They could not have imagined giving anyone these moral dicta without first giving them Jesus, who had spoken them anew "from the heart of the fire, face to face." They themselves had only come to understand largesse and greed, violence and forgiveness, duty and the love that runs past all duty, by knowing Jesus, and him crucified. And to know Jesus they had also had to understand Caiaphas and Herod and Pilate; Mary his mother and James his brother who at first wanted to lock their crazed Jesus away but then stood by him in loyal bewilderment; Simon who needed three tries to become truly Peter, and Paul who wielded and then submitted to savagery; Magdalen and Zacchaeus and the Robber on the Right; Stephen, and Ananias and Sapphira, and Cornelius and Lydia and all those others who stood fast, and were better than the world deserved — a cloud of witnesses who persevered, and neither lost heart nor came to grief. What Christians had learned from them was why they must not lie to or steal from or assault one another. Theirs was an ethic received within the fellowship of the Church, the only place where they could both show and tell their truest moral imperatives. As has well been said, "the Christian must always remember that he is likely to be the only copy of the Gospels that the non-Christian will ever see."[17]

The revisionist claim is that the authoritative documents of the Church, like those of Christian revelation, do not prescribe; they exhort. They can intensify our search for right behavior but they do not affect the

17. Philip Scharper, quoted by James O'Gara, "Fortieth Anniversary Symposium," *Commonweal* 81, 9 (20 November 1964): 280.

rational, moral insight of believers into what that right behavior is. Catholic ethical debate and its resulting moral wisdom claim their rightful place in the open forum of public society, as the Church's contribution to the universal moral concern for human integrity. But it is a public and generic endeavor, not a private or sectarian one.

Schüller urges that Jesus did the Father's will "to the ultimate degree. And since the requirements of morality bind all, all who believe in Jesus Christ are also bound by the commandment: 'Walk in love, as Christ loved us and gave himself up for us, a fragrant offering and sacrifice to God' (Eph. 5:2)." Yet he waffles: if the requirements of morality bind "all," then "all" — not just "all who believe in Jesus Christ" — would be bound to take Christ, not just as their inspiring exemplar but as their norm.

A characteristically Christian ethic, from the first[18]

The Proportionalists claim that neither the intention nor the style of the Scriptures aims to convey specific, normative moral instruction. That is a serious misunderstanding of Scripture. The men and women who first tried to follow the risen Jesus were Jews. They were not entirely unprepared for the moral demands their new allegiance would make on them. The Christian road followed terrain already familiar to Jewish moral teaching. Infidelity was to be avoided in all its forms: adultery and incest and idolatry. They were never to take crafty advantage of others, by perjury or sorcery or usury. And they were to restrain themselves from all violence, whether by drunkenness, gossip, or murder.

This ethical standard here rests on the New Testament but is a close cousin of its contemporary Jewish competition, which shows what a direct lineage there is from biblical and hellenistic Judaism to early Christianity. In the Sermon on the Mount Jesus invites his followers to go even further along the new Way, as I have already argued. It was not enough to spare your neighbor's life; you must not even hurl insult at him. If adultery was wrong, then so was lustful intent. And there was scant advantage from being a person of your sworn word if you were a chiseler whenever you were not on oath. Yet this innovative and prophetic summons to a righteousness higher than that of the scribes and Pharisees would itself have

18. The following discussion is adapted from my "The Defining Ethic of the Earliest Church," ch. 2 of *The Giving and Taking of Life: Essays Ethical* (Notre Dame: University of Notre Dame Press, 1989).

found strong endorsement in many of the better synagogues around Judaea or Galilee.

Christian moral doctrine showed from the first its direct descent from Jewish ethics. It was fitting, then, that its agenda of departure from Jewish ethics would be the further pursuit of teachings they most closely shared. Both Synagogue and Church taught that authentic religion meant coming to the aid of women and children deprived of breadwinners, and of those two other categories of the helpless: the indigent, and isolated aliens. Nothing could be more traditional for a Jew or more fundamental for a Christian than this ancient commitment to provide for the widow, the orphan, the pauper, and the stranger. Yet it was precisely here, on this point of ancient and familiar obligation, that the young Christian community found a distinctive vigor and vision, and set forth from its mother's house on a moral journey of its own.

The alien and the pauper, the widow and the orphan, classic beneficiaries of preferential sustenance since Torah, were suggestive to the Jesus people of four other forlorn categories that they must now safeguard: the enemy and the slave, the wife and the infant — unborn or newborn.

The resident aliens had to be guaranteed shelter, for they dwelt defenseless within the national enclosure of Israel and trusted its people for their safety. But the Christians were commanded to go far beyond protecting the nearby and helpless alien. The Christians were charged to cherish the alien who threatened them as their enemy. They had heard it said that they must love their neighbor and hate their enemy. Jesus told them they must love their enemy even at the risk of being caught in the crossfire of hatred from both countryman and enemy. A disciple was to set no more bounds to her bounty than did the Father who lavished sunshine and rainfall on all fields alike. Their pattern was the Lord Jesus, who had loved to the death those who betrayed and denied and deserted and condemned and crucified him.

The destitute poor were always a special charge on the Christian's conscience. But their endless needs suggested another, even more vulnerable, group. The novice Christians were told forthwith that for those "in the Lord," no one was any longer to be demeaned as mere property of another. Even slaves had to be dealt with as brothers and sisters in the Lord. Thus was Philemon unsettled about Onesimus . . . and Onesimus about Philemon.

Every man was to join in supporting the wives his fellow believers had left behind as kinless widows. But now he was startled to be told that he no longer had a male's freedom of choice to dismiss his own wife. Jesus' rejection of mosaic divorce affected men and women differently, since in Israel only husbands had previously been free to reject their partners. Now women could no longer be chosen and then discarded by their men. Both alike must now be faithful throughout life, if they loved and married in the Lord, and like the Lord.

Beyond the orphan Christians discovered another, more helpless claimant upon their protection: the unborn and the newborn. Roman law in that era offered no protection against either abortion or infanticide, both of which were within the prerogatives of the male head-of-household. But a new hellenistic Jewish tradition had been articulating a strenuous prohibition against both abortion and infanticide. It was in many respects to be both parent and sibling of a nascent Christian belief. Jews were then being enjoined not to abort or to "expose" their children, but to bear and rear them: the defense and nurture of the unborn and newborn was put forth as a notable moral duty. For example, Pseudo-Phocylides writes: "A woman should not destroy the unborn babe in her belly; nor after its birth throw it before the dogs and the vultures as a prey." Neither tradition, Roman or Jewish, offered a protection for infants reliable enough to suit the first Christians, however, and they soon stated their own conviction which was to the point.

Already in the first-century catechism known as *The Didache*, The Instruction of the Twelve Apostles, the obligation to protect the unborn and the infant was included within the roster of essential moral duties:

> You shall not commit murder; you shall not commit adultery; you shall not prey upon boys; you shall not fornicate; you shall not deal in magic; you shall not practice sorcery; you shall not murder a child by abortion, or kill a newborn; you shall not covet your neighbor's goods. You shall not break your oath; you shall not give perjured evidence; you shall not speak damagingly of others; you shall not bear a grudge.

In a later passage the instruction describes what it calls "the way of death":

> It is the path of those who persecute the innocent, despise the truth, find their ease in lying . . . those who have no generosity for the poor, nor concern for the oppressed, nor any knowledge of who it was who made them; they are killers of children, destroyers of God's handiwork; they turn their backs on the needy and take advantage of the afflicted; they are cozy with the affluent but ruthless judges

of the poor: sinners to the core. Children, may you be kept safe from
it all!

These were four radical, prophetic and, if you will, "sectarian" imperatives that the new Christian faith set before all who would live in the
Spirit and fire of Christ: four disconcerting duties that would distance
them from Jews and Romans alike. First: the command to love their enemies struck down forever their exclusionary allegiance to a single race or
nation. Second: the command to acknowledge slaves and masters as
brothers and sisters condemned slavery to a long and sullen retreat, and
ultimately to extinction. Third: the command that husbands and wives
were to pledge an equal fidelity was a first yet crucial rejection of the
corruption of men and women by their respective domination and acquiescence. Fourth: beyond the children orphaned by their parents' deaths
were those still more helpless children whom their parents slew themselves, and now they too were declared inviolable. These were thunder-
claps of moral exclamation that bound the small and scrappy new fellowship to make the very purpose of their lives the liberation of those most
at a loss.

These were not all rhetorical exhortations, as the Proportionalists have
supposed. They were distinctive moral imperatives by which the Christian
Church was willing to be known and judged. It was not a program for
the more strenuous. It was presented as the imperative agenda for the
Church, the test for all discipleship. Abortion, adultery, murder, greed, and
theft: they were all ways to spiritual death. The four Christian normative
innovations were offered as new signs of authenticity. If theirs was not a
community where Jew and Gentile (divided by such ancient hostility),
where man and woman, slave and free, parent and child could show forth
as one, then it had failed as Christian. That was their test. Paul sends
Onesimus the slave back to his master Philemon and tells him to receive
him as a brother, and then charges him: "So if you grant me any fellowship
with yourself, welcome him as you would me." That was their test. If this
was heroism, it was a heroism exacted of every person who would walk
the new Way.

There is a further innovative paradox. Though these moral instructions show a sensitive and compassionate sympathy for the victims, the
principal moral concern is for the oppressors. It is the husband that bullies
his wife whose personhood dwindles even more sadly than hers. The
mother who agrees to eliminate her child destroys her own *philanthropia*
— her humane love — in doing so. The disease of character that follows

from exploitation of others was seen, in Christian perspective, to be more hideously incapacitating than the worst that befell the victims: it was a dying worse than death. In truest normative Christian perspective, it is the oppressor that is destroyed. When Onesimus walked home to his unpredictable fate, it was Philemon who was even more in jeopardy, because now he would have to ponder how to survive morally if he owned a Christian brother.

The early writers know well that any true protection of the helpless and exploited calls for a stable empowerment, so that those same people would not continue to be victimized. This means that the Christian moral agenda demands a price. Oppressors must give up their advantage. It little matters whether the advantage was seized purposefully or inherited unwittingly. There is a forfeiture to be accepted by those in power if the disadvantaged and helpless are to be afforded true protection.

But the victims had to accept suffering as well. The price they must pay — to be Christians — is to forgo resentment and hatred. Empowerment cannot be grasped as the means to take revenge or, still worse, as the way to begin to be an exploiter oneself. The victims must gaze directly upon those who had taken advantage of them, and recognize them as brothers and sisters who themselves may have been pressed by distress of one kind or another. So there is no moral accomplishment possible unless reconciliation extends the hand of fellowship across the front line of suffering. Justice has nothing to do with it. There will be heavy and sometimes bitter things to accept if hatred is to be extinguished, and not merely aimed in a new direction.

The Church's belief is in a Lord who was the spectacularly innocent victim of injustice. Yet Christ caught the impact of that injustice in his own body, his own self. He deadened its force and refused to pass it on; he refused to let retaliatory hatred go on ricocheting through humankind. Truly to follow him one must be committed to doing the same. And the truest test of that faith is whether one has the gumption to share it with others: with victimizers, but more especially with people who are victims. Christians must prevail upon victims to let us catch some of the impact of their distress in our own bodies and our own selves alongside theirs, without permitting the cycle of violence to carry on.

Neither Christ nor his Church punish — can punish — their members' sins. As John Milbank explains it so well, "the only punishment [for sin] is the deleterious effect of sin itself upon nature, and the torment of knowing reality only in terms of one's estrangement from it." This providential self-perversion is inherent in sin, and the Church is meant to be an asylum for those exposed to the alienation and social anger their sins have provoked, so that they may find the nerve to see how their isolation is their own doing. Pursuant to that ministry the Church must do what Christ does: name the sins and confront the sinners. In the sustaining shelter of forgiveness the sinner's imagination is provoked, and courage braced, to do what is necessary by way of restitution without and restoration within, so that sin is swallowed up in the victory of a harmonious reconciliation.[19]

The fire of Pentecost rapidly enflamed the Christian community to a sense of what they were about. They were in so many ways an observant Jewish movement: in their worship, their hopes, their moral way of life. But in two great matters they showed forth as men and women possessed by a new Spirit. They witnessed to the resurrection: Jesus, during whose unjust execution they had been inert and disengaged, was risen to power as Messiah and Lord. That was the first great matter. The second was like it: they witnessed to their own resurrections. They too had been raised to unexpected power, and they stated with vehemence that they would no longer be passive before affliction. That determination was highlighted in the distinctive and innovative moral commitment to befriend the enemy, to dignify the slave, to raise up the wife, and to welcome the child. Their own lives were at stake, for these Christians believed that they would perish in their persons if they proved nonchalant about the suffering of any of these most vulnerable brothers and sisters.

This was a rigorous duty presented to the Church's pioneers. The light was dazzling, and understandably they often preferred to draw back into the shadow. Christians have sinned against that light and continued to relish and even to justify hatred against their enemies. They did not rush to set the slaves free. Women were not welcomed into equal status. And some parents continued to destroy their young. But the imperatives still stood, and still stand, and they tell us *what* is required for eternal life, not just *why*.

This was not the same as being trustworthy, loyal, helpful, friendly, courteous, kind, obedient, cheerful, thrifty, brave, clean, and reverent. When Proportionalists simply stipulate that the model of Christ imposes nothing but the norms of good citizenship — framed to make clean sense to the world at large — they miss how Christian morality can make only tangled sense without Christ. If God in Christ has done no more for the

19. John Milbank, *Theology and Social Theory: Beyond Secular Reason* (Cambridge, Mass.: Blackwell, 1990), pp. 420-21.

believer than "shown him nothing but (moral) goodness and love," the fit response might indeed be something as flaccid as "to show goodness (as far as he can) to everyone." Schüller claims that Christian faith can offer us an "understanding of existence that simply transcends the limits of the insight available to us," but it cannot supply any normative understanding of moral behavior.[20] It is startling to think of the crucifixion of the Son of God for the benefit of those who killed him as an exhortation "to show goodness (as far as we can) to everyone." In pursuit of what he calls an "ethical universalism," Schüller wants his moral method to be no more "Christian" than "Greek" or "German."[21] He succeeds.

The Proportionalists mostly agree that the Church will not find within its own revealed and authoritative sources any truly authoritative moral norms. However: moral insight, moral exhortation, and moral discipline are not much cultivated, handed on by tradition, sustained by conversion and discipline, and preserved by forgiveness, except in a community. Since the Proportionalists deny so explicitly that the Church should be the privileged community where Christians would find and foster a normative moral mandate, the most likely alternative patronage would come from the cultural society of the nation, or the ethnic group, or the socio-economic class. Christians who choose by default to make one of these instead of the Church their primary moral community, will undoubtedly find that their moral influence arouses as little attention as Proportionalism does among the secular philosophers. They will be sucked down in a moral undertow that cares very little for proportionate or commensurate good.

The moral force of actions upon character

Schüller and his colleagues say that the agent's good intention, and the prevailingly good outcomes it foresees and intends, morally define his or her actions, which apart from their intention and intended outcomes can have no existential reality, no moral definition. They argue that a multi-dimensional moral calculus must first determine whether the prospective good and bad outcomes will net out positively. Since the Proportionalists do not offer any workable formula for ascertaining the "commensurability" or "proportionality" of such factors as Richard's violent and untimely death, my inconvenience, Palestinian water rights, bodily injury,

20. Schüller, *Wholly Human*, p. 28.
21. Schüller, *Wholly Human*, p. 126.

emotional exultation, Harry's love for Blanche, money, loyalty, your reputation, my faith, crop failure in Saskatchewan, one child more or one spouse less, a four-day work week, the dignity of refugees, a 1.3 percent rise in the Nikkei Index, or next year's foreseen health care coverage for legal immigrants, one is understandably inclined to fear that in the calculation of outcomes, the interpretive self-concern of the interested party will enjoy a wide perimeter of free play. Good shall be as good seems — to oneself. Since theoretically each action does not even come available for pre-appraisal until all its potential factors are in sight, the Proportionalists have designed the utmost in casuistry: the single case being appraised on its own merits, from the perspective of the person about to act, whose interests are not necessarily congruent with those of whoever else may have most at stake in the outcomes.

But all does not really ride on outcomes. Both Situationism and Proportionalism speak about outcomes, but both theories really pivot on the intention and the perspective and sometimes the "interests" of the person acting. Both suppose that the *finis operis,* the dynamic of the action itself, eventually lies under the control of the *finis operantis,* the designs of the person acting. Neither imagines that the chief moral outcome of a human act is the moral character of the acting human. Both think of how this acting person might influence others through this action. Neither considers seriously enough how the action will affect or even transform this person doing it or — if indeed moral good and evil be incomparably more significant than "nonmoral" good and evil, as claimed — how the moral recoil upon the subject is likely to be even more powerful than its impact upon others. They ignore the dynamic, purposeful power of certain actions and habits to bend in their direction the very purposes of those who submit to them.

Here we behold what is probably the central misunderstanding of Situationism and Proportionalism, these two energetic and contemporaneous attempts to revise Christian moral discourse. It is a misunderstanding that is shared by many of their traditionalist antagonists. Both Situationism and Proportionalism tell us that the good and evil of our behavior hinge on a pure or a polluted intention, insofar as behavior's foreseen results will benefit or blight the world.

Both schools of thought assume that the chief result of our activity is what we achieve, rather than who we become. As John Paul II puts it otherwise in *Veritatis Splendor,* moral actions are deliberate choices of *intrinsic worth.* Thus "they do not produce a change merely in the state of affairs outside of man, but to the extent that they are deliberate choices, they give moral definition to the very person who performs them, determining his spiritual traits." He quotes Gregory of Nyssa: " 'Thus we are in a certain way our own parents, creating ourselves as we will, by our own decisions.' "[22]

The Pope is joined by other critics of Situational and Proportionalist ethics who insist there are such things as "intrinsically wrong acts," and therefore "exceptionless norms," which cannot be redeemed by special circumstances or good intentions, even unforeseen intentions. Common examples are the intentional killing of an innocent, adultery, suicide, slavery, pimping, and contraception. The defenders of the Catholic tradition locate its strength in negative moral imperatives — acts that all moral agents are obliged to avoid. They are neglectful of Aristotle's teaching that moral reasoning is a type of insight that leans neither on universal laws nor on a calculation of net benefits, but on a canny type of instinctive insight that depends upon experience, because it reflects upon human deeds and their results, and upon virtue, because it needs the passions to provide an impulse that enhances insight instead of overriding it. Moral insight, as Aristotle taught (and as the Christian tradition learned), is like the matured instinct of a generous physician, not the crack competence of an adolescent chess champion. It produces convictions ahead of commandments. Commandments construed legalistically had been a preoccupation of the Old Moralists which, by an ironic twist, the New Moralists came to share. They were willing to grant that there might be exceptionless norms, but they then proceeded to raise the requirements so impossibly high that none qualified.

The Proportionalists have labored to bring forth a moral theory that makes its peace with the traditional Catholic moralists (who are mostly what are called deontologists). That Catholic tradition, at least since the Baroque age, has been very weak in scriptural insight, but strong in legalism. The revisionists have worked from within the insights of legalism's comrade, casuistry, in order to disallow ethical absolutes, those single, morally lethal events that had become an embarrassment in these more desirous times. If they had been more creatively revisionist they might have considered more seriously that the primary good and evil effects of right and wrong actions are the reinforcement or the degradation of the acting person's integrity. They might also have avoided focusing their attention (albeit disapprovingly) on a magic moment of serious sin. This might have led them toward a more integral reform.

22. John Paul II, Encyclical Letter *Veritatis Splendor*, 6 August 1993, §71.

Unfortunately, the revisionists may have drawn their traditionalist critics somewhat astray. Fletcher, in his casual way, and Schüller, in his more meticulous way, have tried to minimize specific moral imperatives so as to leave the individual conscience free to be guided by slogans vague enough to allow a wide play of freedom. They agree that there are no acts which by definition alone are lethal: in the traditional terminology, categorically mortal sins. But when the traditionalists react and move in to defend the intrinsic, and thus invariable, wrongness of specific actions, they may be missing a timely opportunity offered by the revisionists to clarify the tradition.

To illustrate: a girl takes up smoking at 11, in order to look mature and sophisticated in the eyes of her schoolmates. At 12 she is smoking a pack of Virginia Slims a day, and she smells like it; but her parents choose not to smell. At 14 she is offered marijuana and refuses, because the drug program at school had been so lurid in its warnings of what it does to motivation. But at 14½ she does smoke a joint, and it makes her mellow. By senior year, when she turns 17 and should be a young woman but is not, her crowd gathers for binge drinking, round-robin each weekend at the home of a different classmate whose parents are out of town. Two or three times a month she passes out on malt liquor/peppermint schnapps/vodka, or whatever. At 18 she goes to college and at an October party she snorts her first line of cocaine and becomes Mary Poppins. At 20 she joins some special companions who mainline heroin twice a week, or maybe more. And at 22 she enjoys a tight circle of friends . . . for whom she is now the primary drug source. She is the only one in her circle who graduates with no student loans outstanding.

Now if, in the Old moral mode, we were to try agreeing on when the lethal moment occurred — the substance-abuse equivalent of mortal sin — it would be very difficult. One might choose the cocaine initiation because there is no way home from that except through detoxification and arduous recovery. One could also say that the point of no return would not come until she turned 24 and ended in the morgue. One could as well argue that the entire process was underway with the first Virginia Slim, and the rest was a long and predictable slide. Or one might put it back to the age of twelve, when her parents evidently decided to go on indefinite furlough. All observers would probably say that by the end she had disintegrated, but they would probably be at a loss to agree on which particular action brought her down. A closer study of her character might draw our attention aside to less spectacular but very correlative trespasses: cheating on exams, lying to her parents, drugging her mind with none but banal thoughts. But what one must recognize is that the entire decline was lethal: the first Virginia Slim was probably incipiently mortal, though not evidently so at the time. To understand such a collapse, which was physical as well as moral, one would have to contemplate each successive diminishment as toxic, even if not terminal. One would have to realize that little insight is gained by identifying one or another of the late, morally mortal lurches as the *definitive* collapse into evil, unless one can also detect those much earlier willing seductions into habit, addiction, promiscuity, and self-imposed blindness that create the *decisive*, continuous undertow that has already begun the extended drowning process.

The shared notion of specifically wrong and seriously evil acts — which the revisionists distrust and the traditionalists defend — is of actions that must be terminal to be truly lethal. That notion ignores patterned acts — habits — that are morally toxic from the outset: addictive, seductive, degenerative . . . and *gradually* lethal. This is unfortunate because the latter is the more frequent way we fall. The definitive point of no return comes too late for there to be much benefit in recognizing it; the decisive stages of disintegration are the entry, not the prelude, to moral death.

That eminent Irish moralist, Oscar Wilde, had much of this in mind when writing *The Picture of Dorian Gray*. Dorian, the ruthless man whose moral degeneration has long been concealed by a preternaturally preserved youthful beauty which never shows his age, can only occasionally find the nerve to gaze on the mysterious painted portrait which shows him actually aging, and displays so accurately every new and brutal deformity in his character, from the first touch of cruelty to his final state: "withered, wrinkled, and loathsome of visage," with a knife in his heart. Throughout the book Dorian soliloquizes on how one must never allow emotion, advice, or conscience much of a hearing, lest life lose pleasure. Though there are murders, betrayals, and seductions along the way, there is something lethal in the entire pathology, which suppurates in the individual actions that betray a deeper death underway, a death that cannot be timed to any single action, and which clearly had preceded the onset of "serious" misconduct. It was Dorian's life that had become intrinsically evil, not the crime of any afternoon. He had foreshadowed the moral imperative expressed by the eminent Jewish moralist, Woody Allen, in his exquisitely autobiographical euphemism: "The heart wants what the heart wants."

Fletcher and Schüller share the view that the normative Christian tradition presents us with maxims, not mandates. Fletcher thought moral imperatives, whatever their syntax, were meant to be maxims. Schüller, though his theory aims to disempower them, knows what moral impera- tives are but assures us they are not to be found in our normative tradition. But if we riffle through only the younger Testament, we find the likes of these:

> Whoever divorces his wife and marries another is guilty of adultery against her. (Mark 10:11)
>
> Anyone who wants to become great among you must be your servant, and anyone who wants to be first among you must be slave to all. (Mark 10:43-44)
>
> When you stand in prayer, forgive whatever you have against any- body, so that your Father may forgive you your failings too. (Mark 11:25)
>
> *You must love the Lord your God all your heart, and with all your soul,* and with all your mind *and with all your strength.* (Mark 12:30)
>
> Go out into the whole world; proclaim the Gospel to all creation. (Mark 16:15)
>
> You have heard how it was said, *You will love your neighbour* and hate your enemy. But I say this to you, love your enemies and pray for those who persecute you. . . . (Matt. 5:44)
>
> Do not store up treasures for yourselves on earth, where moth and woodworm destroy them and thieves can break in and steal. (Matt. 6:19)
>
> *You shall not murder.* (Matt. 19:18)
>
> Love your enemies and do good to them, and lend without any hope of return. You will have a great reward, and you will be children of the Most High, for he himself is kind to the ungrateful and the wicked. (Luke 6:35)
>
> When you have a party, invite the poor, the crippled, the lame, the blind, then you will be blessed, for they have no means to repay you and so you will be paid when the upright rise again. (Luke 14:13)
>
> Be at peace among yourselves. We urge you, brothers, to admonish those who are undisciplined, encourage the apprehensive, support the weak and be patient with everyone. Make sure that people do not try to repay evil for evil; always aim at what is best for each other and everyone. Always be joyful; pray constantly; and for all things

give thanks; this is the will of God for you in Christ Jesus. (1 Thes. 5:13-18)

I, Paul, give you my word that if you accept circumcision, Christ will be of no benefit to you at all. (Gal. 5:2)

You were not to have anything to do with anyone going by the name of brother who is sexually immoral, or is greedy, or worships false gods, or is a slanderer or a drunkard or dishonest; never even have a meal with anybody of that kind. (1 Cor. 5:11)

Make no mistake — the sexually immoral, idolaters, adulterers, the self-indulgent, sodomites, thieves, misers, drunkards, slanderers and swindlers, none of these will inherit the kingdom of God. (1 Cor. 6:9-10)

If anyone is at fault, reprimand him publicly, as a warning to the rest. Before God, and before Jesus Christ and the angels he has chosen, I charge you to keep these rules impartially and never to be influenced by favouritism. (1 Tim. 5:20)

For the sake of the Lord, accept the authority of every human institution: the emperor, as the supreme authority, and the governors as commissioned by him to punish criminals and praise those who do good. (1 Peter 2:13-14)

There is only one lawgiver and he is the only judge and has the power to save or to destroy. Who are you to give a verdict on your neighbour? (James 4:12)

It is no easy thing for us to construe the pattern of the literal obligation passed on to us by these authors who thought in Aramaic, wrote in Greek, were haunted by the Spirit, and speak to us in unfamiliar genres with multiple overtones. But these are neither maxims nor exceptionless norms. They are glints of a great wisdom about a life lived in love for God's Son who was slain by us and died for us, and means to raise us to life to the point where we can be that singlehearted ourselves. One might single out — some surely would — the one apodictic prohibition: *"You shall not murder."* But strewn through these verses are a hundred paces toward murder, just as that first Virginia Slim began a death-march.

There is a paradoxical difference between our knowledge and experience of the right and the good, and our knowledge of the wrong and the evil. Evil is much more discernible and less ambiguous than good, especially when we contrast good and evil imperatives. Pope John Paul, for instance, recites Vatican II's famous roster of invariable wrongs:

whatever is hostile to life itself, such as any kind of homicide, geno-
cide, abortion, euthanasia and voluntary suicide; whatever violates
the integrity of the human person, such as mutilation, physical and
mental torture and attempts to coerce the spirit; whatever is offensive
to human dignity such as subhuman living conditions, arbitrary imprisonment, deportation, slavery, prostitution and trafficking in
women and children; degrading conditions of work which treat la-
borers as mere instruments of profit, and not as responsible persons.[23]

But when he offers a matching array of mandatory positive actions,
the color fades noticeably: "The person must do good and avoid evil, be
concerned for the transmission and preservation of life, refine and develop
the riches of the material world, seek truth, practice good and contemplate
beauty."[24] The mandatory Nays are a lot more specific than these mandatory Yeas.

But the case is reversed when the older tradition compares moral
progress and regress. The smooth slide through self-deception to compromise to corruption is decidedly more gradual than the strain and heave
it takes to clamber out of established selfishness into established love. The
gradient and the gravity clearly draw us one way: one yields to evil; but
one must strain to the good. Thus the climb by grace toward recovery,
resurrection, conversion, is better defined than the glide into deathly sin,
because one is the work of conscience alive and the other is the result of
conscience beguiled. We work to become truly free when our insight is no
longer blinded by a pattern of sin and self-absorption and when we
possess our selves well enough that we have the nerve to see and the
gumption to choose what is truly good. The most valuable freedom, then,
is not the right to be left alone or to be emancipated from unwelcome
truth; it is the capacity to look truth in the eye and then to act on it, at
whatever cost. To abide that truth is to look God in the eye, for it is his
creative will for us, an expression of his wisdom, to which we submit.
This must have been what both Philemon and Onesimus felt when the
imperative began to bear down on them: that their faith would demand
from both of them more than they could ever have imagined.

The Christian tradition has believed that with these inspired cues, and
with the experiences of both the sinners and the forgiven sinners who
became saints for us to learn from, the Church has the wherewithal to

23. *Gaudium et Spes,* §27.
24. *Gaudium et Spes,* §21.

discern right from wrong, and to do good and avoid evil, and ("the sadder but wiser girl was she") to take both warning and encouragement from that wisdom. The Proportionalists are perhaps right in their belief that even the most deplorable actions might occasionally be performed in such situations or states of mind that they do not extinguish a person's grace and goodness. But that may be because the one performing them is long since morally dead. The reason we call mortally sinful acts "mortal sins" is not because they morally kill the people who perform them. Usually you have to be dead to do them. The Proportionalists seem to ignore the fact that actions of an ostensibly petty quality, which draw a person unobtrusively into a sinister and selfish undertow, are the moral equivalent of the Human Immunodeficiency Virus. You are dead long before you hit bottom.

CHAPTER SEVEN

An Ethic Both Personal and Social:
Decisions of Choice

For anyone who believes that the Father of Jesus loves and draws to himself all human persons without regard for their behavior, conventional Christian ethics must undergo profound rearrangement. It is crucial for us to discern good from evil, right from wrong, and to act accordingly. However, the purpose for which we must govern ourselves is not to secure God's gracious welcome, which is assured us in any case. It is rather that we might be transformed and grow and mature into love, lest that infinite cherishing be lost upon us, and we be disabled from making a home within that welcome.

The moral charge of Jesus of Nazareth, peculiar among this world's ethics, is no program for minimal integrity, but an outright demand that humans abandon themselves to generosity. Thus, although the Church may, has, and does frame commandments, they are not divine laws, but inspired human wisdom about how to respond to the divine call. Their publication as from God is a literary and homiletic custom, bespeaking the unchanged conviction that moral insight and behavior are no simple matter between humans, but ultimately creative of bonds with the Lord.

Preachers and theologians who present Christian morality in unrelieved terms of praise or blame, reward or punishment for responsible deeds, tend to obscure the dissimilarity between virtue and vice, sanctity and sin, which respectively enhance and destroy responsibility. They also obscure the intrinsic and immediate outcome of good and evil behavior, in favor of some final resolution at the time of death. Although we are creatures, the Lord who loves us without measure offers the nearly unbelievable invitation to respond with measureless love. It has often been the desire of moral theologians to persuade believers that Jesus had more modest plans.

I should now like to explore some of the paradoxes that deepen the relationship between personal morality and social morality. The ethical enterprise of a creature in the care of her all-cherishing Lord is a venture toward fullest personal growth, and at the same time a commitment to the needs of neighbors. It may arise from within a single person's conscience, yet is beholden to the collective wisdom of the human family. In purpose and in source, morality has to be both individual and social, though in paradoxically diverse ways. Oversimplified understandings of morality have tended to yield to one or another of these poles, and let the other go. The pages that follow will ponder several inescapable features, individual and social, that must be accounted for in any full moral understanding.

How Christians put everyone else on the spot

One of the stories that best conveys this is in the Gospel according to Matthew:

> "When the Son of man comes in his glory, escorted by all the angels, then he will take his seat on his throne of glory. All nations will be assembled before him and he will separate people one from another as the shepherd separates sheep from goats. He will place the sheep on his right hand and the goats on his left. Then the King will say to those on his right hand, 'Come, you whom my Father has blessed, take as your heritage the kingdom prepared for you since the foundation of the world. For I was hungry and you gave me food, I was thirsty and you gave me drink, I was a stranger and you made me welcome, lacking clothes and you clothed me, sick and you visited me, in prison and you came to see me.' Then the upright will say to him in reply, 'Lord, when did we see you hungry and feed you, or thirsty and give you drink? When did we see you a stranger and make you welcome, lacking clothes and clothe you? When did we find you sick or in prison and go to see you?' And the King will answer, 'In truth I tell you, in so far as you did this to one of the least of these brothers of mine, you did it to me.' Then he will say to those on his left hand, 'Go away from me, with your curse upon you, to the eternal fire prepared for the devil and his angels. For I was hungry

166

and you never gave me food, I was thirsty and you never gave me anything to drink, I was a stranger and you never made me welcome, lacking clothes and you never clothed me, sick and in prison and you never visited me.' Then it will be their turn to ask, 'Lord, when did we see you hungry or thirsty, a stranger or lacking clothes, sick or in prison, and did not come to your help?' Then he will answer, 'In truth I tell you, in so far as you neglected to do this to one of the least of these, you neglected to do it to me.' And they will go away to eternal punishment, and the upright to eternal life.'" (25:31-46)

The format of the story follows classic lines of Hebrew apocalyptic: the Lord will send judgment through his chosen people upon all the peoples of the earth. Blessing will be meted out for obedience, and curses for failure to obey. What will merit condemnation among the nations is not their defiance of or disinterest in Torah or Gospel, but their failure to respond hospitably to the needs of the Lord's own "brothers" and "sisters," the "least of his," and in Matthew's idiom that means the needs of Christians. The story clearly does not say that Christians (these brothers of mine) will be judged on how generously they have treated the needs of their non-Christian neighbors (the "nations"). To the contrary: The Son of Man will draw the line of doom between non-believers according as they have or have not come to the aid of the Christians.[1]

Matthew could not imagine a Christian who was not a missionary ("Go, therefore, make disciples of all nations," was Jesus' final command), and he anticipates that all peoples would eventually be approached by Christians who mean to win them over as fellow disciples. How? These Christians would have to put non-believers on the spot by the witness they give in peaceably offering the best they have to give — the best of all good news — and by persisting even when and where they are ignored or even abusively treated. In Matthew's parable Jesus implies that his followers' mission will be twofold: first, to share with all peoples what they have to show and tell about himself, the Messiah and Suffering Servant who will come again to judge the living and the dead; and, second, to present themselves in a manner so forthright yet meek, so persistently loving whether or not they gain a welcome in return, that their antagonized listeners' only possible motive for ignoring their witness would have to be bad will.

1. John R. Donahue, S.J., "The 'Parable' of the Sheep and the Goats: A Challenge to Christian Ethics,' *Theological Studies* 47 (1986): 3-31.

The peoples of the earth are to be faced with the challenge from Jesus' disciples when they disclose to them, in their own flesh, that same relentless love he had once revealed to them in his own flesh. The brothers' and sisters' authentic credential would be a love of Christ-like constancy. They would need to be as helpless before the force of any human who wished to ignore their needs or do them violence as Jesus had been. Yet by their bruises their listeners might be healed. In a word, to win unwitting sinners they would have to love sinners so wittingly, at the same risk and the same cost Jesus had accepted to show *them* his Father's love. In Matthew the moral test of any human is his or her readiness to be converted by the peaceable tenacity of any rightly functioning Christian. And the moral test of any Christian was to be his or her readiness to repay injury with blessing: however much it took to show forth the face of Jesus.

The Parable of the Sheep and the Goats is addressed, of course, to believers. It leaves them with the clear challenge that their lives as individuals and as Church must shine forth so undefendedly and purely and consistently in the public eye that non-believers will have no excuse but their own perversity not to be won over to fellowship in Christ.

Of course we too carry that limitless obligation to see and succor those in need. It is possible for one to affirm that he has supported his parents in their older years, and resisted adultery, and stayed clear of perjury. But who is to say he has given the hungry their fill, housed all the homeless, befriended the imprisoned, and supported the widow and the orphan and the pauper? There is more: to qualify as fully faithful we must love strangers as graciously as Jesus did, and in his name, with no surety of kindness in return. As it was with Jesus, it will only be when people have done their worst to us that we can show them his best.

It would be a mistake, however, to see this as a sideline or an amateur pastime in a busy life. My colleague Robert Rodes makes the point wryly:

> It appears that the professional religionist would like to turn the spiritual energies (such as they are) of the Catholic layperson away from his secular occupation and into what is called the "apostolate." Generally, the apostolate is conceived as an amateur work for social betterment carried on with religious motives. It involves policemen spending their spare time teaching people to read while schoolteachers spend theirs demonstrating against police brutality. It involves students from business schools spending their summers building

houses for Latin American peasants, while construction workers organize cooperatives in the slums.[2]

The parable is disconcerting. God's claim, previously taken to be manageable and measurable, is as unfathomable as both the ills and the ill will of humankind. For the Christian there is neither measure nor limit offered for her observance, though her capacities seem so very measured and limited. The good she is sent to do is not optional, yet it is described in infinite terms. She is sent, not simply to keep herself clear of the world; not simply to break into people's lives and busy herself with their needs to confront them with God's call, but to expose herself to the same rebuff and resentment Jesus encountered from the Twelve and from us.

Moral choices

One very personal feature of this morality that deserves heightened emphasis is the role of *decision,* of *choice.* The call from Jesus to wholehearted service confronts every believer with the vast claims of human need. Yet the believer is so limited in time, wit, and wealth. He will grow, and his capacities will stretch. But even with perception, appetite, and performance enlarging, choices have to be made and so much is at stake in them.

The believer is burdened with all human burdens and exposed to all human heartlessness, and there is no one to tell him just how far his own concrete contribution of action and forbearance need go. And all this is commanded, not commended. Our scriptural mandate is about obligation, not about alternatives. The wrangles between moral traditionalists and revisionists have turned their attention away from alternatives to imperatives. But what has preoccupied them both are exceptionless negative norms, which the traditionalists defend and the revisionists deny. Because of the assymetry between good and evil, negative imperatives about what must be avoided appear to stand out more clearly than positive imperatives about what must be done. The rest of our life, involving most constructive decisions, has usually been considered morally less crucial. Most folks rarely feel under moral pressure in making open choices, since morality is understood only to forbid those sorts of debauchery and addiction they are not bothered by anyhow, or to encourage a less defined generosity.

2. Robert Rodes, "The Bride from the Desert," unpublished manuscript, 1967, p. 27, quoted by permission.

A person will rarely think it is a "moral" issue what career she should follow, what man she should marry, what to read, what prices she should charge, what friends she should be loyal to, or when she should take a stand and when it would be better to be silent.

We have come to think that where there are options, where there is freedom, our choices are ethically indifferent. Not so. It is often our discretionary choices that are the making or the unmaking of us: our education, our careers, our marriages, the rearing of our children, political loyalties, toil, friendships. Here is where our moral character is articulated.

The Gospel puts it to us that our lives must be turned to generous service and to patient forbearance in favor of our sisters and brothers in need. But which sisters? Which brothers? How many needs? Here it is that we turn option into imperative. There is no one who tells a couple they *must* have three more children, or a man that he *must* support a certain candidate for Congress, or a woman that she *must* take in her neighbors' children to make possible a weekend away for their parents. For negative imperatives a person can and should rely heavily upon the experience and wisdom of the tradition, which advises, "Thou shalt not . . ." For positives, sometimes less definitive but often more decisive, the individual must be creative: Not "I must . . ." but "I will . . ." Self-determination can be every bit as fateful in choice as in acceptance, even when it begins from options.

Mother Teresa was trained and experienced as a teacher, and she decided she would leave her convent school in Calcutta to teach the poorest children there. But once having put herself at the mercy of the poorest and their needs, she went on to see their greater needs and her greater call, which was to accompany them in their dying. The whole shape of her ministry was the largest moral issue of her life, and it grew from an imperative she imposed upon herself. She heard the call which decisively assigned her to her neighbors' most definitive need. And the voice was her own.

Negative decisions can also impose the need for personal choice. Thomas More decided at a certain point that he could and would no longer follow his king. Why at that particular point? As chancellor of England he had been the king's minister in more than one transaction that would have troubled a conscience as sensitive as his. On the other hand, it is conceivable that his fine and subtle purchase on the law might have permitted him to tolerate this matter of the king's marriage, only to find some other, intolerable, issue years later. Why was it precisely at *this* point that More chose to dig in his heels, to opt out of the king's obedience? Another man of equal integrity might have said, "I will go no further," over some other issue, earlier or later than More did. But he *chose*. It was not just the intrinsic necessity of events that forced him to draw the line at this point, but it was a necessity for him as an ethical man to acknowledge this as his breaking point and to stay by his honest decision. Here his imperative was a negative one, but it bore within it some elements of the discretionary. He had to sense when and whither and why to choose.

In his novel, *Cry, the Beloved Country*, Alan Paton relates the resolution of a young white man, Arthur Jarvis:

> "Therefore I shall devote myself, my time, my energy, my talents, to the service of South Africa. I shall no longer ask myself if this or that is expedient, but only if it is right. I shall do this, not because I am noble or unselfish, but because life slips away, and because I need for the rest of my life a star that will not play false to me, a compass that will not lie. I shall do this, not because I am a negrophile and a hater of my own, but because I cannot find it in me to do anything else. I am lost when I balance this against that, I am lost when I ask if this is safe, I am lost when I ask if men, white men or black men, Englishmen or Afrikaners, Gentiles or Jews, will approve. Therefore I shall try to do what is right, and to speak what is true.
>
> "I do this not because I am courageous and honest, but because it is the only way to end the conflict of my deepest soul. I do it because I am no longer able to aspire to the highest with one part of myself, and to deny it with another. I do not wish to live like that. I understand better those who have died for their convictions, and have not thought it as wonderful or brave or noble to die. They died rather than live, that was all."[3]

Jesus' own career embodies such an imperative. It was at the arrest of John that he chose to inaugurate his public preaching. As a young man in his early thirties (according to Luke; Irenaeus offers strong evidence he was in his early forties), he might well have made the decision earlier or later or differently. Nor need he have gone so quickly, perhaps within the year, to press the challenge home in Jerusalem. But thus he chose, and saw his decision so merged with the Father's call that on the eve of his arrest he could see his death, not simply as his own freely accepted task, but as the cup being handed to him to drink.

Like Mother Teresa, More, Jarvis, Jesus, we are all commanded to command ourselves, to make the decisive choices that will make us

---

3. Alan Paton, *Cry, the Beloved Country* (New York: Scribner's, 1948), p. 175.

women and men of fullest stature, to take the responsibility for our own moral calling. In this sense, morality is deeply personal. Also, while negative imperatives are guided and authorized by the wisdom of past experience, positive imperatives are authorized and enlightened by the wisdom of future experience, and require a special kind of courage.

Hilaire Belloc put it thus in a letter to Lady Lovat:

> I have desired all the time to clarify and write down for you — for the little it may be worth as service — what seems in my mind in the matter of Decisions. They are taken but rarely in one human life, and these points would seem to be true of each and all.
>
> First, when a true Decision is come to, there has been a full conjunction of the intelligence and the will: that is why Decisions of gravity are rare. Therefore a Decision is a thing reached by sufficient weighing of conditions and its acceptance by the will ratifies that. Every Decision of consequence has grave evils attached to it — or grave risk of evil. We deliberately conclude that the good prevails. In most Decisions there is a great act of merit.
>
> Next there is in any such Decision Peace. Full Peace is not attainable in this life, and the degree of Peace one attains is conditioned by things we cannot foretell: health and accident and the rest. But the contrast lies between the measure of Peace and the tendency to further Peace which a Decision produces, and the increasing lack of Peace which a failure to decide produces — still more a Decision on the wrong side and for the wrong motive.
>
> Next a Decision bears two kinds of fruit, outwards and inwards — outwards, it does good in its effect on all around us: inwards, it fructifies and increases what is in ourselves.
>
> I think when people come to die it is not so much the memory of good deeds that can support them as the memory of Decisions taken.
>
> They are the structure of perseverance. They are creative. And they are in communion with the ruling and directive power of Almighty God.
>
> So they seem to me. And no matter what the unforeseen connections and effects in the future they are never really regretted in the core of the heart.[4]

4. Letter dated 8 August 1930, in *Letters from Hilaire Belloc,* ed. Robert Speaight (London: Hollis & Carter, 1968), pp. 214-15.

Belloc, of course, is not hailing decisions because they are willful: because they are assertions of the self and its wants. He writes of "true" decisions: reached after grave and generous consideration, therefore rare, worthy of persevering gumption, and peaceable. His point is well expressed by Martin Buber: ". . . He who no longer, with his whole being, decides what he does or does not, and assumes responsibility for it, becomes sterile in soul. And a sterile soul soon ceases to be a soul."[5]

There are choices that are frivolous. Columnist John Garvey brought this up in a conversation with a young woman enrolled in a thanatology course who spoke enthusiastically of providing places where people could go to commit an "ethical suicide." He was "bothered by the fact that a young woman who was every bit as much in the pink as I am was so enthusiastic about the idea of suicide. When I said that even suffering might have some meaning, something to teach us, she said, 'Well, dying is a choice. You have a right to make a choice'."[6]

Charles Stuart in Boston was apparently alarmed by his wife Carol's pregnancy. Her plan to leave her job as a lawyer for motherhood would seriously crimp their joint income and comfortable suburban life. When she refused an abortion he shot her one day on their way home from a childbirth class. When his attempt to frame a black man for the murder fell apart, he leapt off a bridge to his own death. Choice all the way down, but never a real life choice.

The *definitive* choices are faced, as the tradition tells us, when we come to those ultimate temptations to commit acts that are gravely and inherently evil. But the more *decisive* choices (as I like to call them) are those many decisions which may not be ultimate, but which regularly either build up the fiber of our moral character or infect and disable us. So the more effectual moral decisions are often not those which which draw the final line between right and wrong, but those which choose among a wide array of alternatives. Right behavior of this latter sort is as imperative for us as that of the former sort. For this kind of choice one relies less upon the tradition. Here morality is both discovered and created. These are the works without which faith falls dead. Thus one's full configuration of ethical decisions will be as peculiarly personal as one's face and fingerprints.

5. Martin Buber, "The Education of Character," in *Between Man and Man* (London: Kegan Paul, 1947), p. 115.

6. John Garvey, "Choice as Absolute: The Highest Morality?" *Commonweal* 119, 1 (15 January 1982): 9-10.

The moral revisionists have confused these two modes of moral choice. They have tried to intrude the decisional postures whereby we choose between good alternatives into the process for discriminating between good and evil, where the good is to be found, rather than established.

The Catholic doctrine is that in the face of the helpless, the vulnerable, the exploited, we have no choice; and in the face of the violent, the hateful, the victimizer, we also have no choice. Or, to put it another way, if we are Christ's we have already made our main choice: to put their several welfares ahead of our preferences and our wants; their survival ahead of our needs. In that is our peace.

To grow is not to depend on our society

Let me come at this individual aspect of morality from a somewhat different direction. As a rule, the classical ethical systems have required *equity*. They call on people to share their substance with their fellow-humans, to support justice, to protect a tolerable guaranteed minimum of necessities and of opportunity. They are, further, ethics of *reciprocity*. They provide a pattern of conduct which, if followed mutually by all in the society, would enable all to live in tranquillity. They are, in fact, paradigms for reconstructing *society*. Most ethical schemes are implicitly meant to supply the minimal requirements for a congenial public order, thus to be agreed upon by all members of society, required of all, and enforced even by coercion in cases of default. In contrast with these ethics of equity, reciprocity, and society, Jesus (differing even from his late master John) preaches a way of life that ignores equity, does not expect to find reciprocity, and could never serve as a formula to be accepted or imposed within world society.

Jesus (like Marx) shows deep concern for the inequalities of material wherewithal. Oddly, however, he frets for the rich person perhaps even more than for the brother she is impoverishing. His goal is not simply an equitable redistribution of all wealth, but the saving of the precious person of every human being. It is in caring for others that both rich and poor are saved, and the sharing of goods and services becomes transfigured as the sacrament of a more valuable inner exchange (unknown to Marx).

In most ethical systems good people must provide for their own protection, knowing that not all people are good, nor are any people always good. Thus these systems are founded by force and maintained by it as well. In order to make room for the good person, the exploiter must be restrained. Jesus, by contrast, suggests no defense against injustice from without except confrontation, and his own experience is put forward as a clear warning to any disciple that he may expect to be exploited, and should provide for it in the belief that this powerful acquiescence is often the only means of touching and healing the heart of the exploiter.

A social ethic is realizable only in a society that has already accepted it. A person will devote himself to working for justice in the hope that one day it will become the working relationship between all people, that one day he may trust his neighbor and count on finding honesty and integrity from him, and finally be able, in the reconstructed society, to relax and be his better self. But Jesus talks little indeed about a reformed society or a better world. He insists that a disciple save his soul right now in the society of the Church, surrounded by the most ruthless of all worlds.

The Christian ethic has customarily been disparaged as Utopian. "It would be wonderful if people could be counted on to live that way, but of course they never will." This, however, is to misconstrue. Jesus claims to have overcome the world, but never suggests that his kingdom would take over the world. The kingdom — God's rule — is no social order to wait for; it is the conversion experience and love-fellowship with the Father available to any person in this world right now. The Gospel is not addressed to all peoples; it is addressed by the Church to any person. The believer rejoices at comradeship of belief from others, but never expects to find so much of it that he can be carried along on its current. As for drawing other comrades to his side, he hopes to do this by his own example, rather than by reorganizing society.

The ethic of Jesus is the most non-Utopian in sight, read to be lived in any circumstances whatever. To be reconciled to the Lord means to dedicate oneself against suffering and injustice, but simultaneously to live and thrive amid them. Robert Rodes has written well:

> I have little understanding and no hope at all except in the passion, death and resurrection of Jesus Christ, true God and true man. Not that the world lacks elements of intelligibility and elements of hopefulness; but absent the passion, death and resurrection of Jesus Christ, they fall short of unifying into an intelligible or a hopeful whole. The world presents itself neither as totally random nor as systematically malevolent, but as a thing of flawed intelligibility, the product of frustrated benevolence. The classic problem of evil — if God could accomplish so much, why could He not have gone the rest of the way and produced a perfect creation along the lines already

175

laid down? Intellectually, He has scant comfort for those who ask that question. . . . God has offered only one answer to the evil in the world — to undergo it Himself. Whatever in this flawed universe challenges man's understanding or belies man's hope, that God took upon Himself through His incarnation in Jesus Christ, and brought to a happy issue through his resurrection from the dead.[7]

The invitation by Jesus to death and resurrection is given to us most personally. It is a call to conversion, and as was said earlier, persons may be converted in groups, yet no group was ever converted. The Church begets us in Christ, and in turn we together make up the Church. We depend on one another, yet only initiative-takers are dependable, not followers. When one makes the commitment to spend her entire strength in service of her brothers and sisters, she makes a choice that is both social and solo: social because made within the Church; solo because she must be prepared to stand faithful for others who may not be. She may group together with others of similar belief and like premises, yet that group needs the free-standing souls and the diverse histories of its many members.

In a sense, the world has no moral history in the way that a single person has. There are no world moments of radical transformation. Some projects may be attempted and succeed. Racial integration may be pushed through the legislatures and the courts, even into some people's hearts. Freedom of the press, surely of high moral value, can be established in an area where it did not previously exist. Security for orphans can be provided, or women's suffrage, or protection for mine workers. But as each real social achievement is realized, the predatory forces dark within human hearts inevitably sidestep into other avenues of exploitation. Improvements must be fought for, and they mark real progress. But despite them all we cannot speak of constant moral growth within society. As an individual one may have his entire life turned inside out morally, and may be radically transformed on various occasions throughout his lifetime. Not so a society; surely not so the world. Global history does not allow of the startling transfiguration that a single person may experience between birth and death. Thus the Christian must pursue his purposes on his own, without waiting for the world to become receptive to them. Morally, the world never edges nearer the kingdom.

The Church opposes both its leftist and its rightist rivals for wanting

7. Rodes, "The Bride from the Desert," p. 1.

to transform society through force. Justice and peace, law and order, are hardly to be established through violence and deceit. But has Christian experience been any more capable than Marxist or Phalange efforts? The Philemons of this world will be deceived by any Utopianism, ruthless or compassionate, which bids them turn their energies toward the abolition of slavery without making a brother of Onesimus.

These, then, are aspects of the moral life which are inescapably individual. The single person must make critical choices in the solitude of his own conscience, and cannot expect society around him to be virtuous, in order that his own integrity might come more easily.

The Gospel is no call, however, to isolate oneself or to provide for one's individual integrity in private. First of all, it is spoken and heard within the Church, and it is in the fellowship of the Church that we take these personal steps. It flings the believer into social service, assures her she will cleave to the Father only by succoring her brothers and sisters, and urges her to make common cause with all possible people in order to serve an ever widening range of brothers and sisters. One is indeed to collaborate: not simply with those who have the same visions and beliefs, but with all people of enough good will.

In any task group he enters, the Christian must realize that his personal goals and those of the Church cannot — must not — coincide with those of the world at large. The world must work for equity, protect itself, and seek to reorganize society. It might coerce, it may sometimes subordinate personal interests to financial need, it may pursue short-term goals. The Christian and the Christian Church can neither despise out-group endeavor nor impose on it the ethic by which, through divine revelation and enablement and Church, we live. Just as there is no ethical code that can contain the full force of the call of Christ, inasmuch as we Christians must always be asking ourselves what is right and wrong (though for outsiders who do not worship Christ together with us, our best moral wisdom may hardly make coherent sense), so there is no group or group activity that can contain and represent the full force of a believer's needs and decisions — not even a family — yet all believers must be ever making common cause in the Church, and with others, for what God would have them struggle for.

This creates particular frustrations for Christians holding public office: statesmen, for instance, or corporate executives; but also for those in more private spheres, like mothers of families. One is caught both ways. On the one hand, since any group moves mostly by consensus, any person with group responsibility is likely to be held back by the sluggishness and faltering motives of her fellows, and drawn to compromise and to bite her lip. On the other hand, so much of her energies and ego are thrown into leadership that she is tempted to submerge all her personal endeavor into the projects at hand, and to reserve no identity for herself other than her corporate person. The service of humankind requires many stewards of the common good, but they have additional reasons for working out their salvation in fear and trembling. Not a few of these wardens have been beguiled into thinking they were laying down their lives for their brothers and sisters, while in fact they were suffering instead the loss of their own souls.

Thus far, in exploring the moral relationship between person and society, I have argued that the irreducible unit of moral concern is the individual person, not society. It is the lone man and woman who must make and enact their ethical decisions; and these decisions as moral are mainly for those same moral actors. It is the person that loves, and lives beyond death. No society is capable of either . . . except the Church. This is one reason why Christians have ever shied away from princes and politics that wished to claim their total loyalty, and why they have held their own churchmen in highest contempt when they degraded the Church herself into a totalitarian or self-serving organization. It is the fellowship of those who are passing over from death to life, from this world to the next.

To grow is to reckon with society

Now, to turn the corner into another avenue of reflection, I want to stress the paradoxical fact that the individual person, if he is to rise from the dead and grow and mature into love, is obliged to turn his care and service toward society.

The newborn child begins in selfishness. If original sin has any meaning it would reside neither in some hereditary curse spoken of by some ancients in the Church, nor in the latent youthful savagery depicted by William Golding in *Lord of the Flies*. It is the thorough egocentricity in which we all were born and out of which, at our peril, we must grow. The child becomes an adult as she encounters and comes to terms successively with parents, siblings, playmates and friends, teachers, spouse, children, professional associates. One's life widens as one comes to care for ever widening circles of people. One becomes a full-grown individual to the extent that one has become socialized.

But that is not enough. In life's course it is possible to become attached only to those who in some way belong to one, who can be trusted. In a word, one can limit love to those who offer some return. There is another step we must take, if we are not always to remain held by the aboriginal selfishness: to reach out in love to the stranger. In the Old Testament the test case of sincere love was the "sojourner in the land." Every village might have a few Gentile members, migrant or resident: not kin of the tribe or the nation, but thrown upon the hospitality and guardianship of the locals, who for survival had had to be wary of any alien folk. One token of unselfish love was to sustain these scattered and unprotected sojourners, who could offer no *quid pro quo*. In the New Testament the test case is the enemy. If the Christian could bring himself to forgive and even to cherish the person who had sought his harm, then one had true Jesus-love.

In our own time, a further test case might be the anonymous stranger, the unknown and unmet neighbor, the public. Recently the concern over environmental devastation has brought to our attention the way we have of mistreating our environment in ways we would never treat our private property. Ecologists accuse us of the "downstream mentality," a willingness to discard our own offal without regard for whomever it will then afflict. The acrid smokestacks of Gary, Indiana, the unrecoverably depleted aquifers under Missouri and Kansas farmland soon to become permanent desert, the strip-mined wastelands of Kentucky, the poisonous public sludge reefing the coast off New York and New Jersey — all this and more testify to our contempt for the anonymous neighbor.

I have seen the same thing at colleges and universities, on a minute but vexing scale. The first week of every academic year, students arrive and work industriously to furnish and equip their rooms. Mothers come with matching bedspreads and curtains; sons repaint the walls; the Salvation Army supplies fourth-generation couches with third-generation resident roaches. There is always much carpentry, and I noticed year after year that for an entire week the public hallways were littered with sawdust and woodscrap and sprayed stain, after the private rooms had been swept and garnished. Inside, Fontainebleau; outside, Les Misérables. I was reminded of more primitive places (so I supposed) where the denizens empty their chamber pots from their windows onto the streets every morning. Evidently the corridor, belonging to everyone, was seen to belong to no one in particular, and thus became a no-man's land, a dump.

One must have a sense of proportion. It is not exactly the same thing when a motorist flips his burning cigarette butt out the window onto the roadside; when 60 percent of the registered voters fail to cast their votes in a federal election; or when 38 people in Kew Gardens, Queens, in 1964 sat at their windows and watched young Kitty Genovese stagger back and forth on the street below, and listened for a half-hour to her screams and moans while she was stalked and repeatedly stabbed and sexually molested and stabbed again and finally died alone in a doorway. Only then did one of them call the police. Others later said they had been tired, or drunk, or afraid, or "didn't want to get involved." But the slant of mind is the same. We are sensitive to those who are known to us, but we easily de-personalize the faceless person, the neighbor. We tend to walk briskly down the road from Jerusalem to Jericho, glancing neither to the left nor to the right. Or, like Philemon and Onesimus, we strain to find some minor re-arrangement in our relations that will spare us anything as radical as what the Lord asks.

Governments in our day have assumed broader obligations to succor the warstricken, to supply help after national disasters, to support the unemployed. But we are easily drugged by the presence of the government and the existence of so many organized social enterprises. Somehow we manage to shift to officials and organizations all responsibility for need beyond our short reach. Thereby are we morally dwarfed. It is surely ironic that in every age when citizens have insisted that their governments be more active in socially constructive activity, individuals have been encouraged to transfer any long-distance moral responsibility to appropriate agencies, and to return to their social torpor, caring not for those who never come — or are never welcomed — into personal touch with them. In this sense, enlarged social programs can anaesthetize social concern in human hearts. And without this loving and active service of those who are neither close enough nor well enough disposed to scratch one's back in return, no one can rise out of that original sin; no one will have left land, house, and kin to follow Jesus.

CHAPTER EIGHT

The Suppleness of Moral Wisdom: A Case Study in Armed Force

Reading over contemporary literature in the field of Christian ethics leads one to discover that many topics of interest derive from the companionate areas of sex and force. What are the debated issues of the day? Abortion, homosexuality, feminism, assisted suicide, adolescent sex and adult policies thereupon, AIDS, manipulated reproduction, domestic abuse, immigration policy: all touch on sex or force, and many mingle them. There must be something about this agenda of concern beyond the native human prurience that has always had its fascination tickled by these two activities.

In the thirteenth century Aquinas commented upon the curious resemblances between what he called the concupiscible and the irascible appetites, which we might call sex and wrath. The former appetite attracts us to other people in pleasure, and the latter repels us from them in anger. Freud as a young man at first linked libido and aggression, on the ground that they were alternate expressions of one basic drive for sexual mastery over others. In his later career he preferred to differentiate them, in the belief that the libidinal drive seeks after life, while the aggressive drive is death-oriented. While not identifying the two, I would agree with Freud *junior* and with Thomas that they are paradoxically symmetrical. "The vicissitudes of aggression resemble those of sexuality to such a degree that the assumption of a constant driving power comparable to that of libido seems appropriate."[1]

---

1. Heinz Hartmann, Ernst Kris, & Rudolph Loewenstein, "Notes on the Theory of Aggression," *Papers on Psychoanalytic Psychology: Psychological Issues* 4, 2 (Monograph 14), 1964, p. 78.

A book critic once wryly observed how lust and coercion are similar by comparing pornography to what he called carnography. "When the meat flies off the head, it must be just right. Through the lens, spraying the viewer with reality. Except that the reader/viewer is safe in his chair. That is the fun of voyeurism — its safety. . . . Carnography's adrenal rush, quickened pulse rate, and readying of muscles for action are nearly as effective as pornography's sexual flush in blocking out all other emotional and intellectual reactions."[2]

One obvious shared feature is that both passions involve physical contact: one must somehow touch the body of another, whether to caress or to assail. These are among the deepest and most direct human relations. In their simplest forms they bring persons into one-on-one, body-to-body, or body-against-body, encounter. Another similarity is that although they natively and rightly embody fidelity and justice, when either goes septic it can tend to inflame the other. Thus we behold gang rape by military units run amok, and abortion as a common outcome of casual copulation.

The close corporality common to both behaviors easily distracts ethical discussion from their wider social implications. Considerations of nuclear weaponry, for instance, document vividly what becomes of the citizens upon whom the bomb falls. Why not reckon with equal vividness what becomes of the politics and economics of nations that invest heavily in weapons which are always poised though not used? Many writers are distressed about the Sherpa-like climb of statistics on teenage pregnancy and sexually contagious disease, without looking behind both phenomena to the decay of the family that gives children little strength to hunger for something deeper than the estranged "intimacy" that festers in our time. Treatises on the theory of just war take for their moral model the scenario of an innocent person being attacked; defensive intervention on behalf of the victim is invoked, and then this miniature model is projected to national scale. That may have enjoyed some analogical legitimacy when wars were private struggles between princes, but as a model it fails to illuminate or resolve ethical problems of national or global armed hostilities.

This lack of interest in the rights and wrongs of social involvement desensitizes one to the massive values of good and evil that resist being reduced to a simple, person-to-person dimension. To understand sex, one must inquire not simply into the proprieties of genital intercourse, but also into the different possibilities of marital fidelity, the rearing of children, the loyalties of kin and clan and town and people which the ancients called

2. John Skaw, review of *First Blood* by David Morell in *Time*, 29 May 1972, p. 82.

pietas, the public status of women, caring for elder grandparents, the conflict of prolonged responsibility caused by education lengthened far past marrying age, and so many other broad issues. Violent force would also become an expanded notion, touching upon slum landlordism, election fraud, international trade imbalances, racial segregation, epidemic malnutrition, and so forth. One would think of violence, not as limited to the simple model of physical assault, but as whatever *violates* integrity. I would propose the term *isometric violence* to depict the brutal, unyielding shove that destroys persons, even when no one is struck or bruised, no one dies, no one is buried.

Ethical discussion has a way of distracting itself from larger issues. Theologians, for instance, are reluctant to scrutinize restraint of trade by labor unions, manipulation of motivation through advertising, increasing monopolies in the communications media, expanding inequities in international development, wastage and pollution of natural resources, or inertia in prison reform. We have given our attention by preference to close, person-to-person behavior, and ignored the social structures, massive pressures, and intricate commitments that also make us the persons we are. We have bothered ourselves with good and evil, but no further than any individual could touch and see and hear.

The Christian rejection of armed service

I should like to explore one normative moral question here, in order both to illustrate what I have in mind by way of an imaginatively proper insight, and to see whether this approach, simultaneously personal and communal, may consistently and usefully serve in the resolution of particular problems. The issue is the proper use of force. More particularly, should one acquiesce in armed service, or should one refuse to bear arms? The question is alive in our time, and illustrative of problems that are in every time alive.

The Gospel represents Jesus as opposed to the use of force, and he raises the issue explicitly in the context of defense. If a man is bent on robbing you of your goods, present them to him as a gift rather than resisting. If he would take your coat, then ask him to wait while you take off your shirt as well. Always round off a transaction in the other fellow's favor. Encroaching evil, Jesus advises, is best not met with a tough resistance or canny retaliation, but with a guileless good that can wear down evil. If you must go before the courts, let it never be as plaintiff. The earth will go to the meek, not to the pushy. On the eve of his own arrest Jesus tells his own following to put away weapons, for whoever takes up the sword will perish by the sword. Since he was knowingly on his way to an innocent death, with all his flights of angels grounded, one infers that it is not the risk of falling beneath an opponent's weapon that is so deadly, but the risk of losing one's soul by the sword in one's own hand. More vividly than by any words, though, Jesus' own acceptance of arrest, perjury, torture, and execution demonstrates that his source of power lies not in coercion or force, but in his disarmament. Only by dying in his innocence might Jesus reach the violent hearts of those who assassinate him. Thus by dying, not by killing, does he wrestle death down. He cares not to defend himself or his followers. Those who need help are the ones with murder in their hearts, and he overpowers them by catching the full impact of their evil on himself, and absorbing it.

There could be no surprise, then, that the earliest Christians saw their message as what a bewildered Peter nervily told Cornelius, an officer in the occupation army that held his country in its violent grasp, was "good news of peace" (Acts 10:36).[3] Justin († c. 165), Irenaeus († c. 202), and Origen (†253/54) saw the Church as a peacemaker people finally fulfilling the messianic prophecy:

> For the Law will issue from Zion
> and the word of Yahweh from Jerusalem.
> Then he will judge between the nations
> and arbitrate between many peoples.
> They will hammer their swords into ploughshares
> and their spears into sickles.
> Nation will not lift its sword against nation,
> no longer will they learn how to make war.
>
> (Isaiah 2:4, repeated in Micah 4:3)

Said Justin Martyr: "For twelve men, ignorant and unskilled in speaking as they were, went out from Jerusalem to the world, and with the help of God announced to every race of men that they had been sent by Christ

---

3. The historical report that follows is indebted to texts assembled by C. John Cadoux, *The Early Christian Attitude to War* (London: Headley Bros., 1919); and Louis J. Swift, *The Early Fathers on War and Military Service* (Wilmington, Del.: Michael Glazier, 1983). Unless otherwise noted, text translations are taken or adapted from these authors, and designated by "C" or "S" and the page reference.

to teach the word of God to everyone, and we who formerly killed one another not only refuse to make war on our enemies but in order to avoid lying to our interrogators or deceiving them, we freely go to our deaths confessing Christ."[4]

That was in 153. Christians would generally have been free not to serve in the army. Those who were Jewish may have benefited by their special ethnic exemption. Conscription was almost never done anyway, since military needs were satisfied by enlistment, and we hear of no Christians serving in the army until the time of Marcus Aurelius (161-80) when the Twelfth Legion, recruited in Cappadocia, was said to have been rescued from dire thirst in battle by a thunderstorm in answer to prayer by Christian soldiers in the ranks. That they were numerous suggests that enlistment was by then (173/74) not uncommon. Yet at that very time the emperor, himself no friend to Christians, was being told by Athenagoras that the Christians were praying for him so that the empire might enjoy a stable peace. They would not, however, join in fighting for it, since that only led to entire cities and towns burnt to the ground, and whole populations put to the sword. Christians, he wrote, could not bear even to sit and watch the gladiatorial games, which served as capital punishment for condemned criminals: "Watching a man being slain is almost the same as killing him."[5] At the same time Celsus, an articulate critic of the Christians, was complaining that their unwillingness to take up arms — even in self-defense, let alone by accepting military service — made them dangerously disloyal citizens: if their example were to spread, the empire would quickly fall to the waiting barbarians.[6]

Christian doctrine and practice were now seemingly at odds. Christians were beginning to be commonplace in the military, yet to read the most influential Church writers you would think enlistment was a great disgrace. The army offered secure lifetime employment (provided one survived), with pension and homestead, and by the end of the second century Christians were serving in considerable numbers; in one province they were said to constitute a majority. At first the evidence suggests that they were men already under arms who had converted to the faith. But now some Christians were beginning to enlist. Tertullian († c. 220) wanly assures us that "many" had abandoned the service after conversion. His efforts to explain how continued service was compatible with their com-

4. Justin Martyr, *First Apology*, 39.2-3: S34-5.
5. Athenagoras, *Embassy*, 35, 5: S35.
6. Origen, *Against Celsus* 8.68.

mitment to non-violence show the strain. Like other Christian apologists he was ready to admit that the spread of the faith and the safety of Christian communities had benefited from the *Pax Romana* instituted by Augustus and maintained by his successors. The price of that peace, of course, was eternal — and well garrisoned — vigilance. The primal Christian objection to military service was bloodshed, horrific to Christians, and Tertullian stretched to the view that soldiering was tolerable for a Christian provided that he did not actually kill. The second objection was that military service required an oath and occasional sacrifice to the Roman gods and emperors, and that was idolatry. The same two compromising duties — imposing death, and partaking in imperial worship — were incumbent on civil magistrates as well, and Tertullian's only solution was that Christians had better serve in the latter capacity only on an honorary basis, to avoid responsibility for torture and execution and involvement in state sacrifices. Thus his practical advice was compromised and had none of the resonance he gave to his more theoretical effusions:

> There can be no compatibility between an oath [*sacramentum*] made to God and one made to man, between the standard of Christ and that of the devil, between the camp of light and the camp of darkness. The soul cannot be beholden to two masters, God and Caesar. . . . the Lord, by taking away Peter's sword, disarmed every soldier thereafter. We are not allowed to wear any insignia that symbolize a sinful act.[7]

Elsewhere he writes that in Gethsemane Jesus "cursed the works of the sword forever."[8] But, like us all, even when he is compromised Tertullian does break open some truth when he unlooses his rhetoric on himself. When one Christian legionnaire refused to take part in the emperor's birthday rites, Tertullian meditated on the unbearable conflict any Christian soldier sustained. Beside the bloodshed and the idolatry, there was a third objection: the daily, degrading moral contradiction:

> Is it right to make a profession of the sword when the Lord has proclaimed that the man who uses it will perish by it? Will a son of peace who should not even go to court take part in battle? Will a man who does not avenge wrongs done to himself have any part in chains,

7. Tertullian, *Idolatry*, 19.3: S41-2.
8. Tertullian, *Patience*, 3: S42.

prisons, tortures and punishments? Will he perform guard duty for anyone other than Christ, or will he do so on the Lord's day when he is not doing it for Christ himself? Will he stand guard at the temples he has forsworn? Will he go to a banquet at places where the Apostle disapproves of it? At night will he protect those [demons] that he has exorcised during the day, leaning and resting all the while on the spear that pierced the side of Christ? Will he carry the standards that rival Christ's? Will he ask his commander for a password when he has received one from God? At the moment of death will he be disturbed by the trumpeter's horn if he looks forward to being awakened by the horn of an angel? Will he be cremated according to the usual practice when this has been forbidden him and when he has been freed by Christ from the punishment of fire? By looking around one can see how many other forms of wrongdoing are involved in fulfilling the duties of military camps, things which must be considered violations of God's law. Carrying the title "Christian" from the camp of light to the camp of darkness is itself a violation.

Therefore, concludes Tertullian, any soldier who becomes a convert must either leave the army immediately or ready himself for martyrdom:

Jesus will save the life that has been given up for his Name's sake but will destroy the one that was saved at the expense of his Name for money's sake. . . . There is no allowance for a plea of necessity. No necessity for wrongdoing is incumbent on those for whom the only necessity is to avoid wrongdoing. Someone, you say, is pressed into sacrificing or officially denying Christ by the inevitability of torture or imprisonment. All the same, Church discipline does not wink even at that kind of necessity because the necessity to fear denial and to suffer martyrdom is greater than the necessity to avoid martyrdom and to make the required offering. What is more, a pretext like this undercuts the whole meaning of the baptismal oath.[9]

By the middle of the third century, while Christian involvement in the military was enlarging, Christian misgivings were persisting. Cyprian of Carthage (†258), Tertullian's disciple, deplores the apparent enlargement of violence: "The world is drenched with bloodshed. When individuals

---

9. Tertullian, *The Soldier's Crown*, 11.1-7: S43-5

slay a man, it is a crime. When killing takes place on behalf of the state, it is called a virtue."[10]

Origen of Alexandria (†253) saw peacefulness as a specific difference between Christians and Jews. Israel had its own land, government, and citizens, and was thereby obliged to maintain freedom from without and order within by the use of coercive force. It was providential that with the coming of Jesus, God's people were no longer bound by primary loyalty to any one territorial or ethnic or civic identity which might require them to take up arms in its defense (or aggrandizement). Christians no longer take up the sword, he says; they have become sons of peace instead. They do struggle, he says, but now it is to keep violence from breaking out:

> Though they keep their [sword] hands clean [of blood], the Christians fight through their prayers to God on behalf of those doing battle in a just cause and on behalf of an emperor who is ruling justly in order that all opposition and hostility toward those who are acting rightly may be eliminated. What is more, by overcoming with our prayers all the demons who incite wars, who violate oaths and who disturb the peace we help emperors more than those who are supposedly doing the fighting. . . . We do not go out on the campaign with him even when he insists, but we do battle on his behalf by raising a special army of piety through our petitions to God.[11]

Origen lived to be tortured so energetically in the savage persecution under Decius that when released because of the emperor's death he soon died of his injuries: a confirmed son of peace.

As the third century rolled on and the empire became more troubled, Christian involvement in warfare increased further, but so did Christian misgivings about it. As the waves of persecution under Decius (250-51) and Valerian (257-59) and the Great Persecution begun under Diocletian (303-13) put their dual loyalties under great strain, Christian soldier-martyrs began to step out of the ranks. At Palestinian Caesarea in 260 Marinus was blocked from promotion to centurion by a rival who objected that he was a Christian and would not offer sacrifice to the emperors. So he was, and so he would not, and after three hours' reflection he was executed. The acts of his martyrdom report that during the interval his bishop was allowed to offer him counsel. The bishop laid the Gospel-book on a table beside

10. Cyprian, Letter to Donatus, 6: S48.
11. Origen, *Against Celsus* 8.73: S55.

Marinus' sword and told him he would have to choose between them. At Theveste in Numidia (now Tébessa in Algeria) in the year 295 Maximilian, age 21, was brought by his father for induction as expected of soldiers' sons, but he refused to accept his uniform or the military badge with the imperial seal. "I am not going to receive a seal that belongs to this world. If you put it on me, I will smash it because it has no power. I am a Christian; I may not carry a piece of lead around my neck now that I have accepted the saving seal of my Lord Jesus Christ, Son of the living God. You know nothing about him, but he suffered for our salvation, and he was delivered by God for our sins. It is he whom all of us Christians serve; it is he whom we follow as life's sovereign and as the author of salvation. . . . I am committed to serve my Lord; I cannot serve in an army of this world." The proconsul objected that the imperial armies had enrolled many Christians, but Maximilian said that was their problem. "I cannot do what is wrong." Thus died the first known Christian conscientious objector.[12]

At Tingis (now Tangier) in 298 Marcellus, a centurion, publicly stripped himself of insignia, arms, and uniform on the emperor's birthday: "I serve Jesus Christ, the eternal king. . . . I cease from this military service of your emperors, and I scorn to adore your gods of stone and wood, which are deaf and dumb idols." To the judge who sentenced him to death he asserted: "I threw down my arms; for it was not seemly that a Christian man, who renders military service to the Lord Christ, should render it (also) by (inflicting) earthly injuries."[13] Pope St. Damasus († *c.* 384) commemorated two soldiers of the Praetorian Guard, Nereus and Achilleus, who "were carrying on their cruel duty," but "suddenly laid aside their madness . . . left the general's impious camp . . . cast down their blood-stained weapons," and won their different "triumphal parade" to martyrdom, probably during the Great Persecution.[14]

Christians in arms for a Christian Emperor

Then fortune turned . . . and more than fortune. In 310 there were four who shared the imperial title of *Augustus*. Their savage competition lasted until Constantine emerged as victor and sole survivor in 323, and since Christians had suffered violence from the other three, they were well

12. *Acts of Maximilian,* 1-2: S72-4.
13. C152.
14. S154.

prepared to honor Constantine whose first decisive victory in 312 — fought under the badge of the Cross — was followed by an official edict granting them religious freedom.

Eusebius of Caesarea († c. 339), his court bishop, in his *Praise of Constantine* declared that Isaiah's prophecy of swords wrought into ploughshares and spears converted into sickles was fulfilled, not by Christians' forswearing of bloodshed and military force, but in the overwhelming success of the bloodshed and military force of their new patron who had taken Christ as his "heavenly champion and ally." Now Christians brought peace *through* arms, not through their refusal to bear arms. In one ominous passage Eusebius specified, not that Constantine's victory was for the Christians, but that it was for "the Romans."

Athanasius of Alexandria (†373), despite his frequent antagonism toward the imperial government, could report a common opinion in 357: "One is not supposed to kill, but killing the enemy in battle is both lawful and praiseworthy. For this reason individuals who have distinguished themselves in war are considered worthy of great honors, and monuments are put up to celebrate their accomplishments."[15]

Ambrose of Milan (†397), former governor of Northern Italy (his father had been military governor and judge of most of Europe), described the resort to armed struggle as morally defined by its purpose, and he was ready to assign high virtue to it. "The bravery which guards the fatherland in war from the barbarians or defends the weak at home or allies from robbers, is full of justice."[16] Ambrose sent his prayer along with the emperor hastening to battle the Goths in 378 (a prayer that General Patton might have found too zealous):

> Almighty God, with your own blood and devastation we have paid enough and more than enough for the death of the faithful, the exile of priests and the horror of such great impiety. It is abundantly clear that those who have abandoned the faith cannot remain untouched. Turn, O Lord, and raise the banners of faith. . . . Show us now a clear sign of your majesty so that with the help of that majesty he who believes that you are the true "power and wisdom of God," not temporal or created but, as it is written, the "eternal power and divinity of God," may win trophies for his faith.[17]

15. Athanasius, Letter to Amun, 13: S95.
16. Ambrose, *Duties of Ministers*, 1.27.129: C257.
17. Ambrose, *The Faith*, 2.16.40-3: S106-7.

Christian success had turned around: now Christ would have as his witnesses, not those who die rather than battle, but those who kill in battle.

Augustine of Hippo (†430) thought that the great moral infection in public affairs was *libido dominandi*, more modernly known as the will-to-power. This was no new notion, but whereas in earlier times Christians had instinctively associated that bully appetite with a zest for violence, Augustine saw military might as a good Christian way to curb the libido in the wrong sort of people: warfare was now a way of striking a blow for peace:

> Surely it is not vain that we have such institutions as the power of the king, the death penalty of the judge, the hooks of the executioner, the weapons of the soldier, the stringency of the overlord and even the strictness of a good father. All these things have their own method, reason, motive and benefit. When they are feared, evil men are held in check, and the good enjoy greater peace among the wicked.[18]

It was *malitia* (evil intent), not *militia* (warfare), Augustine argued, that made military ventures morally hazardous.[19] Thus Augustine saw the possibility of distinguishing good bloodshed from bad:

> What else can we call it but larceny on a grand scale when a nation wages war on its neighbors and then solely out of *libido dominandi* moves on to grind down and suppress other nations that have done no harm?[20]
>
> As a rule just wars are defined as those which avenge injuries, if some nation or state against whom one is waging war has neglected to punish a wrong committed by its citizens, or to reclaim something that was wrongfully taken.[21]

Yet despite this swift and well-recommended legitimation of a life and livelihood at arms on behalf of the imperial authority, there was still a riptide of traditional conviction that combat was morally destructive regardless of the purposes it served. It was during his years of service, c.

18. Augustine, Letter 153.6.16: S112.
19. Augustine, Sermon 302.15.
20. Augustine, *City of God* 4.6: C134.
21. Augustine, *Questions on the Heptateuch,* 6.10: S135.

366-84, that Damasus I of Rome had inscribed those harsh phrases in his retrospective inscription on the tomb of the two soldier martyrs, Nereus and Achilleus: "cruel duty," "bloodstained weapons," military "madness."

There was a conflicted but stubborn sentiment persisting into the latter fourth century and somewhat beyond, that even if warfare could no longer be condemned in itself, it was repugnant to admit its practitioners to sacramental communion. The *Egyptian Church-Order* (*c.* 300)[22] and the *"Canons of Hippolytus"* (also Egyptian, *c.* 338)[23] excluded those with the power of the sword, whether in the army or in the magistracy, from baptism and communion, but they give rise to some doubt about how effective the discipline was, since they also excommunicate those who do hold such offices (whether by enlistment or conscription) and actually shed blood. Basil of Caesarea in Cappadocia (†379) reported that men whose hands were stained by blood should abstain from the eucharist for three years.[24] Siricius of Rome wrote the bishops of Africa (386) that a council had decreed that anyone who enlisted after baptism could not later be accepted into the clergy, and instructed them to maintain a like discipline.[25] Innocent I of Rome (396) affirmed this same policy to a synod at Toledo.[26] The *Testament of the Lord* (probably a fifth-century church order from Syria) forbade a soldier to be baptized unless he left the service, and excommunicated anyone who enlisted.

These statutes betray a queasiness of conscience aroused by the new and militant Christian patriotism offered to Constantine and his Christian successors. This was also the period when Martin († *c.* 399), a Pannonian (Hungarian) conscript and an eager catechumen, demanded to be released from military service under Julian ("the Apostate," then Caesar, not yet Emperor) in order to serve Christ (356). He was given his dismissal and went his way to become a monk and bishop of Tours, and the first non-martyr to be honored as a saint. His comrade Victricius (†407) later left the service out of revulsion for bloodshed, and ended as archbishop of Rouen. Yet Basil of Caesarea († *c.* 379) meets a soldier on his travels and is delighted to find him a true believer. He encourages the young man to

---

22. *Egyptian Church-Order* 11.9-11.
23. *"Canons of Hippolytus,"* 13-14.
24. Basil of Caesarea, Letter 188.13.
25. Siricius of Rome, Letter to Bishops of Africa, 3, 5.2.
26. Innocent I to the Synod of Toledo, 4.

continue in the service: "You convinced me it is possible, even in the life of a soldier, to preserve the fullness of love for God."[27]

Christian patriotism would increase to the time when Theodosius would exclude non-Christians from the army (416). Eventually the only disciplinary measure to which the Church could resort to embody its now heavily compromised abhorrence of careers dedicated to armed force was the injunction against clerics bearing arms.[28]

Christian rejection of armed force

The historic records of this great shift of conscience repeatedly highlight the three moral issues that made military service repugnant to the early Christians: it required men to shed blood and to kill; under the pagan emperors it often demanded participation in idolatrous rites; and it begot a vulgar macho morality. With the advent of tolerant emperors the second problem was relieved, and with the advent of Christian emperors it was seemingly reversed, since the soldiers' religious loyalties could now seem reinforced by their imperial loyalties. In short order they came to the further sentiment that bloodshed on a Christian prince's behalf might now help impose a righteous peace on the barbarian-threatened common-wealth, and this allowed hopeful men to believe that their bloody work might now be a brave one, and indeed a pacifying one.

Now we draw near to the nub of their moral quandary. We can be guided by Paulinus of Nola (†431), whose father had held imperial status as high as Ambrose's father had. Paulinus was the biographer of Martin and Victricius, and wrote the following to a military friend who had doubts about his work:

> Do not go on loving this world and the military service that is part of it because Scripture bears witness that anyone "who chooses the world for a friend is constituted an enemy of God" (James 4:4). The man who fights with the sword is an agent of death, and whoever sheds his own blood or someone else's will have death as his wages. He will be responsible for his own death or for the crime of bringing it on another because, of necessity, the soldier in war, even though he fights for someone else rather than for himself, either meets death

27. Basil of Caesarea, Letter 106.
28. Council of Chalcedon (451), can. 7.

in defeat or attains victory through killing. One cannot be victorious except through shedding blood. For this reason the Lord says, "No one can be the slave of two masters" (Matt. 6:24), that is, both the one God and mammon, both Christ and Caesar, although Caesar himself now wants to be the servant of Christ in order that he might deserve to be ruler over certain nations. For no earthly ruler is king of the whole world. That belongs to Christ who is God because "through him all things came into being, not one thing came into being except through him (John 1–3)."[29]

What Paulinus implies here is that the forbidding aspects of a military life were not three — bloodshed, idolatry, and immorality — but the three fused into one. As that bishop of Caesarea who laid the Gospel and the sword on the table before Marinus and told him it was an either/or choice must have understood, and as Christians had generally intuited: no one had the authority to take life except the one who had authority to give it. Slaying was not understood as evil in itself: it was evil only when and because God was neither the author nor the authorizer. And since Christians soon realized that their break from Jewry was also a break from Judaea, from an ethnic or territorial commonwealth, they were relieved of ever needing to bear arms for their faith community. Throughout that early period they had acquired a new and tenacious sensibility that with or without any obligation to partake in imperial liturgies, the very acceptance of a warrant to slay was idolatry, and carried within it an inescapably corrupting force. The chief issue of immoral behavior by soldiery was not their typically bawdy and brawling disposition. It was their simple readiness to wield death. That was their lethally immoral act, and it was lethal first of all to themselves. This had already been expressed by Lactantius († c. 320), Constantine's elder contemporary:

> How can a man be just if he harms, hates, robs or kills? Those who strive to benefit their country do all of these things. . . .
> We must avoid the [gladiatorial shows] because they are a strong enticement to vice, and they have an immense capacity for corrupting souls. Rather than contributing something to a happy life they are, in fact, exceedingly harmful. For anybody who finds it pleasurable to watch a man being slain (however justly the person was condemned) has violated his own conscience as much as if he had been

29. Paulinus of Nola, Letter 25: S152-3.

a spectator and participant in a clandestine murder. The actual term used by the pagans for these events in which human blood is spilled is "games." They are so alienated from their own humanity that they believe they are playing when they take human lives. In fact, however, the perpetrators are more harmful than all those people whose blood is a source of delight to them. I ask, then, whether anyone can be just and reverent if he not only permits men who are facing imminent death and are pleading for mercy to be slain but also flogs his victims and brings death through cruel and inhuman punishments whenever he finds himself unsated by the wounds already inflicted or by the blood already spilled. . . .

Killing a human being whom God willed to be inviolable, is always wrong.[30]

Lactantius sees that what is peculiarly perilous about bloodshed — whether inflicted on criminals or on aggressors; whether commanded, perpetrated, tolerated, or enjoyed — is that it lays claim to an authority that is uniquely divine. That is both idolatrous and decisively corrupting. It is not even the killing itself, but the oath and disposition and readiness to kill. Paulinus sees that the new military justification — serving under the authority of the Christian Caesar now qualifies as serving Christ — is a deadly scam, for however the emperor's ultimate allegiance might have changed, his political motives were very much those of his pagan predecessors.

Ambrose lets slip how utterly loyalties had been switched. Commenting on the old provision in Deuteronomy that a Jew might exact usurious interest from a foreigner but never from one of his own people, he describes how little solidarity there is between Romans and foreigners:

> You can legitimately demand interest from someone whom you have every right to wish harm to and against whom you can lawfully wage war. . . . Demand interest from him whom it is no crime to kill. The man who demands interest fights, but without a weapon; he who exacts interest of an enemy, avenges himself without raising the sword. Thus, usury is legitimate wherever war is legitimate.

One might imagine at this point that Ambrose was exegeting the ancient text, and explaining what it meant to an Israelite under the Old

---

30. Lactantius, *Divine Institutes*, 6.6, 20: S62-3.

Dispensation. But he immediately defines the contemporary boundary of solidarity that divides comrade from outlaw — in his day:

> "Your brother" in this context is, first of all, everyone who shares the faith and, secondly, every Roman.[31]

Ambrose and his contemporaries could no longer hold to the original warning that the use of force, the power of the sword, was dangerous to Christians, and that it was the handle, not the blade, that was so deadly. Describing their two communities of brotherhood, Christians and Romans, Ambrose implied that his Church was a segment of the empire and there could be little doubt which of the two identities and loyalties and moralities would prevail over the other. Before long — indeed, it is already the case in some of what we have just overheard from the Constantinian period — the brotherhood would be Roman first and Christian second: because a brother is someone against whom you never take up arms, and by definition all those brothers were within the empire, not the Church. When he spoke of "the bravery which guards the fatherland in war from the barbarians" Ambrose took it for granted that Rome was the *patria*, the fatherland, which enclosed his brothers and sisters. To struggle for that empire would certainly require a different sort of bravery than the defense of that other *Patria*, named after the Father who gives all fatherhood its name.

We must note that by the time Augustine was pondering what objectives might justify the use of the sword — to repel invasion, to expand the empire, to punish and correct and deter crime, to assert rights, to repress dissident heretics — it had become clear that he and his contemporaries were allowing the empire and its officers a moral agenda they would never allow themselves as individuals. Augustine repeatedly argues that neither the soldier nor the magistrate sins by carrying out his duty, because they act under a higher authority, and the larger good of the state gives an overriding integrity to these applications of force. This was an almost complete reversal of the Gospel tradition and its centuries of development which had held, to the contrary, that there was much *malitia* in *militia*: armed service itself was an inveterate corrupter of whoever acquiesced in it.

Even those fourth-century attempts to distinguish between the military oath and actual bloodshed had stepped away from the older insight

---

31. Ambrose, *Commentary on Tobias*, 15.51.

that the first act of buckling on the sword and standing to orders was the *decisive* moment when one handed one's soul over to death, and in some respects a more ominous one than the *definitive* moment when one drew it out to slay. The church orders which enacted that distinction were trying to establish bloodshed as the inviolable holding point, the "exceptionless norm." But their gesture was impotent and self-deceptive. The young recruit Maximilian saw that once he accepted the emperor's badge and the emperor's obedience, it was all downhill to death. Death-dealing was the ultimate evil, but he would be decisively compromised long before taking down his first opponent. *Militia* was intrinsically and dynamically evil because it surrendered to death long before there was an opponent in sight. And as young Maximilian saw it, you couldn't get more *malitia* than that.

The onset of imperial toleration and then patronage changed the political fortunes of Christians in the fourth century. In return, their new and cozy deference to the emperor exposed them as never before to the imperatives of state. They had never forgotten Jesus' agreement that Caesar had a claim on their money, and Paul's dictum that "Everyone is to obey the governing authorities, because there is no authority except from God, and so whatever authorities exist have been appointed by God" (Rom. 13:1). They even accorded a divine right to their pagan overlords: "For the sake of the Lord, accept the authority of every human institution: the emperor, as the supreme authority, and the governors as commissioned by him. . . . Fear God and honour the emperor" (1 Peter 2:13-17). The empire is loyally acknowledged as God's handiwork beside the Church by the great writers: Irenaeus, Tertullian, Origen. There are admonitions to pray for the emperor, for the peaceful succession of his heir, and on behalf of his military ventures.

In the story of the martyrdom of the "Theban Legion," which is unreliable regarding fourth-century events in Switzerland but clear about fifth-century views in Rome where it was composed, we read that "These were men well-tried in the tasks of war, noble for their courage yet nobler for their faith. They gave the emperor their bravery, and their worship to Christ. Even in the army they did not neglect their Gospel duty. They rendered unto God what was God's and to Caesar what was Caesar's." When Maximian threatened them with execution for refusing to participate in the Great Persecution, they were said to have replied that they were ready to fight his enemies and criminals, but not their fellow Christians or their fellow Romans. They had fought *pro fide*, by which they meant their military oath, not their Christian faith. Now they will die with weapons in hand, without resistance, as a better thing than living guiltily.[32] On this view of things, the soldier might manage to be faithful to two parallel allegiances which would conflict only rarely.

Until the hopeful days that greeted the close of the Great Persecution, and the emergence of Constantine as their patron, the Christian attitude to the empire had been rather like their attitude toward the Old Testament. They revered and read it as God's inspired handiwork, yet their submission to it was selective (especially after their dispute with the Marcionites). They knew that the newer light of Jesus had put that provisional past into the shade. For instance, they preferred to read the accounts of Israel's divinely directed hatreds and savageries toward their enemies in an allegorical mode, insofar as those motivations and hostilities were so at odds with what Jesus stood for. So they already had another well-exercised and well-justified tradition of acknowledging a great enterprise (Israel and Judah) as God's own handiwork, while at the same time knowing it was alien: it did not direct their minds and souls. In the same mode, they had honored the state as divinely provided. But just as they always interpreted the Scriptures of Israel midrashically as under judgment of the higher law of the Gospel, so they had always warily considered the agents and laws of the empire as under judgment of that same higher law, which it was their highest privilege to have had revealed to them.[33]

The old resistance revives

In our day, perhaps more than at any time since the Constantinian embrace, there has been a renewed exploration of the theme that the service of armed force is inherently corrupt. For instance, Simone Weil, a young French Jewess deeply taken by Christian contemplation, proposed that it was not death itself that was the blackest flower of war. Those who have neither stood nor fallen in battle, but have simply taken up arms and assumed the force that their mere threat offers, invite degradation:

> Here [in death on the battlefield] we see force in its grossest and most summary form — the force that kills. How much more varied in its processes, how much more surprising in its effects is the other force, the force that does *not* kill, i.e., that does not kill just yet. It will

32. *Passio Agaunensium*, 3-9.
33. Cadoux, pp. 218ff., offers insights in this direction to which I am indebted.

surely kill, it will possibly kill, or perhaps it merely hangs, poised and ready, over the head of the creature it *can* kill, at any moment, which is to say at every moment. In whatever aspect, its effect is the same: it turns a man into a stone. From its first property (the ability to turn a human being into a thing by the simple method of killing him) flows another, quite prodigious too in its way, the ability to turn a human being into a thing while he is still alive. He is alive; he has a soul; and yet — he is a thing.[34]

Weil's commentary on the *Iliad* in the war-stricken Europe of 1940 introduces what may be one of the most sensitive studies of warfare written in our time. Her theme is not unlike that of Jesus, who warned men they would die by picking up the sword. "Force," she wrote, "is as pitiless to the man who possesses it, or thinks he does, as it is to its victims; the second it crushes, the first it intoxicates. The truth is, nobody really possesses it." It is the strong-arm man who can be most overcome by force:

> The man who is the possessor of force seems to walk through a non-resistant element; in the human substance that surrounds him nothing has the power to interpose, between the impulse and the act, the tiny interval that is reflection. Where there is no room for reflection, there is none either for justice or prudence.

The intoxication of battle creates a momentum that cannot be stopped, an exhilaration in combat that forgets its own purposes, if ever it had any.

> Thus war effaces all conceptions of purpose or goal, including even its own "war aims." It effaces the very notion of war's being brought to an end. To be outside a situation so violent as this is to find it inconceivable; to be inside it is to be unable to conceive its end. Consequently, nobody does anything to bring this end about. In the presence of an armed enemy, what hand can relinquish its weapon? The mind ought to find a way out, but the mind has lost all capacity to so much as look forward. The mind is completely absorbed in doing itself violence. Always in human life, whether war or slavery is in question, intolerable sufferings continue, as it were, by the force of their own specific gravity, and so look to the outsider as though

34. Simone Weil, *The Iliad, or the Poem of Force,* trans. Mary McCarthy (Wallingford, Pa.: Pendle Hill, 1956), pp. 4-5.

they were easy to bear; actually, they continue because they have deprived the sufferer of the resources which might have served to extricate him. . . . If the existence of an enemy has made a soul destroy in itself the thing nature put there, then the only remedy the soul can imagine is the destruction of the enemy. . . .

Such is the nature of force. Its power of converting a man into a thing is a double one, and in its application double-edged. To the same degree, though in different fashions, those who use it and those who endure it are turned to stone. This property of force achieves its maximum effectiveness during the clash of arms, in battle, when the tide of the day has turned, and everything is rushing toward a decision. It is not the planning man, the man of strategy, the man acting on the resolution taken, who wins or loses a battle; battles are fought and decided by men deprived of these faculties, men who have undergone a transformation, who have dropped either to the level of inert matter, which is pure passivity, or to the level of blind force, which is pure momentum. Herein lies the last secret of war, a secret revealed by the *Iliad* in its similes, which liken the warriors either to fire, flood, wind, wild beasts, or God knows what blind cause of disaster, or else to frightened animals, trees, water, sand, to anything in nature that is set in motion by the violence of external forces.[35]

In war, the misfortune of the victims and casualties is obvious. Weil is at pains to notice the price paid by those who win. It is the wantonness and abandon that destroy even the conqueror, she says. The very use of arms summons up a fury that quickly escapes one's original purposes. "A moderate use of force, which alone would enable man to escape being enmeshed in its machinery, would require superhuman virtue, which is as rare as dignity in weakness."[36] Moderation is possible but evaporates so easily.

The forces of rightful anger (like those of rightful sex) are fired by deep and smoldering passions. Provided these passions be absorbed into one's purposes, provided they be stabilized by temperance so that one acts from the core of one's being, wrath and indignation can find stronger voice in force and temper, just as love and fidelity can be magnified by carnal ecstasy. They are risky but humane forces. It is when they pick up

35. Weil, *The Iliad, or the Poem of Force*, pp. 13-14, 22, 23, 25-26. See also J. Glenn Gray, *The Warriors: Reflections on Men in Battle* (New York: Harcourt, Brace, 1959).
36. Gray, *The Warriors*, p. 19.

a speed of their own, when intemperance causes force and sex to arise, no longer from within the depths of the soul, but with an irrational and berserk fury (this one word describes both violence and lechery) that a person is at the mercy of his passions . . . and they are naturally merciless. Thus even the most sincere and self-sacrificing defender of an unjustly exploited neighbor must realize that if he take up arms to put down an aggressor, the arms may turn upon him if he fail to have that superhuman virtue which could allow him to survive.

One might consider the effects of simply carrying a weapon. There used to be a marked difference in bearing, for example, between a police officer in the United States and a police constable in Britain. Being unarmed, a Bobby was at all times thrown on his or her nerve and wits and muscle. Whether he chased a burglar or tried to restrain a tipsy crowd, he had to come to terms with people. But a policeman who carries a weapon, particularly an exposed weapon, expects to be able to command and subdue anyone in sight, or any crowd. With the best of intentions, one easily develops a sort of moral swagger, a feeling that one never need come to terms with an opponent. When the kinds of violence the ordinary urban police officer confronted were more savage in America than in Britain, Britain took pride in a constabulary that by being unarmed enjoyed strong popular support. They are now learning that one who constantly carries a weapon easily picks up an arrogance that is only intensified in one who is always under orders, and who might hanker after someone else over whom to enjoy mastery.

The moral hazard within the use of force may not be death or a wound inflicted, but the injury — in all directions — of having a rogue force, a passion, provoked. It is not only the violence wrought without, but the violence summoned up within. This is well put in James Goldman's *The Lion in Winter*, in an exchange between the queen and her truculent princelings:

Richard the Lionhearted
A knife. He's got a knife [refers to his brother John].

Eleanor of Aquitaine [their mother]
Of course, he has a knife. He always has a knife. We all have knives.

It is eleven eighty-three and we're barbarians. How clear we make it.

Oh, my piglets, we're the origins of war. Not history's forces nor the times nor justice nor the lack of it nor causes nor religions nor ideas nor kinds of government nor any other thing.

We are the killers; we breed war.

We carry it, like syphilis, inside.

Dead bodies rot in field and stream because the living ones are rotten.

For the love of God, can't we love one another just a little?

That's how peace begins. We have so much to love each other for. We have such possibilities, my children. We could change the world.[37]

Force without passion

There is an alternate version of violence (and of lechery) which is not openly passionate, was not much contemplated by those early Christians who saw warfare as wicked, and does not fit Augustine's alarm about the bullying appetite, or Aquinas's account of the irascible (and concupiscible) appetites run riot, or Simone Weil's hot-blooded account of intoxicating force. It is insensate, but in a sense contrary to the usual one of distracted fury. It is a violence motivated by detachment, nonchalance, impassivity. This is bloodless violence, though on one side only.

In our time Hannah Arendt was the first to draw it to public attention after the trial of Adolf Eichmann when she described what she called "the banality of evil":

> Eichmann was not Iago and not Macbeth, and nothing would have been farther from his mind than to determine with Richard III "to prove a villain." Except for an extraordinary diligence in looking out for his personal advancement, he had no motives at all. . . . He *merely*, to put the matter colloquially, *never realized what he was doing*. . . . It was sheer thoughtlessness — something by no means identical with stupidity — that predisposed him to become one of the greatest criminals of that period. And . . . if with the best will in the world one cannot extract any diabolical or demonic profundity from Eichmann, that is still far from calling it commonplace. . . . That such remoteness from reality and such thoughtlessness can wreak more havoc than all the evil instincts taken together which, perhaps, are

37. James Goldman, *The Lion in Winter* (New York: Dell, 1968), pp. 77-78.

inherent in man — that was, in fact, the lesson one could learn in Jerusalem.[38]

In a similar vein, British mystery writer Eric Ambler reported on his extensive study of murderers as background to his novels. He found they typically have persistent infantile attitudes which make their frustrations feel intolerable. Murder as a relief becomes possible because, like children, they simply take no account of those they eliminate. "One may say they kill because they do not appreciate the deprivation they inflict upon others." One killer said that he was "in a tangle" and "fed up. I wanted to start afresh." By contrast, he had no comparable sensitivity toward his victim, whom he burnt to death: "He was the sort of man no one would miss. . . . I never asked his name. There was no reason why I should do so." Ambler summarizes: "They murdered for severely practical reasons — profit, security, freedom — without feelings of guilt."[39]

To be ready to enter wholeheartedly into the violence of war in this alternative way — not passionately but impassively — a person must be prepared to shut down all normal sensitivities. Instead of unleashed fury there is a nonchalance about death and agony. One must be able to look upon global disaster and writhing suffering with placidity. Which is to say, one must not look at them at all. If the symmetry between force and sex includes this variant on both sides, one imagines that pornographic films and bathhouse sex-without-encounter would provide a telling parallel.

Upon his retirement from the U.S. Air Force in 1966 General Paul Tibbets, who had piloted the *Enola Gay*, the aircraft that dropped the atomic bomb on Hiroshima, commented: "I look back on it purely as a job I was assigned to do. We knew the effects that bomb would have when we dropped it. We looked down from the plane and we could see the havoc it was making. I don't think about the effects of it, though. If you start doing that you would go insane."[40]

Simone Weil might have said it would have restored him to sanity. On her view of it, one may have a cause to struggle for, and a sense of its

38. Hannah Arendt, *Eichmann in Jerusalem: A Report on the Banality of Evil*, revised and enlarged edition (New York: Viking [Compass], 1965), pp. 287-88.

39. Eric Ambler, *The Ability to Kill: True Tales of Bloody Murder* (New York: Mysterious Press, 1987), pp. 11-17, 96-97.

40. Mileva Ross, "A-Bomb Pilot No. 1 calls it a day," *The Sunday Express* [London], 7 August 1966, p. 7.

right worth. But in the course of conflict, both cause and perspective yield to an obstinate and blinded determination to vanquish (Augustine's old bully appetite, the *libido dominandi*), with the whys and the whats and the whos no longer in sight.

Near the close of the Vietnam War the *Wall Street Journal* appraised the moral situation among U.S. Air Force personnel operating over Cambodia:

> Perhaps it is the final irony of America's Indochina experience that a war that has consumed U.S. emotions like no other issue in decades will end (for Americans) with a long distance, button-controlled and supremely impersonal bang. . . .
>
> The B-52 crewmen who are based here seem uncannily similar to a group of American junior executives commuting from, say, Westchester to Wall Street. The bombing crews generally work eight-hour days, six days a week, commuting to war in their B-52s. They seem no more — and perhaps less — emotionally involved in their work than any young engineer or insurance agent. . . . "We're professionals," one young officer says. . . . "I don't think about what the targets are," another says. "We just fly the missions." Are the crewmen curious to know what they have hit? "Well, it would be nice if we had more bomb damage assessment, but the feed-back is kind of limited." . . . The crewmen all appear convinced that they aren't causing civilian casualties in Cambodia: "Our targets are all military targets. . . . We have absolute confidence in the accuracy of the bombing . . . so we can't be hitting villages."
>
> Do they have any particular feeling about Cambodia and the Cambodians? "It's difficult for me to worry about Phnom Penh. I've never been there. I have no personal contact."

The journalist could detect no hawks or doves among the aviators: none who worried they were about to "abandon a friend," or who worried about dropping 60,000 pounds of high explosive on "insurgents" in Cambodia. Their concern was morale, not morality: they missed their families.[41]

Meanwhile, on the home front, armed bands burst into some homes in Massachusetts and Illinois, cursed and imprisoned the families, trashed the furnishings, then left without apology or explanation. They turned out

---

41. Peter R. Kann, "U.S. Crews in Thailand View Cambodia Bombing As an Impersonal Task," *Wall Street Journal*, 6 August 1973, pp. 1, 12.

to be federal drug enforcement officers without warrants or, it turned out, reliable directions. The U.S. Office for Drug Abuse Law Enforcement explained: "Drug people are the very vermin of humanity . . . occasionally we must adopt their dress and tactics." Tom Wicker offered moral commentary in *The New York Times:*

> Well, in Vietnam, people fighting on the other side came to be known as "slopes" and "gooks" — such vermin of humanity that it was acceptable and understandable that they should be mowed down at My Lai and in countless free-fire zones, whether they were women, children, civilians, or soldiers. They were all gooks. At worst, slaughtering them was a matter of occasionally adopting their tactics. The crucial connection is that the mentality of conducting a "war on crime" has been developed here in America, and it is not much different from the mentality of conducting a "war on Communism" or a "war against aggression" in Southeast Asia. In a war, the other side is despised; in a war, anything goes. . . . At worst, this makes "us" understandable victims of righteous zeal. "We" may have committed excesses but "we" — as that exponent of law and order, Ronald Reagan, said of those involved in the Watergate excesses — "are not criminals at heart."[42]

John Le Carré's *The Spy Who Came In from the Cold* is a meditation upon the non-passionate *anomie* of espionage. The protagonist, a British agent named Leamas, has been captured by Communists in East Germany and is being interrogated by Fiedler, his captor.

> Most of all [Fiedler] asked about their philosophy.
> To Leamas that was the most difficult question of all.
> "What do you mean, a philosophy?" he replied; "we're not Marxists, we're nothing. Just people."
> "Are you Christians, then?"
> "Not many, I shouldn't think. I don't know many."
> "What makes them do it, then?" Fiedler persisted; "they must have a philosophy."
> "Why must they? Perhaps they don't know; don't even care. Not everyone has a philosophy," Leamas answered, a little helplessly.
> "Then tell me what is your philosophy?"

42. Tom Wicker, "Gooks, Slopes and Vermin," *The New York Times,* 4 May 1973.

"Oh for Christ's sake," Leamas snapped, and they walked on in silence for a while. But Fiedler was not to be put off.

"If they do not know what they want, how can they be so certain they are right?"

"Who the hell said they were?" Leamas replied irritably.

"But what is the justification then? What is it? For us it is easy, as I said to you last night. The Abteilung and organisations like it are the natural extension of the Party's arm. They are the vanguard of the fight for Peace and Progress. They are to the party what the party is to socialism: they *are* the vanguard. Stalin said so" — he smiled dryly, "it is not fashionable to quote Stalin — but he said once 'half a million liquidated is a statistic, and one man killed in a traffic accident is a national tragedy.' He was laughing, you see, at the bourgeois sensitivities of the mass. He was a great cynic. But what he meant is still true: a movement which protects itself against counter-revolution can hardly stop at the exploitation — or the elimination, Leamas — of a few individuals. It is all one, we have never pretended to be wholly just in the process of rationalising society. Some Roman said it, didn't he, in the Christian Bible — it is expedient that one man should die for the benefit of many."

"I expect so," said Leamas wearily.

"Then what do you think? What is your philosophy?"

"I just think the whole lot of you are bastards," said Leamas savagely.

Fiedler nodded, "That is a viewpoint I understand. It is primitive, negative, and very stupid — but it is a viewpoint, it exists. But what about the rest of the Circus?"

"I don't know. How should I know?"

"Have you never discussed philosophy with them?"

"No. We're not Germans." He hesitated, then added vaguely: "I suppose they don't like Communism."

"And that justifies, for instance, the taking of human life? That justifies the bomb in the crowded restaurant; that justifies your write-off rate of agents — all that?"

Leamas shrugged. "I suppose so."

"You see, for us it does." Fiedler continued, "I myself would have put a bomb in a restaurant if it brought us further along the road. Afterwards I would draw the balance — so many women, so many children; and so far along the road. But Christians — and yours is a Christian society — Christians may not draw the balance."

"Why not? They've got to defend themselves, haven't they?

"But they believe in the sanctity of human life. They believe every man has a soul which can be saved. They believe in sacrifice."

"I don't know. I don't much care," Leamas added. "Stalin didn't either, did he?"

Fiedler smiled. "I like the English," he said, almost to himself; "my father did too. He was very fond of the English."[43]

Perhaps even more clearly than the soldier, the spy becomes an operative within the uninhibited struggle between nations. Blake Ehrlich writes:

> In the world which the spy inhabits, there is no such thing as a friendly nation. In the main, the world of nations is a pagan world, expressing no ethic except that of individual survival. It is dark and cold out there, and nothing grows save suspicion and fear. . . .
>
> A voluntary exile from the organized body of society, the spy is supposed to divest himself of every tenet of the ethic except loyalty. This loyalty is not really an expression of any moral obligation, however; it is merely, like expendability, one of the terms of employment.
>
> What would be a foul, heartless deed for anyone else could be a matter for congratulation in a spy. Unfair, indecent, immoral? These are words for propagandists, for people inside a society. In the frozen void, the dark side of international politics, they are not words with meaning, words such as *gun* or *document* or *orders*.
>
> "The work of an intelligence service . . . is an obscure, ungrateful work; it is composed of the sum of tasks which have about them nothing of the romantic, the amusing or the comfortable. . . .
>
> "It demands an effacement of personality, a modesty and a spirit of sacrifice of which few men are capable, and of which even fewer men are capable for long."[44]

The public conscience has usually been roused about the questionable morality of warfare whenever a new and more sanguinary weapon was introduced and denounced as hideously inhumane, and immoral. One

---

43. John Le Carré, *The Spy Who Came In from the Cold* (London: Victor Gollancz, 1963), ch. 13.

44. Blake Ehrlich, *Resistance: France 1940-45* (New York: New American Library [Signet Books], 1966), pp. 106-7. He quotes from Col. Georges Groussard, *Service secret* (Paris, 1964).

thinks of the crossbow, and of poison gas, and of land-mines, and of Mutually Assured Destruction. But force can arm itself more and more quietly and demurely, too. Texas introduced a new method of execution — lethal injection — in order to dissociate it from the visible violence of the traditional methods: electrocution, hanging, gas, and the firing squad. *Plus c'est la même chose.*

Military strategists took some pride in a very successful maneuver used during the Gulf War. They sent in a phalanx of tanks fitted with plough blades at top speed, sideways from the flank over a ten-mile array of trenches, burying hundreds of Iraqi soldiers alive. Despite its "cleaner" feel, the move aroused strong moral concern. An American colonel, probably not meditating on the irony of his ploughshares having been beaten into swords, commented: "People somehow have the notion that burying guys alive is nastier than blowing them up with hand grenades or sticking them in the gut with bayonets. Well, it's not."[45]

In the ordinary passion of armed conflict public sentiment is aroused through propaganda to support the animosity of those doing the actual fighting, killing, and dying. When, in the midst of the conflict, the spell breaks, and the enemy is encountered as a sympathetic fellow human — still more, as a brother or sister — then the entire undertaking is threatened. One famous occasion for this occurred during World War I when the Germans and Allies were mired in trenches along the entire front. Despite the gas and bombardments and sapper sorties, Tommy and Jerry got to be familiar with one another over the weeks and months, heard one another's songs at night (and sometimes sang back and forth), and alarmed their respective high commands when, on Christmas Day, the opposing troops in one sector managed to play a soccer game in No Man's Land.

A Mississippi warden, despite his conviction that the death penalty was a necessary evil for the worst offenders, worked for four years with a man placed on Death Row for having shot a convenience store clerk. When he came to the prisoner for the final walk, they recited the Lord's Prayer together, embraced, and walked side-by-side to the gas chamber. Just after the cyanide pellets dropped into the sulphuric acid the convict looked up and whispered, "From one Christian to another: I love you." Throughout the ordeal, the warden kept telling himself (as Saint Ambrose or Saint Augustine might have told him) that he was an instrument of the

---

45. Eric Schmitt, "U.S. Army Buried Iraqi Soldiers Alive in Gulf War," *The New York Times*, 15 September 1991.

legal system and just doing his job. But afterward he decided that no matter how humane the state tried to make it, legalized killing was still murder. He confessed his work as a sin, and quit "corrections" work.[46]

Jesus insists that he will be assimilated to no one, least of all to one who takes up a weapon. By sustaining but not succumbing to the violence of Jews and Gentiles alike, he overpowered his aggressors. Unlike warriors who in their pell-mell fury or their bureaucratic lack of intention tend to lose all recollection of what they are about, he pursues his own purpose relentlessly. Perhaps the only man surely possessed of the "superhuman virtue" that would allow him to take up the sword without dying by it, Jesus considers the sword too dull for the conquest of human hearts, and a victory at arms too puny a success to merit his efforts. It would indeed seem that a Christian has every warrant to follow this example: to over-power people with peace rather than lose oneself in war.

The conscientious warrior

But now let the issue be considered from the other side: from the side of a Christian who takes civic citizenship seriously in its own right, and reckons that the Gospel prescription for peace through an overpowering witness to unquenchable benevolence is quite beyond what the nation can demand or even hope for from its wide medley of citizens. What is the Christian to do about those who, despite good witness and example, remain bent upon exploitation, and whose inclination to violence destroys peace and peaceful alike? Though followers of Christ may endeavor to incorporate his disdain of force into their lives, and may seek to ally like-minded comrades with their efforts, they can never look to the day when this will be a consensual conviction of the wider society. It is a stance of high integrity, intense and generous beyond anything Washington and Jefferson had in mind when they spoke of the civic virtue necessary for a peaceful republic.

We can always count on the presence of energetic and aggressive neighbors who will do their worst to victimize and oppress and destroy us. One of the services of government is to contain these people. Christians see it as the aim of the virtuous to convert the voracious, but they know

---

46. Alison Schneider, "Through an Executioner's Eyes," *The Chronicle of Higher Education*, 17 May 1996, A6, reviewing Donald A. Cabana, *Death at Midnight: The Confession of an Executioner* (Boston: Northeastern University Press, 1996).

that they will in large part fail of their aim. Meanwhile the society creates for itself a government that is founded upon coercive force.[47] A law is not simply a declaration of what the society deems ethical, but a proclamation of the terms on which coercion and retribution will be applied. Coercion admittedly never reaches down to the roots of evil; thus we speak of state agencies as merely containing victimizers, and protecting that modicum of order which allows generous citizens to apply other remedies: more potent, perhaps, but less urgent.

Some articulate Christian thinkers say that this is entirely too apologetic a stance. Jesuit James Schall writes in a realistic vein:

> There is evil in the world; we must confront it somehow in an organized way. When we withdraw from the present civil order on the grounds that it is totally corrupt, that no process of the liberal state will really work, or when we, more logically perhaps, seek to create a totally new order with none of the defects of the human reality, when, in short, we render also unto God the things that are Caesar's, we have already taken the leap into the greatest of the social confusions, we have already crossed over the great dividing line that separates this world from the next.[48]

Reinhold Niebuhr was considerably more impatient, for he saw Christ giving us pardon for sin rather than power to be healed of it.

> The good news of the Gospel is not the law that we ought to love one another. The good news of the Gospel is that there is a resource of divine mercy which is able to overcome a contradiction within our souls, which we cannot ourselves overcome. The contradiction is that, though we know we ought to love our neighbor as ourself, there is a "law in our members which wars against the law that is in our mind," so that, in fact, we love ourselves more than our neighbor. . . . Christ is the "impossible possibility." Loyalty to him means loyalty in intention, but does not actually mean the full realization of the measure of Christ. . . .
>
> The question is whether the grace of Christ is primarily a power

47. See Jacques Ellul, *Violence: Reflections from a Christian Perspective* (New York: Seabury, 1969), pp. 84-88.

48. James V. Schall[, S.J.], "Caesar as God," *Commonweal* 91, 18 (6 February 1970): 507.

of righteousness which so heals the sinful heart that henceforth it is able to fulfill the law of love; or whether it is primarily the assurance of divine mercy for a persistent sinfulness which man never overcomes completely.[49]

Niebuhr thought pacifism was a heresy aggravated by self-righteousness. In the forms familiar to him it was grounded, not on the corrupting force of force, but on the presumption that it would really transform the world. He was sure that no activist agenda would transform the world, and he was willing to settle for much less.

The peace movement engendered by U.S. hostilities in Southeast Asia displayed a frowzy moral hypocrisy that gave all pacifism a bad reputation. *Time* editor Mayo Mohs registered his contempt at the New York Moratorium March in the fall of 1969:

> Almost at once I could sense that these marchers were different. There was a fresh new hate in them, a bitterness hurled indiscriminately at the world around them. At one corner a black cop, patient but looking terribly weary, stood with his fellow officers holding back the crowd while the traffic went through. The front line of protesters was shouting the old chant "1-2-3-4 — we don't want your f---ing war"; one girl — she could not have been more that 15 — was taking particular delight in shrieking the obscene adjective [participle, actually] loudly at the cop. The word was hardly new, but her strangely misdirected rage was. It was surely not *his* war.
>
> The Viet Cong flag passed, and I knew what the kids must have been told. Some of the older Vietnamese have been fighting one enemy or another for 30 years, and their despair must be huge. But that banner was no flag of peace for me.
>
> Then came a Cuban flag, bold and bright, for a moment reminding me that once, when Castro was still in the hills, he looked like a hero to many of us. Then I remembered "*Al paredon* [To the Wall]!" and the betrayals that came before the sugar cane. But the kids could not remember — these wispy-bearded caricatures of the sainted Che.
>
> I watched four blocks of the parade pass. Panther flags. Shouts of "Off the pigs!" The Youth Against War and Fascism under a red banner emblazoned with Lenin's portrait. Maybe they had not heard

49. Reinhold Niebuhr, "Why the Christian Church Is Not Pacifist," in *Christianity and Power Politics* (New York: Scribners, 1940), pp. 2, 18.

of the early, ugly Party tyranny that broke the heart of Lenin's romantic young American follower, John Reed. Behind them came another, newer cause, something more to cloud the main issue: "Abolish all abortion laws." That's it, kids. A reverence for life.

I stood on the curb, caught on the knife edge between two unhappy worlds. Behind me was a bank window, offering joyless, useless prizes for opening an account. Across the street were the kids, ramming their way into Bryant Park. Later, the militants — the YAWFs, the Progressive Labor S.D.S. wing and others — fought their way onto the platform and kept off speakers they did not approve of. If that was the future, it, too, would be a joyless prize.[50]

Meanwhile, in San Francisco, a pretty young radical shouted out her own considered formula for peace: "You don't do it by hollering peace. You got to pick up the gun."[51]

An entirely different and more credible argument for the use of armed force by the state was written by an American priest who spent his life working among the poorest Bengalis in what was once India, then East Pakistan, and after the Bengalis declared their independence from West Pakistan in 1971, Bangladesh. Both sectors of the former nation, split off from either side of India at independence time, were predominantly Muslim but separated physically by 1,200 miles, and culturally by ethnicity and language. After the East drew off on its own the Pakistani Army, dominated by the West, poured into unarmed Bengal on a punitive mission, and was finally neutralized only by the intervention of the Indian Army. This is the letter that Father Edmund Goedert, C.S.C., wrote home:

All I got for Christmas was my life — a gift from Mrs. Gandhi. We endured eight months of terror while the nations of the world did nothing. Finally India came to our aid. You may question her motives but this war has saved millions of lives; and one of them was mine. For eight months the West Pakistan Army carried out a program of extermination, with orders to loot and burn and rape and kill until they had destroyed forever the courage of the Bengali people. This savagery was not against a rebel army, but against the unarmed men, women and children of Bengal. I was in the middle of it. I saw them

50. Mayo Mohs, "End of the March," *Time*, 27 April 1970, p. 27.
51. "Make War, Not Peace," ibid.

die: women and children deliberately shot by the most savage and cowardly army in modern times. I saw their homes put to the torch. I saw thousands fleeing in terror. In our instant hospital for bullet wounds only, I watched a five-year-old boy take a month to die, in pain and in fear. Every time a gun went off, he whimpered, "Mummy, will they shoot me again? Please, Mummy, don't let them shoot me again." And this is the brutality that, incredibly, the U.S. Govt. supported. Father Bill Evans was brutally murdered by the Pak Army. We hoped the U.S. Govt. would protest strongly; but he was just one more of a million human sacrifices offered on the pagan altar of State Dept. Policy.

Our agony isn't over yet. If the past is believable, the present is unbearable and the future uncertain. Our people's homes are destroyed; they are hungry; they are mourning their dead. They need massive help. But at least we no longer live in terror of the Pak Army. And the kids will be fleeing and screaming and dying, only in their sleep.[52]

Neither law nor force can establish tranquillity of the heart, nor should it be the ambition of the state to do so. But it can strive to hold victimizers sufficiently at bay to permit people to work for that further peace which neither the state nor indeed the world can give. As Niebuhr put it: "The whip of the law cannot change the heart. But thank God it can restrain the heartless until they change their mind and heart."[53] Shakespeare puts it more imperatively: "Mercy but murders, pardoning those that kill."[54]

It is important to see that this is a common good. When a man walks down Main Street on a dark night and is mugged, that may simply be a matter of his head and his pocket cash. But if matters on Main Street are at such a pass that a man is often mugged there, or likely to get mugged, then Main Street is effectively removed from public use. It then becomes a deprivation for everyone, whether or not any particular person actually braves the street and makes his assertive way from end to end with his

52. Letter circulated in January 1972 to other members of the Congregation of Holy Cross.

53. Reinhold Niebuhr, "The Montgomery Savagery," *Christianity and Crisis* (12 June 1961): 103.

54. William Shakespeare, *Romeo and Juliet* 3, 1. Speaking is the Prince of Verona, deploring the great carnage resulting from his failure to enforce the law.

head intact. What the public needs is to be able to count on their medicines being precisely measured, their drinking water uncontaminated, their basic commodities purchasable, fire protection always on duty, foreign travel protected, bank drafts honored, children unmolested, and the public thoroughfares open. Briefly, everyone needs to be able to enjoy a calculable trust in her neighbors, to know that in a minimal way she is protected from molestation. She needs to be free from consuming all her attention and temper in defending herself and her own.

These are not material values of a second order simply because they are not the goods within a person's soul. Someone with superhuman virtue, that inner peace which permits one to confront violence and survive it, to be tempered and annealed by it rather than bent or crushed by it, may well contemplate and suffer these deprivations and insecurities without letting them harm one's soul or discompose one's peace. For a person who has not so composed herself in love, but might, to live under such oppression can well pierce through the skin to the soul. Despotism can destroy both the body and the soul. If there are sacraments of grace and love, material exchanges that enliven humans' hearts, there are also dark sacraments of evil: material oppression and outrage that can twist and break the human person.

Wars have been fought for so many reasons, most of them ignoble. But if one would seek the cause that might most easily justify taking up arms, it would be the liberation of an oppressed people, whether from exploitative overlords or from invasive foreigners. Although people can undergo victimization of various sorts and still somehow manage to bear it, there does seem to be a breaking point, an explosive moment when suddenly people deem their own lives cheap by comparison with freedom. To be sure, it is one thing to consider one's own life expendable, and quite another to call down the runaway horror of war upon nations and people. But people have deemed such monumental misery a worthwhile price to pay for freedom. As the Declaration of Independence observed:

> . . . all experience hath shown that mankind are more disposed to suffer, while evils are sufferable, than to right themselves by abolishing the forms [of government] to which they are accustomed. But when a long train of abuses and usurpations, pursuing invariably the same object, evinces a desire to reduce them under absolute despotism it is their right, it is their duty, to throw off such government and to provide new guards for their future security.

So many other peoples beside the colonial Americans have decided it right, and even dutiful, to put into jeopardy their lives, their fortunes, and their sacred honor. Admittedly, mixed with their motives have been some desire for vengeance, envy for possessions, and just anger. But the decision has justified itself on the rational conclusion that despotism destroys the life of the spirit, and so becomes a moral evil that can at least be held at bay by physical resistance.

In the ordinary course of events, force exercises more influence simply by being at the ready than by being brought into action. A police force, for instance, is far more significant for the crime it deters than for the crime it seeks to punish. So the issue of armed warfare must be pressed back to the issue of a standing armed force with dominance sufficient to restrain aggression. If one waits until the last bitter moment of abuse before acting, then it is nigh impossible to act, and the destructive force that must be unleashed has to be much more intense than had the abuse been confronted earlier.

There are, then, gentle and reasonable people who resort to armed struggle, sadly but not grudgingly, to gain or regain a freedom they consider almost as morally necessary as love. At its conclusion they visit the cemeteries with grief but without desolation, and reckon themselves and their fallen comrades as virtuous — whether or not they have reported a victory. They would consider themselves cowards and moral dwarves had they not been willing to risk the sacrifice.

Why doesn't it usually work out that way? In the midst of a geyser of sexual scandals in the U.S. military the former Secretary of the Army, himself a Vietnam veteran, explained: "We became vicious and aggressive and debased, and reveled in it, because combat was all of those things and we were surviving." Military trainers added their comments. "Basically my guys are practicing how to throw a guy down and kill him." "It's tough to bring in these young men who don't have a wealth of experience and teach them to kill and annihilate and also expect to be able to teach them all these shades of sexual gray — you can see the friction in their faces." A former Undersecretary of Defense said, "Military life may *correctly* foster the attitudes that tend toward rape, such as aggression and single-minded self-assertion." One journalist's own observation of troops on hostile police duty was unsettling: "They were like a tribe with a terrifying and feral need for sex and violence, preferably combined." His reflection on it all was remarkable:

> In other words, at one level the military's, any military's, existence is perhaps subconsciously *predicated* on the kind of aggression

associated with rape; remove that, and you don't have an army. *This scary thought sounds like an argument for not having an army at all.*[55]

That is a ponderous thought. It spurs one's imagination to wonder why so many wars are initiated by "Defense Forces"; why so many "People's Liberation Armies" become the enforcers of dictatorship; why so many police are expected to be the chief criminals in their districts; why so many peoples who have their ancestral lands, homes, fields, and their children seized violently by overlord peoples (one thinks of the Jews, the Congolese, the Khmer Rouge) and then are led to independence by brave leaders, find the brutal habits of their oppressors vested in their new rulers. This had already been seen by William Blake:

> "Thy Father drew his sword in the North,
> With his thousands strong he marchèd forth;
> Thy Brother has arm'd himself in Steel
> To avenge the wrongs thy Children Feel.
>
> "But vain the Sword & vain the Bow,
> They never can work War's overthrow,
> The Hermit's Prayer and the Widow's tear
> Alone can free the World from fear.
>
> "For a Tear is an Intellectual Thing,
> And a Sigh is the Sword of an Angel King,
> And the bitter groan of the Martyr's woe
> Is an arrow from the Almightie's Bow.
>
> "The hand of Vengeance found the Bed
> To which the Purple Tyrant fled;
> The iron hand crush'd the Tyrant's head
> And became a Tyrant in his stead."[56]

55. Richard Rayner, "The Warrior Besieged," *New York Times Sunday Magazine*, 22 June 1997, pp. 25ff. (emphasis added).
56. William Blake, "The Grey Monk."

Hubris

As one meditates upon the hubris of armed force, one must take seriously the blind momentum of struggle and the training for struggle that reduces the warrior to inert aggressivity. Americans do well to remember how this befell us in the immoderately swift decision to drop the atomic bomb on Hiroshima on 6 August 1945, resulting in 100,000 deaths, followed by 40,000 in Nagasaki three days later. President Truman was given the final recommendation by his counsellors to use the weapon against the enemy only six weeks after he first learned of its existence, and the order to proceed was issued six days after the Alamogordo test explosion showed that it would work. The official rationale was as follows:

1. The necessary invasion of the Japanese mainland would incur unacceptably large Allied casualties at the hands of a fanatical land army (powerfully revealed by the kamikaze strategy) ready to die rather than accept defeat. Only the atomic bomb could avert that carnage, by forcing surrender.
2. Japan would be given another opportunity to surrender unconditionally.
3. And Japan would be warned of the destructive power of this new weapon that would be used if surrender were refused.
4. The President had been assisted in his decision by the combined counsel of the scientists, military commanders, and statesmen involved.
5. The target was stipulated to be one of strategic military importance, not a large population center.

The facts, however, were all different.

1. It had already been arranged that the Soviet Union would declare war on 8 August, and its massive land offensive in Manchuria would have greatly reduced the ability of the Japanese Army to resist a homeland invasion. The U.S. Strategic Bombing Survey later judged that even without Russian participation, or the bomb, or the contemplated invasion, Japan would have surrendered.

2. The United States concealed its readiness to accept a conditional surrender (assuring the preservation of the imperial dynasty), which Japan was already prepared to offer. The Potsdam Declaration by the Allies, threatening "prompt and utter destruction" if unconditional surrender were not forthcoming, was issued on 26 July, two days after the Strategic

Air Forces had already been directed to proceed with the bombing as soon as possible after 3 August.

3. The President accepted his advisors' recommendation that the bomb be dropped "without specific warning."

4. A petition from hundreds of the scientists in the Manhattan Project, expressing their moral and political misgivings over the use of the bomb without convincing warnings, or an effective demonstration, or a realistic opportunity to surrender, was forwarded to the President but intercepted by General Groves, the director of the Project. Groves later explained that many of the scientists were Jewish refugees from Hitler, and after his demise "they apparently found themselves unable to generate the same degree of enthusiasm for destroying Japan's military power."

Admiral William D. Leahy, Roosevelt's and Truman's most experienced military advisor, deplored the bomb as the moral equivalent of bacteriological warfare and poison gas:

> Wars cannot be won by destroying women and children. . . . These new concepts of "total war" are basically distasteful to the soldier and sailor of my generation. Employment of the atomic bomb in war will take us back in cruelty to the days of Genghis Khan. It will be a form of pillage and rape of a society, whereas in the Dark Ages it was a result of individual greed and vandalism. These new and terrible instruments of uncivilized warfare represent a modern type of barbarism not worthy of a Christian man.

5. Henry Stimson, Secretary of War throughout the war, publicly justified the decision soon after the war. A million casualties were expected from an invasion, he said, and the consequent decision was to bomb "military objectives as far as possible." No mention of the scheduled Russian offensive was made. McGeorge Bundy, who later aided Stimson with his memoirs, shows how his military subordinates had effectively sidelined the Secretary from their strategic decision-making, and what resulted:

> For thirty years Stimson had been a champion of international law and morality. As soldier and Cabinet officer he had repeatedly argued that war itself must be restrained within the bounds of humanity. As recently as June 1 he had sternly questioned his Air Forces leader, wanting to know whether the apparently indiscriminate bombings of Tokyo were absolutely necessary. [The first of these

carpet-bombing raids on the civilian population had killed more people than died at Hiroshima.] Perhaps, as he later said, he was misled by the constant talk of "precision bombing," but he had believed that even air power could be limited in its use by the old concept of "legitimate military targets." Now in the conflagration bombings by massed B-29s he was permitting a kind of total war he had always hated, and in recommending the use of the atomic bomb he was implicitly confessing that there could be no significant limits to the horror of modern war. The decision was not difficult, in 1945, for peace with victory was a prize that outweighed the payment demanded.

Payment by whom? As part of his own final justification Stimson observed that by destroying the civilians in Hiroshima and Nagasaki the United States had halted those deplorable fire raids on the civilians in Tokyo, Nagoya, and Osaka. Along with Admiral King, he appears to have been one of the few in our military apparatus who did deplore them. It was a pathetic *apologia* for the Secretary of War to explain how the civilian extermination in Hiroshima and Nagasaki now gave the Americans a justification for discontinuing the civilian extermination in Tokyo. He explained — or hoped that he explained:

> The face of war is the face of death; death is an inevitable part of every order that a wartime leader gives. The decision to use the atomic bomb was a decision that brought death to over a hundred thousand Japanese. No explanation can change that fact and I do not wish to gloss it over. But this deliberate, premeditated destruction was our least abhorrent choice.

President Truman explained that "the first atomic bomb was dropped on Hiroshima, a military base. That was because we wished in the first instance to avoid, in so far as possible, the killing of civilians." But the official Bombing Survey Report stated that both target cities were chosen "because of their concentration of activities and population."

A Japanese statesman later recalled that when the Emperor reacted to the liquidation of Hiroshima by saying defense was no longer possible and an immediate peace should be sought without haggling, "the Army, as ever, was a stranger to common sense. . . . They were, as ever, riding on a hot steed headlong to destruction." This would serve just as well to describe the military attitudes in Washington, where the consideration of alternatives, surrender terms, warning, consultation, and targeting were all so hustled and hasty as to lack all due sincerity. General Groves said that President Truman "was like a little boy on a toboggan" with no real opportunity to make a decision, and General Groves had had more than a little to do with his headlong inability to stop.[57]

This brief review of the most devastating single military strategy in history is a parable that helps us better to understand Simone Weil's description of the wantonness and abandon and fury produced by war. It also illuminates her conclusion that "a moderate use of force, which alone would enable man to escape being enmeshed in its machinery, would require superhuman virtue, which is as rare as dignity in weakness."

Dorothy Day, writing immediately afterward, may have had the best last word on the bomb:

> Mr. Truman was jubilant. . . . He went from table to table on the cruiser which was bringing him home from the Big Three Conference, telling the good news; "jubilant" the newspapers said. *Jubilate Deo.* We have killed 318,000 Japanese. That is, we hope we have killed them. . . . The effect is hoped for, not known. It is to be hoped that they are vaporized, our Japanese brothers, scattered, men, women, and babies, to the four winds, over the seven seas. . . .
>
> "We have spent two billion on the greatest scientific gamble in history and won," said President Truman jubilantly. ("UNRRA . . . will open its third council session tomorrow, hoping to get enough funds to carry it through the winter.") . . .
>
> Today's paper with its columns of description of the new era, the atomic era, which this colossal slaughter of the innocents has ushered in, is filled with stories covering every conceivable phase of the new discovery. . . . In the forefront of the town of Oak Ridge, Tennessee, is a chapel, a large, comfortable-looking chapel benignly settled beside the plant. And the scientists making the first tests in the desert prayed, one newspaper account said. Yes, God is still in the picture. God is not mocked. . . . Our Lord Himself has already pronounced judgment on the atomic bomb. When James and John (John the beloved) wished to call down fire from heaven on their enemies, Jesus said: "You know not of what Spirit you are. The Son of Man came

---

57. The primary sources for this account are all collected in *Hiroshima: The Decision to Use the A-Bomb,* ed. Edwin Fogelman (New York: Charles Scribner's Sons, 1964).

not to destroy souls but to save." He said also, "Inasmuch as ye have done it to the least of these My brethren, ye have done it unto me."[58]

Warfare is only one of so many human enterprises which are so dynamically capable of inciting the *libido dominandi* or one of its libidinal companions. If the Hiroshima massacre was enacted by men already snared in the undertow of anger and fear, to the point where they lacked the superhuman virtue required for moral survival, then surely the *decisive* season when they resolved what kind of men would make this *definitive* judgment in 1945 might have begun as far back as when Admiral Leahy (born 1875) was being taught not to make war by killing women and children. As Fiedler told Leamas, "Christians may not draw the balance"; they may not be Situationists or Proportionalists. And when they believe they must, and end up making their "least abhorrent choice," they seem long since to have died.

Choosing life, making peace

What we have seen yields three sobering lessons.

First: What is our primary community of moral discourse and fellowship? The earliest Christians who lived subject to the Roman Empire (and it is they who have left us a documented past) were quite clear that they were aliens. Many were citizens, some were gentry, some even of the nobility, but their initiation into Christ made them table-fellows with slaves and commoners of the poorest sort, and drew them into a community of belief and worship and practice that guaranteed a perspective as divorced from their surrounding and governing culture as that of a Lubavitcher rabbi is from that of a Calvin Klein commercial. They did not apparently draw attention physically to themselves, but their understanding of God, marriage, death, sacrifice, ethnicity, and honor made them a people apart. Whatever their respective zones of socioeconomic comfort or their sociopolitical influence, the occasional persecutions and the memory of those past were sobering reminders that they enjoyed a provisional and revocable membership in that civic world. As already mentioned, their acceptance of the Jewish Scriptures in their canon prepared them to understand what it was to treat a reality as divinely provided, yet not on a par

---

58. *By Little and By Little: The Selected Writings of Dorothy Day*, ed. Robert Ellsberg (New York: Alfred A. Knopf, 1983), pp. 166-70. I owe this reference to my confrere, Michael Baxter, C.S.C.

with their latter-day Christian insights and commitments. They could pray for the emperor the way they prayed for the crops and against the plague, but not the way they would pray for the coming of the Kingdom.

The Roman legions and their work were triply repugnant to these Christians: they claimed the emperor's warrant to have power over life and death, a power which these folks could not believe had been delegated by him who was the Giver and the Reclaimer of all life; to make the arrogance more explicit, they expected their warriors to worship these emperors and their idolatrous gods; and the arbitrary exercise of this much force invariably corrupted the manners and morals of the soldiery. With the coming of Constantine and his eventual baptism this compounded sense of moral estrangement cracked, and Christians imagined that a military under Christian command and purposes had, as it were, been relocated from the Old Testament to the New. The old repugnance to the work of the sword was thrown into confusion, and only the sacramental sanctions on actual killing, or on participation by clergy, remained to express the older sentiment that this was no place for a Christian to be: at the violent mercy of a sovereign's not-very-Christian imperatives.

In 430 the co-regnant Emperors Theodosius and Valentinian declared (in their writ convening the Council of Ephesus):

> The integrity of our commonwealth depends upon religious fidelity to God. Each is closely related to the other: they are inseparable, and when either thrives the other advances. Thus religion yields honest hehavior, and the public welfare benefits from both. Since God has appointed us to govern, we have a stake in both the religious and the civic behavior of our subjects: we serve as mediators between Providence and our people and zealously protect their twofold welfare. We act as God's servants in fostering the common good, and we marshal our subjects to assure that they are devout in their belief, and lead their lives as devout belief requires.[59]

Since then there have been various Christian attempts to clothe government in the divine prerogatives: the Carolingian Holy Roman Em-

---

59. Letter of Theodosius II and Valentinian III on convocation of the Council of Ephesus (430) in *Sacrorum Conciliorum Nova et Amplissima Collectio,* ed. Johannes Dominicus Mansi (Florence: Antonio Zatta, 1760 & 1761), 4:1111-14; 5:531-32; *Acta Conciliorum Oecumenicorum,* ed. Edward Schwarz, vols. 1, 2 (Berlin & Leipzig: Walter de Gruyter, 1925-26), p. 31.

pire, the Baroque divine right of kings, and the notion of One Nation under God with liberty and justice for all. American Christians today are as befuddled as Constantinian Christians in their persisting and absurd belief that there is divine sanction for doings on the Potomac. Christians seem ready to limit their moral discourse to whatever makes sense to their civil community, and to repress any unintelligible Gospel leftovers as an awkward "sectarian" remainder.

These are the normal results of our taking the nation, or the State, as our primary community of moral discourse, instead of the Church.

Second: We are faced with two complementary callings. We are born, willy nilly, into a violent world where the strong manhandle the weak, the cunning defraud the simple, the successful trample the struggling, and overlords of many sorts — legal and outlawed, vast and mean — maintain dictatorships, sweatshops, cartels, prisons, cults, republics, and households where helpless victims are subdued to their pleasure. In this world of forced advantage there are two lethal temptations: to take an active part, and place ourselves to best advantage; or to find what shelter we can, and accept what we cannot avoid. Both of those two alternatives are what the *Didache* meant by the Way, or the Ways, of Death.

Conscientious objector or conscientious warrior

But there are two life-giving options, both of which risk death, except that this risk and death lead to eternal life. One, the way of the conscientious objector, is to have an eye for every exploitation and injustice and persecution, to find a voice to expose it all to all consciences that dare to listen and look, and to refuse utterly to manhandle anyone ourselves. The second way, that of the conscientious warrior, is like the first, though apparently its opposite: to gather courage and strength and to use counterforce to repress the violent and release their victims. The objectors forbear to engage in the use of force, and must always beware of letting their conscience rest, for violence never rests. The warriors meet unjust force with just force, and must always beware of letting their anger sweep them away.

One may refuse to have anything to do with force. There is no evil abroad in the world that is not exceeded by the force-turned-violent that is so riskily applied as remedy. By taking up arms against the tyrant or the criminal one so readily succumbs to the criminal's worst threat: one agrees to become as the tyrant or the criminal is. No sufficiently radical change is made in human affairs by the use of force. The only heart-deep transformation comes when people agree to renounce force and claim a greater power: to overcome the victimizer by defiantly being loving victims. One's brief life would be ill-spent if one did not have ambitions beyond survival and a fictive tranquillity of order. It is important to realize that conscientious objection is not simply the refusal to use force. It is not being a passive spectator. It is actively *objecting:* to the use of force, but firstly to the outrages that tempt good people to take up arms. It is not a safer alternative, because conscientious objection is at least as dangerous as military service.

Or one may choose to wield force. The world, one observes, is infected deeply by greed and cruelty, which can rise into a tyranny that eats out the human heart. Those who crave justice and freedom must therefore organize and hold in readiness armed forces: police within and armies without. These they must control and direct as best they can, for armed forces are capable of wreaking far more harm than good. Indeed, since the breakaway use of force has so often provoked incalculable harm, since most deprived groups that rise to power use it in their turn to deprive others, peoples must use their forces with forbearance and patience and fear. But force there must be. The goal of coercion is admittedly meager: to provide a public tranquillity wherein people may sleep without terror, eat the bread they earn, publish the truth, and preach and worship from their conscience. None of this is ultimately worthwhile without the deeper peace that grace brings, but for most people these freedoms are themselves graces that make room for all others.

The conscientious objector and the conscientious warrior stand at great variance, yet they are secret comrades. Both have chosen a pathway of service to walk upon; both are willing to follow it through danger to the death. Together they stand in almost equal opposition to the ordinary objector, who declines equally to take up arms for the abused neighbor or to suffer imprisonment or death as a witness, and to the ordinary warrior, who may perish in the fury of armed conflict. As should now be clear, it requires similarly superhuman virtue to be a truly conscientious objector or an authentically conscientious warrior, and the numbers on either side are pathetically few. Otherwise there would be more imprisonments and courts martial. Either choice must be made with deep regard for one's own moral self, and with deep disregard for one's physical self in service of one's brothers and sisters. Each should regard the gift given to those brothers and sisters as invaluable, yet incomplete. Both will be held in some public contempt, unrecognized in their respective and symmetrical heroisms. Perhaps only the one could understand and honor the other.

Third: We have seen that recourse to force, especially deadly force, has within it a deadly power to corrupt, and organized military force may have the power to corrupt absolutely. I refer, not simply to bloodshed, but to the promise to kill as ordered, which is the *decisive* act while the actual killing would be the *definitive* act within a destructive continuum. What is especially revealing in our study of the early Christian instincts on this issue was their growing conviction that to enlist in the military was sordid, desecrating. They might not have thought of armed service as an exceptionless negative norm, but would have feared it for its unavoidable, morally lethal, undertow. It would make no difference what moral convictions or inadvertence one brought to enlistment: life in the legion, in time, would surely work its way with your conscience. In that respect they left us a helpful way to understand other sinful patterns of behavior.

It might seem that the pre-Constantinian tradition has nothing to teach us about the conscientious warrior, and that the post-Constantinian tradition is not to be trusted on the subject. But the New Testament itself is full of injunctions never to ignore or neglect the cry of the poor, the cheated, the manhandled. The reason it never could be, and never was, applied to honest military or constabulary service is because under their imperial auspices these state agencies were unimaginable as sponsors of saving justice. But if imagination would be turned to the question, it should be able to appreciate that the moral requisites for courageous and evangelical service in arms were about the same as those for resistance to the predominantly ruthless use of arms.

A conscientious witness

Germany's Third Reich quickly took advantage of national patriotism to put together a Protestant *Reichskirche* and young Pastor Martin Niemöller was among some clergy who opposed the puppet bishop Hitler had installed over these "German Christians." They were called in to be lectured by the Führer, and when Niemöller professed that he had "no other object than the welfare of the Church, the State, and the German people," Hitler said brusquely: "You confine yourself to the Church. I'll take care of the German people!" Niemöller rejoined:

> *Herr Reichskanzler*, you said just now: "I will take care of the German people." But we too, as Christians and churchmen, have a responsibility towards the German people. That responsibility was

entrusted to us by God, and neither you nor anyone in this world has the power to take it from us."

Niemöller thought of Germany as a Christian country, and hence his moral constituency. Hitler thought it was *his* constituency, and he was proven right. To frame his objections for a national audience Niemöller accused Hitler in political terms of putting "the service of the community above the rights and interests of the individual." He opposed the "German Christians," for being Germans first and Christians second, yet he addressed them as Germans first and Christians second. It was after the War, which he had spent in Dachau and Ravensbrück concentration camps as Hitler's personal prisoner, that he realized his country was not Christian. "In fact we in the Christian Occident are not 'Christian' at all. Our political conceptions are not based on Christ and Christianity, but on Roman imperialism."

After World War II, when Niemöller addressed his fellow Protestants, he spoke much more forthrightly than when addressing his fellow Germans on the much more limited terms they shared. For instance, his political stand on the Cold War was a religious stand. He rose in opposition to the idea that the West should go to war with the Soviets. "I am only against the often-heard statement that a war against bolshevism is necessary to save the Christian churches and Christianity. But it is unchristian to conduct a war for the saving of the Christian church, for the Christian church does not need to be saved."

In 1933, when the Nazi repressions began, there had been 14,000 Protestant pastors and nearly as many parishes in Germany, with an enormous capacity to speak prophetically. But Niemöller said that by refusing to speak out they "had again betrayed their Lord":

> If we had then recognized that in the communists who were thrown into concentration camps, the Lord Jesus Christ himself lay imprisoned and looked for our love and help, if we had seen that at the beginning of the persecution of the Jews it was the Lord Jesus Christ in the person of the least of our human brethren who was being persecuted and beaten and killed, if we had stood by him and identified ourselves with him, I do not know whether God would not then have stood by us and whether the whole thing would not then have had to take a different course.[60]

60. Dietmar Schmidt, *Pastor Niemöller*, trans. Lawrence Wilson (Garden City, N.Y.:

I have taken this issue of armed warfare to exemplify the kind of moral decision-making that must be at once utterly personal and expansively social. Philemon — the Christian — must determine his own course, knowing that his overriding concern is to grow to the fullest human stature, ready to meet the consuming love of his Creator. For the larger turnings of the way, he will have some help and example and advice — but only some — to help him choose the road rightly. He must summon to himself considerable independence, for he must become human in a hostile world, one which will certainly not keep pace with him as he grows from birth through death to rebirth. Knowing well that he can never transform enough people within it, he turns the brunt of his generosity on his neighbors, reaching wider and wider from Onesimus outward, in increasingly sensitive and costly concern, reaching out with his sympathy and his substance to those who crave his service. He will come to have an ethic that is both personal and social, and driven by unmanageable imperatives.

At the end, which is never the end, he will wring his hands and admit that he is but an unprofitable servant. But in the end he knows he is welcome in the kingdom.

Doubleday, 1959), pp. 92-95, 170-75; James Bentley, *Martin Niemöller, 1892-1984* (New York: Free Press, 1984), pp. 164-67, 208-9; Clarissa Start Davidson, *God's Man: The Story of Pastor Niemöller* (New York: Ives Washburn, 1959), pp. 146-48, 180-81, 190-91.

A Distinctive Worship

CHAPTER NINE

When a Gesture Isn't Only a Gesture: The Good of Ritual

The Christian vision is of a Father whose relentless love revealed in Jesus elicits a similarly relentless love from his children: a love engendered and embodied in their service of one another. It might seem that in such a belief system, the stress upon moral action and forbearance would derogate from any serious attention to ritual. If the real business of growth from selfishness into love is the outcome of selfless service, then worship would easily appear as a distraction, a diversion, and possibly a delusion. Yet it is not so. The mind and imagination and conscience of Philemon — and of any Christian — are stung precisely by the devout accomplishment of ritual. What is unfortunately so prone to routine should be, and rightly is, the believer's antidote to routine.

The Gospels do report a hesitancy on the part of Jesus toward his people's worship. He was known to be meticulous about the fulfillment of temple obligations. Yet when his companions newly come to town were ogling at the extravagant new sanctuary, he pooh-poohed the temple, suggesting that many of those attending it to offer sacrifice made a farce of the place by harboring hate in their hearts; anyway, it would be torn down far more swiftly than it had been built. It was common knowledge that Jesus prayed a great deal; in fact, he frequently annoyed his disciples by disappearing into the countryside on just those exciting occasions when they had managed to draw a decent crowd to listen to him. Yet when he talked about prayer his forehead furrowed and there was a note of caution. Be wary of prayer, he warned . . . many people pray with their eye on the crowd. Jesus gave alms; one of the designated tasks within his close group was to hold the common purse and look after beggars and the destitute in the name of them all. When he spoke of almsgiving, however, he had sharp criticism for philanthropists who extended their hand only before an appreciative audience. Regarding the priests, he encouraged his people to do their duty by them in all correct observance; as for their personal worth, he spoke of it mostly with frowns and complaint. He frequented the synagogues, but was on the outs with the scribes who taught under their auspices.

Jesus was a regular and devout participant in all the customary worship activities of his people. Yet he constantly warns his followers about what a sham worship can be. Why so? One reason is fairly obvious, then and now: worship, though directed toward God, is done in the company of one's fellow humans. Hence a temptation to play to the gallery.

Hypocrisy is recognized and feared in most churches as the great spoiler of worship. But there is another interpretation of cult which is well received within most religious traditions, though it runs clean athwart the purpose and policies of Jesus. It is this: Worship is seen as a submission to the service of God, as the chief means of reconciling believers and their Lord. It is at worship that humans meet God, appeal to him, have explicit and articulate interchange with him, have their offenses lifted, and make their peace with him. Worship is the occasion to turn aside from human affairs, and to treat directly with the Lord.

One cannot deny that this view would be at home in many Christian assemblies. But it conflicts with insights from the Gospel elaborated earlier in this book. If Jesus reveals a Father whose acceptance of us is perpetual, we need no ceremonies to draw him to us, to atone, to merit his good pleasure. And if we grow to be able to receive and respond to God's love by costly service of our neighbor — especially our needy neighbor — then no prayers or rites could take the place of this service.

There are two common misunderstandings about ritual. It has been a recurring temptation for Christians to consider moral behavior as a means of changing God: by proper comportment one would win the divine favor. The same temptation is endemic to worship: people would use ritual or prayer to turn God's head, to wear him down, to abate his wrath. One would thereby effectively disbelieve what Christians must believe: that the Father can't help loving us. The second misunderstanding is that the disciplined and energetic moral conduct whereby one grows to be a loving man or woman could somehow be replaced by worship. It is this twofold twist — that worship can manipulate God, and that it can redeem sinful behavior — which makes for magic.

Worship seems to be the target of chronic complaint — primarily, perhaps, because so much worship is unworthy. In church one hears prayer sung and bawled with words which, if one fastened one's attention on them with much care, would be embarrassingly insipid. Prayers are too often uttered in a style that suggests a flat EEG. Among all genres of human discourse, perhaps no other is regularly less intelligent or communicative than the sermon. Novelist J. F. Powers writes, "I have suffered all my adult life from something I can only describe as My Sunday Sickness. This is what comes from listening intently during the sermon. Sleepers and the Indifferent Awake are never afflicted, and that they are dead or indifferent to the preacher is no test of their faith: it could be a testament to their wisdom."[1] It is not clear how much the faith of Christian congregations has suffered from all this flaccid exhortation. Perhaps most of them, either unwittingly or as an instinctive gesture of self-protection, have suspended belief upon entering the church. Or, worse yet, while at their public prayers they may be in the habit of protectively shutting down those faculties of mind and spirit where belief resides.

No less incredible, though more appetizing, is the recently developed preaching in the mega-church. This more carefully crafted oratory, with halogen-highlighted glitz and hairspray halo and monster TV monitors above the palms, lifts the mind and heart to Las Vegas, in a liturgy that finds its climax, not in the sharing of the Lord's Supper, but in the sharing of the collection. In this worship environment the life-signs are in crescendo, not coma, all rising to a jubilant banality.

Superficiality and humbuggery we shall always have with us, but there is, I would argue, a further cause of our chronic disaffection which may entail more snarled theology than atrocious performance. The foolish objection one hears is that worship is "ritual." "Ritual" is in this context a dirty word, a slur, like "ceremony," "rite," "formality," "observance." The implication is that even if intelligibly and devoutly undertaken, it cannot escape a certain intrinsic impotence. My purpose in discussing it further is not to inquire into how worship can go bad, leaving this to the ample evidence available to every worshipping reader. I would rather pursue the point that liturgy is of highest consequence precisely because it *is* ritual. And it is by ritual that we define who we are, what we live for, whom we would die for, and which loyalties dominate our lives. So there needn't be any surprise that we need highly tuned instincts about the integrity of our rituals and our worship.

Ritual would include performative gestures of many sorts. The pre-

---

1. J. F. Powers, "Short and Select," *Commonweal* 50, 17 (5 August 1949): 415.

sentation of the Belgian ambassador to Queen Elizabeth II is a ritual. So is the donning of the champion's blazer at the end of the Masters Tournament in Augusta. Thomas and Mary's wedding last Saturday was ritual, as was its sexual consummation — though maybe not, if it happened a hundred Saturdays before. The burial of a soldier's remains recently unearthed at Gettysburg, attended by two Civil War widows — one each from the Union and the Confederacy — was a ritual. Since each Ottoman Sultan begat scores of sons in his harem, and left most of them behind when he died, the heir who succeeded him would relieve the Sublime Porte of instability by immediately ordering all his brothers and half-brothers removed as possible rivals, but they were eliminated with requisite dignity: each was strangled with a scarlet silken cord. This too was ritual. So too were so many handshakes: between the Rangers and the Maple Leafs in the courtesy line after their match with the Stanley Cup in the balance; between Yasir Arafat and Yitzhak Rabin; between Monica Seles and Martina Navratilova; between Herbert von Karajan and his concertmaster; and between President Reagan and the returning U.S. hostages from Teheran.

The question then arises: Do rituals *do* anything? It is easily seen that they *show what is done;* but are they then only the shadow cast by the substance? A shadow, though long, is still but a shadow. Does anything transpire in a ritual?

The national flag: an item of ritual power

Take, for example, the flag of the United States, a ritual artifact that incites all manner of ritual usages. In 1956 the segregationist Georgia legislature had protested against civil rights demonstrations by inserting the Stars and Bars from the old Confederate flag into their State flag, and it was taken by blacks as the insult it was intended to be.[2] Its neighbor, Alabama, flew the Confederate flag atop its Capitol along with the Alabama flag for years, and relegated the U.S. flag to a lower mast off to the side. Segregationists were cheered in 1976 when a federal judge dismissed a black legislator's lawsuit to restore the federal flag to its place in chief, and then were bitterly confounded when George Wallace, then in his third term as Governor, put the Stars and Stripes at the top of the central staff (he had

2. William E. Schmidt, "Rebel Flag Setting Off Civil Wars," *The New York Times,* 22 April 1985.

once considered taking down both the Alabama and Confederate flags and replacing them with a black flag of mourning during the Selma March). One Alabama official grieved: "I think it's pretty shabby when you fly the flag of a defeated nation on the same pole below that of its conqueror. It's a demonstration of defeat on a pole."[3]

In the autumn of 1969, deep in the prairies of Kansas a gathering of demonstrators against American warfare in Vietnam marched from town to town for about 30 miles. The story was told me by an elderly woman, wife of a Russian who had fled the Bolsheviks and his homeland nearly 50 years earlier, and later brought his Swiss wife to find and cherish freedom in being American. They and many of their fellow marchers were Mennonites, devoted pacifists, many of whom had been interned or otherwise maltreated for their beliefs during World War II. Feeling still ran sharp against them in that part of Kansas: since so many of the males of military age in the county were Mennonites, the draft quota had to be drawn from a much smaller pool, which meant that the proportion of their neighbors sent to Vietnam was much larger than otherwise. As they marched along, the lady told me, the road was lined to left and right with onlookers, most of them antagonistic, and many of them waving — or brandishing — small American flags at the silent marchers. She noticed that the same faces would reappear: evidently some were running forward from place to place to demonstrate against the demonstrators. It was all she could do, she confessed, to keep from asking for one of the taunting flags, so that she could hold it in front of her: the flag she had come across continent and ocean to make her own.

As they trudged along an enormous bell was borne on a wagon, to toll once for each American dead thus far in the war. When it struck, she said, she imagined some young man, with a mother and family and an emptiness of grief left behind. It took only a few seconds for the echoes to reverberate away across the prairie, and then it tolled again, and again, and relentlessly again. "Each time, it struck my heart: *another* boy, *another* family, and perhaps a young wife and little ones." The ritual had its effect: those who called for the war and those who grieved for it both found their hearts rising within them as they marched to the clash of symbols. And as for the bell: everyone there *knew* there had been 38,000 Americans dead, but somehow that pierced the heart when the bell struck those many, many times.

3. Ray Jenkins, "U.S. Flag back at Alabama Capitol," *New York Times,* 14 October 1976; cf. ibid., 15 February 1976, p. 47.

When a group of demonstrators against the Vietnam War lowered the flag in front of the Federal Reserve Bank on Wall Street, in sympathy with the students killed in their peaceable demonstration at Kent State, a team of construction workers working nearby climbed down from their scaffolds, trooped up the street, raised the flag, went back to work, saw the flag hauled down a second time, went back to their patriotic duty with an even more muscular resolve, and mounted a hardhat guard around the mast, eager for a more direct defense of the nation. In Shea Stadium, where some Mets fans had been calling for the flag to dip, a detachment of wounded soldiers and sailors in wheelchairs came out in force, and Bowie Kuhn said he thought it would be best to leave the flag alone.

Up in Scituate, Massachusetts, where people tend to be less demonstrative than in Manhattan, the selectmen of the town wrote a quiet but official letter in 1973 to tell President Nixon that they were "weary, frustrated, angry, saddened, confused and yet determined how tragic it is that human emotion is spent on war when there is so much yet to be done in the world of peace." Their local constituents, many of them fishermen, stood behind them in their urgent call for a negotiated peace. But when the selectmen voted in addition to lower the town flag as a public protest, thereby making Scituate a target for NBC, CBS, the VFW, and the American Legion, the town was torn in two. Some said it should be lowered for the boys of Scituate lost in the war; but others insisted that since the flag was the symbol for them all, it should never be brandished divisively by some against others.[4]

Desert Storm, our country's military venture in the Persian Gulf in 1991, caused millions of yellow ribbons to be worn. Author Russell Banks was at his ease with this new symbol. It meant "We would keep dinner on the stove, sheets on their beds, until our kids were brought home again. The yellow ribbons expressed loyalty to our military on an individual basis, one young man or woman at a time, and not loyalty to the whole, the coalition forces, as the Pentagon calls this armada. And certainly not loyalty to something as abstract and out of our control as Republican foreign policy in the Gulf." So thought he. But as the Storm became daily more violent the flags finally came out, and this made Banks nervous. "Flags signify a wholly different relation to the war than the yellow ribbons do. This is Us vs. Them. The flags express a Super Bowl mentality — identification with a team (in our case, the visiting

4. Bill Kovach, "Scituate, Proud of Its Historic Symbolism, Is Split by Flag Dispute," *The New York Times*, 17 January 1973.

team) instead of with the individual players. From hoping that the Republicans or God or Jimmy Carter or Jesse Jackson — anyone — would soon bring our sons and daughters home alive, we'd gone to declaring our collective desire to kick collective butt."[5] Columnist Tom Wicker thought the ribbons themselves were ominous, because even they celebrated the war as a "national rejuvenation. . . . Instead of the long national agony over the 'morality' of the war in Vietnam, Americans saw themselves this time in their chosen role — waging a crusade for the right, against a devil figure who tortured captured U.S. pilots and blighted the Persian Gulf with oil. Instead of stalemate and defeat in the jungle, television brought them an American technological triumph of smart bombs, Patriot missiles, and magnificent flying machines. Instead of ever-lengthening rows of body bags arriving from Indochina, casualties in the gulf were light and largely unseen." After the humiliation of Vietnam, here was a glorious war, a victorious war.[6]

The basketball coach at Seton Hall University thought it would be good for the team to support Desert Storm by American flag patches sewn onto their uniforms. Marco Lokar, a foreign student from Trieste, Italy (with a 3.8 grade-point average), and a reserve player, would not wear it. "From a Christian standpoint I cannot support any war, with no exception for the Persian Gulf war. I have heard many people saying the flag should be worn in support of the troops and not in support of the war. This is a foolish argument, though." He said he held governments on both sides responsible for any loss of innocent life. Lokar was booed in Madison Square Garden each time he touched the ball, and finally he was left on the bench. Threats began to come in, directed toward him and also his pregnant wife, so he took her home to Italy. The Italian media wanted him to say he protested because he was a Slovene nationalist. George Vecsey of *The New York Times* complained: "Did anybody at any one of these schools think any of this out? Or was it a willy-nilly decision to make the athletes once again fly the flag for the rest of us? Of all our institutions, college is the place where beliefs are challenged, where new information is examined. In his deeds and in his statement, Marco Lokar was the teacher rather than the student." A Catholic newspaper in New Jersey editorialized in his favor, not questioning the war but supporting his democratic right to question it.[7]

5. Russell Banks, "Red, White, Blue, Yellow," *The New York Times,* 26 February 1991.
6. Tom Wicker, "Yellow Fever," *The New York Times,* 27 February 1991.
7. Al Harvin, "College Player Quits, Citing Threats Over Flag," *The New York Times,*

A month later a fierce ruckus was raised in a small county courtroom in Queensbury, New York, where a local was being tried for illegally connecting his cable television. The judge ruled that the prosecutor could not wear a 5/16" American flag pin in his lapel when addressing the jury because it might prejudicially associate the current flush of patriotism with one side of the trial. A higher judge angrily reversed the ruling and suggested disciplinary proceedings against the defense attorney who had objected.[8]

Stories of such incidents invariably speak of "strong emotions," which is about all that could be expressed in a country where each citizen claims the right to unlimited dissent yet wants *his* dissent to be regarded with honor. The government in power, unlike any other group in the country, claims the right to raise the national flag over its policies and endeavors in the name of the entire nation, not just of the party. But when that flag goes up over any matter of moral controversy, dissenters sense themselves implicitly obliged either to slight the flag, or to brandish it defiantly. There are some issues and some moments when a failure to demonstrate publicly is an act of public submission. Americans must appreciate that the flag is an even more compelling ritual symbol in countries where the citizens cannot elect their government.

Rituals of national solidarity

When great violence has been done, it becomes important for us to declare ourselves, to take a stand — if only ritually — and claim co-responsibility or abhorrence.

While that Mennonite woman was marching in Kansas in October of 1969, a quarter-million protesters had marched in Washington. One month later they were back: "Thousands after thousands after thousands," said the *Washington Post*, gathered at the National Capital to renew their protest at the Second Moratorium.[9] In one of the most poignant rituals of the three day observance, 40,000 people were given placards bearing the name and home state of one of the fallen. From Arlington National Cemetery they

---

14 February 1991; George Vecsey, "Lokar's Last Point Was His Best," ibid., 15 February 1991; "Lessons to learn from Lara and Mario," *Catholic Star Herald* (Camden, N.J.), 22 February 1991; Ken Shulman, "A Man of Principle Pays the Price," *The New York Times*, 3 March 1991.

8. Kevin Sack, "Prosecutor Wins Right to Wear Flag Pin," *The New York Times*, 23 March 1991.

9. *Washington Post*, 16 November 1969.

slowly filed across the Potomac, past the White House, up to Union Square Park facing the Capitol. As each name-bearer passed the White House he or she would call out that name, and home, and then lay the placard in an open coffin. Each witness mourned privately. One told the rest of us what it meant for him.

Hour after hour names were called out into the night, slicing through the cold rainy air across the helmets of marines guarding their President from his people, then bouncing with just a faint, faint echo off the wet, white walls of the White House. Charles Green, Jr. . . . Robert James . . . Karl Rollins . . . echo and the drums, those ever rolling drums reminding one of the black horse prancing behind John F. Kennedy's flag-covered casket or the sounds of wailing at Martin Luther King's funeral, a hundred taps being sounded.

Raymond A. Thomas . . . Joseph Pulaski . . . and then "Philip J. Grant" . . . the name called out in a half-hoarse young woman's voice. It shook me — for I knew Philip J. Grant. He always insisted on using J. as a middle initial even though he didn't have a middle name.

The drums rolled his 30-second funeral as the young girl passed on. But in that space of time, my mind raced back to my home town, Georgetown, South Carolina, back, back when my brother, sister and I were 10, 11, and 12 and an older childless couple, Anna and Jeff Grant, had adopted this three-year-old baby boy. We called them Mrs. Anna and Mr. Jeff in accordance with local tradition. Mr. Jeff and Mrs. Anna were poor and illiterate. . . .

The last time I was home Mama told me that the Army men from Columbia, the state capital, had come to tell Mrs. Anna that Philip had stepped on a land mine in Vietnam, that he had died suddenly, without pain, and bravely.

Mama said Mrs. Anna just stood and looked as the Army men — one white, one black — told her she could fill out the papers and the government would give her $10,000.

Mama explained how Mr. Jeff was already dead two years . . . and how Mrs. Anna was so alone when Philip had gone to the war. She used to say how Philip was her "only anything."

When I went to see Mrs. Anna we sat and talked. Once in a while she would recall how we would never get his diapers straight and how Philip loved us — and she would cry, or I would.

Now here I was listening to Philip's 30-second funeral and thinking how fitting that someone should notice and remind the American

President about Philip. But he was watching a football game on television.[10]

The rite was simple, yet one young woman recounted that as she stood in the somber mortuary line for those slow-paced hours, the name in her hands slowly came to life, as a very personal young man from some town in Illinois. The longer she held him the more he quickened, until the grieving moment when she had to let him go to his death — in the coffin. Briefly a ritual had touched her at the quick: she had felt a boy die; the terror of the war had flared up in front of her.[11]

Not all shared those feelings. One man sued to prevent anyone from reading out his dead brother's name. The word went round that to dissent from the dissenters people should drive with their headlights lit during the day, and people began taking private opinion surveys on the highway.

In 1973, just as the Vietnam War was ending, a Jesuit educator explained powerfully why the national anthem was sticking in his throat:

I am an enthusiastic singer of national anthems. Possessed — I am not going to change that word — possessed of a sturdy baritone which some have found too self-indulgent but in which the more thoughtful have recognized a Cremona timbre, I have borne my gift through the heedless marketplace.

As a freshman at Holy Cross, I tried out for the glee club and was rejected. I report this fact, which my friends find hard to credit, without rancor. Others who applied at the same time, some under the impression that they were trying out for working beagles on the Myopia Hunt, were accepted. I was reduced by nameless prejudice to singing in boisterous quartets and despairing church choirs, even to competing with the bell-ringers on Beacon Hill on Christmas Eve.

My private sorrow has not burked my pleasure at joining in national anthems. I remember Coronation Day in 1953 when hundreds of well-wishers crowded Symphony Hall to watch a review of a hastily assembled company of veterans of the Queen's service parading in the beautiful slow march. Then we heard Her Majesty speaking from overseas to "my people," and responded by lifting the coffered ceiling with "God Save the Queen," and, for good measure, "The Maple Leaf Forever."

10. Clarence Funnye, ". . . Give Peace A Chance," *The Village Voice*, 20 November 1969.
11. Stanley Karnow, *Vietnam: A History* (New York: Viking, 1983), pp. 598-601.

When a Gesture Isn't Only a Gesture: The Good of Ritual

I remember Lily Pons, like a girl from Donremy on a white horse, singing the *"Marseillaise"* in Rockefeller Plaza the day Paris was liberated. I was in the new Abbey Theater for its opening in July, 1966, and sang to all the suffering and glory that had made Ireland a nation again. That was "The Soldier's Song" (rather wide-ranging for the voice, and rough terrain for the bagpipes):

Soldiers are we whose lives are pledged to Ireland;
Some have come from a land across the wave.

Indeed we had; half the audience were Americans.

I remember when Pope Paul VI made his fourteen-hour visit to New York to preach, like Paul on the Areopagus, to the General Assembly of the United Nations. It was an incredibly crowded day, climaxed with a moving liturgy in Yankee Stadium. For Catholics of the old school and the old parish, like myself, it was a time as historic as the naming of a new planet. It seemed to bring America's infinity of neighborhoods together, to make us one fold for an hour, knowing one shepherd.

When, before his departure, he had circled the stadium with arms lifted to the crowd, and the Dunwoodie Seminary choir had sung "Now Thank We All Our God," and Archbishop Sheen, announcing for television, had said with pardonable sentimentality, "Good night, sweet Prince," — then the choir did a stunning thing. They sang "The Star Spangled Banner."

It was as if they were saying thanks to the great Pope who had called the world to a higher cubit of dignity. No more feuds between the nations. No more plundering of colonies for gold and copper and oil. No more bullying the weak and enforcing honor by mallard-fleets of bombers staining the sky. "If you wish to be brothers, let the weapons fall from your hands. . . . No more war, war never again."

Peace was no longer a pedantic illusion but a future we could plan for, as a man plans security and education for his children. So the creaky old patriotic words of the song rang like a carillon, and we thought what a dawn it indeed was, and how that early light would enlarge and flood like the morning of the world. That was Oct. 4, 1965.

Oh, my country! I cannot sing your anthem now.[12]

12. Francis J. Sweeney[, S.J.,] "Now Hushed the Voice," *The New York Times,* 17 January 1973; reprinted as "Anthems," in idem, *It Will Take a Lifetime* (Boston: Charles River Books, 1980), pp. 65-66.

This was 17 January 1973, when U.S. planes were bombing Hanoi and Haiphong, and no one yet knew that within days the peace accord would be signed. For Father Sweeney the anthem had lost all relish — it was the bawdy, martial taunt of an outlaw band. To sing it then was to shout down peace.

Six months earlier everyone's imagination had been stung by the news photo of nine-year-old Phan Thi Kim Phuc, running toward the camera naked and screaming with the napalm eating her back with its fire, after an American commander had ordered South Vietnamese planes to drop napalm where the people of her village happened to be huddled. Two of her brothers had been killed and a third burned. The AP photographer, who would win the Pulitzer Prize for his picture, took the little girl to a hospital for a long period of grafting: third-degree burns had destroyed more than half the skin on her body. The pain during those 14 months was so intense that any touch made her lose consciousness. Other complications followed — asthma, migraine, and diabetes — and always the clinging background of pain. With the help of Quakers she and her husband were eventually granted asylum in Canada. Twenty-four years after her Hell she accepted an invitation by American veteran groups to visit the Vietnam Veterans Memorial for the Eleventh of November. Accompanied by a retired colonel who had been a prisoner in Vietnam, she joined him in laying a wreath of carnations, iris, and amaryllis at the wall. She had become a Baptist and hoped someday to go to a Bible college. These were her words on that occasion:

> Behind that picture of me, thousands and thousands of people, they suffered — more than me. They died. They lost parts of their bodies. Their whole lives were destroyed, and nobody took that picture. . . .
>
> God saved my life and gave me faith and hope. Even if I could talk face to face with the pilot who dropped the bombs, I would tell him, "We cannot change history, but we should try to do good things for the present and for the future to promote peace."[13]

Her tribute on that Veterans' Day was an act of ritual. It was no all-purpose gesture of mourning or melancholy. This young woman *enacted* forgiveness, in response to a plea from former enemies for recon-

13. Elaine Sciolino, "A Painful Road from Vietnam to Forgiveness," *The New York Times*, 12 November 1996.

ciliation. Their encounter — given loud resonance and representational authenticity by the Wall of the Lost, the scar tissue, the assembled military units, the flag, the flowers, and the exchange of graced words — muffled those bombs, healed that hate, and transacted a peace even beyond what the secret negotiations of Henry Kissinger and Le Duc Tho had first transacted so many years before. Rituals have been making that peace by remaking people.

A Catholic priest from Liverpool visited Rwanda soon after the first wave of fratricidal massacres of hundreds of thousands of Tutsi and Hutu people, and faulted his clerical brethren there. Pointing out that many of the bishops and priests had been deeply involved in ethnic militias and thereby in their bloodshed, he faulted them for their guilt — a ritual guilt, he called it. Their ethnic patriotism, he said, had stifled their ecclesial responsibility.

> No one from the Catholic Church, the predominant Church in Rwanda [on both sides], has ever spoken of the mass graves, the thousands of unknown graves, the pain of just not knowing whether loved ones are alive or dead. No one has led the people in a solemn Requiem or directed how the many graves in back gardens, in ditches, in every corner of the country can be held as sacred, or given direction for re-interment in sacred ground those remains which can be moved. I was the first priest to come from outside Rwanda and say to these men, "I am sorry." I was the first priest to visit the former cesspit into which the bodies of a priest's parents had been thrown, along with the bodies of 24 other people, which had now become the holy ground of a grave, and the first to come and pray at the grave he had dug himself to re-inter the remains of four of his brothers.[14]

Obviously there could be no peace, not even an overture toward peace, until the complicit clergy did their duty and led their people — their peoples — in mourning as Catholics know they must. No requiem: no rest. And in this case, the only requiem tolerable for Catholics would be one where *all* people regardless of their ethnic group would be obliged by the Church — in the name of Christ who bled for them *all* and to whom they owe a paramount loyalty — to mourn *all* the victims regardless of their ethnic group.

Consider the amnesty program in South Africa. After the white government accepted that they could no longer sustain themselves in power behind Apartheid, and the African National Congress swept into

14. Peter Morgan, "A Time to Grieve," *The* [London] *Tablet,* 28 October 1995, p. 1366.

power with free elections, they faced the pent-up rage and bitterness on the part of so many victims of violence by the rogue state. The socio-economic fabric of the country was too fragile to sustain a generation or two of hatred and reprisal. The nation was now led by Nelson Mandela, who had miraculously emerged from his decades of imprisonment as a man of peace. With his support an amnesty program was entrusted to the Truth and Reconciliation Commission, which was legally empowered to forgive any South African, white or black or "colored," who publicly and voluntarily and completely confessed and apologized for his or her crimes of violence. They were thereby freed from any further legal liability, even past convictions. One of Apartheid's most notorious hit men, Dirk Coetzee, an Afrikaner terrorist who had made a career out of assassinating ANC members on government orders, took timely advantage of the amnesty program. But the brother of a black attorney who had been dragged out of his car and stabbed 45 times joined with families of other victims determined to close down the amnesty program. "President Mandela wishes that people will forgive and forget and life goes on. But unless justice is done, it is difficult for any person to think of forgiving."[15]

This raises the obvious question: can there be any forgiveness and reconciliation on the strength of a ritual confession without reparation? It is even more complex after wrongful death, when no restorative amends are possible. But the greater question would still remain: is South Africa, as a country, capable of sustaining such a sacrificial program of forgiveness on pragmatic grounds alone — that the nation must put the past behind them? Or is such forbearance only possible in an explicitly Christian community that knows we have to forgive as Christ forgives us, which believes that forgiveness is the provocation, not the sequel, of repentance?[16] Would this make any sense except to a people who knows already that forgiving always leaves justice behind?

Rituals for the dead, and for the living

The rituals of death are enormously powerful: powerful in what is revealed, but also in what is thereby realized. Anna Quindlen caught some of this in her account of what is called an Inspector's Funeral in New York:

15. Tina Rosenberg, Editorial Notebook: "A South African Killer Goes Free," *The New York Times*, 11 August 1997.

16. See L. Gregory Jones, *Embodying Forgiveness: A Theological Analysis* (Grand Rapids: Eerdmans, 1995).

the traditional full-dress burial of a policeman killed in the line of duty, from Blessed Sacrament Church. Jerry Scarangella and his patrol partner had had 30 bullets pumped into them by a pair of gunmen in Queens, and Police Commissioner McGuire was there at the head of the police who had come from all over the region.

> Always there is the long blue line, badges and white gloves catching the sun. Always there are the patrol cars, their red lights glowing. A piper plays a thin tune that sounds like the cry of a wild bird; the men salute when the hearse comes by, and the silence is complete as the drums in their black coverings are beaten by the Emerald Society Band. Always taps splits the air. And always Mr. McGuire stands at the center of his men, with his hand over his heart and his heart in his eyes.

The dead man had left a wife and four children, the eldest only 14. He might never have been gunned down had he not changed his service schedule to be able to take his wife for her cobalt treatments.

> The only spot of color on the street was an American flag hanging from the porch of one small frame house, and the red and yellow flowers on the car ahead of the hearse. Mr. McGuire leaves the church at department funerals before the widow, so that when she finally comes out, spread on the street before her will be thousands of people wearing the uniform her husband always wore, and at their center the police brass, and at their flanks police cars and motorcycles and curious onlookers.
>
> When Mrs. Scarangella came out of the church yesterday, limp as a rag between her husband's brothers, she was at the absolute center at the top of the steps, and the Police Commissioner, straight and grim as a tin soldier, was at the absolute center at the bottom. There was nothing between them except Officer Scarangella's coffin. . . .

The Commissioner privately explained what those funerals meant to him. "You've done it before, sure, but there's a widow standing there who's never done it before. Everybody goes back to their business and all the men go back to their precincts, but there are these people who have never done this before and who never will forget."[17]

17. Anna Quindlen, "About New York: The Commissioner Attends Yet Another Funeral," *The New York Times*, 6 May 1981.

Patrolman Kenneth Nugent, another New York officer, was shot by three youths, none over 20, in the midst of a candy store hold-up. He was buried with all honors, but for him there was an unusual memorial. Hugh Curtin, his partner, submitted a request to be assigned Nugent's shield. He said his own shield had no history, but now this one did. "For 10 years we spent eight hours every day in the patrol car. It was like a marriage. In the department you know very quickly if you can make it with someone or not, and we did. I guess we'd have lasted forever." No one in the Department could recall such a request, but it was eventually approved, and that weekend Curtin took some of his eight children and the badge out to show it to Mrs. Nugent and her children. The widow remarked, "Hughie and Kennie were closer than brothers, and now Hughie is keeping me from cracking up. [The Curtins] are taking care of me." The children of the two families had talked it over, and 12-year-old Brian Nugent said: "The shield goes on working. Otherwise it would just be in a drawer somewhere."[18]

The shield goes on working. And all the thousands of police go on working, reinforced by the honor they have shown to their slain comrade, and by the honor shown to his wife and children. That same honor, they know in moments such as this (there really *are* no moments like this), is meant to be theirs. The Commissioner and the Mayor are there to embody the honor and thanks of the people of the City, and through the cameras they stand before all the citizens to bring home to them how costly was the valor that tried to protect them.

In June 1943, navigator José Holguin was the only crew member to survive the crash of a B-17 bomber in the South Pacific. Injured and frightened, he was imprisoned by the Japanese, but beside praying for his crewmates he resolved to come back some day and see that they were buried. After his retirement he returned twice to New Britain and searched the area. The wreckage was eventually found, but without human remains. Holguin persisted, exhausting his retirement savings, and 42 years after the fiery crash his mates' bones were traced to an unmarked grave in Hawaii and brought home to their families for burial. The brother of Lieutenant Herman Knott, now himself a grandfather, said at his graveside, "This man is like a missionary from God. Without him, my brother would still be lost." Holguin pinned the Distinguished Flying Cross, the Air Medal, and the Purple Heart on the flag draped over Knott's coffin, and told the mourners it was not a day of sadness, but one of

18. Lacey Fosburgh, "City Policeman Wearing Shield of Slain Partner," *The New York Times*, 24 September 1971.

appreciation. "We know where he is now. We can come and say a prayer, bring some flowers, and that is something we should be thankful for. . . . These were men I had learned to love, men I had depended on for my survival. Their skill was my insurance policy. To make it home with them still out there weighed very heavily on me." After the mourners left red carnations on his grave, his two sisters walked over and laid two carnations on their parents' graves, several rows away. They had always waited for their brother's body, the sisters said, and never had peace of mind without it.[19]

The war hero was back now: they "knew where he was now." They realized, of course, that it was not *him* there, only some of his bones. Yet there was a powerful difference for them in having that grave. Is this a ritual that evades, or one that embraces, reality?

There would seem to be much too little in the short life of an eight-year-old to make his funeral powerful, but this story tells it otherwise.

Gandhi John would have been nine years old soon. But far away in some distant, colorful fantasy of his imagination, he could not see the dull steel and rubber of a car, or if he had in that last second, would he not have simply slain it with his ray gun as he had so many other fearsome monsters who had attacked him in his world of heroes and super deeds?

Except for those painful, five hours in Children's Hospital, Gandhi often commanded the world and all its intergalactic forces: ants were his pets, the Detroit River flowed past Belle Isle so he had a place to swim, and Buck Rogers was his favorite co-pilot. How confusing it must have been for him when his parents could not tell him how the pain would soon go away; or why they could not take him in their arms and hold him and make him feel better.

The evening before he died, Gandhi John McMahon spent the night with a neighbor. They dressed in matching pajamas and pretended they were twins. On other nights, with other friends he could pretend: "You be Spider Man and I'll be Superman." "Let's be soldiers." "Let's pretend we didn't fight." "I'll be Father O'Hara and you be the altar boy and we'll have church."

Church was his long time favorite. As with any eight-year-old, a blanket could be a tent in the desert, a box could be a cave in the

19. Jane Gross, "War Hero Laid to Rest on L.I. After 42 Years," *The New York Times*, 23 April 1985.

woods, but Gandhi had a special affection for saying mass. The coffee table was his altar and he would gather up candles and plates and cups and books and offered mass with many amens and alleluias. As his mass progressed the amens and alleluias grew louder, hopefully to attract more followers but more often gaining him exile to a back bedroom. His disdainful exits left no doubts about his opinion of those sinners who could not appreciate and join his fantasy.

His death was the greatest fantasy and this time hundreds of friends, relatives, neighbors and schoolmates joined him.

They entered slowly. Before midnight his parents were alone in the surgery waiting room at Children's Hospital when the surgeon told them he had died. They wept together. Then a neighbor and co-worker came to inquire about Gandhi and stayed. Fr. Bill Cunningham was called and came. Gandhi's grandmother and his brother were told. In the early hours of Thanksgiving morning mass was said for Gandhi John around the kitchen table of his home.

Later that morning, from the real world came a few, then dozens, then hundreds of friends, neighbors and relatives who would give up the pressing reality of their day to spend a little time remembering him and consoling his parents. But they only imagined they were consoling his parents because it was they who were giving strength to the mourners who did not yet understand. George and Patsi understood. Soon they were joined by others. Planning the liturgy, the meals, the logistics, telephoning friends and relatives, going to the morgue, meeting the funeral director, choosing the gravesite, picking up people at the airport, building the coffin, keeping an all-night vigil, choosing the Scripture readings, blowing up balloons, collecting toys were all steps into Gandhi's fantasy. Each step found more persons remarking, "This is unreal," but they still joined.

Building the coffin by hand brought not only raised eyebrows at Harris Funeral Home but also cooperation. Fourteen men and women, some strangers to each other, worked off and on for 12 hours cutting, mitering, gluing, scraping, stripping, staining and finally burning his name onto the lid of the coffin. By one a.m. strangers had become friends and old acquaintances had new insights about their friends. Gandhi's fantasy was working. Twice others called St. Patrick's Center where Gandhi laid in rest and inquired if the family was too poor to afford a casket. One offered to buy one. They didn't understand.

His coffin sat on a low, wood platform between two candles in the lobby of the St. Patrick's Senior Citizen Center on Parsons Avenue.

His classmates and friends came to see him for the last time. They would lean against the coffin, with arms on the walnut molding and reach over and touch him and stroke his hair. At first, one did not look directly into the coffin when he approached it. Later, alone, he went back and stood silently looking down on his "wrestling partner" and held his hand for a few seconds.

They understood. They drew their feelings on paper with crayons that Gandhi's parents had placed in an adjoining room for them. They inscribed their drawings:

"Peace be with you Gandhi. Have a happy time in heaven with GOD." Monica

"I miss you Gandhi. I no you are in heaven." Lena

"I love you Gandhi." Bridget

"Gandhi will rise." Hobson

"Eric is his brother. Gandhi is the angel."

"Gandhi was a beautiful cousin. He was taken by the Lord Jesus Christ." Monica Richeon.

They joined his fantasy.

On the day of his funeral hundreds understood and came to be with him one last time. With balloons and banners and singing "March On Down" they followed his cousins, boys and girls, who carried him into the church. They attached clusters of the balloons he loved so much to the sides of his coffin and his favorite fantasy character came to life as Fr. Michael O'Hara offered Mass for Gandhi. Lena Bright who lived in the apartment below Gandhi sang a solo of "Yes, Jesus Loves Me." As Mass ended George and Patsi and their son Eric passed out Gandhi's toys to the children in church.

At last his father told the congregation, "We were happy in his life; we should be happy in his death. The Lord giveth and the Lord taketh away. Blessed be the Lord." And it was over. When they were alone Eric told his father, "Gandhi had a race and he took a short cut. We gotta take a long time."

Under the grey skies and cold rain, a few went to the grave site and watched the coffin lowered into the concrete box. Then they shoveled dirt on top of it, and went home.[20]

But was this a fantasy, or was it a transaction?

20. Jim Stackpoole, "When a little child dies," *The Michigan Catholic* [Detroit], Special Supplement, 30 November 1979, pp. 2-5.

By contrast: rituals gone wrong

To grasp how much is at stake in strong rituals, we need to contemplate some that are disfigured, or dishonest, or deceptive.

In a small town in Louisiana a gold-and-white corrugated steel funeral home can be approached by a paved drive that brings the motorist up to a large plate-glass window, in which the open casket of the person next to be buried is on display, surmounted by a small cross fringed in blue neon light. The motorist can lean out the car window and sign the guest register on an easel. The funeral director, customarily dressed in matching white jacket, slacks and tie with a gold shirt, explains that the drive-up option was meant for working people who didn't have time to dress but wanted to offer condolences. "It's so nice to know someone cares." The ambience, he explained, had proven so attractive that groups have been asking to rent the facility for social functions. The Future Young Women of America had recently held a wine and cheese party there.[21]

Emulating Mae West's dictum that too much of a good thing can't be all that bad, a funeral director in Chicago provides a more versatile drive-up feature. Visitors first approach an outside speakerphone, and at the prompt they name the person whose body they want to see. While a digital voice instructs the driver, "You may proceed," an attendant inside flips on the lights and video camera over the desired casket (among those at the ready) and when the automobile advances slowly to the display window the driver beholds a head shot of the embalmed loved one flashed on a 25-inch screen. The logistics are generous: the picture is displayed for only three seconds, but mourners are welcome to press the repeat button: more than once, if that is their need.

The proprietor is vexed when visitors grateful for this convenience compare it approvingly to ordering fast food at a drive-through. However, he is not an entrepreneur who lacks imagination. He had already installed a shop to sell flowers and sympathy cards to visitors who arrive without evidence of their solidarity with the bereaved. Videotaping funerals was an obvious next step now in the planning stage.

> He explains that that setup can ease those sticky situations where the deceased had a wife and a girlfriend and they both want to pay their respects. "This way the girlfriend can go through the drive-

---

21. "Drive-Up Funeral Home Gaining Acceptance," *The New York Times*, 31 January 1977.

through and pay her respects in whatever name she chooses, while the wife is inside with the deceased. It happens all the time. . . .

One elderly lady left behind a number of contemporaries who could not get to her funeral service.

> About a dozen of them in wheelchairs boarded a bus to see the deceased on the drive-through. "The bus drove down on one side, then it had to back up and turn around so people on the other side could see. It was like watching a good picture on television."

A nearby sociologist, when asked for the social-science opinion on these innovations, made the statutory comment: "There has been a loosening of our communal ties. Still this is a way of putting in an appearance."[22]

When cremation is preferred to burial, there are other innovating options, one of which is having one's cinders sprinkled across the countryside of one's choice. Sweet Chariot Helicopter Services in Stone Mountain, Georgia, was reported as offering such a service anywhere within a 50-mile radius for $750. To avoid the ashes being scattered in the downwash of the rotor they are mingled with carnations "because they fall more truly and help validate the promise of pinpoint accuracy. Afterward the company will provide an aerial photograph and a 'burial certificate' with date, time, and the longitude and latitude of the place." Not all states allow this expression of mortuary devotion. California banned the practice because of alleged abuses. The director of the California Cemetery Board explained: "There's a problem when you're out at some picnic in Yosemite and the ashes of somebody's uncle Charlie come floating down on you."

Still, Sweet Chariot was signed up to swing low for a number of expectant mortals. One woman who had chosen the frequently bogeyed 16th hole of the golf course in Big Canoe as the place of her final lie told why she found it so attractive. "I'm 44 years old and have two teenage children, and the thought of their feeling they had to visit a gravesite grieves me."[23] A swift post-putt salute while playing the back nine must have been the better thought.

---

22. Isabel Wilkerson, "New Funeral Option For Those in a Rush," *The New York Times,* 23 February 1989.

23. Ronald Smothers, "To Last Resting Ground From a Long Way Up," *The New York Times,* 29 May 1990.

There is an instinctive resistance by some people to many of the recent accommodations. One Catholic priest remembers his surprise the first time he went in cortège to the cemetery and was directed, not to the grave, but to a new building for committal rites, "like an old, locomotive roundhouse. Ours was called Resurrection Chapel and, as Winston Churchill said, 'If that depicts the bliss of the resurrection, then I can face an eternal sleep with equanimity.'" They were seated on metal folding chairs around a metal, hydraulic wagon. A man came in with a clipboard, and when asked if they would be going to the grave he replied, "We don't do that anymore." The priest mused: "I admit that I began wondering just what they did do, and the first image that came to mind was the Mike Nichols and Elaine May $15.00 funeral — 'Two men come in a green pick-up, and God knows what they do.'" After the prayers the man with the clipboard adroitly pressed a taped label onto the nether side of the coffin and the wagon bore it away on its track through swinging doors and disappeared. Curious mourners risked a peek through the doors and what they beheld in the Beyond was not eternity, but some startled grave diggers eating their lunch before burying the half-dozen coffins gathered in the round.

The priest mused about the ritual adaptations this might require. He recalled the traditional graveside prayer:

> Lord Jesus Christ, by the three days you lay in the tomb you made holy the graves of all who believe in you; and even though their bodies lie in the earth they trust that they, like you, will rise again. Give our (brother/sister) peaceful rest in this grave until that day when you, the resurrection and the life, will raise (him/her) up in glory. Then may (he/she) see the light of your presence, Lord Jesus, in the kingdom where you live for ever.

He imagined the adaptation the hydraulic chariot seemed to require:

> Lord God, as you watched over and guarded the bodies of the (patriarchs/matriarchs) until they could be brought to rest in the land you had promised, so we ask you to watch over the body of our (brother/sister) as it enters upon its own unknown voyage from here to its grave. May your holy angels keep the label with the name and plot numbered from falling off; may the martyrs keep the gravediggers alert and bring them to the right grave; and may all the saints guard this body until it should be laid to rest and buried.

252

Sometime later the challenge became more real when he was asked to preside at the burial of the cremated remains of a non-religious man — a scientist and generous philanthropist — who had obtained permission to be buried with his relatives in the Catholic cemetery.

> Again we were in Resurrection Chapel — same wagon, same man, same clipboard. The little bronze box looked lost on the hydraulic wagon so we packed it through the oven doors and placed the box on a small stand. At the end of the service a sister-in-law, still quite feisty despite her eighty years, asked, "Well, when do we go to the grave?" Again, the same answer, "Oh, we don't do that anymore." "Oh yeah? I don't leave here until I see my brother-in-law's ashes in the ground." And, warming to the battle, added, "And the grass put back on top!" "But we can't do that." "YOU can't do it," she shouted, "But I can, and I'm gonna!" Within what seemed like a matter of seconds we were walking, single file, up the grassy hillside to the near-by grave — relatives, bronze box, clipboard, shovels over pin-striped shoulders, startled gravediggers running to catch up. Before long the dead man's colleagues were helping with the burial, highly polished cordovans shoving the spades into the soft soil. Soon it was over. The sod was patted back into place. And it was completed. The man's colleagues were smiling. And the sister-in-law said, "Good, we've finished. Now we can go home."[24]

What was completed, what finished? What does it matter whether a body be burnt or buried or both? And what is gained or lost when people must grieve at a distance? Or when they keep their distance and pretend to grieve?

Make-believe rituals

Consider — at an even farther remove — the alternate efforts of those who compose rituals that are purposely designed by atheists as surrogates for religious rituals. Some years back the British Humanist Association published *Funerals Without God.* The BHA staff explained: "The church has

24. David O'Rourke[, O.P.], "Into the Roundhouse and Over the Styx to Grandmother's Grave We Go," *Commonweal* 105, 18 (15 September 1978): 589-90. Inclusiveness supplied.

had a stranglehold on social ceremonies. But Britain is now essentially a secular country, so we are filling a gap. . . . Increasingly, families are getting fed up with vicars who say the same generalized earth-to-earth and dust-to-dust words for everyone, words that have nothing to do with the person who died. And people have grown up. They don't believe we are all going to fly off with little wings on our shoulders when we die." The bishop who chaired the Church of England's committee on funerals replied that the BHA clientele was a rather limited "sophisticated minority" in London. Most Britons were not atheists, he said, although they didn't go to church much. "Underneath the surface their residual faith makes them want to turn to an authorized God man at points of bereavement." He was evidently unaware that once BHA's volunteer funeral presiders began to receive the standard clerical fee their ranks doubled in less than six months.[25]

Humanists in the U.S. have had their funeral format in print for nearly half a century, in defiance of religious conformity and claptrap. Suggested musical selections make that point right off, e.g., Gluck's "Dance of the Spirits" from *Orpheus and Eurydice,* the "Londonderry Air," Wagner's "Liebestod" from *Tristan und Isolde,* and Kern's "Wandering Westward" by Mark Twain. One of the suggested meditations, to be led by a non-God man (or, more likely, a non-God woman), gives a sense of the new and heavy Humanist vitality:

> Although it is premature death that is most tragic, the final parting signified by death is bound to bring shock and sorrow whenever the ties of love and friendship are involved. Those who feel deeply will grieve deeply. No philosophy or religion ever taught can prevent this wholly natural reaction of the human heart.
>
> Whatever relationships and enterprises death breaks in upon, we can be sure that those whom we have lost are finally and eternally at peace. And whatever length of time we have had a friend, we always remain grateful for his having lived and for our having known him in the full richness of his personality.
>
> Nothing can now detract from the joy and beauty that we shared with _____; nothing can possibly affect the happiness and depth of experience that he himself knew. What has been, has been — forever. The past, with all its meaning, is sacred and secure. Our love for him

25. "London Journal: At the Secular Funeral, a Tango May Be Tasteful," *The New York Times,* 10 January 1990.

and his love for us, his family and friends, cannot be altered by time or circumstance.

We rejoice that _____ was and is a part of our lives. [We rejoice that he lives on in his beloved children and grandchildren.] His influence endures in the unending consequences flowing from his character and deeds; it endures in our own acts and thoughts. We shall remember him as a living, vital presence. That memory will bring refreshment to our hearts and strengthen us in times of trouble. These are reflections that we treasure; for there can never be too much friendship in the world, too much human warmth, too much love.[26]

Of this kind of prose, there can be too much.

More energetic was the effort in the USSR, after the first Soviet Conference on Socialist Rituals in 1964, to replace rather than repress religious rites. The traditional Easter Cake became Spring Cake; the Ten Commandments were the model for the Moral Code of the Builders of Communism, Geologists' Day and Truck Drivers' Day took their inspiration from old feasts such as those of Saint Basil and Saint George. Throughout the Republics a chain of opulent Palaces of Festive Events was constructed for such ritual celebrations as the Ceremonial Registration of the Newborn, or of the First Job (signifying entry into the working class), or of induction into the Army. "Religious ceremonies are withering away by themselves," observed the chairwoman of the Commission on the Composition and Implementation of New Rites in the Ukraine. "People needed new ceremonies to mark major occasions."

The most popular new Socialist ceremony was that of marriage. At one of these rites in Kiev, presided over by a handsome woman in a floor-length gown, fur-trimmed cape, and badge of office hung on a broad chain about her neck, the couple's entrance was accompanied by a choir in the balcony singing a Ukrainian song, "Look Upon Your Bride, Your Wish, Your Fate." The officiant stood beside an enormous white marble bust of Lenin and a handsome marble table that looked like nothing if not an altar. After her extensive instruction, the taking of rings and signing of the certificate, and six more songs climaxed by "How Broad Is My Beloved Land," the all-but-Reverend Ms. Galintsovskaya intoned: "You have given your hand to each other at a happy time, under the peaceful

26. Corliss Lamont, *A Humanist Funeral Service* (Buffalo & New York: Prometheus Books, 1954, 1977), pp. 16-17.

sky of the motherland of the Soviet People, led by the party of Lenin along the bright path to the Communist future." She concluded with an injunction "to raise children as worthy and industrious citizens of our motherland."[27]

Not entirely unrelated has been a concerted effort among mainline Protestant churches in this country to offer some liturgical celebration of divorce. A Methodist specialist in worship resources explained: "Although we had centuries-old ways of giving support at other critical moments of life, we were finding the church had nothing to offer at this very painful time." One Methodist divorce service had the minister witnessing the couple's promises to free each other from "claims and responsibilities" and from "the burden of guilt and sterile remorse." Those first efforts proved disappointingly unpopular, mostly because the liturgists couldn't climb out of their marriage rut. "The divorcing couple are expected to recite the prayers together, usually in the company of friends or relatives, as is traditional in the celebration or sanctification of many other major events in life. The problem is that such recitations require a spirit of unity that might not be possible." What they needed was some of the resourcefulness of that funeral director in Chicago who knew how to arrange for obsequies à trois. But there are few motivations more tenacious than that of a cleric to be needed: ignoring this first market-test they redoubled their efforts to find some meaningful ministry: no wedding come to grief need be a complete loss if they could somehow solemnly bless its demise.

What most troubled the divorcing couples, some ministers finally realized, was the promises that they had once solemnly vowed: "to love and cherish till death do us part." The chief witnesses to those vows, of course, had been these same ministers, so now the ministers had to find some way, "with dignity and compassion," to help the faithful be unfaithful and feel better about it. Too often their divorcing congregants felt shame and humiliation at their infidelity and withdrew from their ministers. Nothing worse than that! So the clergy redoubled their efforts to take divorce into their repertoire. As one fortunate man divorced with benefit of clergy put it, "We had started out in a church, so we felt the dissolution should be something that happened before God." The wife, whose invited children and in-laws did not attend, said it was very emotional (no higher index of sacramental success is known in this sort

27. Serge Schmemann, "New Soviet Rituals Seek to Replace Church's," *The New York Times*, 15 March 1983.

of thing) yet it gave a sense of peace. But one United Church of Christ minister (her church has taken a lead in this pastoral gambit) who took part in a promotional role-play of such a ceremony at a national conference had such a disastrous experience that she set out to devise a service designed for only one of the divorcing partners, or perhaps a group of unrelated divorcees. That would be immensely more comfortable, she explained.

A Methodist Sunday School teacher on her way out of marriage was very positive about just such a ceremony she had devised and shared with her friends. "I needed the congregation to tell me I was still O.K. because I was doing something that my upbringing had taught me was very sinful." A pair of New York ministers, one also a "mind-body therapist" (is not every sacramental minister a mind-body therapist?), marketed a $400 divorce package that included a prayer from the wedding, the ritualistic burning of a "small, meaningful item" (the marriage certificate is favored here), and "a moment when the vows are broken and the rings returned." No further ritual detail on the vow-breaking was provided. As for the rings, the National Organization for Women solicited them for their ERA drive: tokens of discarded loves for the Scarlett O'Hara Fund, in memory of Scarlett tossing hers into the collection for Confederate wounded.[28] Making a ritual virtue out of marital necessity is a true challenge for any clergy.

Catholic ventures in ritual divorce have tended to be wordy, since in a Church that ostensibly takes "for better, for worse, until death" more straightforwardly, there is more that needs to be said in a service that explicitly subverts the Catholic rite of marriage. The Paulist Center in Boston showcased such a rite (though in experimental mode only), entitled "Divided We Stand." The Mass begins with appropriate song: "All my trials, Lord, soon be over." The spoken parts ensue:

Priest: My brother and sister, John and Mary, you have come here today in the presence of this Christian community and in the presence of myself, the community's minister, to declare publicly,

---

28. *Ritual in a New Day*, in "Rites of Parting," *Newsweek*, 17 January 1977; Andree Brooks, "Finding Solace: Prayers Accepting Divorce," *The New York Times*, 31 August 1987; David Behrens, "Methodist study suggests a ritual for divorce," [Louisville] *Courier-Journal and Times*, 6 March 1977; "Celebrating Divorce," *The New York Times Sunday Magazine*, 13 May 1995, p. 9; "You can't give away memories," *Miami Herald*, 26 February 1981.

with heavy hearts, that your two lives have not grown together, that you two have not become one flesh, that your two hearts have not become as one — you have come here to declare that your marriage has ended, and you come asking God's help and the help of this community as you begin a new life apart, a new life as divorced persons.

The church will ever proclaim the ideal of permanent commitment of man and woman to one another, and the ideal of married love that lasts till death for this example of the Lord himself who laid down his life for those he loved. But the church must also recognize the harsh realities of human life and the fragility of our human nature, which often wounds the noblest of human interventions and separates the most genuine attempts at love.

To those whose marriages have ended, the church reaches out in love and understanding, following the example of the Lord, and bids those whose marriages have ended to choose life — to love again — to forgive one another — and to make a new life — no longer sharing the intense relationship of marriage, but a new life of mutual love and concern for one another.

The Christian community reaches out to you, Mary and John, at this moment of truth, this moment of painful self-examination, and offers you the healing love of Christ bidding you to reach out to each other in healing love. And so I ask you to declare your intentions before this Christian family.

Couple: I, (John/Mary), declare before all present that our marriage has come to an end. I beg forgiveness for all I have done that has wounded this relationship and I promise to love you even though we are no longer husband and wife. I ask you, my brothers and sisters, to love us and support us as we face our new life with uncertainty. Yet we pray that God will give us the gift of married love again and that he will bring to completion what he has begun in us.

Priest: I call on all here present to witness the end of this marriage and to reach out in brotherly and sisterly love to these two, our brother and sister, who have struggled so hard to find peace and happiness.

May God bless and strengthen you both. May he give you the courage to choose life and to love again. And may his blessing be upon us all.

The service was consummated by "It's Too Late, Baby" (with all lights out) and ended with "I Get By with a Little Help From My Friends."[29]

In a like spirit the Catholic Diocese of Autun in Burgundy attempted to deal with its marriage problem. Disappointed that some of the locals were content with a merely civil marriage while others preferred a church ceremony, and that there seemed to be very little difference of conviction between the two groups, the diocese began in 1978 to experiment with a new alternative: a non-sacramental rite called *mariage avec acceuil,* "invitational marriage." If in time a couple in this sort of "come-on" union were disposed to upgrade their commitment with the sacrament of matrimony, the point was clearly made that though there would be another rite, it was not considered another wedding or another marriage: just development. The Church was ostensibly trying to free a large proportion of its members from their situations of bad conscience: from the standpoint of Catholic faith those intentionally married at City Hall only were living in a state of fornication, while those married in church but without much religious conviction were living in a state of superstition. On balance, the new policy feared superstition more than fornication, but created a third, even more equivocal alternative that combined fornication with superstition.[30]

By rituals we define ourselves

What is at stake in all these tales of rituals that were authentic, or contorted, or dishonest?

Rituals — in any case, the deep rituals — are nothing we create. They are functions of communities, observances given their form and meaning and sponsorship by those communities. The most powerful rituals are acts whereby we define ourselves according to the mind of our community. At the invitation of the community and within its ambit of shared insights, they enable us to declare ourselves, align ourselves, commit ourselves, pledge ourselves. Those police officers standing in white-glove full dress at attention, eight deep on either side of the street, were repledging themselves to protect the people of their city at the hazard of their lives. That

29. " 'Divided We Stand' — 'Rite of divorce' enacted during mass," *National Catholic Reporter,* 3 November 1972, p. 17.

30. Brother Bede Hubbard, O.S.B., "French Diocese Experiments with Non-Sacramental Marriage Rite," National Catholic News Service press release, 17 February 1978.

English priest praying over the grave of Catholic Tutsi massacred by Catholic Hutu was recommitting himself as an officer of a people of higher loyalty than any ethnic people or national state. The police would probably doubt that anyone outside their fellowship could understand it fully, yet they took their stand and affirmed their commitment in public view for what the public could make of it.

Most of us belong to a variety of ritual communities: scouting, the United States Golf Association, Greenpeace, the Veterans of Foreign Wars, the Soroptimists, the National Association for the Advancement of Colored People, the Evangelical Lutheran Church in America, the Amalgamated Garment Workers Union, Friends of the Chicago Art Institute, Rotary International, the Vassar College Alumnae Association. Amid that variety there could be some conflict of perspective, conviction, and loyalty. The fellows at the VFW bar on Saturday night might have some fun with their brother who carries a Greenpeace card. The supporters of the Art Institute might have their imaginations dislodged somewhat to find an AGWU officer among their number.

But that would be mild by comparison with one person's attempt to be active in the Communist Party and the American Legion; or Planned Parenthood and Right to Life; or Hell's Angels and the Sierra Club.

Most people with serious commitments in their lives receive them, share them and nourish them in a community, and usually their involvements are integrated within some working understanding of which ones have the higher claim. Usually one community will be paramount. Others will tend to be judged by its lights — though that need not make it immune to reciprocal challenge from time to time. This is the community one is more willing to trust about elements of its shared life that may not yet be adequately understood. Usually such a community-in-chief of conviction and fidelity is also a community of ritual, and its rituals are the rituals of first instance in the lives of its communicants.

The Vassar College Alumnae Association probably disavows any ambition to serve in this primary way in any member's life-loyalties. Likewise the USGA, though wives might wonder. But ethnic groups do, and totalitarian parties do, and nations do, and churches do, and militias do, and terrorist organizations do. These are natural competitors for primacy, then, and their rituals are charged — consciously or unconsciously — with that rivalry. A paramount community does not extinguish or control other communities, but it does provide the master perspective whereby its communicants evaluate it, and the others. It is the explicator; they are the explicands.

There are many competitive strategies, and the strong players often combine them. First the Communist Party took direct control over the Russian Orthodox authorities, then it executed or imprisoned prophetic or obstinate clergy, and after that it used The Soviet Palaces of Festive Events to imitate and replace the traditional Christian rituals. The NAACP dressed in good suits and gold jewelry and rallied Negroes behind lawsuits and sit-ins and coalitions of Christian churches to achieve integration, by contrast with the Nation of Islam who dressed in quasi-military outfits, identified themselves as Blacks, rejected Christianity and coalitions with whites, and talked austere lifestyle, armed struggle, and separation. The United States at one time treated membership in the Communist Party as a federal crime, while the leftist Communists worked effectively in their necessarily conspiratorial environment to see America as the most repressive of societies. Recently the rightist militias have done the same. The priest who presided and preached at Jerry Scarangella's funeral was so engulfed in the powerful civic pageantry that he would have been a courageous man indeed to introduce any rival or dissonant Christian theme into his eucharistic rites.

In the various dynamics whereby rival claimants for paramount loyalty stake their claim on people and, consciously or unconsciously, devise their rituals so as to trump others, the two basic strategies are confrontation or cooperation. It seems clear that in the long pull the compromisers lose. The pathetic efforts to find a way to bless divorces, or to dignify legal cohabitation, or to devise an atheistic pseudo-funeral, show the Methodists, Catholics, and Humanists degrading ritual with their folly. They imagine themselves to be adapting, but they have been assimilated. If Methodists bless divorce they can no longer truthfully witness marriages. If Catholics welcome to Christian eucharist those who reject Christian matrimony, they are extinguishing a credible faith. Since the Humanist efforts to deny resurrection have outdone the Christians in banality, they may well drive people back to the churches out of taste, if not conviction.

To illustrate this need for ultimate loyalties to trump all rivals through ritual, I offer a reminiscence of Elie Wiesel:

> All of us — I wasn't the only one; when I say "I," I mean all of us — were taken away from the Yeshiva, from the Talmud, straight to Birkenau. And for three days I was in a daze, I couldn't believe what I saw. Then I awakened and I remember that immediately after, it must have been on the fourth or fifth day, I was sent to a commando

[labor team]. I have never told this story, because I consider it too personal. I was sent to a commando to carry stones. The man with whom I carried stones — I never saw his face, only his neck and I remember only his voice — the very first day he asked me, "Where do you come from?" I told him. "What do you do at home?" I said I was a *Yeshiva Bocher;* I studied. He said, "What tractate did you study?" I told him. He said, "What page?" I told him. He said, "Let's continue." I said, "Are you mad? *Here?* Without books, without anything and *why?*" He said, "We must continue. This is the only way." And believe it or not, we continued. He was a famous *Rosh Yeshiva,* the famous head of a famous Yeshiva Talmudic school in Galicia. He used to recite a passage and I would repeat it, day after day. We studied Talmud to the very end. That a man like this not only studied but also taught Talmud in Auschwitz, that is a source of wonder to me. Also the fact that he was not the only one.

There was a man who smuggled in a pair of *tefillin,* phylacteries. It cost him I don't know how many rations, portions of bread. He smuggled them in and there were at least two hundred Jews who got up every day one hour before everybody to stand in line and to perform the Mitzvah [reciting daily prayers with the leather prayer-cases strapped on the forehead and arm]. Absurd! Yes, it was absurd to put on the phylacteries. Do you know there were Jews there who fasted on Yom Kippur! There were Jews who said prayers! There were Jews who sanctified the name of Israel, of their people, simply by remaining human!

Within the system of the concentration camp, something very strange took place. The first to give in, the first to collaborate — to save their lives — were the intellectuals, the liberals, the humanists, the professors of sociology, and the like. Because suddenly their whole concept of the universe broke down. They had nothing to lean on. Very few Communists gave in. There were some, but very few. They had their own church-like organization — a secular church, but very well organized. They were the resisters. Even fewer to give in were the Catholic priests. There were very few priests who, when the chips were down, gave in and collaborated with the torturer. Yet there were exceptions. But you could not have found one single rabbi — *I dare you* — among all the *kapos* or among any of the others who held positions of power in the camps. . . .

What the Germans wanted to do to the Jewish people was to substitute themselves for the Jewish God. All the terminology, all the vocabulary testifies to that. And in spite of all, here were these men who remained human and who remained Jewish and went on praying to God.

These Jews persisted in their first loyalty, and found reinforcement in their rituals to defy the destruction of their souls.[31]

The earliest contemporary memoir of a Christian martyr also illustrates Wiesel's point. Polycarp, who as a boy had been a disciple of the old Apostle John, was still a young man when he became bishop of the church in Smyrna, where he served for more than a half-century. One day in the late winter of either 155 or 156, the crowd at the public games in Smyrna had got its blood up for more Christians to throw to the wild animals, and they began to yell: "Away with the atheists! Find Polycarp!" The Christians refused worship to the gods, and were charged with the crime of atheism. A search party located him at a local farmhouse, and he came downstairs and asked his hosts to lay a meal for the arrest party, in return for which they gave him time to pray, which he did out loud for two hours, standing in the same room with them, and confiding every single person he had ever cared for, to the Lord's care. The squad began to feel sympathy for the old man, who was venerated throughout the eastern Mediterranean. When they brought him in the police chief took him aside and, despite the frenzied impatience of the stadium crowd, argued with him. "What is the harm in simply saying, 'Caesar is God,' putting some incense on the embers, and walking away?" Polycarp refused, and was hustled into the stadium.

> [The Proconsul] tried to persuade him to disown Christ. "Have some regard for your age," he said, as they usually do, "Swear by the Fortune of Caesar, repent, and say 'Away with the atheists!'" But Polycarp took a good look at the lawless heathen in the arena, raised his arm in salute, sighed, looked up to heaven, and declared, "Away with the atheists." When the Proconsul urged him, "Take the oath

---

31. Elie Wiesel, "Talking and Writing and Keeping Silent," in *Holocaust: Religious and Philosophical Implications,* ed. John K. Roth & Michael Berenbaum (New York: Paragon House, 1989), pp. 365-66.

There are unresolved issues in Wiesel's eloquent memoir, since he himself has remained faithful to his Jewishness but only equivocally to the God whom those Jews were worshipping. Indeed, the far better known Auschwitz reminiscence we owe him is the anonymous murmur, as a young boy was being garrotted in front of the entire camp: "Where is God now?"

and I'll release you; damn Christ!" Polycarp answered, "I have been his slave for 86 years, and he has never harmed me; so how can I blaspheme my king, who saved me?"

He persisted: "Swear by the Fortune of Caesar!" Polycarp replied, "If you imagine that I will swear by Caesar's Fortune, as you put it, and keep pretending you don't know who I am, then listen clearly: I am a Christian. If you want to take instructions in Christianity, set a date and give me a hearing." The Proconsul said, "Convince the people." Polycarp replied, "You I would think a worthy interlocutor, for we have been told to honor rulers and authorities assigned by God, if they do us no harm. But I do not reckon that crowd deserves to hear my defense."

The Proconsul told him, "I have wild beasts, and if you do not repent I will have you thrown to them." "Call them, then, for we are not allowed to repent of better things in favor of worse; a proper conversion is from evil to uprightness." He tried again: "If the animals don't persuade you, I will have you burnt alive, unless you repent." But Polycarp said, "The fire you can threaten me with burns quickly and goes out. You are ignorant of the fire that is waiting for the evil in the coming judgment, to be a punishment that never burns out. But why this delay? Do what you decide."

The conversation filled him with courage and joy, and his face was lit by a grace untroubled by the threats. The Proconsul was the one unsettled, and he sent the herald onto the field to announce in all directions: "Polycarp has confessed he is a Christian." After the announcement the crowd of heathen and of the Jews resident in Smyrna could not contain their anger and shouted: "This is the teacher of Asia, the father of the Christians, the liquidator of our gods, who teaches many people not to sacrifice and not to pay reverence." Then they shouted to Philip, the governor of Asia, to let loose a lion on Polycarp, but that was not allowed since the "Animal Sports" had been concluded. So they shouted in unison that he should burn Polycarp alive. . . .

The crowd lent a hand in scavenging for wood and kindling from workshops and baths; the Jews were, as usual, especially energetic about all this. When the wood was arranged Polycarp undressed. He had some difficulty bending over to remove his shoes, since the faithful usually vied for the privilege of doing him that service, to reverence his body. Long before his martyrdom they had treated him with that exquisite respect. He was quickly lashed to the pyre; but when they went to nail him to the post he said, "Leave me as I am: He who strengthens me to endure the fire will make me able to hold fast without any need for nails."

So they bound him instead, hands behind his back, as a noble ram selected from a great flock as an offering, a holocaust offered and acceptable to God. He looked up to heaven and said,

O Lord, almighty God,
Father of your beloved and blessed Child Jesus Christ,
through whom we have come to know you,
God of angels and of powers and of all creation
and of the family of the righteous, who live in your sight!
I bless you, that you have honored me with this day and hour
to share with the company of martyrs the cup of your Messiah,
and so to rise, body and soul, to everlasting life
in the immortality of your Holy Spirit.
And may I today be received by them in your presence
as a rich and delectable sacrifice
as you, the truthful God who never deceives,
have prepared in advance, and disclosed, and accomplished.
Therefore I also praise you for all things,
I bless you and I give you glory
through the eternal and heavenly high priest,
Jesus Christ your beloved Child,
through whom be glory to you with him and the Holy Spirit,
both now and into the ages yet to come. Amen.

After he had reached his Amen and finished his prayer the crew lit the fire and a great flame billowed up and we, who were given the privilege, saw a wonder, and were preserved in order to pass it on. The fire enclosed him in a sort of tent of flame, billowing like a sail in a high wind, and there he was, sheltered inside, not as burning flesh, but like bread baking in the oven or gold and silver being purified in the furnace. We breathed a fragrant scent, like incense or fine spices.

Finally the outlaws, seeing that his body was not being burnt, had an executioner go up and stab him, and then a dove came forth, and so much blood that the fire was stanched, and the entire crowd noticed the difference between the unbelievers and the chosen. The awesome martyr Polycarp was certainly among the chosen: in our day he was a teacher in the spirit of the apostles and the prophets, a bishop of the Catholic Church in Smyrna.[32]

The account was written by contemporary witnesses in Smyrna, who cast it into the literary form of a great ritual. The town is howling against atheists, and Polycarp enters the stadium and throws the charge back in their faces: they are the atheists, the ones who will not bend the knee to the real God. He is handed on from one authority to the next, and it is they, not he, who are on trial. Repeatedly he is invited to renounce Christ and recant, even if insincerely, and go home a free man. His enemies become the ones who chant his honors: a venerable old man, a Christian and the father of Christians, the teacher of all Asia Minor, the trasher of false idols who teaches many people not to offer them sacrifice or reverence, the eager victim of a fragrant sacrifice, the witness filled with the Spirit who is now on the loose in Smyrna. Polycarp is bread for the eucharist, refined treasure for the Church, with blood stronger than fire. And the servants of Christianity's rival, the Empire, have been stared down.

Wiesel's account applies here too: What the Romans wanted to do to the Christian people was to substitute themselves for the Christian God. All the terminology, all the vocabulary testifies to that. And in spite of all, because of all, here were these men who remained human and who remained Christian and went on praying to God.

The old man died rather than finesse a ritual. If he had falsely feigned worship to Caesar, he would truly have become Caesar's man. It is in our community's rituals that we establish our identities and accept our commitments. Or reject them. Or compromise them. Or blur them.

No one has explained this proper power of ritual more crisply than Robert Bolt. He took the unusual step of writing a preface to his play, *A Man for All Seasons*, to answer the obvious question: why he, neither Catholic nor Christian,

> take[s] as my hero a man who brings about his own death because he can't put his hand on an old book and tell an ordinary lie?
>
> For this reason: A man takes an oath only when he wants to commit himself quite exceptionally to the statement, when he wants to make an identity between the truth of it and his own virtue; he

---

32. *The Martyrdom of Polycarp: Letter of the Church in Smyrna to the Church in Philomelium*, 7-16.

offers himself as a guarantee. And it works. There is a special kind of shrug for a perjurer; we feel that the man has no self to commit, no guarantee to offer. Of course it's much less effective now that for most of us the words of the oath are not much more than impressive mumbo-jumbo than it was when it made obvious sense; we would prefer most men to guarantee their statements with, say, cash rather than with themselves. We feel — we know — the self to be an equivocal commodity. There are fewer and fewer things which, as they say, we "cannot bring ourselves" to do. . . .

Thomas More, as I wrote about him, became for me a man with an adamantine sense of his own self. He knew where he began and where he left off, what area of himself he could yield to the encroachments of his enemies, and what to the encroachments of those he loved. It was a substantial area in both cases, for he had a proper sense of fear and was a busy lover. Since he was a clever man and a great lawyer he was able to retire from those areas in wonderfully good order, but at length he was asked to retreat from that final area where he located his self. And there this supple, humorous, unassuming and sophisticated person set like metal, was overtaken by an absolutely primitive rigor, and could no more be budged than a cliff.[33]

The reason for More's adamantine sense of his own self was that throughout his life he had — with an honesty evidently unmatched by most of his contemporaries — celebrated the rituals of the Church and really meant what he said and did. The self he celebrated in those sacraments was that of a believer, a disciple, a sinner, a husband and father, and the king's good servant but God's first. And by celebrating that self, he became himself.

33. Robert Bolt, *A Man for All Seasons* (New York: Vintage, 1960, 1962), pp. xii, xi.

CHAPTER TEN

The Rituals of Jesus, the Anti-Ritualist: Worship, the Real Make-Believe

Several of the rituals described in the previous chapter are rituals of the Church. An innate instinct drives the Church to act out her convictions in ritual, which we first considered generally, and now do more specifically.

It is in her sacramental life that the Church professes her faith, embodies her convictions, and enacts her commitments. This is most obviously so in the sacraments.

That embodying instinct was already active in those who left us the Gospels. One sees it in their stories: Jesus is himself a sacrament. He is the benevolence of the Father begotten in eternity, and now fleshed out as man and thus in humanity. In his humanhood Jesus reveals God: incompletely (as must always be so within the confines of this world and of our cramped insight), yet tantalizingly, invitingly. Otherwise put: Jesus is God displaying himself and his Father. As Jesus passes from village to village he feeds the hungry, raises the dead, fraternizes with the whores and collaborators, heals the paralyzed and the sickly, and washes away the sins of those who repent. His every act is a ritual, for the incarnation discloses the Father, not only in the words of the Son, but in his every gesture and kind service. What is more, even though it is through the touch of his body that he reveals the love of the Father and conveys his life, Jesus makes flesh — his and ours — the conveyance of gifts more inward than flesh alone could receive. His Church is therefore a people who truly know that one can convey forgiveness with the sign of the cross, and who have seen that one can wash the soul with water and anoint a person — not just a body — with oil. To believe in Jesus is to see that there is more to him than meets the eye: and that he who is man is much more than man. Just so: to believe in his sacramental rituals is to see that there is more to the sharing among humans than meets the eye; further, that all service of neighbor is more than human service, in what it reveals and what it enacts.

Consider the eucharist, for example. The ritual of the eucharist is that of a community meal. Any disciple emerging from the Last Supper could have explained right out that he or she had been to a meal. It was no ordinary meal, because on that night unlike all other nights, Jews commemorated at supper their liberation from bondage in the Exodus. But within that commemorative occasion it was, with all its special dishes and prayers and observances, a meal. Unfortunately, most Christian worshippers issuing forth from the eucharist on Sunday morning would be unlikely to have that basic an understanding of what they had just shared in. It is a sacred meal. At the head of the table stands one who stands for Christ. He shares among his fellow believers hallowed bread and wine. What binds this fellowship together around that table is the common belief that through Jesus is revealed to us the Father, the Creator of all humankind. We further believe that whenever any human being shares the substance of life with a brother or sister, more passes between them than simple nourishment, or goods of the body. Just so what appear to be but bread and wine are by their profound new inwardness now truly the Body and Blood of Jesus crucified and risen. Thus these believers celebrate as brothers and sisters their common belief that whenever they give generously to their neighbors, their gifts are conveyances of their own flesh and blood, and in turn conveyances of the divine life of the Son.

Sacraments are celebrations of the Church's faith. They are not the events by which we are rescued, and emerge from our sins, and are transformed into loving men and women. That we must do by the daily, substantial exchanges of life with our brothers and sisters. In fact, our worship is an interlude in the actual transformational and formational work of salvation. It deals in symbol, not in substance. Sacraments, like Jesus, reveal, and precisely by revealing they are powerful in the dynamic of salvation. In the eucharist no concrete, substantial sharing of bread, or of all the supports of life that bread represents, is given from one human to another. What is shared is a token bread, a sacramental nourishing by the body of Christ. It is only in the pragmatic order of work and sacrifice that humans are transformed. Yet it is this sacramental "interlude" that awakens in us the energy to serve. Revelation incites salvation. It is the pause we need to glimpse the inwardness and the purpose and celebrate the eternal worth of what we do when we work for one another.

Sex, the ritual of marriage

To appreciate how the sacramental rituals of the Church provide both direction and energy for the service that saves us and one another, contemplate the comparable dynamic between sex and marriage.

Sex, by the nature of things, is the oldest of human rituals, more primitive even than speech. It is also powerful: powerful enough in the lives of individuals to fuel deep love or deep hate, powerful enough in the life of the human species to beget the social institutions of marriage and family. Men and women can seek to convey in sex any number of relations. It can mean nothing: only a nonchalant exchange of orgasm — if indeed there is exchange. It can mean a man and a woman are attracted to one another. Or that they love one another. Or that they belong to one another. Or, in that further reach of sexual possibility celebrated by Christianity, that they rejoice in unconditioned, mutual fidelity, for better or for worse, for richer or for poorer, in sickness and in health, until death.

The conviction within the Christian tradition has been that, whatever the purposes sex may be put to by men and women, it offers and allows right fulfillment only when it embodies outright and settled fidelity. Not only does it give no right rest otherwise: it deceives, it corrupts, it lures us to destruction. This view is treated with disbelief and contempt by those who believe that sex is meant to embody love — not to mention any of those lesser appetites and expectations. To contend against that bleak belief — which Christians do believe to be true but deceptive if taken for the full truth — one would have to observe that we have many loves in our lives that are of a most intimate and intense kind, yet they do not crave, or perhaps even allow of, sexual exchange. Does a man love his mother the less because he declines to sleep with her? Or his son? Does a woman love her Ob-Gyn the less for relating only professionally? Does the love between lifelong best friends fall short of the mark for want of sex? In the insight of the Church, what sex craves — indeed, needs to embody — is not simply "I like you," or "I love you," but "I belong to you and you to me . . . as long as we both shall live."

The innate symbolism of sexual intercourse is the sharing surrender of privacy. A man and woman give their bodies in diverse ways to all their friends and loves and associates, but they surrender their selves, their whole bodies, their "private parts" (as quaintly and rightly called) only to the partner with whom they share unqualified privacy. Children and parents may exchange the fullest love possible, yet their mutual need is that the children be acquiring their own privacy, to be able to move off into healthy independence (and then adult dependence). Only with a spouse does one pool all privacy and purposes and decisions and home. Thus sex craves to embody and celebrate the mystery of a man and a woman who have surrendered their individual lives to one another for the sake of that deeper and more fruitful life they must have in common. It is not just any generic sort of love, nor need it be the most intense (it is considerably outdone by crucifixion); but it is a peculiarly dedicated type of love that can unite about as closely as humans can, and in its own proper way. And this, we believe, we could not have seen so boldly or clearly were it not for our Christian revelation.

It is not sex, though, that holds wife and husband together. The actual business of life — partners becoming two in one flesh — is the exchange of mutual service. A man *makes* love to his wife when he senses without being told that she probably has a headache, when he mows the lawn before it gets shaggy, cares for the runny noses of the children when he is there, supports her own growth in interests and career, offers once in a while to come home early and fix dinner, gives his infant the last bottle of the night, puts down the remote and turns the TV off to talk with his wife, and wipes the ring out of the bathtub. (I must confess that the dismaying obsolescence of the bathtub in our culture threatens the vitality of this best-remembered of all images in *Philemon*'s first edition.) A woman *makes* love to her husband when she uses some imagination in the kitchen, lets him go for a round of golf even though the lawn needed to be cut last week, gathers up his shirts to drop off at the dry cleaners, risks asking how his day went (and really listening to the answer), and knows when they both need to get away from the children. It is not in bed that spouses *make* love to one another. In bed they *celebrate* the love that grows between them while on duty: the love that, in those concluding words of Dante, "moves the sun in heaven, and all the stars, and the hand that wipes the ring out of the tub."[1] It is urgent that they *do* have sex with one another: in this ritual they both release and impose the meaning that their mundane adventure together has for them, lest it end disappointingly in being nothing more than keeping the tub immaculate. What marriage and fidelity and two-in-one-flesh require is not only that spouses wash the ring out of the tub, but that husbands and wives thereby grow into one, and in *love*. That love grows, not merely from the services done, but from their having been done as services.

The two become one by bodily union. A wife and husband enjoy and

1. Dante Alighieri, *The Divine Comedy,* Paradiso, 33:135. Inclusiveness added.

foster two kinds of physical exchange: those that are substantive and those that are symbolic. By mutual bodily services they grow into loving persons; by joint rituals they ignite and fan the flame of love within those services. The ritual is actuated by service, yet the service is quickened by the ritual. It is in sleeping with her husband that a woman enjoys the confident glimpse of what is at stake when she too (excuse it again, but it *is* the point) washes the ring out of the tub. It is in washing the ring out of the tub that she becomes the loving woman who can with full honesty sleep with her husband. And once in a while it is incumbent on one or the other of them to come upon the tub dishearteningly defiled by a delinquent, scummy ring, patiently to forgo the opportunity to call down fire from heaven, and forgivingly to make the universe right by wielding the soap and rag vicariously. Christ asks no less.

Ritual, then, is neither self-ratifying nor self-sufficient. It is the celebration that gives us insight into our lives, and incites us to live up to that insight. It is not merely an expression of our beliefs and values. Like ethical activity, it works from the inside out, and also from the outside in. It expresses what lies within us, but it also shapes us to our revealed ideal. Of every true ritual it can be said with paradox — and Catholics say this about their chief rituals, the sacraments: it effects what it signifies . . . provided that what it signifies is already in effect. Where ritual is not ratified by service, there we have hypocrisy, sham, magic. Where service is not given meaning by ritual, there we have drift and drudgery and an end of human civilization.

Sex is a vital interlude in the real business of love, which has as its purpose to make spouses two-in-one-flesh. Yet it is in sex that they have to rediscover and refresh their belief that these enduring and costly services are tokens of something even more precious. So too in the eucharist. It is not in church that we make love, that we are saved, that we emerge from selfishness into charity. Worship is one activity in life wherein one does not work out one's salvation. The church is not the place set aside for us to encounter God, for we are unremittingly reminded to find the Lord in our neighbor. The church is the essential and sacred place where we draw aside momentarily to rediscover and refresh our faith: that it is in serving our neighbor that we cleave to God.

It is entirely appropriate that Christians would and did eventually devise the custom of rededicating a recurring day to leisure. We have our own compelling reasons for valuing work and service and duty, but we also have a specifically Christian reason for needing time free to draw back from that work, as Jesus did. For without worship — sacred, even playful leisure — benefits passed from hand to hand will cease to become gifts, and are in danger of degenerating into commodities, or commercial transactions. A token is a token only so long as the giver sees it as a conveyance of something he cannot hold within his hand. The eucharist, a celebration within leisure, is the secret of those who believe that we cannot live by bread alone, and that by our gifts of bread we can and do receive more than bread alone.

What was said earlier about the Church must be said of the Church's rituals. The specific purpose of our liturgy is not to save, but to reveal that there is a God who is at all times saving. Sacraments are not meant to draw one's attention away from one's pursuits and involvements, as from a distraction. On the contrary, what they reveal and celebrate is the salvific power of common activities performed with uncommon generosity, by God's grace. One draws away from one's work, not to forget it, but to contemplate what God lovingly enables us lovingly to accomplish. Leisure is not just a rest before going back to work; likewise, liturgy does not afford us an occasion of retreat, to step aside momentarily and attend to our intimacy with God, which is then neglected during those workaday times when we are preoccupied with matters mundane. Worship was never intended as a refuge from the mundane. It does not offer access to the Father any more immediate than one has elsewhere. Nor does it offer a privileged forum wherein one may remedy faults and shed sins. Worship reveals the Lord to his creatures, and reveals his heart to us, and also ours to us. It offers no escape from the world and its activities. Instead, it casts over those activities the high-intensity insight of faith.

Rituals that make demands

As the faith of the Church is not at home in this world, it is in our sacramental celebrations that the believing community should sense our conflicted uneasiness toward the world and its cultures. To illustrate: in a nation where bride and groom are commonly asked to vow to remain faithful to one another only as long as they care to, a really authentic marriage in Christ would be startling. In a world where unwelcome children are fair game to be destroyed by their parents, and where children can be manufactured to order in order to be welcome, an authentic baptism of infants which welcomes them with reverence as God's own children and our sacred peers takes on an abruptly countercultural aspect. In a society where people no longer able to maintain themselves are generally not welcome to live in their children's homes, and where the elderly or sickly who become too bothersome can usually be put out of their bother (and, of course, ours too), a full-strength anointing of the sick might become an underground activity. In a Church whose charity budget is mostly funded by state and federal tax moneys, where would we ever find the nerve to break the bread and share the cup of the eucharist?

In those intimate sacramental times, however, when we are meant to be *mano-a-mano* with the Mystery revealed in Christ, we do not really seem to be very sharply at odds with our odd culture. In a word, our rituals may be unwittingly as phony as a drug enforcement officer on the take.

If vacant-minded and half-hearted ritual does not alarm us, we nevertheless can sense that sacrilegious ritual, ritual that is offensively false, grates against the soul like a fingernail against a blackboard. Why? Why is it that we recoil when Napoleon crowns himself? When Judas betrays Jesus with a kiss? When Scobey, in Graham Greene's *The End of the Affair,* receives communion sacrilegiously? When Elmer Gantry seduces his new converts in the tall grass? Because our rituals impose heavily on us to honor their true meaning.

Jimmy Breslin, prominent public moralist and liturgist, put his thumb in the Catholic eye on this subject in 1979. Cardinal Cooke of New York, whom Breslin saw as too uninvolved in public issues, had stunned the city by denying a requiem mass for Carmine Galante, a mobster who was gunned down.

> There are in New York about 3,000 ugly men who trade in narcotics and in murder over narcotics. They form the Mafia, or whatever it is you call them this week. . . . All but a handful of these men were baptized as Catholics. Nearly all of their families and friends are Catholic. And these drug peddlers murder in the shadow of their church and the church, until now, has never uttered a word against it. . . .
>
> A sign of approval of the man's life would disturb the flock, Cooke said. At first, this seemed to be a point so small as to be ridiculous and the feeling was that if this were the only reason he could advance for not holding the requiem Mass, then one should be held.
>
> But then I began to think of Knickerbocker Ave. in Brooklyn on the day Galante was killed. The large crowd outside was nearly all Puerto Rican, and for them the shooting was a celebration. Dead in the backyard of the restaurant was a person who controlled the heroin

that infests the young of poor neighborhoods. Glance past them down the street and you saw the entrance to Knickerbocker Park, which has become a swamp, a place where young girls sell themselves to get drugs. If a religious institution were to give an outward sign of honoring the death of this Galante, then in Knickerbocker Park and the streets around it, and on the streets of Brownsville and central Harlem and the South Bronx, the cardinal's theory of [scandal] would be more than just a tiny detail of canon law on which he could hang his mitre. . . .

[Cooke's] weapons of excommunication and scolding from the pulpit could accomplish more than all the federal agencies. It is Cardinal Cooke's job to hold these mobsters up in public, hold them up in front of family and neighbors, and pronounce their ways as being those of the Devil. No longer should a mobster, or those who support them, feel an ease and graciousness in their relationship with their church. The obvious question is, once you start this, where do you stop? The answer must be found in Cooke's conscience.[2]

Breslin rightly sees that sacraments are given both to confront us with the demands of Christ and to invite us into them. Not all people are ready to accept that dare, nor does the Church do well to finesse it and pretend they do.

Moving in quite another direction, the Church of England's Board for Social Responsibility seems to have flinched in a major way in its three-year-long effort to "make it plain that the love of God is loved out in a variety of relationships":

Cohabitation is now common behavior before marriage, [and the Church has too often] spoken about families in ways which are sentimental, or excluding, or which do not connect with people's lives as they are really experienced. . . . Many of the people who wrote to us had sought welcome and haven in the Church in times of darkness but had instead encountered disapproval and sometimes downright rejection. . . .

[The] first step the Church should take is to abandon the phrase "living in sin." This is a most unhelpful way of characterizing the lives of cohabitees. . . . Theologically and ethically, it represents a

2. Jimmy Breslin, "Galante's followers need a Cooke reprimand too," [New York] *Daily News*, 19 July 1979, p. 4.

serious failure to treat people as unique human beings [and] perpet-
uates the widespread misconception that sin is only about sex. . . . A
more positive approach, involving a genuine recognition that some
people choose cohabitation as a way of expressing their deepest commitments, could transform the current awkward embarrassment.[3]

One cannot imagine Breslin coming to the defense of drug dealers who
"encounter downright rejection," or chiding the Church in the Bronx for
thinking "that sin is only about" addiction and murder, or feeling "embarrassed" for the junkies and druglords as "unique human beings who have
chosen heroin as the way of expressing their deepest commitments."

Rituals that invite responsibility

The traditional teaching, of course, even among Anglicans, was that if
cohabitation were the deepest commitment two people are able to make,
then sexual intercourse badly overstates their relationship: that is, it falsi-
fies it. This is not an "excluding" way of speech, as the Board for Social
Responsibility thinks. The Church *should* welcome them. But it should not
deform its Gospel to compliment all "people's lives as they are really
experienced" (a remarkably passive way of putting it) because, for all she
knows, some of those lives are lethal. The Church welcomes people into
Christian rituals and commitments, which are meant to oblige them to
make all the other rituals and commitments in their lives happily congru-
ous with them. The Church is commanded, not to force that choice upon
them, but to offer it to them — explicitly. That is its astringent welcome.
It is nothing to be awkward about.

The welcome is always meant to transform us insofar as our lives and
our selves are not worthy of welcome and haven. Even in the evening of
life the ritual welcome is meant to be energizing, not just palliative. A
theologian in his middle — and last — age, who had been a priest but left
and married, and had become snarled in every way with the Church,
wrote powerfully of the Hail and Farewell he received:

> It was a slow Sunday afternoon when a local priest whom I
> admire as a genuine pastor ambled into my room. He delivered

3. Fred Barbash, "Anglican Panel Eases View on 'Living in Sin'," *Washington Post*,
7 June 1995.

himself of a few stories, his equivalent of small talk, and then asked what priests had been visiting me. I laughed and reported that spiritual ministrations had been minimal. Irritated, but not surprised, he asked if I would like to be anointed. With no thought, I said yes. So we went through a spare, adapted version of the Church's ancient ritual that asks God's help for the seriously sick — begs divine support and comfort for both body and spirit. Although it began almost shamefully casually, this anointing . . . has lodged itself among the half-dozen most moving religious experiences of my entire life.

When I took religious vows as a Jesuit, I thought my future would run as straight as a pair of railroad tracks. When I was ordained a priest, I knew my future would be hopelessly tangled, because I had lost faith in the church's rules about celibacy. In both cases, though, I assumed that I had time, that things would sort themselves out, that the wilderness could prove habitable, the desert could bear fruit.

Lying in my narrow hospital bed, feeling the oil of gladness and healing, I knew I had little time. More importantly, though, I felt, by your wondrous grace, that this was the first time in my effective memory that the Church, in the representative figure of one of its priests (who, at a still deeper level of representation, stood for Christ), was praying for me individually, by name, to deal with painful circumstances, suffering, and needs uniquely my own. . . . I realized, on my hospital pallet, that "Mother Church" had not been my mother for a long time. Psychologically (not theologically), Mother Church had kicked me out, waiving visiting rights, and said the divorce from my role as "father" (due to my independent convictions about love and Christ) suited her fine. In a dozen ways Mother Church shouted that I was a big disappointment. Through the twenty-odd years of estrangement my typical response, usually thrown imaginatively toward the tubby clergy claiming to represent Mother Church, was a simple Italian hand gesture, bawdy and amused.

Anointing was a very different business. Something maternal really did appear. I felt taken to the bosom of a holy mother, a loving family that cared for me. It knew about my muscle spasms and dismal prognosis. It loved me despite my manifest failings and my worst sins. And it dismissed the past history, the tubby clerics, the mutual antagonism of mother and child, as irrelevant.

For once, the church did not point to itself but was transparent to God. For once it was a community of prayer, offering the praise and petition that have always been its primary reason to be. For what seemed to me to be the first time, I, little John, weak John, competent John, mixed-up John, strong John, very sick John had a name in this community. My pain aggrieved it. My dying would sadden and diminish it. I mattered. For once, I mattered. . . .

The church at prayer in my anointing said, "We ask God, who is wholly good, to strengthen your body and spirit, for we love you and care about you, as God does infinitely more. We are not clerics, bureaucrats, bloodless functionaries. We are your family, your brothers and sisters, mortal and sinful like you, sure one day to need anointing ourselves. Come close, into our embrace. Become part of the communion of saints as we intercede for you with God. Be at peace."[4]

It would be impertinent to suppose, though perhaps not to imagine, that it was good John, more even than Mother Church, who was drawn the farther distance into that sacramental embrace. For the welcome made demands on him. Still, what an open yet truthful heart the Church needed to display, through the man at his bedside and the old rite they shared, for all that to happen.

Weddings without much marriage

It takes nerve for us to celebrate the sacraments honorably. It takes a clean conscience for the Church to enact with dramatic and prophetic truth what Christ gives us to celebrate, instead of being sucked into the presumptions and predilections of a culture that needs an exorcism to be able to look into the face of the Mystery. It takes Christ in our rituals to bring people to belief, and all sacraments, in this best sense of the words, should *make-believe:* should make us believers.

Nowhere could this be more clearly seen than in the sacrament of Matrimony. We live within the confines of a culture whose sensibilities toward marriage have been so deranged that the traditional vocabulary — courtship, marriage, vows, childbearing, family — evokes in the public mind images and expectations that are repugnant to the Gospel. And we who live surrounded by that alien culture have tended to minimize that alienation. We have searched for a public discourse vague and ambiguous

4. John Carmody, *Cancer and Faith: Reflections on Living with a Terminal Illness* (Mystic, Conn.: Twenty-Third Publications, 1994), pp. 54-56.

enough to sound as if we really shared the same hopes. We hardly dare admit that the culture finds the Gospel toxic. The *New Yorker* cartoon caption in 1972 was not entirely fanciful: a bridal couple surrounded by shaggy friends in the park vow: "Also in all times and at all places to condemn war, pollution, and non-biodegradable containers, to support the Third World, and to fight for a better life for the migrant farm worker."

Consider the range of sensibilities toward courtship, for instance. It is commonly understood that a sensible approach to a marital decision will involve sexual partnership and cohabitation. Social scientists tell us that premarital cohabitation (granted, of course, that most "premarital" sex is not "pre-" anything) is the predictor of a divorce rate considerably higher than— sometimes double — that of couples who did not cohabit. Social scientists also tell us that many of these live-ins were, to begin with, motivated by worry about the high divorce rate, and had the idea that sleeping and living together would provide a more reliable hunch about whether theirs would be a durable marriage.[5] Most clergy responsible for helping people into marriage know that the large majority of those who come to them today are sleeping and living together. The clergy may have their own convictions that this is wrong, but they usually avoid questions that might bring it out into the open. There is just enough cultural memory around for young cohabitants still to feel a need to justify their practice. "I was aware of what the church teaches, but it wasn't the religious thing that made me hesitate. I was afraid my parents would kill me. I believe in God and I believe in the commandments. Sure, I'm living with my fiancé, but I don't think that's bad. I'm a moral person. I'm living with one man. It's not like I was going with other guys too."

Speaking from a much deeper fund of experience is actor Eddie Fisher, married in yesteryear "only three times" for a total of 6½ years. Of his four children, actress Carrie Fisher (born to Debbie Reynolds) is best known and

5. Judith S. Wallerstein & Sandra Blakeslee, *Second Chances: Men, Women and Children a Decade after Divorce* (New York: Ticknor & Fields, 1989); Neil G. Bennett, Ann Klims Blanc, & David E. Bloom, "Commitment and the Modern Union: Assessing the Link Between Premarital Cohabitation and Subsequent Marital Stability," *American Sociological Review* 53, 1 (February 1988): 127-38; Alan Booth & David Johnson, "Premarital Cohabitation and Marital Success," *Journal of Family Issues* 9, 2 (June 1988): 255-72; Larry L. Bumpass & James A. Sweet, "National Estimates of Cohabitation: Cohort Levels and Union Stability," National Survey of Families and Households Working Paper, No. 2, Center for Demography and Ecology, University of Wisconsin, 1989; Bumpass, Teresa Castro Martin, & Sweet, "The Impact of Family Background and Early Marital Factors on Marital Disruption," *Journal of Family Issues* 12, 1 (March 1991): 22-42.

most outspoken. She told Fisher: "I didn't have a father and I didn't have a mother. You did what you wanted to do and I raised myself." Fisher's current philosophy: "It's awful when you're not (living) with someone. I hate going out on dates. I really am the marrying kind — that is, I have to live with a woman. I'm a one-woman man, one woman at a time." This sounds very much like Proportionalism, though at Tenderfoot rank.

Another form of preventive care to avoid marital conflict is the legal prenuptial contract, known as a "pre-nup" in the trade, and as the "death knell" by one attorney who has made it a specialty. Previously a resort of wealthy, aging, multi-divorce men marrying showgirls, pre-nups have now become a staple item in prophylactic marriage. Couples can negotiate beforehand how income is to be available severally to the partners; how many children they will have, by birth or by adoption; who controls abortion in case of excessive conception; how paternity will be determined if the husband demurs; what are the rights of children from previous unions; how life insurance benefits shall be distributed; alimony, child support, division of assets, and occupancy of the family home after separation and/or divorce; whether extramarital sex is acceptable; how much continuing education or travel is assignable to either partner; how household chores are to be divided; more intimate agreements such as that "Ralph shall not urinate before putting the seat up," or "derogatory terms such as 'married,' 'married to,' 'husband,' and 'wife' shall be avoided"; and how eventual disputes over the contract itself are to be arbitrated. There is also a trend in the opposite direction: pre-nup "supervows" promise more than the law requires: e.g., to wait at least six months after asking for a divorce, to see if there is a reconciliation. For those who are parrying but not marrying, there is the "non-nup," drawn up for specific time periods to provide for or protect from palimony, and to assign a monetary value to unsalaried mutual services.

The wedding itself, which often bears very little discernible relation to marriage, can be the focus of extravagant concern by the parties. The soft-porn section of every magazine rack displays a number of magazines fixated exclusively upon brides and brides' mothers and brides' marriages. Veils and nails, invitations "and accessories," bed and bath essentials, makeup, hair, skin, bachelor parties, gift returns, formal-daytime/formal-evening/semi-formal-daytime/semi-formal-evening/informal-daytime-and-evening variations, contraceptive menus, remembrances for attendants, place settings, who-pays-for-what, groom's duties ("buy an engagement ring," etc.), limos, "how to talk about money," kitchen I.Q., rebates after cancellation — it is all there, except for the What and the Why.

For those with a more structured personality there is the more intensive format: trade shows known as "bridal seminars." One typical seminar featured a week of presentations by a Certified Stress Management Counselor; a Renowned Caterer; a Renowned Caterer and Party Planner; a pair of professional party and wedding planners (strictly lowercase); an Internationally Recognized Gem and Jewelry Expert; the Author of best-selling "Winning by Negotiation"; and the national bridal directors of Gorham, Noritake, and Wedgewood U.S.A. Promised were Celebrity Tablesettings by Ivana (then) Trump, Kathie Lee Gifford, Regis Philbin, Sally Jessy Raphael, Michael J. Fox, Arnold Scaasi, and Adrienne Arpel, plus a betrothal ring retrospective display, a flower arranging demo, a tea tasting, and drawing for the Grand Prize: a fabulous Caribbean honeymoon for one couple in the store's bridal registry ("You could be our couple of the year"). But Why?

The press has begun to notice the durable trend to designing weddings which manifest ritually that these marriages are going to be exactly what *this couple* wants, and exclude the prospect that there is any tradition they are making their own. Presiding clergy tend to be hired from one of the churches that deal in ceremonies but not in God. One celebrant who "specializes in unusual unions" began by helping troubled teenagers, and started her own church when those to which she took the girls "proved too judgmental." She has joined couples — on a need-to-know basis, of course — aboard motorcycles and helicopters and boats, roller coasters and hot air balloons, in mid-bungee-jump, and while scuba- and sky-diving, in golf courses, cemeteries, and sewers.

One couple staged their wedding across a seven-hour walking tour of Manhattan to recap the high points of their courtship, beginning at the Morning Star Diner, and segueing through six other locations: Bryant Park where they had once watched a movie in the rain, a Korean restaurant where the wedding party and guests all lunched and blew soap bubbles, down to a ride on the No. 1 Subway where a nondenominational minister boarded and pronounced them man and wife. Another showcase wedding took place as a fashion show where a Party Promoter was preceded down the runaway by 43 bridesmaids (one for each year in her life) in, er, idiosyncratic dress. The Promoter herself arrived clad in a flesh-colored leather body suit and a great, billowing, egg-shaped veil that enclosed her entirely from top to toe, to be met by her husband, a Gym Entrepreneur, in a matching leather G-string. Said she: "We didn't want a traditional wedding per se. After all, we've been living together for three years and have a 14-month-old baby. But neither did we want to go to a registry office. . . . But this is for real. We really wanted to be married, to be a family, to fit in with the masses." The Unity Fellowship provided the presider, and *Playboy* magazine sponsored the event. Then there was the bride in leotards and the groom in a "Let's Go Mets" T-shirt whose nuptials took 8.5 seconds in a municipal Wedding Chapel; the Chicago bus driver who chartered ten buses to bring all his friends to his wedding (as it turned out, there were only 15 friends who came), and walked away from the judge single because they had never thought to procure a wedding license; the couple who married in the Twin Gables Tavern, after a round of pool, because that was where the groom had first seen the bride. The groom wore an open sport shirt and the bride wore blue slacks and a blouse. "The blouse, naturally, was white." The minister from the Universal Life Church presided with the mike from the bandstand shortly after 11:00 P.M. "Under the circumstances, he thought it best to omit the prayers." Patrons expected drinks on the house, or at least on the groom, but he left them to pay for their own.

Readings, traditionally from Scripture, began already in the 1960s to be drawn from alternative authorities such as *The Velveteen Rabbit*, Kahlil Gibran, and *Are You Running With Me, Jesus?* Now the repertory has enlarged to include Ralph Waldo Emerson, W. Scott Peck, e.e. cummings, Elizabeth Barrett Browning, Ben Jonson, and "Go placidly, amid the noise and haste. . . ." But it is in the vows themselves that the rite of marriage has made a thousand didacticisms bloom:

> "I pledge to share my life openly with you. You can trust my love, for it is real. I promise to share and support your hopes, dreams and goals. I vow to be there for you always. And when you fall, I will catch you."
>
> "Although we journey on the same path, your journey will be your own, and my journey will always be my own."
>
> He: "It is therefore our glorious and divine purpose to fly mountains, to sow petalescent . . . to glorify glory, to love with love."
>
> She: "We hereby commit ourselves to a serenity more flamboyant and more foolish than a petalfall of Magnolia."
>
> They: "This is the purest double helix of our us-ness."
>
> "We promise to love and accept what is different in each of us, recognizing that love must always be ready to accept otherness, the mystery of the other. In its purest form, one loves to the extent that one permits what is different from oneself to exist.
>
> "We promise to recognize the need in the other for silent and

independent growth. Such growth alone can give vitality and further renewal to our relations with one another. . . .

"We promise to recognize the need for personal relationships outside the circle created by our relations with one another. . . .

"We promise to give ourselves as much as is possible in love, remembering the dangers and contradictions in the tendencies to possess or to give oneself away absolutely. . . ."

One mayor says he tailors the traditional ceremony. "There used to be a line, 'till death do us part,' but that was too morbid. I use 'for all our days together.' When I say it, it sounds like an eternal commitment." [Though not if anyone is listening.] The Anglicans in New Zealand deleted " 'till death do us part," as well as "love, honor and obey." The syntax of the entirely more amiable service was shifted from promises to wishes: "All that I have I offer you. Wherever you go I will go. What you have to give I will receive. I pray God will grant us lifelong fidelity and so I take you for my wife/husband." The cleric presiding also avoids asserting that they are now married. Instead, he prays that they might be: "May God so join you together that no failure nor misfortune shall ever part you."

Alternative rites have produced alternative vows. The San Francisco Chapter of Dignity, a gay activist group for Catholics, after lengthy deliberation devised Guidelines for the Blessing of Committed Relationships, which by the nature of things are quite meticulous. There are three levels of commitment, which require progressively long previous periods during which the "life-partners" have defined themselves as a "couple." Level One, a "declaration of relationship," requires a prior longevity of three months; Level Two, a "Blessing of Commitment," requires six months; Level Three, the ultimate "Rite of Blessing of Life Commitment," requires one year. Those declaring a Relationship stand up after the homily at the Sunday Eucharist and declare whatever it is in words of their own choosing, and are introduced to the community. Those asking for a Blessing on their Commitment are treated more formally: the community is asked to witness the blessing; the couple do not declare their intentions but are questioned about them; everyone extends hands over them to join in the blessing; they are introduced and also centerpieced in the Sign of Peace. Those who rise to Level Three must meet three times with a pastoral team to work out the terms of their contract of covenant, e.g., work, money, property, living together, standing obligations (parents, children), debts, wills, medical examinations, fidelity, substance abuse. They also discuss "religion and their faith," and plan the ritual. The format is basically that of a wedding, with or without Eucharist. The Guidelines do not specify what is Committed.[6] Critics have noted that with the tragic record of homosexuals for promiscuity, these rituals seem to celebrate in the optative mood what is rarely realized in the indicative. The criticism is well made; it would be even better made if it went on to observe that the same disability is now befalling heterosexuals.

Most tortured of all are Interfaith rites: not those of a single church or religion which a spouse and family and clergy of another religious community find that they can honestly join, but effortfully equivocal rites that try to manage a worship service without community of faith, in order to enact a wedding without community of faith — which initiates a marriage without community of faith. When an Armenian groom and a Jewish bride encountered strong Armenian and rabbinical policies against interfaith weddings, they found a United Church of Christ minister and a Reform rabbi who wove them a ceremony "influenced by the traditions" of the couple: the groom placed an Armenian crown of flowers on his bride's head, under a Jewish canopy. And since nothing serious was dealt with, in order to avoid any disagreement, the general opinion was that it "created a warm feeling and brought the families together. It seemed to cross all the boundaries." More likely it was trapped in No Man's Land and never got inside either set of boundaries. It would have to be a very powerfully warm feeling to make up for real faith. One straight-talking rabbi got to the point: "What you're really saying is that all religions are the same when they are not. Christians, for example, are married in Christ and Jews are married in accordance with the covenant of Moses and Israel — and those things don't mix."[7]

This collage of deviant ritual is suggestive — though no more than that — of the disintegration of the celebration and thus of the commitment of marriage. In the culture of the United States the archetypal doctrine and rite were Catholic. Even American civil ceremonies were overshadowed by the Anglican ritual, which was itself derivatively Catholic. The tradition tenaciously clung to those rites, and especially to their invocation of lifelong monogamy, long after that ceased to be enforceable at law or preached (except as a hope) by most denominations. But now we live in a culture that simply disbelieves in monogamous, faithful marriage. This

6. "Dignity/SF Guidelines for the Blessing of Committed Relationships," 16 August 1992.

7. Ari L. Goldman, "Interfaith Couples Pick Ways to Wed," *The New York Times,* 16 February 1985.

state of affairs is humorously depicted by Calvin Trillin: "When I asked a friend of mine recently how his twenty-fifth college reunion had gone — he had attended with the very same attractive and pleasant woman he married shortly after graduation — he said, 'Well, after the first day I decided to start introducing Marge as my second wife, and that seemed to make everyone a lot more comfortable.' "[8] Tiny indeed is the believing community today that preaches marriage in Christ as a revealed gift and challenge, and empowers its officers to witness and bless that kind of marriage only, since it knows nothing of any other kind.

This was brought out well when Louisiana enacted an optional "covenant marriage" available to couples who wished to make divorce less quickly obtainable. The new arrangement is a wistful half-gesture to recover Christian marriage, under civil auspices. But Louisiana lacks the revelation, the mandate, and the community to sustain such an endeavor. "The Lousiana law invites couples to lash themselves to a morality the broader culture does not support."[9] Psychiatrist Peter Kramer quickly observed that the American divorce rate is the normal outcome of a culture which has valued autonomy over mutuality, self-assertion over community, self-reliance over mutual reliance.

The disintegration of marriage in Christ allows — indeed, promotes — subsidiary follies. One recalls the Surgeon General of the United States encouraging instruction in masturbation in the schools.[10] Helpful instructional aids already used for equivalent purposes are Hand-Made Anatomically Realistic Dolls and Celebration-of-the-Clitoris Dolls (specify whether fluffy or velvety hair) advertised in *Ms.* When some Episcopal clergy inclined toward same-sex church marriages as a curb against promiscuity, one of their number criticized their motives. "If we want to have blessing ceremonies to stop the spread of AIDS, then we're asking them to be monogamous. That doesn't sound like a blessing. It sounds like a negative approach."[11] A videotape called Video Baby has been marketed for any who want "the full, rich experience of parenthood without the mess and inconvenience of the real thing." Owner-parents receive a 13-

---

8. Calvin Trillin, "Old Marrieds," in *If You Can't Say Something Nice* (New York: Ticknor & Fields, 1987), p. 40.

9. Peter D. Kramer, "Divorce and Our National Values," Op-Ed Page, *The New York Times*, 29 August 1997.

10. Kay S. Hymowitz, "We've Educated Sex to Death," *The New York Times*, 13 December 1994.

11. The Rev. Robert Williams; see Kate DeSmet, "Some Episcopalians extol virtues of same-sex 'weddings'," Religious News Service press release, 19 January 1990.

minute tape, along with birth certificate and medical record sheet. They are prompted to name the little 9-month-old girl, and she will interactively smile, wave, eat cereal, clap hands, play Peekaboo! and throw the toys out of her crib (not to worry: the reverse button brings them all back). Her older tape-sibling, Video Dog, will allow the owner/master, even while sitting in his chair, to walk him at various speeds. There has been some talk of a new product: Video Husband.[12]

The question for Catholics amid all this disintegration is direct and crucial: is there any evidence that the Church — in either her preached faith, her moral behavior, or her ritual enactment — has kept her convictions about marriage in Christ intact?

Orthodoxy, orthopraxy, and ortholiturgy

There has been plenty of open conflict during the past decades about the authenticity of the Church's teaching, and of her moral convictions. Liturgical reform has also aroused strident controversy, particularly in reference to how it may be re-inculturated. For many, this last element of Church renewal has seemed to have had the least at stake. But the sensibilities of the Church in its communal celebrations and rites are perhaps that element in her life that most needs to be culturally detoxed if the revelation entrusted to us is to be rightly refreshed.

As things stand, our sensibilities seem to have little independence from those of our civic neighbors. Divorce rates among Catholics do not seem to single us out as conscientious objectors. Abortion rates embarrass us. Income statistics in Catholic households are also among the highest in the country, and that is not a finding irrelevant to our concerns here. Perhaps the most unsettling statistic tells us that every year our Church's marriage tribunals give about 60,000 divorced ex-couples the assurance that their marriages were never valid — like vaccinations that never puffed up — and they usually attribute the misfire to "lack of due discretion." They may be on target. Maybe these examiners should be assigned to our baptisms and funerals to see how many of them labor under a like lack. But if these annulments *are* honest judgments, then what do they imply about the due discretion of a clergy that is charged with preaching

12. Roger Ricklefs, "What a Darling Baby! Let's Push Rewind And See Her Again," *Wall Street Journal*, 24 November 1987; Douglas Martin, "An 80's Baby Simulated On Videotape," *The New York Times*, 19 March 1988.

a startling kind of marriage almost no one else in America has the nerve to believe in — a clergy that is willing to retail whatever appeals to the walk-in trade, and lacks the gumption to look them in the eye and suggest that what we Catholics are obliged to celebrate is probably not what *they* want to celebrate?

A tiny fragment of counter-evidence is the stunning story of Mother Teresa's visit to Radcliffe College, now the women's activist center at Harvard.

> In the *Radcliffe Quarterly* of September 1982 we read the news that Mother Teresa was invited to address Radcliffe's graduating seniors at Class Day. Mother Teresa, the *Quarterly* reports, "made a bid for virginity." The *Quarterly* quoted her as having said to the seniors that on "your wedding day . . . the most beautiful thing is to give a virgin heart, a virgin body, a virgin soul." The reporter, a member of the graduating class of 1983, added in straightfaced language: "Many questioned the appropriateness of the choice of Mother Teresa as Class Day Speaker."[13]

13. Norma Rosen, "Hers: Everybody wants to do something about baby-making," *The New York Times*, 2 December 1982.

Four years earlier and several hundred yards away, Alexander Solzhenitsyn had inflicted a comparable *angina* on Harvard graduates gathered to hear his Commencement address, entitled "The Exhausted West," which described America's failure as a moral community:

> I have spent all my life under a Communist regime, and I will tell you that a society without any objective legal scale is a terrible one indeed. But a society with no other scale but the legal one is not quite worthy of man either. . . .
>
> No, I could not recommend your society in its present state as an ideal for the transformation of ours. Through intense suffering our country has achieved a spiritual development of such intensity that the Western system in its present state of spiritual exhaustion does not look attractive. . . .
>
> In early democracies, as in American democracy at the time of its birth, all individual human rights were granted because man is God's creature. That is, freedom was given to the individual conditionally, in the assumption of his constant religious responsibility. Such was the heritage of the preceding thousand years. Two hundred, or even fifty, years ago, it would have seemed quite impossible, in America, that an individual could be granted boundless freedom simply for the satisfaction of his instincts or whims. Subsequently, however, all such limitations were discarded everywhere in the West; a total liberation occurred from the moral heritage of Christian centuries, with their great reserves of mercy and sacrifice. State systems were becoming increasingly and totally materialistic. The West ended up by truly enforcing human

288

The Rituals of Jesus, the Anti-Ritualist: Worship, the Real Make-Believe

The late moralist Erma Bombeck, using more familiar terminology but no less strange a message, spoke for the tradition . . . or, more accurately, the faith. Faced with phrases like "Love doesn't need a piece of paper," and "Look how many people get stuck in unhappy relationships," she was trying to define what makes marriage different from cohabitation. "In both relationships, one shares the same bathroom, feeds the collective dog, eats together, shops together, sleeps side by side, and yet. . . ." Then she saw the difference in a TV play, when a widowed father didn't want to continue with a spice instead of a spouse. Why not? "Because we don't worry about things together."

> You have to be married to understand that line. Anyone can play house, but a couple struggling to pay for one is something else. A philosopher once said, "Marriage is our last — our best — chance to grow up." He could be right. Everything up until the time you walk down the aisle has been polite, guarded, and a little superficial. . . .
>
> We've gone through three wars, two miscarriages, five houses, three children, 17 cars, 23 funerals, seven camping trips, 12 jobs, 19 banks and three credit unions. I stopped counting slammed doors after 3,009. What do I have to show for it? A feeling of pride and contentment for having done something that isn't easy. A realization that there is someone outside of myself without whom I do not feel whole.
>
> Maybe the difference between living together and being married is that the former is a spectator sport and the latter is playing the game by all the rules. Marriage has no guarantees. If that is what you're looking for, go live with a car battery.[14]

Wendell Berry, another great moralist of our age, is even less circumspect:

> Marriage, in what is evidently its most popular version, is now on the one hand an intimate "relationship" involving (ideally) two

---

rights, sometimes even excessively, but man's sense of responsibility to God and society grew dimmer and dimmer.

Harvard Magazine, July-August 1978,
pp. 22, 24, 25-26

14. Erma Bombeck, "Living together can't measure up to marriage," *Chicago Sun-Times,* 4 February 1988.

successful careerists in the same bed, and on the other hand a sort of private political system in which rights and interests must be constantly asserted and defended. Marriage, in other words, has now taken the form of a divorce: a prolonged and impassioned negotiation as to how things shall be divided. During their understandably temporary association, the "married" couple will typically consume a large quantity of merchandise and a large portion of each other.[15]

Jesus taught that those who marry may not divorce, and that those who do divorce and marry another commit adultery. That gave his disciples as much whiplash as Paul's instruction to Philemon to take back his slave — as his brother. It was a doctrine that took people's breath away. If we cannot easily identify with that stark an independence by a faith community, we can always find an example in the small Hutterian Brothers community known as the Bruderhof, who have remained committed to fidelity in marriage, but were faced with the issue in a new way when some new members claimed that their first marriages had not been meant as acts of faith, and wanted the community to consent to new unions celebrated after their conversion:

> Again and again we have to consider this question before God. We know that already in the Old Testament, God speaks of adultery, meaning also the unfaithfulness of the people of Israel. (Micah 2:10-16) The Apostle Paul lifts up marriage by comparing it to the relationship between Christ and His Church. It is only on this basis that we can consider the question. We take very seriously Jesus' words in the Sermon on the Mount about love and about divorce and remarriage. (See Matt. 5:27-28, 31-32; see also 1 Cor. 7:10-11.)
>
> Therefore no Bruderhof member may divorce and remarry, and no remarried person may become a Bruderhof member while maintaining a marriage relationship if a former spouse is still living. For this reason also we are unable to offer overnight accommodation, except separately as singles, to couples who are not legally married. We do not want dogma. We want to be faithful to Christ. . . .
>
> We feel called not to lose the clear direction of the Sermon on the Mount, which says, "You are salt to the world. And if salt becomes tasteless, how is its saltiness to be restored? It is now good for nothing

15. Wendell Berry, *What Are People For?* (San Francisco: North Point Press, 1990), p. 180.

but to be thrown away and trodden underfoot." (Matt. 5:13 NEB) This is a serious warning for us to embrace the whole truth of Christ. Otherwise our Christianity would lose its salt.[16]

If the Church today gainsays Christ's radical teachings on marriage, the defection is sure to be visible in the ways we celebrate weddings. It would mean that those whose office it is to articulate the Christian way of marriage and to preside when people have daring enough to commit themselves to it, will be at constant odds with the degraded sensibilities that afflict all of us who live in these times. They would have to confess that in the name of the community they had been presiding at the unworthy marriages of people who were not whole enough to possess themselves or give themselves to another.[17] Then they would have to promise that in the name of that community and with a much more active participation by that community they mean to reform this pastoral ministry. For the sake of those they serve they shall have to stand firm. If they do, they will encounter great stress and resentment. They will need to initiate a further and much more strenuous liturgical movement, and for their pains in restoring marriage in Christ they will understandably be accused of trying to undermine what the tradition had become. But only a ritual life that peaceably and harmoniously enacts this crazy Gospel that Christ left us will give us any peace.

Moral attention in the sacrament

The sacramental life of the Church has a deep link with its shared moral commitments. This is illustrated by a story told by the neuropsychologist Oliver Sacks, the last author in this chapter to be honored as a distinguished moralist. Sacks wrote in *The Man Who Mistook His Wife for a Hat* of Jimmie G., his hospitalized patient who by 1975 had totally lost all memory of events since 1945. He could remember his youth, his military service, and Truman's inauguration, but everything since then was utterly lost to his memory. Jimmie was found to be afflicted by a syndrome identified a century earlier by Korsakov, and described in this century by

16. Johann Christoph Arnold, "Divorce and Remarriage," *The Plough* (Rifton, N.Y.), No. 2 (1983), p. 14. Quotation from the *New English Bible*.

17. See Maggie Scarf, *Unfinished Business: Pressure Points in the Lives of Women* (Garden City, N.Y.: Doubleday, 1980).

Luria. His mind was bright and his recall from the early years was prodigious: for instance, he could recite from memory all the chemical elements, in order and by number, but he stopped at Uranium, no. 92 in the
Periodic Table, the last to have been discovered before Jimmie's high
school chemistry class. Since his memory cannot retain any new impressions for more than a few seconds, every person at the hospital where he
has lived since 1975 is a stranger to him each time they walk into the room.
The only person remaining from Jimmie's youth and available to be recognized, with emotion, is his brother, though Jimmie cannot understand
how he got so old. "None of us," wrote Sacks, "had ever encountered,
even imagined, such a power of amnesia, the possibility of a pit into which
everything, every experience, every event, would fathomlessly drop, a
bottomless memory-hole that would engulf the whole world." Sacks encouraged Jimmie to keep a diary, but it was of no interest to him since he
retained no notion of a "day before" and did not even recognize his own
handwriting. Because of this utter isolation Jimmie was chronically unen-
gaged, and chronically sad.

One tended to speak of him, instinctively, as a spiritual casualty
— a "lost soul": was it possible that he had really been "de-souled"
by a disease? "Do you think he has a soul?" I once asked the sisters
[who directed the hospital in which he practiced]. They were outraged
by my question, but could see why I asked it. "Watch Jimmie in
chapel," they said, "and judge for yourself."

I did, and I was moved, profoundly moved and impressed, because I saw here an intensity and steadiness of attention and concentration that I had never seen before in him or conceived him capable
of. I watched him kneel and take the Sacrament on his tongue, and
could not doubt the fullness and totality of Communion, the perfect
alignment of his spirit with the spirit of the Mass. Fully, intensely,
quietly, in the quietude of absolute concentration and attention, he
entered and partook of the Holy Communion. He was wholly held,
absorbed, by a feeling. There was no forgetting, no Korsakov's then,
nor did it seem possible or imaginable that there should be; for he
was no longer at the mercy of a faulty and fallible mechanism — that
of meaningless sequences and memory traces — but was absorbed in
an act, an act of his whole being, which carried feeling and meaning
in an organic continuity and unity, a continuity and unity so seamless
it could not permit any break.

Clearly Jimmie had found himself, found continuity and reality, in the absoluteness of spiritual attention and act. The sisters were right — he did find his soul there. And so was Luria, whose words now came back to me: "A man does not consist of memory alone. He has feeling, will, sensibility, moral being . . . it is here . . . you may touch him, and see a profound change." Memory, mental activity, mind alone, could not hold him; but moral attention and action could hold him completely.[18]

Sacks's description of the frail but primal capacity which Jimmie somehow retained, and which revealed itself at Mass, would seem to be a wonderful account of what any one of us aspires to at worship: he "was absorbed in an act, an act of his whole being, which carried feeling and meaning in an organic continuity and unity, a continuity and unity so seamless it could not permit any break." Sacks sees a power in moral activity which transcends that of the mind: "Memory, mental activity, mind alone, could not hold him; but moral attention and action could hold him completely." We might carry that insight a little further and observe that our ritual activity is what unites and activates the work of both the mind and the will — and it was still so even for Jimmie.

If that be so for us, then ritually we shall have to be a Christ community that initiates and enjoys rituals which would allow no one to be at home who did not coherently and powerfully share the doctrinal convictions and the moral commitments of our faith. For Philemon and Onesimus that must have been a burning imperative each time they shared the eucharist. Worship is make-believe: not as a fantasy, but in the very opposite literal sense: it generates and nourishes our beliefs. It should allow us no good peace when we cheat on them.

18. Oliver Sacks, "The Lost Mariner," in *The Man Who Mistook His Wife for a Hat, and Other Clinical Tales* (New York: Summit Books, 1985), pp. 22-42, at 36.

CHAPTER ELEVEN

Close to the Prodigal Father:
Case Studies on Penance and Prayer

To illustrate the manner and power of the Church's rituals, I should like to dwell upon two: the sacrament of Penance, and the practice of prayer.

Penance

Since the 1960s, one practice that has largely eluded renewal is confession. Indeed, it has undergone a sustained decline. There has been no public campaign against confession, no dissuasion in the press, no bitter complaint. But by an almost spooky simultaneity most Catholics in North America and Northern Europe have indefinitely postponed the sacrament, and that postponement eventually became a moratorium. The stoppage was not, it would seem, the result of some negative conviction. The scent of sulphur puckers the nostrils much less in church nowadays and it may be that, with the prospect of punishment so dimmed, people feel under less of a constraint than they once did. Perhaps Catholics were not really as fond of this rite as those pamphlets used to boast, when they chided Protestants for discarding this necessary sacrament.

An inquiry into Penance would be timely even if the confessionals were being mobbed, however. It has suffered from confusion for centuries. At first, deadly sin after conversion was not seriously contemplated, and no formal provision for subsequent re-conversion was made. Mark's "explanation" of the Parable of the Sower (Mark 4:13-20) is illuminating in this matter.[1] It offers three different reasons for defections: some had

---

1. Its primitive form (Mark 4:1-9) dealt with a question that bothered Jesus' original

abandoned their commitment because Satan had undermined it; others, because their faith was shallow and had never taken root; still others, because their commitment had been choked by wealth and other worldly seductions.

This preserves for us an early Christian meditation on sin in the lives of those who have already renounced Satan and all his stratagems and allurements. Paul's warnings about sexual immorality, intramural rivalry, stinginess or finagling with the common funds, and vindictive civil litigation between believers, followed by James's sarcasm about how the clergy were pandering to the wealthy, and 2 Peter's alarm about independent preachers creating their own sectarian conventicles, are all evidence that the Church was not long in its first fervor before finding there were still old abscesses in their souls that needed lancing and healing.

The formal discipline of penance once used to reconcile defectors from persecution or heresy begot in the third and fourth centuries a new process for restoring those guilty of the great sins: adultery, apostasy, and murder. By then it was undeniable that Christians could sin gravely, but it required time for Christians to be as convinced that these sins could be truly forgiven and the sinners reliably reconciled. Penance became known as a sacramental life-preserver, the "second plank after shipwreck." It was a public form of discipline, and to safeguard sincerity it could not be offered more than once in a lifetime. The emphasis was on *penance* and *reconciliation:* a stringent discipline to be undergone, not for communal retribution or public humiliation or even as a cautionary warning to others, but to purge out the evil passions that had gained the mastery over the sinner's heart, and to reactivate him or her in the worshipping community. One had sinned; now one had to unlive the sin. One was on the outs with the Lord and the community; now one sought reunion.

Churchmen (especially the Celts) began at the turn of the seventh century to supplement the ancient discipline with other pious rituals put to penitential use: prayers, pilgrimages to shrines, enlistment in the crusades (later), etc. As the consciousness of sin became vastly enlarged, penitential discipline was imposed, not only for public crimes, but for the

---

disciples: what hope did their movement have if so few of the crowds who listened to his preaching became real disciples? In later years the parable was given a "second edition," so to speak, to answer a question those first disciples never asked, but which arose years after Jesus had ascended: how could any Christian defect? The rewrite was entered into the text as an explanation of the original parable, but it puts the parable to very different use.

numberless infringements of the lengthening catalogue of commandments published by preachers. Now the emphasis shifted to *confession.* The act of reconciliation became private, and was acknowledged as a sacrament. One had to tell all. In the Eastern Church confession was sometimes confided to lay monks respected as spiritual guides.

The sacrament had thus detached itself from what Christians first knew about the discipline of moral rehabilitation. Penance was originally an energetic and painstaking transformation of a person misused. What it gradually became was an instant cure, a magic rite. It may be that the present disaffection among Catholics is a reaction to latent inadequacies that led Protestants to reject the custom and Orthodox to neglect it. Thus an inquiry is doubly opportune: the Church membership has largely discontinued using it, and there may have been good reasons for them to do so. But there is better reason for us all to refresh and renew our understanding of the gift of Penance.

Another reason for venturing these remarks is that I can find no other single point across the field of Christian thought and practice where more misunderstandings converge. The sacrament of Penance, as expounded and as understood, is afflicted by most of the misunderstandings this book is at pains to identify and relieve.

To begin with, most folks have come to confession with the idea that it is God whom the sacrament is going to change, rather than themselves. The penitent approaches God to solicit his forgiveness. She presents herself, and once she has admitted her fault and pleaded her sincerity, the words of forgiveness are offered: from the confessor, and from the God by whom he is deputized. If anyone undergoes ethical transformation it is the Lord. The operative idea is that the Father withholds forgiveness until the sinner has sought and deserved it. First the sinner repents; then God forgives her. But this is all a denial of what Jesus discloses about his Father: that he *is* Forgiveness, that reconciliation between ourselves and him requires no change in him, but one in us: a divinely enabled healing to allow his extravagant love finally to permeate us. Reconciliation does not involve our seeking him, or our placating him. It is *he* who must take the initiative, he who seeks *us* out. Jesus offers forgiveness, urges it upon his hearers, always makes the overture to them.

This is nowhere better expressed than in the parable of the Prodigal Son in Luke 15. Actually, we misname the tale: it is the father who is the main character in the story; *he* who is prodigal. Little is said of the son save that he stalks out of home and family and squanders his share of the fortune (the proceeds of his father's land and toil) in circumstances suggestive of Club Méd. Ruined and desperate, he heads home again, not as a son — no hope or thought of that now — but possibly as a hired hand, with a full belly for a change. The story never suggests that he has a change of heart, only that he is hungry. He is the same Schlemiel of a son when he comes up the path. But the father has been waiting. He does not let the son walk up to the door. He runs out to meet him. He does not allow him to finish his prepared apology and job application, but sweeps his fool of a son into his arms and orders a household celebration. If that were not enough, the story then continues on to describe the outrage of the elder brother, whose sense of justice provides an even sharper contrast with the prodigal affection of the father. The story ends in frustration, because the father cannot make either son understand how and why he loves them. The younger son thinks he is beyond loving as a son, and hopes only to be a hired hand who earns what he gets. The elder son thinks he has earned his father's love, and has thought of himself all along as a hired hand. Neither realizes that the old man loves them both for the same reason: they are his sons.

Our understanding may be no better. As the sacrament is conventionally understood, the penitent is summoned to submit himself, to humiliate himself for his misdeeds before priest and Lord. But in the parable, if anyone humiliates himself it is the father, who throws himself without guile upon the hearts of his two sons. They may treat him as a fool, or be overwhelmed by his love and respond with like sincerity. Likewise in the sacrament: the person who would be deputized for Christ, as Christ was for the Father, has no business summoning his weak and sordid brothers and sisters before him to be forgiven. He must at his own risk offer open affection to them in the face of their offenses, and draw them into forgiveness. That is why the service of eucharistic preacher is joined to that of penitential forgiver. His task is not to sit in the confessional ready to administer the protocols of reconciliation to those who have already come to terms with their failures, but first to reach out from the pulpit to touch and stir those who had not given it much thought before his overture. The initiative in the sacrament, then, must lie with the minister, who must represent a God who in no way will alter his love for the sinner through the sacrament. He will not relent, he cannot be placated, he demands no prior atonement: because, like his deputy but ever so much better, he does not turn away in disdain in the first place. The initiative is from and for the Lord. The sinner, wanting to be back in the family, responds.

Another feature of Penance that has been twisted wrong way round is that of revelation. By rights a sacrament, like Jesus himself, should bring a beneficial disclosure to the believer: a disclosure of her own character and of the Father's. But in confession as poorly practiced all revelation has been by the penitent. Nothing is discovered; she comes to tell what she already knows. The minister has nothing to reveal. And such disclosure as there is, leaves no one much the better for it. Not even the confessor comes away much the wiser.

The structure of the sacrament has been turned into something reminiscent of a tribunal. The confessor sits in judgment on the misadventures of the penitent, and assigns a token penalty. It is a thorough embodiment of the forensic metaphor discussed in Chapter Five. And it is a sad confusion. For the one thing a judge can never do is to forgive. A judge can condemn, or acquit, but never forgive. And the one thing Jesus does not do on behalf of his Father is punish. Thus the dynamics of a criminal court are perhaps the least apt to serve as an embodiment of what God is trying to do in his forgiveness.

Sin

The sacrament reaches deeply into beliefs about morality, and here it has managed to institutionalize some of our worst confusions about sin. For example, the catechism recounts that a serious sin, one that would separate a person from amity with God and destroy all graced love in her heart, has three distinct elements: grave matter, full knowledge, and full consent. Surely this is misleading.

There is a dismal amount of sin in life, but not always "grave matter." Most of the sordidness and selfish neglect take less spectacular forms than grand larceny, aggravated assault, or perjury. As Rose Macaulay put it so vividly, sin begins with the sneaky thieveries of a child, and need not have grown into a front-page felony to have eaten out a person's heart. But as I tried to argue in Chapter Six, there are patterns of action that are morally toxic, addictive, seductive, degenerative, and progressively lethal. The descent into evil through seduction into addiction, promiscuity, and self-imposed blindness, may create an undertow that has already begun the drowning process. That *decisive* time when a person is morally terminal may be more important to recognize than the later, *definitive* moment when he or she is morally dead. Action can be morally grave before actions are.

As for "sufficient reflection," it is the last thing we possess when messing in evil. When we are up to no good, reflection is the last thing we permit ourselves. A clear head and an open eye are what we shun. We confuse ourselves with double-think and double-talk; we never look our-selves in the eye. We blur our vision. Evil has no relish for reflection. We manage to harbor within ourselves far more sin than malice.

And as for "full consent," apparently no one ever fully consents to evil. We sidle into it, we back up to the edge of the cliff and wait for a stiff wind to blow us off the edge, and then shout "Whoops!" We speak of our embarrassments as "having happened to us," or simply as "having hap-pened." "Mistakes were made." Sin does not involve determined acts of the will. It involves a lurching, disabled will. It is virtue that enables us to make decisions; sin is our way of ricocheting through life by avoiding decisions.

The *Catechism* states:

> Mortal sin requires *full knowledge* and *full consent.* It presupposes knowledge of the sinful character of the act, of its opposition to God's law. It also implies a consent sufficiently deliberate to be a personal choice. . . .
>
> *Unintentional ignorance* can diminish or even remove the impu-tability of a grave offense. But no one is deemed to be ignorant of the principles of the moral law, which are written in the conscience of every man. The promptings of feelings and passions can also diminish the voluntary and free character of the offense, as can external pres-sures or pathological disorders. Sin committed through malice, by deliberate choice of evil, is the gravest.
>
> Mortal sin is a radical possibility of human freedom, as is love itself.[2]

This is the perspective and language of criminal justice (and probably not very helpful there), but not of moral ministry. Love is a radical possi-bility of human freedom, but sin is not; it is a radical inevitability of sub-human bondage. Love and sin are contraries: they are the characteris-tic attitudes and acts of self-possession and self-alienation.

We are misled if we search for responsibility as the hallmark of sin, for the serious selfishness in our lives is more likely to be furtive and impulsive than deliberate. A penitent asks himself what he has done that is monstrously evil, contemplated soberly, and then after mature con-sideration committed — with the forethought and intention of flinging affront to God. Faced with that question he will rarely find anything to

2. *Catechism of the Catholic Church* (1994), §§1859-61.

reproach himself for. That fourteen-year-old we considered earlier, who began with a Virginia Slim and ended as a major junkie, had burnt out morally long before the end, and however grave the nature of her dysfunction by then, her knowledge had been buried beneath a trash heap of incoherent and self-serving confusion, and her consent had succumbed as the victim of addiction. As a woman, as a sinner, she had perished and had taken her disabled mind and will down with her.

Our problem is not what is on our conscience, but what we don't let get on our conscience. If serious sin were the work of people who were knowledgeable and deliberate, rescue might be easy work. But we are not, and it is not. The Church has to take the initiative for the Lord because true self-knowledge can be dared only as we gain the nerve to believe we are loved no matter what we shall find.

The particulars and customs that invested confession had added their own frustrations. For example, the old confessional itself seemed designed only to thwart the purposes of the sacrament. If the minister was to embody the forgiveness of the Father, not simply in words but with his entire person, then the thoroughgoing personal exchange that is wanted could often be blocked by the closeted anonymity of the confessional. It was argued that the very character of people's offenses would lead them to prefer anonymity. But the point of the sacrament is that someone is sent to embody the Father as Jesus embodied him, and one is opened to the Father's forgiveness insofar as he or she is actually present to the person of the minister: not words through the wall, but a forgiving fellow sinner face-to-face.

Then there was the traditionally approved custom of very frequent confession. This had sometimes encouraged a trivializing of sin. People are unlikely to scrutinize their lives in serious depth if they are doing it every week or so. If one does try to give an account of himself too often, he may begin to talk about the surface odds-and-ends instead of overall trends or significant behavior. The Church encouraged this by suggesting quite specific lists of sins and information as to frequency and circumstance. What emerged was not so much a report from the conscience as a bookkeeper's tally: dutiful but without insight or conviction.

There was the further custom of making one's confession to any priest available. A confessor need not be as devout and shrewd as St. Philip Neri or Father Zosima (in *The Brothers Karamazov*) before one dare open one's conscience to him. But the sacrament makes demands upon its minister. If it is perfunctory and routine, then priestly ordination is probably the only qualification needed. But if one person is to ask into the heart of another with the candor and forgivingness of Jesus, then it is a highly personal task, and calls for a person of sensitivity, honesty, savvy, and compassion. These are qualities that do not abound in wasteful profusion among our clergy. Perhaps this is to be expected in a rite that deprives itself of good ministers by ordaining only those who are willing to forgo marriage, rather than choosing those persons who have already displayed the graces one looks for in a servant of God. In any case, the custom had too often been to bring one's sins to the nearest priest available, or to the least inquisitive.

One early attempt to renew the sacrament was the general penitential service with generic group confession and general absolution. Good priests rightly distressed at the sight of honest folk in their congregations hanging back from communion yet loath to come to the confessional, seized the expedient of offering everyone in church general absolution, on the express but perfunctory injunction that those with sins on their consciences should submit them to confession at some early occasion. If one is content simply to augment the headcount at communion, this would serve. But it reinforced all those vexatious misunderstandings that spook people away from confession and, worse, from Christ. First, they are confirmed in their belief that many may be in mortal sin, banned from communion, for having missed Mass on Sunday or (in yesteryear) eaten meat on Friday. Meanwhile some of the more subversive features of human conduct went all unnoticed. Second, one continued to believe that release from sin is achieved with the waving of a hand and the invocation of words. Trivial sin: trivial repentance. And the community went on, sadly ignorant of that intimate sacramental encounter wherein one person learns joyfully to share his conscience with another. They were led to prefer mass meetings where anyone's conscience can be lost in a crowd.

Most difficult, yet most forgiving

Ministry to women and men involved in abortions has provoked some of the most serious pastoral reflection on the ministry of Penance. Once, when confronted with the sorrow of a woman in the aftermath of her abortion, by some instinct I suggested, after our long conversation, that what we might need to do to free her from the many complications of that one painful moment required more time. She agreed that instead of concluding the confession prematurely we would call a recess for a few weeks. I also asked her, during whatever time we found it took, to fast from the eucharist, and she agreed to that too. We went on together for months, until one day it seemed right to us both to move to the exchange of expressed contrition and absolution, and the next day she returned, intact, to the communion of the Church. My last request from that long confession was that someday she write me about it all, which she did with a deep and edifying understanding. Indeed, by then I knew how much I owed my own deeper understanding to her. She also expressed her satisfaction with the pace of reconciliation we had followed.

This taught me that some experiences which tear one's life to shreds are treated trivially if we compress a confession into a single sitting, and that a progressive recovery of conscience and a patient penitential fast from the eucharist can sometimes be appropriate. When a person whose moral disability is beginning to show on the Richter Scale ventures toward reconciliation, one is unlikely to be capable of assisting him or her into forgiveness in a brief encounter. The remedy need bear no resemblance to the fall. The *decisive* disaster may have been provoked by chance, sickness, or ignorance. The *definitive* event may have been abrupt, inadvertent, frivolous. Not so the recovery: that must be as intensely purposeful as the fall may have been thoughtless. A transformation of character pursues its own thoroughgoing pace. The time is not needed for the penitent to put sin into words; it is the much more strenuous search for the feelings, sentiments, recognition, and reconciliation that would then find a settled and settling expression. Real confession can be a long experience, and the joyful reconstruction that follows can be longer still. It takes one-fiftieth of a second to go through a windshield, but years to get a new face.

At the right pace, deep realization ripens. One woman, after a long and powerful account of how she had accompanied a friend to the abortion clinic, and was allowed a brief visit to her in the recovery room, ended her narrative letter: "The operation is over. However, only one of the victims has survived." A man wrote: "I know that I am sorry for my action, and I think you know that too; and I'm willing to bet God knows I'm sorry. But I think you are calling me to do something more than 'be sorry,' to have a self-realization of why I did what I did. What quality permitted me to go through with it?" Another woman reflected at greater length:

> I *knew* in my heart and guts and innards, that I didn't have the right to deny that child life, even out of concern for its own welfare: I didn't have the right to protect it to the point of killing it. When I look at the situation I was born into, living on the streets with a mother who was a drunk, in and out of asylums, and a father who

was often hysterical, it would have been easy for someone to say that I should have been aborted, because I wasn't a wanted or planned child. And indeed, I was not: my father tried to kill me when I was two. But I couldn't for a moment say that I wish I had been aborted, the joy and wonder that life has given me is a thousand times a thousand greater than the childhood suffering, although that left its hang-ups, to be sure.

So you see, I knew what I needed to know, in my conscience. I knew on a level far deeper than personality or logic that the child should be born, but I didn't live up to what I knew because of fear and selfishness, that's all. I was afraid of losing _____, I was afraid of trying to raise a kid alone, I was afraid of the loneliness that might involve, and I was too selfish to want to change my life in the ways that a child would force me to.

Now she *was* seeing and saying what earlier she could not bear to see or say. She was coming to sufficient reflection with time and grit, and with Penance she was recovering full consent of her will.

I have spoken all to one side of the issue, putting the finger on the faltering features of the sacrament of Penance as conventionally understood and practiced. Many devout and shrewd priests still sit in forgiveness, and many believers find new depth to their sincerity and compunction in the sacrament. But for the most part the rapid disaffection across whole fields of the Church that had previously been peculiarly attached to this sacrament only shows that many faithful Christians had not really experienced the gift given in Penance. For many who had given themselves faithfully and regularly in confession, no great discovery had been the reward, because the sacrament had been misconstrued and misministered.

As one young man, a high school student on retreat, once wrote: "But now I am astounded by the possibility for sin, by my personal uselessness; how can I express all that I know is wrong in me? My incapability to express this results in my 'shopping list' confession, my reeling off a series of 'sins' purely symbolic of the inner wrong I feel. But is my duty done? My confession has on the one hand satisfied the basic requirements of my religious scruples and yet my ego is still intact!" His reflection is a potent reminder that some of the most authentic confessions involve matters with none of the life-and-death issues like abortion, yet call the conscience to serious confrontation.

A burden to conscience, not a relief

The Gospel speaks often of forgiving, but perhaps the most fetching forgiveness tale is that of Zacchaeus (Luke 19:1-10). He was a squat man, but held high rank among the publicans in Jericho who acted as agents for the Roman overlords, to tax their fellow Jews. They paid the Romans a set amount up front for the right to collect taxes from a district, and then it was up to them to extort all they could from the residents, to recoup their outlay and take everything beyond that as profit. They were understandably pariahs among their countrymen. One day Zacchaeus wandered over to watch the hubbub when Jesus came to town. To his surprise the prophet singled him out of the crowd and invited himself to lunch and lodge *chez* Zacchaeus. In the midst of the entertainment Zacchaeus blurted out to his guest that he was ready to give away half his fortune to the poor, and would make over fourfold damages to those he had over-assessed. At the close of the story Jesus observed that this was why he preferred to seek out the company of sinners.

In the story Zacchaeus approaches Jesus with common curiosity; it is Jesus who makes the real overture. There are no reproaches, no accusations, not even innuendoes. It is simply the presence of this overwhelmingly simple and honest man of God that gets to Zacchaeus, who had spent his wit and work on gouging his townsmen. Jesus is hosted at his home, and leaves a transformed man behind.

Likewise in the Church. Men and women of profound and single-hearted affection must speak out the simple call and confrontation of Jesus, and must ask for the fellowship of everyone they pass, most particularly the offensive and the inert. Those whom they touch to the heart will accept their readiness to be invited into their consciences. In this intimate encounter, people will come to priests to help them be freed from what perturbs their consciences. But that is just for starters. What they must further do is ask the priests — and others who share their ministries, for forgiveness is a widely shared power — to help them discover what never gets on their consciences well enough.

The revelation in Penance is twofold. Someone calls on another to help her search her heart with comradely honesty. Together they discover the furtive sins, the craft and familiar selfishness, the offenses that are unforgiven because unsuspected, unrepented, unforsworn. On the other side of the exchange the minister reveals to the penitent that in the face of her pettiness and fault he loves her all the same, all the more. And so we can embody the love of the Father and the Son, by dint of their Spirit at work in us. As in all sacramental encounters there is the twofold discovery: God's grace and our sin. And the two are intertwined. A person opens her heart and allows herself to discover fault never earlier acknowledged, because she is in the company of one who she trusts will not hold her in contempt. The love of the Father comes across to her strongly because it is incarnated in one who knows her weakest self, yet takes her as a sister in faith, a friend in Christ.

Thus confession is no mere apology to the Lord for acknowledged failure, nor the comforting response that one's sin is set aside. The servant of the Lord approaches someone in the first place to help him *find* his sin, and conveys to his brother that the Lord loves him no matter what his faults. The forgiveness has always been there, but it may be in this encounter, discovery, and purgation that it penetrates the bones of the person who needs it.

Sacramental Penance is by no means the only means of forgiveness. God has but a single attitude toward us humans: he forgives. Better: he *is* Forgiveness. Reconciliation takes place whenever a person withdraws from selfishness into love. This need involve no religion, no sacrament. A person is forgiven simultaneously as she is transformed into one who loves. It can be done with the help of anyone with candor and care. What the sacrament does is to enhance this transformation with the revealing disclosure of how much is at stake. When one human speaks to another the words of absolution and forgiveness that Jesus Christ charges us all to say, he reveals to his brother that *whenever* he ceases ignoring and exploiting his neighbors, his sisters and brothers, he is being restored thereby to the Father. In every aloofness from brother or sister one is holding back from the Father. So too whenever any person turns afresh toward his sisters or brothers, he thereby — whether he knows it or not — cleaves closer to the Father. Any moment a person takes new counsel with himself or another, and breaks through some trammeling by his ego, forgiveness finds its way into him. What is peculiar about sacramental reconciliation is that it brings faith to bear: one celebrates how eternally it matters that one human cherish another.

Eucharist and Penance call one another forth. In both, the summons of Jesus is uttered: publicly in one and privately in the other. In the one, a spokesman puts the challenge to the entire community how they are loved and how they need to love in return. At Eucharist one minister embodies Christ to the community of believers. At Penance the minister singles people out one by one and seeks entry to their consciences. Eucharist is the invitation to Penance. Penance is the threshing floor where

306

grain and husk are beaten apart, where we are protected from being those who merely chorus "Lord, Lord" at Eucharist.

Guilt and Shame

One often hears that the purpose of confession is to relieve guilt. Yet in the Gospel story Zacchaeus approaches Jesus without any particular guilt; only when Jesus draws near does the publican find himself beset by guilt on every side. The sacrament is gifted to us in order that we may have our sin revealed to us, and incur guilt. The Church insists that guilt is a gift, not a penalty. It is particularly so in the sacrament, where one simultaneously discovers the support of the Lord and of the Lord's go-between. C. G. Jung has spoken very favorably of the practice of confession. He had almost no psychiatric patients who were practicing Catholics, and he explained that they had their pathological guilt feelings relieved in the confessional. Many practitioners of psychology and psychiatry feel differently, though, and some accuse the Church of worrying people into unnatural seizures of scruple or guilt. Perhaps this crisscross of attitude arises from a confusion between what I should like to distinguish as guilt and shame.

Shame is a fear of the contempt of others. It arises from one's own misbehavior. The weaknesses need not really be public knowledge, but there is the fear that they might be exposed, a brooding uneasiness that others might see through me. It surges up most troublingly from the cousin sources of sex and violence. Misadventures of these kinds arise from passion: one feels he has been "beside himself," and is anxious to disclaim his failure since he was not his "real" self. These are the faults we are most reluctant to publish. Craving for privacy is commonly recognized in reference to sex. Our country's bad conscience over various recent military incursions may give us fresh insights into the working of shame regarding violence. In any case, there are things we loathe ourselves for, and since we hunger for the respect of others, we are ashamed for them to know what we have done. But that is not guilt.

Those who care for us try to take the edge off shame by reassurance. They put it forward that what we do is not so contemptible, or that they and others commonly fall into the same shame. This kind of acceptance can be very welcome, especially if one is in a mighty hunger for it. One is relieved to be able to unburden to another, and suffer no disdain. But this does nothing for guilt, and I doubt that the alleviation of shame alone is of much service in the deeps of the heart. Today one hears passionate ballyhoo for the various devices of instant intimacy — sensitivity sessions, pentecostal prayer groups, therapeutic weekends — which can beguile the anxious into thinking they have found reassurance for their lives in a hasty encounter. Relief of shame is a worthwhile endeavor, but I doubt it can be done without resolution of the deeper problems of guilt.

Christianity itself should contribute to the resolution of shame, for it believes in a Father before whom there can be no disgrace. He can have no contempt for us, since our infamies are nothing in his eyes. Yet churchmen have ever been tempted to use people's native shame to maneuver into a position of advantage with them. The Lord whose cherishing should be our greatest source of peace is again and again disfigured by morbid preachers who prefer a god of wrath.

Now guilt is a very different kind of dismay. In guilt one is not so much afraid of being despised, as regretful for having damaged one's neighbor by being self-serving, and sorrowful for having been impervious to the neighbor's needs. My shame makes me worry what my neighbor will feel, whereas my guilt fastens on my neighbor's loss from my neglect. It is a more substantive concern.

At first sight shame appears more easily lifted than guilt, for my neighbor can easily assure me that I am accepted, whereas the real personal harm that guilt sorrows over is not put right by cheerful words. But first appearances deceive; it is actually the other way around. The kindling of shame is the beginning of a trouble that can be endless. But guilt never really arises in one's heart unless the person is moving toward the point of purging himself of his fault. Guilt leads a person to determination, to repentance, to unliving his pettiness. We try to brush away shame by distracting ourselves; guilt fastens firmly on fact. Shame we try to efface by a change of attitude; guilt, by a change of life.

And it is the grace of the Church to give us guilt, to open our eyes to ourselves, to tell us the things our best friends should be telling us but won't. It invites us to confess our sins at the very moment of turning away from them. It urges no embarrassment on anyone in her misery, for it also reveals to her, through the resolute affection of the ministers themselves, the unflinching love of the Father who cannot despise. Not only does the Church seek to bring people guilt; it magnifies guilt, by revealing that to exploit one's neighbor is not simply a misfortune between one human and another, but a foolish flight from God.

The King of Israel called Elijah the Prophet "my enemy, the Troubler of Israel!" The person who accepts to be sent as preacher, confessor, and friend must be such a troubler. Yet when he stings the conscience with true guilt it is consoling, not embarrassing. What a person that must be. He must be so clear of conscience that he helps open the eyes of men and women to secrets of their own, without hedging to keep from playing the hypocrite. Blunt and candid must he be, the sort of friend who cannot conceal to console. And gentle, gentle as befits one who co-sorrows over the unrecoverable past while giving the courage to unlive it. His gift is to replace despair with repentance. It is a task of joy.

In Penance the sinner should not be commanded on threat of punishment to seek the sacrament, but warmly met and invited as by the father in Luke's tale, who is the Father of Jesus, and should be embodied in every minister. It is a gift; it is no imposition.

The gift of Penance is the work of a lifetime. No one ever comes away from confession with all sin removed. But every graced exchange should plough deeper into the soil of the soul than before. One can be forgiven as one grows.

The Gospel implies, as I have earlier suggested, that the Lord does not sit in judgment of us, in the sense that he would make a decision who shall be called to him and who dismissed. In that sense, a human is even less empowered to make such a judgment over fellow humans. But Jesus did claim to be judge, in that he revealed the stance of people's hearts by provoking them to respond to him. In this sense one can, one *must*, be a judge for her brother and sister. We can decree the eternity neither of ourselves nor of others, but we can ascertain with ever clearer honesty who we are and how we are growing into the full stature of a graced humanity. In this way Penance is the judgment in time that prepares us for when there will be neither time nor judgment any more.

I would like to say a word in favor of penance also. It has been the custom for the confessor to assign the recitation of certain prayers as a "penance." This is no penance at all, nor is it often likely to be prayer. Indeed, it has been a harmful counterfeit. Ritual is where a person makes discovery of his sin, but real penance must then send that person back from ritual to the substantive order of work and service. I suppose the idea of penance in this sense is of little appeal today, for it smacks of penalty, and punishment is not the fashion. People have somehow got it into their heads that the evil in their lives will evaporate at will. But we are born in selfishness and we nurture that infection within us by years and years of action for our own convenience. The way to purge the evil of years of action is by action. I have no advice for the civil judiciary and its responsibilities toward criminals, but Dostoevsky's insight into crime and punishment sheds light upon both punishment and penance. As Raskolnikov is being sent to Siberia under sentence of double murder, it dawns on him, on Sonya, and on the reader that somehow the blood will not be expiated save through suffering. The suffering is not to appease an angry people, but to repair the heart of a murderous man. In a way the murder has been uprooted from Raskolnikov before he ever sets a foot toward the East. In another way, it will never finally be plucked up until he actually serves those years of banishment whereby he works out his freedom. Grieving for his crime, Raskolnikov confesses:

> "Did I murder the old woman? I murdered myself, not her! I crushed myself once for all, for ever. . . ."[3]

And as he sets off for his long and rigorous punishment:

> At the beginning of their happiness at some moments they were both ready to look on those seven years as though they were seven days. He did not know that the new life would not be given him for nothing, that he would have to pay dearly for it, that it would cost him great striving, great suffering.[4]

A recent public debate over this very subject, initiated by Jewish intellectuals, is helpful to our understanding of penance. Simon Wiesenthal, a Jew from the borderland between the Ukraine and Poland, survived the concentration camps and led the worldwide determination to bring the Nazi malefactors of the Holocaust to justice. As an inmate in his early twenties he had been pulled out of his hospital work detail one day and summoned to the room of a dying SS officer his own age, who wanted to ask him clandestinely, as a Jew, for forgiveness. An active Catholic youngster, he had joined the Hitler Youth at 14, volunteered for the SS when the war began, and served on the Russian front. In one town they had rounded up 300 local Jews, crammed them into a house already soaked with gasoline, and set it afire. A man holding a young child alongside his wife jumped together from a second storey window after they had caught fire. The young soldier quickly obeyed a command to gun them down where they fell, along with other desperate victims. Since that day he had been

---

3. Fyodor Dostoevsky, *Crime and Punishment*, trans. Constance Garnett (Atlanta: Communication and Studies, 1968), p. 341.

4. Dostoevsky, *Crime and Punishment*, p. 449.

deeply grieved by what he had done. His uneasiness was not contained by that day, either, as he reflected painfully on the Nazi years of his life. Young Wiesenthal was disconcerted by this appeal. They wrangled back and forth for several hours, and he finally walked out without any word of forgiveness. The soldier died that night. Wiesenthal carried the memory with him for years and finally published it, followed by responses of fellow Jews and several Christians, in answer to his question: "What would you have done?" A new edition has added more than 30 new responses.[5]

In the 1967 edition every Jewish respondent said Wiesenthal was right not to have forgiven the Nazi, and every Christian said he was wrong. In the 1997 edition the responses sort out the same way, with a few variants. Some judgments are stark. "Such an act of mercy would have been a kind of betrayal and repudiation of the memory of millions of innocent victims who were unjustly murdered, among them, the members of his family" (Moshe Bejski). "How can you possibly forgive monsters who burned people alive in public; in ceremonies, staged in the open, with typical Teutonic pomp and precision? Could we even expect the Almighty to exonerate them? . . . I would have silently left the deathbed having made quite certain there was now one Nazi less in the world" (Mark Goulden). "Let the SS man die unshriven. Let him go to hell" (Cynthia Ozick). The Dalai Lama, by contrast, brought a Buddhist voice into the conversation. He recalled that a Tibetan monk who had spent 18 years in a Chinese prison, when asked what his greatest danger had been, told him what he had feared most was "losing his compassion for the Chinese." "If asked to forgive, by anyone for anything, I would forgive because God would forgive" (Theodore Hesburgh). "We are under obligation to forgive our neighbor even though he has offended against us seventy times seven. . . . 'Tis God shall repay. I am safer so" (Christopher Hollis). As one respondent observes, this clear split among the respondents was not because the Holocaust was enacted by Christians upon Jews. It brings out into the open the remarkably different views of these two communities on evil and on forgiveness.

Many Jews saw the Gentile instinct to forgive as suspiciously continuous with the prewar anti-Semitism that had made the Nazi movement possible. Wiesenthal himself reflected:

> But ere long priests, philanthropists, and philosophers implored
> the world to forgive the Nazis. Most of these altruists had probably

---

5. Simon Wiesenthal, *The Sunflower: On the Possibilities and Limits of Forgiveness*, revised and expanded edition (New York: Schocken, 1997).

never even had their ears boxed, but nevertheless found compassion for the murderers of innocent millions. The priests said indeed that the criminals would have to appear before the Divine Judge and that we could therefore dispense with earthly verdicts against them, which eminently suited the Nazis' book. Since they did not believe in God they were not afraid of Divine Judgment.[6]

Forgiveness offered so gratuitously seemed false for being frivolous: it failed to take evil seriously. Radio show host Dennis Prager angrily remembered a time when that came through clearly to him. A woman jogger in Central Park had been raped and beaten and left to bleed to death by a gang of youths.

> After their arrest, a *cardinal* of the Roman Catholic Church visited the boys at prison to tell them only one thing: "God loves you." I was so furious that I publicly noted then that someone ought to write an article "How to Get a Personal Visit from the Cardinal." . . . For four weeks I asked the clergy what they would say to these torturers if they had to meet with them. Every Protestant and Catholic clergyman, liberal and conservative, essentially echoed the cardinal's words. All the rabbis, Reform, Conservative, and Orthodox, said that they would not meet with the youths, but if forced to, they would tell them of their disgust with them, that they should be severely punished and spend the rest of their lives seeking to redress their evil; and they certainly would not tell them that God loved them.[7]

Two enormous unspoken differences help explain this divide. The Christians believe that the God of Abraham, Isaac, and Jacob gave a more definitive glimpse of his love in Jesus, dying for the sake of those who killed him, and rising to seek and reconcile them. One of the aspirations of an authentic Christian is to be capable of forgiving such a person as that pathetic young Nazi. The second difference is that Christians continue to believe what was once a salient doctrine among Jews: that after death those who have lived in justice and love will be raised to live in God's presence, and that all accounts will be rightly settled only then. The Jewish respondents were generally agreed that God can and will forgive the unjust only if and after they have sought out, apologized, and given

6. Wiesenthal, *The Sunflower,* p. 85.
7. Wiesenthal, *The Sunflower,* pp. 218-19.

satisfaction to their victims, and received their forgiveness. No one else is qualified to forgive in their name. Since, on that view, all life ends at death, by definition murderers must go to their deaths with no possibility of forgiveness. Murder thereby becomes by definition the most cursed of crimes.

The Christian participants in this symposium have not stated their communal beliefs about forgiveness fully enough to be well understood by their Jewish symposiasts. That may be because they answered the question exactly as posed to them, rather than restating it. They consent to speak of forgiveness as an intransitive act: the forgiving person adopts and expresses the position of affirmation and acceptance. But if that is an account of forgiveness, it is hardly adequate as a Christian one. For forgiveness is transitive: it may begin with a unilateral initiative, but it strains toward its true conclusion: a response by the guilty person. I cannot forgive effectively by simply assuring someone that there is a forgiving God; that would be like assuring a famine-stricken Ethiopian that Kansas has just brought in a record harvest. Nor do I forgive by saying to a woman that I personally bear her no grudge. To forgive is to rehabilitate, like my former assistant now rehabilitates stroke victims, and my brother sponsors alcoholics through recovery. By God's grace we can bring the dead to life, and we can report on those experiences of resurrection.

Making amends

The penitent must admit to what he has done in the now-acknowledged fullness of its evil, must move to make possible amends, and must ask both the victim and the Father, on the strength of the love shown in Jesus, to take him back into their peace. On this account of forgiveness, the transformation must be so thorough that the perpetrator will no longer exist: he will have died and risen. The Jews had good reason to draw back from the "cheap grace" offered, for there was little Christian discussion of how this young man, on the brink of his death, might sincerely and effectively make that transformative response. True repentance entails true conversion: a rigorous course of generosity to discipline one's heart and passions into service. Penitence without penance is little more than a wish.[8]

8. The Twelve Steps of Alcoholics Anonymous are a remarkable model of what is required for penance.

A confessor represents no one but Christ and the Church. He cannot speak for other victims, or listen for them. To the contrary, his duty is to send his penitent back to make amends "whenever possible, except when to do so would injure them or others," as Step Nine of Alcoholics Anonymous wisely provides, or when death has intervened. In the case of Wiesenthal's dying SS man, amends are also impossible, but forgiveness may not be denied him on that account.

Hamlet's Uncle, King Claudius, who had slain Hamlet's father to claim both his throne and his queen, falls to prayer in chapel one day, and sees there how he can have no forgiveness without amends:

> O, my offense is rank, it smells to heaven,
> It hath the primal eldest curse upon't,
> A brother's murther. Pray can I not,
> Though inclination be as sharp as will.
> My stronger guilt defeats my strong intent . . .
> My fault is past, but, O, what form of prayer
> Can serve my turn? "Forgive me my foul murther"?
> That cannot be, since I am still possess'd
> Of those effects for which I did the murther:
> My crown, my own ambition, and my queen.
> May one be pardoned and retain th' offense?
> In the corrupted currents of this world
> Offense's gilded hand may shove by justice,
> And oft 'tis seen the wicked prize itself
> Buys out the law, but 'tis not so above: . . .
> My words fly up, my thoughts remain below:
> Words without thoughts never to heaven go.[9]

Obviously Claudius cannot make amends to his dead brother, but without divesting himself of all that he seized, he cannot even address God honestly to ask to be forgiven.

Something of the same problem was faced by Harriet, a woman whose alcoholism had strewn her life with wreckage. Her mother, whom she had hurt the most, was the most determined in her loyalty to her: "She's my baby, and I love her," she would tell the exasperated family members. "I don't care what she did." Her mother would always ask one of her sisters to look in on Harriet whenever she had been on a binge, or lost a job.

---

9. William Shakespeare, *Hamlet, Prince of Denmark*, 3, 3.

Harriet had been through treatment programs six times before sobriety took hold. As she made her shaky way through recovery she was stymied by the Ninth Step, the making of amends, because by then her mother was dead and no amends were possible. Then one day she realized she could make restitution by taking care of the person her mother had loved the most: her own widowed father. And to the end of his life that she did faithfully — "with exquisite grace," as one of her brothers says.

One powerful penance story occurs in the film, "Gandhi," during the Calcutta riots when the old man is refusing to eat in penance for the violent Hindu-Muslim slaughter. A Hindu man distraught to the edge of insanity comes to him. Muslims had killed his son, so he had gone out and killed a Muslim child, by smashing his head against a wall. "I am going to hell!" he cries. "I know a way out of hell," Gandhi faintly murmurs. The man gapes at him. "Find a child . . . a child whose mother and father have been killed, a little boy about this high," says Gandhi, gesturing with his hand to the same height the man had, when telling of his own son. "Then, raise him as your own. Only be sure that he is a Muslim. And that you raise him as one!"

The authentic Christian tradition about sin and forgiveness, then, seems to resume itself thus. We are created and nurtured by a Father whose very name is Forgiveness. Our sin is that we yield to the inclination to serve ourselves, and to feel for no one but ourselves. Through his Son, his Spirit, and others whom he has begotten, the Father reaches out to touch us, to smite us with guilt. The power and presence of our neighbor's purity opens our eyes to our befouled selves. Conscience comes alive; we turn our eyes upon ourselves, now in repentance rather than fixation. We hear the Father's call. He has but one commandment: he demands all our heart, all our strength, all our self — all, that we might recover. We find the courage to allow into our heart a neighbor who approaches us in Jesus' name, and together we stumble upon shabby and petty scenes. It is I who am guilty. And I am light-hearted to be found out! This neighbor never compels me to submit: it is a favor offered, and we both know it is. I am released from the very sins we discover, not simply for the admitting of them, but by finding it within me, by God's grace, to purge these sins and the resultant pathologies I at last allow myself to see, and by making amends. And since it is revealed to me that eternity is at stake, I become myself a more forgiving person. It will be my chief penance to bring forgiveness to others, whether or not they see this as cleaving to God. To forgive them I must bring them a love that surmounts what is contemptible in them, and is forceful enough to transform them beyond contempt.

To be a minister of such a rite is to be a profoundly forgiving and forgiven person. To be a penitent of such a rite is to be a profoundly forgiven and forgiving person.

Prayer

Sir Lawrence Shipley, writing to Lord Armiton, once sniffed at an item he had found in a daily newspaper:

"The Dean and Chapter of X have decided to discontinue, for the present, weekday morning service *in order that the cathedral clergy may devote themselves to work of national importance!*" (the note of exclamation is mine).

I need not remind you, who read the morning press so carefully, that this item of news was not given the honor of having a sensational black headline at the top of the page or column. It had no headline of any degree of blackness. It was a minor ingredient in a long column of Home News, which included news of such national importance as that "Bumbledom has collected £37 12s. 5d. for Red Cross Flag day," or that "Jane Shook has died at the age of 123," or that "a salmon weighing 35 pounds has been landed at Pangbourne."

What does this paragraph mean?

Or perhaps I had better ask: "What might this paragraph mean?"

1. It might mean that someone with no sense of fitness had attempted a miserable hoax at the expense of the Dean and Chapter of X.

2. It might mean that the Dean and Chapter of X were suffering so deeply from war-shock that they had temporarily lost their reason.

3. It might mean that the Dean and Chapter of X had not lost their reason but had lost their faith to such an extent that public prayer seemed as useless to the national welfare as an allotment [garden plot] at the North Pole.

4. It might mean that the Dean and Chapter of X had lost neither their reason nor their faith, nor both, but had been compelled by their secular masters to a course of action which they meekly undertook as the price of their establishment, and as a reflex of the national conscience. Hence —

5. It might mean that the national conscience had for all practical purposes disowned God, as of no national importance for six days

out of seven; at least, in competition with Mars, who for good or evil was now the supreme deity to receive the nation's supreme worship in sacrifice of goods and blood offerings of human life.[10]

It might indeed have meant that Sir Lawrence's nation had got its priorities in a snarl. Alternatively, it might have meant that upon consideration the public acknowledged the Dean and Chapter in question to be more valuable as bandage rollers than as men of prayer. But he does raise a question that rises above his particular pique: is prayer of value, for the national welfare or for anyone else's? There are some attitudes of prayer that make easy sense: when we render God thanks for everything we are and have, or crave his forgiveness for being faithless, or simply speak our love to him. But when we start to *ask* for things, to pray *for* something, several problems arise.

First of all, what business do we have asking for most of the things we pray for? We pray for a better job, or a raise in pay; but isn't prosperity exactly one of the things Christians are being warned not to be clutching at? And we pray to be rid of a headache, or cured of asthma, or even of cancer. But will God protect us from suffering and pain when he gave up his Only Son to be crucified? And we pray when we've had an auto accident, or when we are trying to find something lost, or when we are about to take an examination (which often amounts to the same thing). But isn't this forgetting the lilies of the field and the birds of the air? All of this praying for the good things of this life seems natural enough, but the Gospel suggests that we may be beguiled by them.

> So do not worry; do not say, "What are we to eat? What are we to drink? What are we to wear?" It is the gentiles who set their hearts on all these things. Your heavenly Father knows you need them all. Set your hearts on his kingdom first, and on God's saving justice, and all these other things will be given you as well. (Matt. 6:31-33)

Prayer of petition, after all, would simply be asking God to aid and abet our comfort and contentment — and possibly vanity — in the world.

A second problem arises from the custom of praying for other people. We pray for the woman who will shortly give birth, or for Uncle Ralph who is too fond of beer, or for grandmother's high blood pressure. In aid

10. From a letter quoted in the diary of Sir Lawrence Shipley by Vincent J. McNabb, O.P., *The Path of Prayer* (London: Burns, Oates & Washbourne, 1939), pp. 23-25.

of even graver needs we solicit family and friends to pray for us. We declare national days of prayer for this and that, and gather in groups to lobby heaven about the war, or the mentally ill, or the bishops. Is there really any strength in numbers before God?

The third problem is yet more crucial. What good does it do to pray for favors at all? God is believed by Christians to be more anxious to give than they to receive. He does not need to be told what we need, he does not need to be persuaded to give it, and he is presumably not interested in what we want but do not need. Is it not absurd in the first place to suppose that creatures could ever persuade or cajole or entice God to change his mind? And if that be so, then what could possibly be accomplished by any sort of prayer of request? Does it make matters any different than had we not prayed?

When I was a research student in Jerusalem one of my colleagues, later a professor of Old Testament in Paris, told us a tale of his brief career as a conscript in the French Artillery. One day while acting as forward observer he got his coordinates somewhat skewed (by 180°) and targeted in a salvo of howitzer fire on their own field headquarters. Far more devastating might it be if our human whim and will were able to call down the divine favor where it seemed best to foolish us. Indeed, does not the entire spectacle of prayer of petition somehow imply that God is not quite as discreet, nor yet quite as generous, as we? It is as though God's more modest and reticent plans for the furtherance of the world's welfare might stagnate without our words to the wise. But who are we to counsel the Most High, or to presume that our hearts are more extravagant than his own?

These are the problems of prayer that asks for things. We tend to ask for the very things we should be detached from. We try to bargain with God by rallying more support behind us. And we humor ourselves that we could (or should) have any influence upon the divine largesse.

Writers in our era have offered a resolution that goes somewhat like this. Despite the fact that our prayers can visit no change upon God's purpose, still our *own* minds can yield to change. The more someone sinks to her knees to beg the Father for help and rescue, the more vividly she comes to realize how completely dependent she is upon the Creator for life itself. Prayer plants within her an appreciation of what it means to be a creature. And when she prays for cessation of a feud in the family or relief from starvation in Bangladesh or for disentanglement of the confusion in our government, she gains from that prayer a streak of deeper sympathy for her neighbor's misfortune, she acquires a fuller sense of fellowship even with people never seen. She feels she is, after all, her brother's and her sister's keeper, and is drawn to serve them all the more energetically in Christian love. And though the effect of her prayer be not in God or in Bangladesh or in the persons confided to God's care, it issues in a change within herself. She is gradually transformed by her own prayer; she is the better person, the better believer, for it.

Even if true, this is feeble. On this view, God might as well not exist. One pretends that he listens to prayers, but beneath the postured exchange one would be listening to one's own impressive echo. It may seem to some a useful therapy, but the Christian is in a poor way psychologically if his transactions with God are staged in fantasy and pretense. A person can hardly gain from prayer a telling sense of dependence upon a God with whom he can never communicate.

The New Testament knows no embarrassment about prayer. The man with an epileptic child falls on his knees before Jesus and craves cure for the boy. Bartimaeus, the blind beggar, and the band of ten lepers, and the Lebanese woman with the addled girl-child, and the four friends who manhandled their paralytic companion and at last tore off a roof to get him proper attention — all these ask favors, and physical favors at that. The promise was there for them: "Anything you ask from the Father he will grant in my name. . . . Ask and you will receive, and so your joy will be complete" (John 16:23-24). Jesus urges his party to pray and never lose heart, like the widow who pestered the judge so often that he finally granted her relief just to be rid of the nuisance (Luke 18:1-8). Their prayer should be humble, though: more like that of the tax collector than that of the Pharisee (Luke 18:9-14).

Paul closes most of his letters with a promise of intercession, and a claim on his protégés' prayers. Timothy is told that petition should be made for public officials, so that the national life might be tranquil. James sends elders to pray for the recovery of those who lie abed.

Jesus himself was one to spend whole nights in the hills, alone to pray. At the great moments in his hasty life he was said to be praying: at his baptism, during the transfiguration, at the last supper, in the garden, on the cross. For what did he ask?

> I am not praying for the world
> but for those you have given me,
> because they belong to you. . . .
> I am not asking you to remove them from the world,
> but to protect them from the Evil One. . . .

I pray not only for these
but also for those
who through their teaching will come to believe in me.
May they all be one. . . . (John 17:9, 15, 20)

What says all this belief to our problems with prayer? First, Jesus' prayer walks pace by pace with his work, as left foot and right tread beside one another on one trail. Christ who cried by the grave of Lazarus, Christ who found food for his followers, Christ who loved the lepers and cleansed them, cares deeply for every human need. There is no spite about the physical, indeed no desire to spare it. But there is little interest in these things of the body for their own sake. When he heals a cripple or raise's a widow's son from death, or provides *Château Lafite* for the feast, it is all with an eye to drawing people most personally into the Father's love. The hand holds out more than the hand can hold. Man cannot live by bread alone, yet through bread Jesus supplies the nurture that provides me with eternity.

Hilaire Belloc writes:

> I am never content with the admonition to treat temporal affec-
> tions as unimportant. It seems to me false with the falsity of a half
> statement. It is, in itself, unimportant, compared with the eternal
> business of the soul, but it is, itself, part of the eternal business of the
> soul. The major human affections are immixed with eternity. That is
> their very quality. If it were not so they would not be major things;
> when the physical side comes in, as with parents and child, or lovers,
> or husbands and wives, the sacramental quality appears at once: a
> thing that never appears save where the temporal and eternal are
> mixed.[11]

Jesus' prayer was as absorbed in temporal gift as was his work. Indeed, his prayer was a cry to the Father about what he was struggling for: to uproot the hearts of humankind from the rancid swamp of ego, and plant them in the sweet soil of love. His prayer is as word to his gesture, the consecration formula for the bread he holds out. He prays for those he serves, and also for those he reaches out to serve with other hands that lend themselves to him. It is not simply his prayer that spurs him to serve;

11. Hilaire Belloc to Mrs. Reginald Balfour, Candlemas 1932, from *Letters from Hilaire Belloc,* ed. Robert Speaight (London: Hollis & Carter, 1958), pp. 225-26.

the one Spirit that gives him force for his task also gives breath to his utterances. The more any believer's prayer is absorbed into this same Spirit, the more it will leave off being simply an expression of selfish whims and cravings, and claim from the Father those gifts that give flesh spirit. The more readily we set our mind upon the kingdom and its righteousness before all else, we shall pray for all else as a means of making that kingdom come.

That point is grittily illustrated in a friend's account of his sharp converse with God, whom he peevishly insults as god:

> Some months ago my wife delivered twin sons one minute apart. The older is Joseph and the younger is Liam. Joseph is dark and Liam is light. Joseph has a whole heart and Liam has half. This means that Liam will have two major surgeries before he is three years old. The first surgery — during which a doctor will slice open my son's chest with a razor, saw his breastbone in half, and reconstruct the flawed plumbing of his heart — is imminent.
>
> I have read many pamphlets about Liam's problem. I have watched many doctors' hands drawing red and blue lines on pieces of white paper. They are trying to show me why Liam's heart doesn't work properly. Blue lines are for blood that needs oxygen. Red lines are for blood that needs to be pumped out of the heart. I watch the markers in the doctors' hands. Here comes red, there goes blue. The heart is a railroad station where the trains are switched to different tracks. A normal heart switches trains flawlessly two billion times in a life; in an abnormal heart, like Liam's, the trains crash and the station crumbles to dust.
>
> There are many nights just now when I tuck Liam and his wheezing train station under my beard in the blue night hours and think about his Maker. I would kill the god who sentenced him to such awful pain, I would stab Him in the heart like He stabbed my son, I would shove my fury in His face like a fist, but I know in my own broken heart that this same god made my magic boys, shaped their apple faces and coyote eyes, put joy in the eager suck of their mouths. So it is that my hands are clenched not in anger but in confused and merry and bitter prayer.
>
> I talk to god more than I admit. Why did you break my boy? I ask. I gave you that boy, He says, and his lean brown brother, and the elfin daughter you love so. But you wrote death on his heart, I say. I write death on all hearts, He says, just as I write life. That is

where our conversation always ends, and I am left holding the extraordinary awful perfect prayer of my second son, who snores like a seal, who might die tomorrow, who did not die today.[12]

Others are not so easily inclined to back off and presume benevolent management. In some pentecostal traditions one would not wait for a capital event like Liam's birth to notice a purposeful divine message. This pentecostal is attentive to the most everyday occurrence. He or she looks to Jesus to relieve high blood pressure, find lost car keys, and secure employment. Pain, poverty, and illness are interpreted as sequelae of sin or the work of Satan or evil spirits. Thus healing prayer begins with the exorcism of demons and an appeal for the alleviation of sin, so that serious sickness can be relieved. This Lord of Pentecost is expected to incline his ear to the most earthy and particular supplications. That could betoken a belief in his exquisite care: if no lily flowers but under his watchful eye, surely he cares distinctly about your sister's shingles and the current price of your GM stock. Yet somehow this CPA does lack something of the grandeur of the sparrow-eyeing Lord. He seems diminished by the notion that he is at our beck to remedy our paltriest concerns.

The craving to construe every auto accident and upturn in the business cycle as a skirmish between Jesus and Satan for possession of each one of us has too little in common with our received faith in the Father Almighty. It is the Gospel writ tiny. For if an influenza fever broken or a new furnace donated to a convent are, to true believers, sure signs of God's periodic affection, then the hit-and-run death of a young father of three, or dry rot in the basement beams, must be darkened by God's wrath. If all the give-and-take of welcome and dread events is spoken by God in a decipherable stream of good and bad news, of digital 111111111's and 000000000's, if weal and woe mean blessing and curse, then this is a puzzling world and that is surely a god you would want to be wary of.[13]

As for praying in unison, the point is not to sway the Father, but to give wider utterance to a shared belief. The thrust of Christ's desire is that his address to the Father infiltrate into every human desire on earth, that the voice of humanity be put into counterpoint by the Spirit with the voice of the Son, that more and more we echo in chorus the eternal dialogue of

12. Brian Doyle, "Two Hearts," *Portland* (The University of Portland Magazine) 14, 1 (Spring 1995), inside front cover. And Liam lives.

13. James T. Burtchaell, C.S.C., "The God of Our Calculations," *Commonweal* 60, 2 (28 January 1983): 54.

intimacy between Father and Son. If others be asked to join our prayer, it is in awareness that the body mystical of Jesus Christ binds us all in as limbs and members, organically quickened by a common instinct. Paul says to the Colossians:

> It makes me happy to be suffering for you now, and in my own body to make up all the hardships that still have to be undergone by Christ for the sake of his body, the Church. . . . (1:24)

The suffering of Jesus was finished on the cross, but the suffering of the fuller-fleshed Christ goes on in every human who lives in Christian faith. Paul might equally well have said that his prayer was meant to complete, in his petitions, the full tale of Christ's converse with the Father. If suffering is handed down, so must prayer be.

To understand the ritual dynamics of Christian prayer, which give petitionary prayer a distinct new sense, we must appreciate that the initiative in prayer is never ours. The Spirit who raised Jesus from the dead has made a home in us, without which we would not have the power or conviction to confess that Jesus is Lord. This same Spirit cries out in us to the Father, "Abba," giving us our share in the affectionate relationship Jesus has always had with him. It is this Spirit of Christ which makes us Christian, and which makes our prayer an echo of Jesus' converse with his Father. The Book of Revelation offers a lovely image: in the heavenly court angels regularly pour bowlsful of the prayers of the saints (that is, of the faithful Christians on earth) as incense on braziers which then send up clouds of smoke to perfume the atmosphere of the heavenly assembly.

On this understanding of it, our prayer is God's work in us, and while we give expression to all our concerns, the Spirit is drawing us ever more deeply into the heavenly agenda. In prayer we do approach the Father, but only because the Father had first invested us with the Spirit of his Son. Our sensibilities, our priorities, our basic sense of what is blessing and what is curse all derive from that Spirit, so that our prayer life bends us to the Father's most ardent will, rather than him to ours. This is what Paul prays for in his disciples: that Christ will live in their hearts through faith, and that with an ever enlarging grasp of God's breathtaking plan which stretches beyond our imagination, we may be filled with the utter fullness of God. That is why the most urgent and persistent prayer will eventually tail off into acceptance.

What the distinguished theologian Julian Pleasants has said of the Mass is true of prayer. Recalling the old words he and his wife had exchanged in their wedding vows, "With my body I thee worship," he observes that these originally spoke for Jesus on the cross, who was worshipping us with his body. So in our prayer and Eucharist it is the Lord appealing to us, opening his heart to us, displaying to us that we are worth the life and death of God. Our prayer is no magic rite that compensates for neighbor service. It is the great stimulus to love God back by loving our neighbor. That is the sense in which Benedictines called their prayer *opus Dei,* God's work. As God was at work in Christ, reconciling the world to himself, so through our prayer God is at work is in us, reconciling the world to himself.[14]

We could never imagine ourselves trying to extort favors from a grudging god. We know no such god. It is none of our charge to rebuke the Father for being niggardly with his children, or to complain that too little largesse, or ill-chosen graces, have been unleashed upon our earth. What we pray for, what we strain to work for, is that men and women would within themselves learn to walk upon the earth as a place graced for us. What one person steps over as a stone, the next will stoop to discover as a warm and fresh loaf. Our path is strewn with favor, and could be even more crowded with kindness, were we no longer disposed to call it wilderness. As we pray "through Christ our Lord," we are the chorus to his desire, and his desire is that we discover the gifts that do lie to hand, that we be fed, healed, and resurrected by the food, folly, friendship, and fearless death we try to share with one another in Christ. Our task is never to draw God's favors to the measure of our requests but — on the contrary — to stretch our petitions to the measure of his generosity. And this involves us in the same mystery as does gratitude: we always need to see more clearly what is a benefit to thank him for, and what is a calamity from which to ask relief. We so easily confuse them.

God inspires our prayer as he inspires our service. Only those who believe, pray. Only those who work, may pray. Only those who pray, work that others may believe and serve. We pray for those we serve, and our prayer strains even to outreach our arms, to solicit for those we cannot touch. Our prayer is the muttering of people busy, yet never preoccupied. Prayer does not accomplish what we cannot; it is not our only resort when confronted by our own limitation. We are in large part an answer to our own prayers, the gift God provides to those we commend to him. We do not take some matters into our own hands, and leave others for the more

14. Julian R. Pleasants, "A Father's [Day] Reflection," *Commonweal* 102, 11 (15 August 1975): 331-34; letter, ibid., 117, 18 (26 October 1990): 594, 623.

powerful devices of the Lord. We achieve nothing but by God's gift; and we are ourselves God's gift insofar as led by his Spirit. It is all one: we pray for what we work for, and we are given what we wreak.

A distinctively Christian sense of prayer reveals that, prior to being an appeal to God, it is itself a reply to his call. It is not we who solicit his generosity; it is he who summons us forth, in word and work harmonized. We are only distracted if always trying to validate prayer by its effects: by a God persuaded, by a neighbor enriched, or (by rebound) by a self made sensitive. Prayer itself is an effect more than a cause. Though cast into the syntax of request, prayer to the Father of Jesus is addressed to the one who is supremely giving — giving even the faith wherewith we pray. Our concern for prayer should not be in what it will produce, so much as in how resonant it is with God's work in the world, and our own.

Jesus' intimates long remembered that when fallen to prayer, he forwent the ancient courtesies of their people and addressed the Lord with startling familiarity. "Abba," he called him, in the affectionate way a son at any age calls his father Papa or Dad. It made them bold to think that they too might speak to the Lord of Hosts, the God of Abraham, Isaac, and Jacob, as friendly Abba. Nor was it merely a matter of titles. As they found themselves being transformed by Jesus' affection, and found others transformed by theirs, to their immense and ecstatic astonishment, they burrowed into the comforting secret of a common purpose and power with the Father, and addressed him with confidence, calling insistently for his favors as a son might who knows his father inside and out, and is sure that his appeals are part of a wiser and subtler scheme than he can yet know, but in which he plays his intended part. They ask the very one who bade them ask, that their joy might be made complete.

So it was with Philemon. He could hardly summon himself to squander all his security for love, if he had no intimacy of conversation with the Father and the Son who had taught him what cherishing might be.

And so it is for any believer, who might sit up some day with astonishment to find that what he or she had got themselves into was far more consuming than they had expected. And so it is.

CHAPTER TWELVE

Our Problem

The theme to which this book speaks is our ability — our calling — to be as outright in love of Lord and neighbor as Jesus has shown himself outright in becoming our Neighbor. This means we must be able to sustain the language of endless obligation, an·imaginative idiom in which we are only awkwardly fluent.

Language of obligation has traditionally been at the center of our moral tradition. In the Bible, for instance, the Lord presented Israel with a dire choice. "I am offering you life or death, blessing or curse. Choose life, then, so that you and your descendants may live in the love of Yahweh your God, obeying his voice, holding fast to him" (Deut. 30:19-20). This language continued in the teaching of Jesus: "Enter by the narrow gate, since the road that leads to destruction is wide and spacious, and many take it; but it is a narrow gate and a hard road that leads to life, and only a few find it" (Matt. 7:13-14). The message was preserved in the earliest nonscriptural Christian writings, which spoke of the "Way of Life" and the "Way of Death" *(Didache; Letter of Barnabas).*

This destiny of choice with blessing or curse, life or death, in the balance got its bite from the specific commands of the Torah tradition. The man caught gathering wood on Saturday must be stoned to death (Num. 15:32-36). Anyone who curses father or mother will be put to death (Lev. 20:9). The man who gives perjured testimony is answerable for it with his life, and to escape retribution he must make good on his deceit, and offer an unblemished sacrifice of expiation (Lev. 5:22-26). Homage to Baal brings assured disaster on the two-timing people who flout Yahweh's jealous love (Jer. 11:13-16). Sexual vice, sorcery, drunkenness, and the like will forfeit the kingdom of God (Gal. 5:16-20).

This moral tradition spoke in a grammar that was continuously imperative: those who heard and followed the call of the Lord in Israel and now in the Church believed their very salvation was at stake. So the fundamental idiom of Jewish and then Christian morality was written in the imperative mood.

Paul, however, began to speak on behalf of virginity, celibacy, and widowhood, not as obligations but as options he commended (1 Cor. 7), while making clear they were not commanded by the Lord. He was weaving into the fabric of obligation a new moral grammar with room for non-imperatives. Yet Paul's very assurance that these counsels were advisories only showed that the dominant moral idiom was one of imperative obligation.

The early Christians were "atheists" at Roman law, and thereby at risk of falling afoul of the state. Martyrdom itself, as the price of fidelity, was therefore an imperative duty. One need not provoke arrest, and one might use sharp wits and careful words under interrogation; but if commanded to forswear the faith by word or worship, a Christian must undergo torment and death rather than apostatize. Even the avoidance of confrontation could be thought sinful. Cyprian, the bishop of Carthage (†257), went into hiding during a savage outbreak of anti-Christian violence, and encouraged his community by letters from the underground. But after a while he was criticized for the safety he enjoyed while they were dying, so he came back to encourage them by his own witnessing blood. Once again, the accent was on unshirkable duty.

Eventually Christianity would be tolerated, then authorized, and then made the official religion of the Empire. By the time Christianity came out from under the ban, many churches already had members of high social standing and affluence. Once the risk of persecution was lifted, a new inclination to casual religious conformism provoked an ascetical reaction which began in Egypt and peopled the desert with anchorites. Their harsh life, however, was not embraced as something optional. The monks said they were penitents struggling to be saved. Anthony (†356) and his fellow hermits deprived themselves of possessions and comfort, family and companionship, simply to make room in their lives for the grace of continence. When Pachomius (†347) led most monks from the solitary into the communal life, he saw himself as intensifying their regimen, not softening it, for obedience was an added undertaking meant to lead them even more deeply into single-hearted allegiance. They saw themselves as unprofitable slaves, doing no more than their duty.

The movement of austerity in the desert was further focused by Basil of Caesarea (†379) and Benedict of Nursia († *c.* 550). Their monastic rules in both East and West were undertaken by men and women who accepted them, not as counsels, but as "Precepts of the Master" meant to make them "partakers of his kingdom" (*Rule of St. Benedict,* prologue).

But those who explained Christian duty to the wider public now began to explain it differently, and the change was more radical than then seen. Ambrose of Milan (†397) in his *Moral Responsibilities* borrowed from Cicero a Stoic distinction between "perfect" and "moderate" fulfillment of responsibilities, and he used this distinction to interpret the gospel.

Ambrose made a particularly unfortunate use of this distinction in his reading of the story of the rich young man in Matthew 19. In the native, prophetical sense of the story, the youth had consistently kept the commandments, only to be told by Jesus that eternal life was still beyond his grasp: in addition he must abandon his wealth and follow Jesus in search of those in need. The original point was that salvation required more than Torah: the young man had done all that was prescribed, but to qualify for resurrection he must venture beyond specific imperatives, to serve the limitless needs of his neighbor.

Ambrose flinched from this story's boundless sense of duty. He interpreted Jesus' "If you would be perfect" to mean "If you wish to exceed what is required," instead of "If you wish to pursue this through to the end." In his exegesis, this youth who would not commit murder, adultery, theft, or perjury, and would be grateful to parents and fair to neighbors, was already a "moderately" (and adequately) observant disciple. Were he to exceed what obligation required — by loving his enemies, praying for his detractors, and returning blessings for curses in imitation of the Father whose sun and rain make the earth indiscriminately bountiful for the honest and the depraved — then he might become a "perfectly" observant disciple.

What Jesus had called for as a prerequisite for eternal life, Ambrose now changed into an optional extra. His innovation was to propose two standards — one sufficient and the other supererogatory. The gospel and its early disciples, however, had seen the prodigality of Jesus, the apostle, the martyr, and the monk as the prophetic standard for every believer.

Ambrose may have taken a miscue from Paul's willingness to issue invitations to optional ascetical practices. He did not see that Paul construed a life of Christian celibacy to be as committed to endless duty as that of Christian marriage.

Later writers created a new vocabulary for Ambrose's divine double standard: the precept (usually a negative prohibition) was an explicit obligation, and the counsel (usually a positive invitation) was only a recommendation. In practice, this notion of precept comprised the morals and manners required for peaceable living in civil society. The counsel then became suggestively modeled upon the vowed practices of religious orders (voluntary poverty, celibacy, and obedience). Ambrose thought he was borrowing the format of his book from Cicero the Stoic, and taking its substance from Jesus. But Cicero was getting the better of Jesus here. Ambrose had tamed the biblical notion of God as a consuming fire. He had converted the language of prophecy into that of legislation, and had deprived the rich young man's question of its urgency.

Moral discourse was thereby cloven in two, with pastoral and homiletic exhortation expanding the moral claims of Christian counsel, while theological and penitential writing tended to constrict those claims within closely defined negative precept. Some medieval Scholastics even opined that the "works of supererogation" performed by more eager Christians yielded a "surplus" of merit that church authorities could divert to the account of supplicants of mediocre zeal.

Ambrose's treatment of precept as an acceptable minimum, and of counsel as a program for a perfectionist elite, had disordered mainstream moral discourse. The gospel thus gone limp gave scandal to Christianity's more fervent reformers, and threw their own doctrines somewhat off balance. John Wyclif (†1384) believed that the gospel comprised imperatives alone: counsels were simply precepts directed to certain specific individuals. Luther, for autobiographical reasons, rejected the monastic tradition of "counsels of perfection," and for theological reasons inveighed against the very notion of counsels, because the implied allowance for human choice compromised the primacy of the will and command of God. Every individual Christian, he argued, was obliged to give the cheek to the smiter, walk the extra mile, give cloak and coat as well, lend without interest, and swallow calumny in silence. That was echoed by Thomas Cranmer (†1556), who derided the possibility that any actions could "do more for (God's) sake than of bounden duty is required."

The wrangle would continue, contentiously dividing those who accented the idiom of precept from those who distinguished that of counsel: Waldensians *v.* Franciscans, the Synod of Pistoia *v.* the Council of Trent, Jansenists *v.* Jesuits, Bossuet *v.* Fénélon.

Catholics continued to distinguish moral imperatives from moral exhortations, and clung to a double standard which invited the "average" believer to a moral standard that was hard to distinguish from the criminal code of most civil governments. Among Protestants the doctrine of a single morality tended in practice to mute or marginalize the stronger forms of single-hearted witness, whether to asceticism or to pacifism. In neither tradition, Catholic or Protestant, has the disorder yet been fully rectified.

By insisting that rigorous moral maxims are only advisory, the Catholic tradition has encouraged laity to find a level of mediocre satisfaction. By assigning to all moral maxims the status of commands, the Protestant tradition has unwittingly made room for a Liberalism which paradoxically considers them all as choices. Casuistry and laxity are the two polar results. In both traditions charity, which the Lord had made the greatest precept, or commandment, of all had been degraded to "charity," the broadest counsel, or suggestion, of all.

Jesus' use of the prophetic idiom deserves a more attentive hearing. He spoke in every genre of speech and tone of voice: commanding, threatening, wooing, shaming, goading, raging, ridiculing. Every claim was an ultimatum though few were prescriptive, in the sense of a defined directive. He issued an undifferentiated summons to service beyond the easy reach of human imagination. His use of analogy was an invitation, not to deconstruct his imagery into minimized specifics, but to surrender to its unpredictable range of moral urgency and energy.

Some theological masters, like Thomas Aquinas and François de Sales, accepted Ambrose's reading of Matthew that the rich young man was being invited, not commanded. But they went on to observe that there was not much difference between precept and counsel — between, for instance, fidelity in monogamous Christian marriage and fidelity in a community of vowed discipleship and poverty.

In Christ, precepts could sound like proposals, and counsels could sound like commands. On this view of it, "Thou shalt not steal" might offer less insight into whole-hearted moral duty than "Sell what you have, give it to the poor, and come, follow me." Instead of taming the text by disengaging precept from counsel or letting counsel be swallowed up in precept, a Christian moral wisdom would listen to it all as an open-ended moral incitement meant to allow us a literally endless satisfaction.

Prophetic precepts

What, then, if Paul had simply told Philemon to do the right thing and let Onesimus go?

Paul knew how to cut to a conclusion. He had directed the Thessalonians to strike from the welfare rolls the sluggard who refused to work

(2 Thess. 3). He instructed the Corinthians to hand over to Satan the man who was cohabiting with his stepmother (1 Cor. 7). He forbade the Colossians to join in angel-worship (Col. 2). Jesus had done the same, as when he forbade husbands to divorce their wives (Matt. 19; Luke 10). Why, then, do Paul and Jesus impose specific imperatives so sparingly?

In the three chief elements of faith which we have surveyed — doctrine, morality, and worship — these two masters left to their disciples only occasional — no, rare — definitions. Jesus dodged clients who came at him for specific answers, taunting them instead with riddles and tales. Matthew, by strewing his memoir of Jesus' death with allusions to Isaiah's Songs of the Suffering Slave, invests his text with iridescent meaning: Jesus is portrayed as the suffering/triumphing Holy One sent by Yahweh to bring his people to their rest, without that ever being stated in such flat and conclusory prose as this. Go to the Scriptures to have a question answered, and you come away with your imagination and your mind provoked, not pacified. When Jesus' answers sound most evasive and vague, he is ignoring the puny question that expects and welcomes only a puny response.

The Church, despite her present reputation, has been similarly inclined. Not that she is incapable of defining an issue and closing a debate when obliged. But even when in-house quarrels over load-bearing elements in our belief become so neuralgic that they have to be resolved, the Church moves with exquisite reluctance, and usually defines (and, perhaps, is then able to define) only the minimum required to avert some massive subversion of the truth.

Even in those moments of crisis she has had the good sense to know that though the faith needs timely definition, it can be protected by those definitions but not carried in them. When the fathers at Nicaea fastened upon the formula that Jesus was "of one substance with the Father," and imposed it as a loyalty oath required for membership, they were not stuffing our revealed understanding of the Lord Jesus into their one critical distinction. The definition was not the carriage on which revelation rode; it was a patch on a slow leak in the rear tire.

We don't go to the Creed for our creed, or to the Catechism, or certainly — God help us — to "Father Frank's Question Box" in the diocesan newspaper. We go to our Scriptures and our lives of the saints and our living community which is the Church. The basic language of faith speaks to our imagination and sensibilities and our wonder. We carry our convictions in poetry and anecdote and parable with less loss of power than in definition. And just as we know the difference between Shakespeare and a

Shakespeare scholar, so we must know the difference between revelation and doctrine. The faith cannot survive in a Church which loses or forfeits its charism to define the faith once delivered to the saints, but when confusion inclines us to fasten upon the clarifications more than to what is clarified — then our definitions go limp because they all draw their life from experience and insight and expression that are of a prior and more venerable blessing.

I have offered here several extended reflections on some great issues: Jesus as the Revealer of a Father who loves sinners irrepressibly; armed force as a test case for Christian morality; penance as a celebration of what God has been forgiving. All three are issues whereupon the Church has accumulated some pretty specific convictions and commitments. Indeed, they are matters upon which Catholics have been obliged to cultivate a defined orthodoxy, protected by a closely patrolled zone of disciplined debate. Yet if we fasten our attention, mostly through controversy, upon these interpretive specificities we Christians have lost some of our familiarity with that primary mode of faith which feeds on our Scriptures and liturgy and ascetical discipline and mysticism and polyglot witness.

We live in a time when the vital communion between the ancient sources of faith and its later doctrinal re-statements suffers from muscle spasm. That is why I have taken Philemon as patron and guide. Had Paul simply (I emphasize the *simply*) sent him an emancipation proclamation, who knows what would have followed? In America we had Emancipation followed by Reconstruction followed by Jim Crow, followed now by who-knows-what. Even those of us who now can see without any doubt that Philemon and Onesimus ought never be master and slave, must contemplate what difference it made for Paul to send Onesimus to Philemon as his brother in the Lord, with the assurance that he was thereby much better, much more, and much dearer. Was that more than sending him as his freedman? I think it was. Even for Onesimus.

This book wonders how it was that Paul asked more, not less, by framing his moral injunction as he did. This book is a meditation on Christian faith as incarnated in convictions, commitments, and ceremonies that function like an emigration to a foreign land, leaven in the dough, a trust fund, a kiss before dying, a marriage vow, a borning child. Who knows how such things as these will work in us, and on us, and varyingly affect us?

If the Father of Jesus loves sinners, and if we let this belief burrow into our minds, our imaginations, our consciences, and our sensibilities, then — like Philemon — we will be hounded by all that might mean. Our faith and discipline and celebration will not lose the sharper definition each has had to acquire through seasons of confrontation and crisis, but neither will they confuse all that with the fuller bloom of the Mystery.

The older generation that reads this book was raised to be able to give a satisfactory account of our belief, to answer typical questions (or at least to retain the approved answers), to define where we stood, and especially where we stood apart. The middle generation wearied of that, and has preferred to present ourselves in terms that made better sense to neighbors who do not share our faith. The younger generation seems cloven by the two caricatures we seem to have created for them: attracted by either antiquarian or secular formats for understanding the Church, and often by neither.

This book's aspiration is to take the cue from Paul and to focus on the more spacious imperatives . . . because they have more bite to them, not less. What might it all mean to serve a Father who loves us regardless of whether we love him; Jesus his Onlybegotten Son who died as our victim to reveal how unlovely we are, yet are loved even so, even so; and their Spirit who fosters within us the strength to become powerfully gracious, to become a fellowship who forgive, reveal, and inspire our way together into the Kingdom?

What might it mean to take our fellow Churchfolks as our dear brothers and sisters in Christ . . . including junkies, those with brains burnt out by Alzheimer's, those on Death Row, those who despise us, those who cheat, and those we have cheated? What might it mean to be goaded to find what we owe to these dearest brothers and sisters? Then, what would it mean for us to confess that even those many others who do not know they are our brothers and sisters begotten by the same Lord, and those who do not even wish to be our brothers and sisters, really are?

Once we figure that out, we will know that the *Postcard to Philemon* was a divinely benevolent letter-bomb.